MEMOIRS OF THE
MARQUISE DE CUSTINE

Delphine de Sabran

MEMOIRS OF
DELPHINE DE SABRAN
MARQUISE DE CUSTINE

FROM THE FRENCH OF
GASTON MAUGRAS
AND
LE C^{TE.} P. DE CROZE-LEMERCIER

WITH FRONTISPIECE

London : **WILLIAM HEINEMANN**
New York : GEORGE H. DORAN COMPANY
1912

Printed in England.

PREFACE

IN the course of my studies on the eighteenth century I came into communication upon several occasions with the Comte Pierre De Croze Lemercier, who possessed a rich collection of autographs. For years this kindly scholar, a man whose charming nature was most attractive, continually showed me the greatest courtesy in placing at my disposal, with unwearied readiness, the documents in his possession.

A man of keen literary tastes, De Croze Lemercier took the greatest interest in intellectual subjects, and in 1894 published a delightful volume upon the Chevalier de Boufflers, which was successful, as it deserved to be. As we shared the same tastes, our intimacy naturally increased, and though at the outset our relations were purely literary, they soon became a deep and cordial friendship.

De Croze Lemercier had long intended to write a life of Mme. de Custine, and had collected numerous documents for this purpose. One day, when we were talking of our work, he happened to speak of his intention; the idea of a collaboration was mooted, and on either side it was readily accepted.

We considered that though much had been written about Mme. de Custine, she had none-the-less remained comparatively unknown. Her family papers, of which we possessed many in their entirety, would allow us to present this uncertain and changing figure in the light of reality. We were attracted by the idea of relating and of basing upon indisputable evidence the narrative of this strangely romantic life which began with hopes of permanent happiness, was disturbed by tragedies unnamed, and finally ended in suffering and despair. We thought that we might point a sound moral lesson to our contemporaries, who are so ready to groan under the miseries of our own times, by showing them what the life of a woman was during and after the Revolutionary tempest, and to what degree of mental misery a being might be reduced who was charmingly pretty, an attractive character, who believed herself destined to all the delights of this world, and who, rather by the force of circumstances than by her own fault, knew little of life but its bitterest sorrows.

Unfortunately, in the course of our work De Croze Lemercier was attacked by a most serious illness which carried him off in a few months from the loving care of his family and the affection of his friends. It has, therefore, been my sorrowful task to conclude this study of Mme. de Custine alone. But the pleasantest part of it is the opportunity of rendering this deserved tribute to my valued collaborator whose wide and profound erudition I have so often been able to appreciate, and to my faithful friend whose intellectual powers and charming and loyal steadfastness will never fade from memory.

G. M.

Almost all the letters collected in the course of this volume are unedited and belong for the most part to the papers bequeathed by Colonel Gibert to the Comte de Croze Lemercier.

M. Paul Prat, who also possessed a number of unedited documents concerning the Boufflers family, kindly authorised the Comte de Croze Lemercier to copy such as might be useful to us. We take this opportunity of expressing our warmest thanks to him.

We have also to thank no less warmly M. La Caille, who with unusual kindness had placed at our disposal his valuable collection of autographs.

CONTENTS

CHAPTER I.
1770–1784 1

CHAPTER II.
1785–1787 14

CHAPTER III.
1787 23

CHAPTER IV.
1787 30

CHAPTER V.
1788–1790 37

CHAPTER VI.
1790–1791 44

CHAPTER VII.
May to December, 1791 53

CHAPTER VIII.
January—June, 1792 67

CHAPTER IX.
January—June, 1792 78

CHAPTER X.
June—December, 1792 84

CONTENTS

CHAPTER XI.
January—July, 1793 94

CHAPTER XII.
July—August, 1793 106

CHAPTER XIII.
August—December, 1793 116

CHAPTER XIV.
December, 1793—January, 1794 129

CHAPTER XV.
1794 142

CHAPTER XVI.
1794 157

CHAPTER XVII.
January—September, 1795 166

CHAPTER XVIII.
September—December, 1795 183

CHAPTER XIX.
1796 191

CHAPTER XX.
January—June, 1797 201

CHAPTER XXI.
July—December, 1797 212

CHAPTER XXII.
1798 221

CHAPTER XXIII.
1799–1800 231

CONTENTS

CHAPTER XXIV.
1801–1803 240

CHAPTER XXV.
January—June, 1804 248

CHAPTER XXVI.
July—December, 1804 262

CHAPTER XXVII.
1805–1810 271

CHAPTER XXVIII.
1810–1812 282

CHAPTER XXIX.
1813 294

CHAPTER XXX.
February—October, 1814 303

CHAPTER XXXI.
October, 1814—July, 1815 313

CHAPTER XXXII.
July—December, 1815 323

CHAPTER XXXIII.
January—December, 1816 333

CHAPTER XXXIV.
1817–1820 348

CHAPTER XXXV.
1821–1825 359

CHAPTER XXXVI.
1826 368
Index 373

The following are the works which have been especially useful to the authors of this book :—

Le Chevalier de Boufflers et la Comtesse de Sabran, by the Comte Pierre de Croze-Lemercier. Paris : Calmann-Lévy, 1895.

Madame de Custine, by A. Bardoux. Paris : Calmann-Lévy, 1892.

Correspondance du Chevalier de Boufflers avec Madame de Sabran, by MM. de Magnieu et Prat. Paris : Plon, 1875.

Lettres du Chevalier de Boufflers à la Comtesse de Sabran, by Prat. Plon-Nourrit et Cie.

Chateaubriand et Madame de Custine, by E. Chedieu de Robethon. Paris : Plon-Nourrit et Cie., 1893.

Trois Amies de Chateaubriand, by André Beaunier. Paris : Charpentier, 1910.

Rahel, Madame Varnhagen von Ense, by Jean Edouard Spenlé. Paris : Hachette, 1910.

Lettres du Marquis de Custine à Varnhagen d'Ense et Rahel Varnhagen d'Ense, published by Ludmilla Assung. Brussels : H. Merzbach, 1870.

Mémoires d'outre-tombe, by Edmond Biré. Paris : Garnier Frères.

La Marquise de Boufflers et son fils le Chevalier, by G. Maugras. Paris : Plon-Nourrit et Cie., 1909.

CHAPTER I

1770-1784

Birth of Delphine—Her family—Her brother Elzéar—Death of her father—Education of the children—Intimacy of Mme. de Sabran with the Chevalier de Boufflers—Visit to Spa—Comedy at Bel Œil—Return to Paris—Delphine is sent to a Convent.

DELPHINE DE SABRAN was born at Paris on March 18, 1770. She was entered upon the Paris register in the names of Louise Eléonore Mélanie, but among her family, for some unknown reason, she was never known by any name except Delphine, and this she retained all her life. Her father, the Comte de Sabran, belonged to a family of Provence, as famous by marriage as by military exploits. He had himself worthily continued the brilliant traditions of his ancestors. He had covered himself with glory at the battle of Santa Maria off Gibraltar on August 7, 1759, when he held out to the last in order to cover the retreat of the squadron. For seven hours he sustained a desperate combat with four English ships, and his vessel, the *Centaure*, was simply riddled, and had eleven feet of water in the hold; but de Sabran still held out; when his projectiles were exhausted the commander ordered the cannon to be loaded with his silver plate. He did not strike his flag until the *Centaure* was beginning to sink, by which time he had himself received eleven gunshots.[1] Louis XV. congratulated him upon this exploit before the whole court, and presented him to the

[1] He had already distinguished himself in the Battle of Minorca in 1756 when he commanded the *Content* in the squadron of the Marquis de La Galissonière.

2 MARQUISE DE CUSTINE

Queen and the Dauphin with the words, "This is one of our relatives."[1]

Such was the father of Delphine. Her mother, Françoise Eléonore Dejean de Manville, was born at Paris on March 3, 1749. She belonged to an old and wealthy family of Languedoc, and on the day of her birth she was so unfortunate as to lose her mother. Her father soon married another wife of a morose and peevish temperament. Brought up in the Convent of the Conception in the Rue St. Honoré, the orphan spent all her childhood and early youth in that pious retreat. She then returned to her grandmother in the Rue des Vieilles-Haudriettes. There she led an austere life without any opportunity for amusement. At a later date she told her son how painfully difficult was her life at this period.

"At the age of fifteen, my dear, I had to nurse a father who loved me tenderly and who was left under my care. I had a grandmother who did her best to prevent me from accompanying him to the watering-place, a hundred leagues from Paris, which he had been advised to visit, under the pretext that I was young and pretty, that my father might die on the road and that I should be too unprotected among the numerous visitors to the watering-place, and so forth and so on, while there were talks and assertions on every side that such a journey would ruin my prospects in life. At that time prudery had reached its height. Struggling between so many contrary desires I was brought to the last extremity and, in despair, for the first time in my life I resisted the tyranny of my grandmother and took my unhappy father to the waters. He nearly died, but my care prolonged his life, and the recollection of it is still dear to my heart."

From this quotation we may see what the girl had to suffer from the prudery of her grandmother, and that she was

---

[1] Saint Louis and his brother Charles, the Comte d'Anjou, King of Naples and Sicily, had married two sisters, Marguerite and Béatrice of Provence, grand-daughters of Garsende de Sabran, Countess of Forcalquier, the wife of Hildefonso of Aragon, sovereign Count of Provence. The other two grand-daughters of Garsende de Sabran had married two English kings. Eléonore of Provence married Henry III. of England, and Blanche married Richard King of the Romans, Emperor of Germany and brother to Henry III. Thus the Sabran family were connected with almost all the reigning families of Europe.

ready to accept anything to escape from an intolerable yoke. In 1769 the Comte de Sabran was introduced to her, a man of famous family and with a splendid reputation, but of narrow means and older than herself by some fifty years. None the less she thought the match a suitable one and offered no objection; so she became the Comtesse de Sabran and lived happily for several years with her old husband. They had two children, Delphine born in 1770 and Elzéar on May 18, 1774. Then this renowned sailor, no doubt under the impression that he had fulfilled his duty to his young wife, succumbed to an attack of apoplexy during the Coronation festivities, on June 11, 1775. He died at the age of seventy-five.

Thus Mme. de Sabran was left a widow at the age of twenty-five with the responsibility of bringing up two children. This duty was no sinecure; though Delphine's health was good, Elzéar had been extremely delicate from a baby and only by constant care was his mother able to rear him. And unfortunately their physical health was not the only difficulty. Their father's advanced age had impaired their blood to such an extent that their moral weakness was equally pronounced and caused them cruel suffering throughout their lives. Hence we must not be surprised if we find them constantly subject to inexplicable nervous attacks and to fits of depression which they certainly owed to the circumstance of their birth and for which they cannot reasonably be held responsible.

Mme. de Sabran, who had shown herself a wife in every respect worthy of her old husband, led at first a retired life of widowhood. She withdrew, with her children, to an uncle on her husband's side, Mgr. de Sabran, Bishop of Laon, and spent the first year of her mourning at his house.[1]

Space will not allow us to say as much of Mme. de Sabran's youth as we should like. It may be stated briefly, however, that Eléonore de Sabran was a charming woman, intellectual, attractive, and talented, while she remained one of the most exquisite of the many seductive feminine figures which were seen during the eighteenth century. Her letters are unrivalled,

[1] Louis Hector Honoré Maxime de Sabran (1739–1811), bishop, duke of Laon, ecclesiastical peer and First Almoner to the Queen.

and are marked by unimaginable sound sense and gracefulness.[1] The reader will soon be able to appreciate and judge Mme. de Sabran in the course of this narrative, in which she plays an important part. He will then observe that though she was an admirable mother she was also an adorable woman.

At the end of a year of almost monastic life Mme. de Sabran considered that she was very young thus to retire from the world, and resolved to return to Paris. She had at that time no house in the capital; at that moment a residence was for sale in the Rue du Faubourg St. Honoré—a magnificent house which had been built for the financier Bouret. Financial embarrassments forced him to sell it in a hurry before it was entirely finished. There was an immense garden with old trees, looking on to the Champs Elysées. Mme. de Sabran visited the residence, was pleased with it, and bought it at once.[2]

As soon as she was actually in the capital the young widow began to re-visit her relatives and friends, and gradually, though timidly, resumed her place in society. Unfortunately for her, or fortunately, according to the reader's point of view, Mme. de Sabran in 1777 made a chance acquaintance which influenced the whole of her future life. One evening, at the house of the Marshal of Luxembourg, she met the Chevalier de Boufflers. Although she had lost the attractions of her early youth and was not precisely pretty, her face was so striking, her mind so original, and her attractions so irresistible, that she was altogether seductive. Boufflers was pleased, charmed, and enthusiastic. He was also a man of infinite cleverness and liveliness, and, in spite of his plainness, he also made a keen impression upon the young widow. This he speedily perceived, and in order not to let an acquaintance so happily begun grow cold he called the next day at the residence in the Faubourg St. Honoré to

[1] We refer those readers who may be interested in the subject to our work *La Marquise de Boufflers et son fils le chevalier* (Plon Nourrit & Co., Paris, 1908), and also to the *Correspondance de Mme. de Sabran avec le chevalier de Boufflers*, by Messrs. Prat and Magnieu (Plon Nourrit & Co., 1875).

[2] If we are not mistaken this residence, which is no longer in existence, was situated between the present English Embassy and the Rue de L'Elysée.

declare his affection. Relying confidently upon his past
successes, he expected speedily to storm the stronghold. He
was soon undeceived. Mme. de Sabran, in contrast to her
contemporaries, prided herself upon her virtue and a siege in
full form became necessary. Begun in the harmless guise of
"brotherly friendship" the intimacy ran the course common
to all such idylls and at the end of a few months
Boufflers was able to proclaim himself the happiest
of men.[1] On neither side, however, was it a case of mere
caprice or *passade*, as the age neatly styled such friendships;
they adored one another and their intimacy, which was to be
lifelong, was cemented twenty years later by a happy
marriage.[2] From that moment the course of Mme. de
Sabran's life was fixed; she had only two delights in the
world—her children and the man she loved. She devoted
herself to the task of securing their complete and exclusive
happiness with the most touching self-denial. Her tender
affection for her children was without parallel and she
surrounded them with limitless care. We shall see that to
their education and their happiness she devoted all her
thoughts, all her strength and all her courage. She was
unwilling at first to leave the care of their instruction to any
stranger and herself gave them lessons in English, music, and
morality. She also taught them drawing and painting, for
she had real talent and has left several charming works
behind her.[3] "Every day," she writes to Boufflers in 1778,
"a kind of Academy is held at my house, when scraps of
history which may interest the children are read. Elzéar's
memory, attention, and cleverness are astonishing; he already
knows more than his sister." There was a complete difference
between the two children. While Delphine was vigorous,
fat, and chubby, a "little scamp," Elzéar was weakly, timid,

---

[1] See Chap. XVI. ff. in the *Marquise de Boufflers* for an account of the
first charming years of this intimacy.
[2] The Chevalier was unable to marry Mme. de Sabran at once because
he was a Knight of Malta, and to this position certain revenues were
attached which he would have lost upon his marriage and he had no
private means. When the revolution had swept away these revenues and
everything else, he legalised the situation without delay.
[3] Among others she painted for Mme. de Rocheforte, afterwards the
Duchesse de Nivernais, a picture in which she represented herself as
painting Mme. de Rocheforte's portrait. Her two children are near,
Delphine holding the palette and Elzéar mixing the colours.

and a "great thinker," as his mother calls him. She compared him to a little lamb; "he has the whiteness, the gentleness and the candour, but he will not allow any bird to pick the wool from his back, as the proverb goes, for his mind is greater than his body."

If Elzéar's intellectual powers were brilliant, the same cannot be said of his physical qualities. His health was always precarious, and he was afflicted with a defect in his speech which caused Mme. de Sabran great grief. She attempted to get rid of it by making him recite poetry, and while she thus cured him she unfortunately gave him an inordinate taste for verse. While he was still quite a child he composed rhymed tags, fables, and couplets. It became a regular disease. At the age of eight he wrote a mock heroic poem in six cantos, the "Charrietiade," which he dedicated to a great friend of his mother, an Englishwoman, Mrs. Buller.[1] Mme. de Sabran not only did her best to complete the education of her children as far as possible; she also sought to give them social talents which might help them to succeed in the world. Among other things she taught them to act. Both of them, Elzéar especially, showed remarkable talent for this form of art. In the month of August, 1778, at Anisy,[2] when staying with the Bishop of Laon, Elzéar played a tragedy before the whole village. Naturally his performance was the most brilliant success, "the whole audience melted into tears and also into moisture," his mother gaily writes, "for it has never been so hot as to-day."

About this time Mme. de Sabran, who was anxious that her children should have a more complete education than she herself could give them, conceived the unfortunate idea of employing a resident tutor, and, on the recommendation of d'Alembert, she took into her house without making proper inquiries concerning his moral character, a certain Abbé Bernard who was a considerable scoundrel, and possessed nothing of the Abbé but the name and costume. At a later date we shall see the unfortunate consequences of this

[1] Mrs. Buller's maiden name was Susannah Yarde; she belonged to a noble family as did her husband, an eminent lawyer.

[2] A little residence which Mgr. de Sabran possessed near his cathedral town and where he spent every summer.

imprudent choice. Elzéar, in despair at being separated from his nurse, of whom he was very fond, frowned considerably upon the Abbé Bernard at first. We need no further proof than this charmingly simple letter which Delphine wrote to the Chevalier.

To the CHEVALIER DE BOUFFLERS, *Colonel of the Regiment of Chartres Infantry at Dunkirk.*

DEAR SIR,

It seems a long time since we have seen you. We are at Anisy, which I like very much. Bonne Amie, ugly as she is, wins the affection of everyone; she is adored by the whole of Anisy, including myself who am very fond of her. She is very nice but not nicer than you. I think it is difficult to be as nice as that.

Elzéar is now a big boy; he is with his tutor. He was very sorry to be separated from his nurse and it made him ill, but he is better. I am at present reading with mother the tragedies of Corneille. I have read "Polyeucte" and "Cinna." I find them very amusing because I think they are very ridiculous. Especially when Émilie says, " softly, my passion now becomes less strong,"[1] and when Polyeucte says to Pauline, "Softly, Pauline."[2] I admit that I prefer Voltaire and Racine to Corneille and I hope that you will be of the same opinion.

Your letter gave me great pleasure and I hope that you will sometimes write to me. My brother sends you a thousand good wishes. Mother has been very ill for the last two days and has stayed in bed; she sends you her best wishes and is very sorry she cannot write.

DELPHINE DE SABRAN.

The amusing reflections of Delphine upon Polyeucte are the best criticism upon the intensive system of education which she received. It is futile to try to make a child of eight or nine years of age understand literary masterpieces.

[1] *Cinna*, Act I. Scene II.
[2] *Polyeucte:* Die for one's God! And how should that be death?
  Pauline: What God?
  Polyeucte: Softly, Pauline! He hears thy words.
    Polyeucte, Act IV. Scene III.

Mme. de Sabran would have been better advised to read to her daughter "Mother Goose's Tales" as more suitable to her age.

Boufflers, before rejoining his regiment at Dunkirk, to secure the goodwill of Elzéar and Delphine, had given them a little dog which they called Bonne Amie. It was by no means pretty and not particularly intelligent, but this did not prevent the children from becoming passionately fond of it. A short time afterwards the Chevalier was informed of an unfortunate accident which had happened to Bonne Amie.

"Your poor Bonne Amie has been in tortures for two days. I wanted to smarten her up and have her shaved like the most distinguished dogs. Unfortunately they shaved so close that they almost skinned her alive. She spends all her time scratching and howling and is so ashamed of her nakedness that she is always hiding. And she will not eat or drink and would lose her intelligence if she had any. But she is certainly more stupid than ever."

In 1782, Mme. de Sabran was very ill and the doctor urgently advised her to visit the watering-place of Spa. Although it cost her a great deal to leave her children she resolved to go. "I have been ill for so long," she writes in weariness, "that I have not the courage to face further illness; I must now die or live." So she went to Spa, where she was to meet again her old friend Mrs. Buller, "the most pleasant woman upon the face of the earth," she wrote to Boufflers; "she takes second place in my heart, the place you have kindly left her."

Spa was the great watering-place of the eighteenth century. Visitors came there from every part of Europe and the smartest and most select society made it their meeting-place. For this reason all the adventurers in the world were to be found there. The Prince de Ligne, with his usual liveliness, has left a pleasant description of this celebrated watering-place. "I made my way into a large hall where I saw one-armed men offering their arms to ladies, lame men displaying their paces, ridiculous names, titles and countenances, amphibious animals from the Church and the world jumping and running in the English fashion. Valetudinary lords were wandering sadly about. Women from Paris came in with loud bursts of laughter in order to be thought agreeable and at their ease and hoping thus to become so. There were young men from every country believing themselves English and aping English manners; talking through their teeth and dressed like grooms, with close-cut black and greasy hair and mutton-chop whiskers round their dirty ears. There were French bishops with their nieces; a doctor with the Order of St. Michael, and a dentist with the Order of the Spur; dancing or singing masters in the uniform of Russian majors; Italians dressed like colonels in the Polish service walking about with young bears from that country; Dutchmen looking in the newspaper for the rate of exchange; thirty Knights of Malta with Orders of every colour right and left and in their buttonholes, medallions of every size and greatness; old duchesses coming back from their walks with long sticks à la Vendôme, with paint and powder three inches thick; marchionesses doubling their stakes, frightful and suspicious in the middle of a mountain of ducats, devouring every coin staked in fear and trembling upon a great green cloth.

"There were two or three Electors dressed as huntsmen with bits of gold braid and hunting knives; some princes travelling incognito who would have been just as impressive under their real names; some old generals and officers retired on account of wounds which they never received; some Russian princesses with their doctors and Palatine or Castilian counts with their almoners. There were Americans, burgomasters from the whole neighbourhood, escaped prisoners from every jail in Europe; impostors of every species and adventurers of every class, abbés from every country; twenty invalids dancing like madmen for their health; forty lovers, or pretending so to be, vigorously perspiring, and sixty ladies waltzing with more or less beauty and innocence, more or less skill or coquetry, more or less modesty and attractiveness. This is known as a 'dancing lunch.'"

This brilliant description may give some idea of the society of Spa at that time.

Mme. de Sabran, however, lived a very retired life with Mrs. Buller and a few intimate friends and was little troubled by this strange assemblage of bathers and gamblers. In a short time her health had obviously improved and she felt so well that she committed an involuntary act of imprudence which nearly destroyed all the benefit she had received. The following is the account of this misadventure which she gave to the Chevalier.

"For the last two days I have been in bed with fever. I shall get off with a heavy cold, which I owe to the Princesse d'Orange who did me the honour, for some whim or other, to ask me of all people to accompany her upon a ride, when she always goes at full gallop in fearful heat and an abominable wind. I came back half dead with fatigue, coughing, feeling my sides badly bruised and cursing all the princesses of the earth who can never act like ordinary people."

A few days' rest were enough to overcome the unpleasant results of this expedition, and Mme. de Sabran, delighted with her recovery, wrote, "if I had no children and no husband in the world, I should never wish to leave this place. I like it, I am well and spend my life in very pleasant society which no longer wearies me—a great proof of my cure. I spend a part of the day in the woods and on the mountains. Were it not for the cold which I have just had I should be dreadfully fat." She felt so well and so far restored that she resolved to send for her children who could only derive advantage from the change of air in that fine country. But unfortunately, the delight with which she expected them became a painful surprise. She writes to Boufflers, "I find Elzéar much thinner, taller and uglier. As for Delphine, she has got so surprisingly stout and thickset that you would never recognise her. She is a diminutive copy of the young Princesse de Rocheforte and it suits her very badly. The truth is, I thought she had grown very ugly. Her figure has lost all its elegance and, in fact, it is all very horrible."

During her stay at Spa, Mme. de Sabran had grown very intimate with the Princesse Charles de Ligne, whose husband was a close friend of the Chevalier de Boufflers. The Princess was anxious that she should come and pay them a visit at the Château of Bel Œil,[1] with her children, and, knowing the weight of the argument, she had pointed out to

---

[1] A magnificent residence which the Prince de Ligne possessed between Mons and Tournai.

her that it would be easy for the Chevalier to leave his
regiment at Valenciennes and come and spend a few charming
days with them. Mme. de Sabran could not refuse so
attractive an invitation, and as soon as she had finished her
cure she started for Bel Œil with Elzéar and Delphine. No
sooner had her guests arrived than the Princess, to amuse
them, proposed to play a comedy. This was the great form
of country-house amusement in the eighteenth century. The
proposal was enthusiastically accepted, but what piece should
they play ? The choice was a delicate question. At that
time the "Mariage de Figaro" was all the rage in Paris; as
amateur actors are usually not afraid of difficulties, there was
a unanimous desire for the fashionable play, and rehearsals
began. Hélène de Ligne played Susanne, Mme. de Sabran,
the Countess, and Elzéar, Chérubin, the Chevalier de
Boufflers, Figaro. As for the Prince de Ligne, the father,
he contented himself with the modest part of the clerk,
Doublemain. But it must be admitted that if he gave good
advice to the other actors he acted very badly himself. He
was generally given the part of the notary who draws up
contracts or the lackey who brings in a letter, and he
regularly missed his cue. On the other hand, once on the
stage it was impossible to get him off. He whispered in
supplicating tones to the other actors, " you won't mind my
staying." [1] At last, after numerous rehearsals, the performance took place. Hélène de Ligne was charming and
Elzéar delightful, but the Chevalier surpassed them all with
his malicious sprightliness.

After a delightful stay at Bel Œil, Mme. de Sabran
returned to Paris and resumed the usual course of her life.
Elzéar and Delphine continued their dramatic success and
acted at their mother's house and at the houses of several
of her friends—Mme. de Champcenetz, Mme. de Clermont-
Gallerande, etc. They were triumphant everywhere; in
fact, the Queen heard of them and was anxious to see the
two little prodigies; so, to satisfy her curiosity, a private
evening was arranged at the house of the Duchesse de
Polignac, but, at the request of Mme. de Sabran, it was
agreed that only the Royal family and the particular friends

[1] *La Princesse de Ligne*, by Lucien Perey, p. 180, Calmann-Lévy.

of the Duchesse should be present. In order to allow the
two young comedians to display their talent in different
styles it was resolved that they should play, successively, a
tragedy, and a lively little piece.[1] In "Iphigénie en Aulide"
Elzéar and his sister gained a real triumph. The Queen was
affected to tears and applauded continuously. They were
no less successful in the comedy, and the King was charmed
and wished himself to wait on the young actors at the
ensuing supper. He gave Elzéar a present and asked him if
he did not feel nervous when he first came on. "Why
should I feel nervous, Sire?" replied Elzéar proudly. From
that day the two children became constant figures at court.
The Bishop of Laon, delighted with their success, continually
invited them to stay with him.

The years 1783 and 1784 passed peacefully away without
any incident worthy of note except the family troubles of
Mme. de Sabran. Her inward life was happy and her
intimacy with the Chevalier de Boufflers was a great source
of pleasure; but her maternal tenderness was cruelly deceived.
It will be remembered that she had taken as tutor a certain
Abbé Bernard. From the time of his entry to the household
this man behaved himself abominably. He beat his pupil,
set him the worst possible example and left him alone
for hours, sometimes in churches, sometimes in gardens,
while he went away to visit his mistresses. Notwithstanding
his behaviour he obtained great influence over the two
children, which he used to estrange them from their mother.
Mme. de Sabran, who was hood-winked by the pious and
reserved appearance of the Abbé, saw nothing except that
he was producing a profound change in her children. Her
grief may be imagined when she saw these two beloved
children turn away from her and display a hostility which
was almost uninterrupted. She made vain attempts to
discover the reason for an aversion so strange and undeserved,
but her heart was broken. She tried to recover their affection by love and tenderness, but in vain. Delphine was even
more intractable than Elzéar.

[1] The principal actors were Elzéar, who took the part of Oreste;
Delphine, the Comte Strogonoff, Mlle. d'Andlau, and Mlle. de Montault-
Navailles.

On the advice of the Chevalier, Mme. de Sabran resolved to take strong measures. Convinced that she would never reduce the rebelliousness of Delphine to order in her own house, she resolved to part from her for some years, and it was decided that the girl should enter the Convent of the Présentation. This resolve was a crushing blow to the kind and sensitive heart of Mme. de Sabran; she wrote to Boufflers on April 17, 1784, " I am spending my sad life in anxiety and grief, and I see the moment approaching with mortal dread when my Delphine is to go to the Convent. It is to be next Saturday. I went there yesterday for the first time and was quite ill the whole day. I do not know what it will be like on the day when I have to leave her there. I have never felt myself so weak in body and mind."

The fatal day arrived and both mother and daughter were reduced to such despair that Mme. de Sabran, in spite of her justifiable cause of complaint, was upon the point of yielding to the lamentations of Delphine and taking her home again. She writes sadly, " I have had to yield once more to that vexatious sense of reason which tortures us throughout our lives without ever doing any good and to stifle the love and pity which spoke to me on her behalf. I do not know how I ever had the courage. I must have a heart of stone and I have not yet recovered from the painful impression which I have received." [1]

The Convent does not seem to have produced in Delphine's character the rapid improvement that was expected. She bore the yoke impatiently and was overwhelmed by her separation from Elzéar, whom she adored. But her mother suffered no less. She went often to see the young schoolgirl and was grieved to find in her always, "that air of constraint which candour and frankness never wear." Delphine showed herself compliant and docile but nothing more, and there were none of those natural outbursts of affection so dear to a mother's heart.

[1] All Mme. de Sabran's letters quoted in this chapter are taken from the *Correspondance de Mme. de Sabran*, published by MM. Prat & Magnieu (Plon Nourrit & Co., 1875).

CHAPTER II

1785—1787

Departure of Boufflers for Senegal—Delphine returns to her family—Visit to the Polignac family, at Montreuil—Presentation at Court—The Abbé Bernard is dismissed with ignominy—Proposals for marriage with Armande de Custine—Visit to St. Amand.

IN 1785 Mme. de Sabran, already so severely tried, was to feel grief perhaps even deeper. The Chevalier de Boufflers, anxious for glory, and perhaps no less eager to escape a crowd of creditors who pursued him constantly and pertinaciously, applied for the post of Governor of Senegal which he obtained without difficulty, thanks to the support of his uncle, the Marshal de Beauvau. "My glory, if I win any, shall be your dowry and your decoration," wrote the new Governor to Mme. de Sabran to console her. But isolated and unable to feel for ambition, she was in despair at the departure for several years of the man whom she loved so passionately. The feelings of de Boufflers may have been deep but were now much less keen, and in the month of November, 1785, he cheerfully took ship and sailed for his new post.

This separation, which left Mme. de Sabran heart-broken and inconsolable, induced her to withdraw Delphine from the Convent, where the girl had remained in unhappiness for eighteen months. "She now has it in her power to do me a great deal of harm," wrote the poor anxious mother. Delphine, however, left the Convent and resumed her position in her mother's house. But at first her mother did not find her entirely satisfactory, though with touching self-denial she devised every means to regain the heart which she feared that she had lost.

"Delphine is daily growing tamer," she writes on December 30th, "my patience, my care and my love will, I hope, have effect some day. At present she is too much of a child to know what a mother is. As regards gentleness, docility and, I might almost say, devotion, she is always the same. Her mind, like her ideas, develops slowly; her ideas are few but they are very reasonable."[1]

While waiting for Delphine to recover her better nature Mme. de Sabran was at her wits' end to amuse her children and win their affection. She took them to the theatre and for excursions and left them as little as possible. In the spring of 1786 she was invited with them to stay with the Comtesse Diane de Polignac at Montreuil. She took them daily for long excursions into the neighbourhood, and showed them the curiosities of the country. She must have kept a firm hand upon herself to hide the vexation of her heart and to seem gay and cheerful. She writes resignedly:

"*May* 31, 1786.

"I am obliged to speak when I should like to be silent, laugh when I had rather weep and my fear of boring Delphine obliges me to find every possible means of amusing her at my expense. For everything which pleases her calm, innocent soul is not equally tolerable for mine and my only thoughts should be for her. The best that I can do at present is to bear with my sufferings so as to keep them to myself and hide them from society and especially from my poor dear children."

On the day of Pentecost the whole family went to Versailles to be present at the procession of the Cordons bleus. The heat was very great, the crowd enormous and there was a momentary risk of suffocation, "but the pleasure of amusing my children supported me in this horrible crowd," writes the devoted mother, "and though pushed and hustled I took them into the gallery to see the procession go by."

Her vicinity to Versailles secured for Mme. de Sabran

[1] Communicated by M. Prat.

many invitations to Court. She was delighted with the success of her children there and speaks of it with pride to the Chevalier. "The Queen saw Elzéar as she passed and kissed him on his two little rosy cheeks. This morning she said to me, 'do you know that I kissed a gentleman yesterday?' 'Madame, I know it, for he is boasting of it.' She began to laugh and told me that she thought he had grown and greatly improved, and that she had pointed him out to the Arch-duchess at the theatre where I had taken him to see 'Didon.'"

Delphine was no less appreciated. Her first appearances at Court were charming. "This evening I went to supper with the Duchesse de Polignac for the first time with my little nun who was terribly nervous. There were quite a number of people; the Arch-duke and Arch-duchess were supping as well as the Queen. I went away a short distance from her for a moment to speak to someone when the Arch-duke took it into his head to come and speak to her. She was so disconcerted that she understood not a word of what he said and, finding no answer, she fled to the other end of the room blushing, and in a dreadful state. The Comte d'Artois, who noticed it, began to laugh heartily and explained to the Arch-duke, who was astonished at her flight, that she was a very timid young person making her first appearance in society. He told the story to the Queen who was greatly amused. They laughed all the evening at the expense of my little savage, who did not know where to hide her face. As she was looking very well I was the less disturbed. Her grace, her simplicity and her youth secured her the favour of the whole company; they were unanimous in her praise. You can imagine what pleasure this was to her good mother; it made me feel quite young again, and the world has never appeared so charming."

Festivities followed almost uninterruptedly. On June 10, Mme. de Sabran and Delphine were invited to a hunt at Rambouillet by the Comte d'Artois; "our hunting party was superb. We reached Rambouillet at mid-day and found an excellent dinner, a kindly host; we met a boar whom we pursued from two o'clock in the afternoon until six. We had covered an enormous amount of ground and I was thoroughly tired; I still feel it this morning. But Delphine was so interested that she felt nothing."

On June 17 there was another diversion, this time at Bagatelle. "Yesterday the Comte d'Artois gave us a charming party at Bagatelle—I mean to the whole of the company—an excellent dinner and a drive through the Bois de Boulogne, when we went as quickly as the wind. Proverbs were played by Dugazon most laughably, and, by way of conclusion, there was an illumination in the style of Trianon. It was a wonderful success. The weather was very mild and the night almost as fine as one of your Senegal nights. The Comte d'Artois was as kind as possible and did the honours of his house with all the grace which is his. It was nearly three in the morning when we got home."

This country life near good friends, and these great festivities provided the happiest diversion to the course of Mme. de Sabran's existence, and somewhat diminished the sorrows which were caused by the departure of her friend. It now became necessary to return to Paris and resume her serious life. When she arrived Mme. de Sabran was agreeably surprised to find at her house, a letter from the Chevalier de Boufflers saying that he was sending one of the products of his province. Great was the astonishment of all when some days afterwards a little negro arrived, " as tall as a boot and as black as ebony." This little negro, practically the only product that Senegal sent out, delighted Elzéar and Delphine, became their plaything and the joy of the whole household. Mme. de Sabran writes to Boufflers, "I must tell you of your little savage, whom my children call Friday. He is a great delight to them, and no joy can be equal to that which he showed on the day when he found himself in a fine livery. He looked so strange in his new garments that we almost died of laughing. He looks like a cat with curl papers tied to its tail; he turns round, looks at himself, and is afraid to move for fear of making himself dirty. He can hardly walk in his shoes and is a source of amusement all day long, and is therefore the more valuable to us as he is our only resource for pleasure and distraction."

The year 1786 was concluded in a manner almost tragical. We have already spoken of Mme. de Sabran's blindness on

c

the subject of the Abbé Bernard, and how the latter's hypocrisy had enabled him to delude her concerning his morals. Suddenly, by a mere chance she discovered that he was spreading the most scandalous rumours concerning her, that it was his influence that had turned the heads of Elzéar and Delphine for several years, and that he was using the power he possessed to estrange them from their mother. Once upon the track there was no stopping, and thanks to an intercepted correspondence it was discovered that the Abbé proposed to poison his pupil in order the sooner to enjoy the pension which had been assured to him when Elzéar's education was finished. This worthy tutor was acting with a chamber-maid who was his mistress and his accomplice. As she was married it was agreed that he should take the same opportunity of poisoning her husband and then marry her. Such were the hands in which Mme. de Sabran had left her children's education. Naturally this little domestic drama could not pass unnoticed; there was a dreadful scandal, and there was no lack of kind friends ready to spread the worst slanders about Mme. de Sabran. The poor woman, alone, helpless and overwhelmed by this unexpected catastrophe, bitterly reproached herself for her want of foresight and was reduced completely to despair. Her sole consolation was to confide her sorrows to Boufflers.

December 16, 1786.

"I learnt to-day that one of the last atrocities of which I am accused is that I got my brother put in prison in order that I might have all his property. They say that the Abbé Bernard, being touched with compassion and knowing his innocence, had undertaken to defend him, and that he was about to produce a pamphlet unmasking the whole of my conduct; that, further, to prevent the appearance of this I had quickly secured M. Bernard's confinement. You see what fine opinions they have of your wife, and as you know her inmost secrets and thoughts and how far she is removed from self-interest or malice or revenge, you must be furious at this injustice. I myself am overwhelmed, not so much for my own sake, for I can console myself behind the shield of my innocence, but on account of my poor children to whom all this may do dreadful harm, especially to my daughter at the time of her marriage. I seek in vain but cannot find any reason under Heaven why I should be treated so cruelly." [1]

The Abbé Bernard was unmasked, convicted of criminal intentions and thrown into prison, after which no more was heard of him. His departure from the family in which he had played so fatal a part produced the happiest results. "I seem to have driven the devil out of my house," writes Mme. de Sabran, cheerfully, "I see none but smiling faces dancing and singing round me. My children have recovered their natural cheerfulness, and we all feel like shipwrecked sailors rescued." Elzéar and Delphine were also enlightened and realised how blameworthy their conduct had been. They went on their knees to ask their mother's pardon.

December 30, 1786.

"They feel so deeply the suffering they have caused me that they try to repair their wrong-doing by their care and tenderness and you may imagine that the past is already forgotten. Delphine especially was the more to blame in view of her age and is so touched by the gentleness and patience with which I have borne for eight years all the harm she has done me, that she does not know how to express her shame and her remorse. The sincerity of her repentance repays me a hundredfold for all I have suffered, and I begin to think that there is still perhaps some special happiness in store for me. I hope that I may have time to remove the last trace of the poison which has been introduced into her heart, and that I may succeed in making her a charming person in every respect."

In spite of her recent sad and cruel experience, Mme. de Sabran was obliged to agree to the formal wishes of the Bishop of Laon and to choose another Abbé as Elzéar's tutor. Her choice fell upon a professor at the Collège de Montaigne, the Abbé de Vaux, twenty-eight years of age, whose learning

[1] Communicated by M. Prat.

and moral character were universally recognised. We may say at once that the Abbé de Vaux gave every satisfaction and helped her to forget the dreadful scoundrel who had preceded him. The painful incidents resulting from the scandal of the Abbé Bernard were the more unfortunate at that moment, as for some months a marriage had been thought of between Delphine and Armand de Custine, the son of General de Custine,[1] himself a captain of cavalry in the Queen's Regiment. Mme. de Sabran was delighted with the proposal. The young man was charming, unusually clever, and his father enjoyed considerable wealth. It seemed possible that the scandals in circulation might have modified the General's views, but fortunately nothing of the kind happened. M. de Custine did not seem to attach any undue importance to the scandals invented by social malignity and the negotiations continued. The young people often met and seemed to like one another greatly, while Mme. de Sabran's appreciation of the serious and lofty character of her future son-in-law increased. Thus everything seemed to be going well; but unfortunately upon every attempt at a business talk the General escaped upon one pretext or another. Considerably exhausted by these continual delays which prevented any decision, Mme. de Sabran resolved, in the month of May, to pay a visit, with her children, to the Bishop of Laon at Anisy. Then, in order to rest from the painful emotions through which she had passed, she decided to instal herself at Raismes [2] near the Comtesse Auguste d'Arenberg with whom she had been intimate for a number of years. "Excessive solitude no longer satisfies me," she wrote to Boufflers; "my soul is frightened at it, like a poor invalid who feels the need of company."

The doctors warmly recommended Mme. de Sabran as she was in the neighbourhood of St. Amand,[3] to take mud baths,

---

[1] Armand Louis Philippe François de Custine (1768–1794), son of Adam Philippe, Comte de Custine (Field Marshal of the King's armies, Governor of Toulon and of the town of Dieuze), and of Adélaide Céleste Louise Gagnat de Longny. General de Custine owned the famous porcelain factory of Niederviller, near Sarrebourg.

[2] A little village in the neighbourhood of Valenciennes.

[3] A watering-place near Valenciennes.

which might be beneficial to her rheumatism. The lady's
first care, therefore, was to visit the bathing establishment
with her friend and she was horrified at seeing the promiscuous
nature of the arrangements to which the unhappy bathers
were condemned.

" We have been for a drive to St. Amand, with the
Comtesse Auguste to see the waters which I am to take and
the baths. The latter seemed to me very filthy and inconvenient, but necessity can put up with anything. I was
greatly astonished to see the mud and to think that sensible
living beings have the courage to bury themselves up to their
necks in such a heap of filth. The thought of the bequests
which every bather must leave in succession made me quite ill,
for everything contributed to the bath by Providence and mankind must be there still. This valuable mud, apparently, has not
been cleaned since the deluge, in which it doubtless originated,
and I feel that I would not plunge into it for anything unless
my life were concerned." Fortunately Mme. de Sabran,
thanks to her connections, was able to avoid this repulsive
bathing station which very reasonably disgusted her, and was
able to follow a course of treatment under conditions which
were primitive enough, though not unnecessarily shocking.
"I have just got out of my bath. It is midnight, for,
contrary to the custom, I prefer to bathe at this hour rather
than in the morning, as otherwise I should have to leave my
children for too long. The baths, like the rest of the
establishment, partake of the rustic simplicity of the place.
A miserable tub is buried in the earth though covered with
a clean cloth. There is a little canvas bed, with curtains
only half wide enough and four very white walls, and little
faggots of willow twigs which crackle and give off a brilliant
little flame." Delighted with her stay, with the rest and
with the beneficial effect of the baths, and equally anxious
to avoid Paris where she found only cares, Mme. de Sabran
resolved to remain at St. Amand for part of the summer.
With this object she hired a little house in a charming
situation. She there spent delightful days, dividing her time
between reading, painting and excursions in full enjoyment
of her adored children and in the neighbourhood of a beloved
friend.

May 15, 1787.

"I am now at St. Amand, in the prettiest little house in the world and in the wildest district. Nothing is to be seen but meadows bejewelled with flowers, little cottages at intervals to rest the eye and nothing to be met but pretty little sheep and young shepherds, far prettier than our modern shepherds, crowned with lilac, eating large slices of black bread and butter with very white cheese, or singing in unison the simple charms of their shepherdesses. The peace that reigns in this solitude goes to one's heart." She feels so perfectly happy that "it is a pleasure to think, to reflect, to look and to talk, to read, to sleep, or to do anything." Every day she took long walks with her children in the neighbourhood. One day they went to visit the Abbey of Bonne Espérance situated in the middle of the woods. The visit inspired her with amusing reflections. "Here are stout monks by no means pale with watching and prayer, but with rubicund faces, who snooze all day and sleep the better for it at night, and are more inclined to wear out the table-cloth than the altar steps. Far from considering sadly their past errors they fully enjoy the pleasures of the present when they meet them. But enough of the monastic life. These people are too happy to inspire much thought."

Notwithstanding the delight which she took in a semi-solitary life, and in the pleasures of the country, Mme. de Sabran could not remain for ever amid the sweets of St. Amand; she was bound to come to some decision upon the proposed marriage for Delphine and resolved to return to Paris in order to bring General de Custine to the point.[1]

[1] The letters of Mme. de Sabran which are quoted in this chapter without references are taken from the volume published by MM. Prat & Magnieu, *Correspondance de Mme. de Sabran* (Plon, 1875).

CHAPTER III

1787

Difficulties with General de Custine—Anxiety of Mme. de Sabran—
Delphine is betrothed—Signing of the contract—Departure for
Anisy—Misadventure of the bridegroom—Marriage ceremony—
Rustic ball.

No sooner had she returned to the capital than Mme. de Sabran resumed negotiations for Delphine's marriage. But owing to the carelessness or unwillingness of General de Custine, discussions were prolonged, nothing was done and the poor mother, who was anxious to see the matter concluded, became nervous and anxious.

July 3, 1787.

" I have not a moment to myself," she writes to Boufflers, "the position of mother-in-law is very tiring, and I do not know how to acquire all the prudery required to fill the post with dignity. The father-in-law is still more tiring, as I cannot find phrases with which to answer him or patience to listen to him. I would readily give a year of my life to be rid of the whole business. I am sometimes tempted to pack up and run away."

A few days afterwards, worn out by M. de Custine, she exclaims, " This father-in-law is a scourge sent from Heaven to finish my life. He does not know what he wants, what he says or what he does." Mme. de Sabran became quite ill owing to this constant hesitancy, which made her fear that negotiations might be broken off at any moment. "This uncertainty causes me great uneasiness," she says, "I fear that my evil star may be predominant and I have no rest. It must be admitted that there is not, perhaps, in the four quarters of the world, such a man as this, and that it is a great misfortune to have the happiness of one's child and her career in his hands." At the end of her patience, after an almost violent scene, she drove the General into a corner. She told him that she could wait no longer, that there was no further excuse for delay, and that a decision must be made. "Fix the date of the marriage yourself," she said, " and let it remain unchanged. Or else let us abandon the proposal and resume it when you can agree to accept a definite date." Before this decisive language the general became compliant, affable and accommodating, difficulties vanished and the marriage was definitely fixed for the end of the month of July. By that date the bridegroom would be nineteen and the bride seventeen. Some small difficulties remained, but the Comtesse Diane de Polignac and the Duc showed unlimited kindness in overcoming them, and at length the day for signing the contract could be settled. In spite of all her vexation, Mme. de Sabran was delighted to see how entirely worthy of her daughter was the man she had chosen for her; "my dear little son-in-law makes up for everything," she cried, and a few days afterwards she writes these charming lines.

July 17.

"What is all the wealth in the world compared with this close union of two souls made for one another, purified in the fire of love like gold in the crucible. What strength and courage are needed to meet all the troubles of life. How easy it is to do without everything when one has everything. Love is the philosopher's stone, but those initiated into its use are very few."

Delphine seemed to show the warmest affection for her young fiancé and to grow more attached to him every day. Armande de Custine was in fact, a charming character, made to inspire love. His bearing was most distinguished and his powers of sympathy and intellect were unusually great. He had been thoroughly well educated and seemed destined to the most brilliant future. His only fault was his extreme youth, but this was a defect on the right side. He had already travelled considerably and, among other tours, he had made a long stay in Germany, where he had studied the art of war in the school of Frederick. Mirabeau, who had met him in Berlin in 1786, had been delighted with him, and had predicted that he would be one of the coming diplomatists. The increasing affection of the two children completed Mme. de Sabran's delight and made her regard the future with complete confidence. "Their happiness is reflected upon myself, like the rays of the sun upon the moon and makes my life calm and serene. It is long since I have felt so entirely at peace with the world. I daily see my little household united by deeper attachment, while the heart of my little girl is softened and melted by the fire of this formidable god who can do her no more harm as he has expended his bitterest arrows upon her unhappy mother."

An unexpected accident nearly put an end to these delightful marriage proposals. "I was completely thrown out of my carriage to-day in the Place de Louis XV," writes Mme. de Sabran, "the axle of my carriage broke and the wheel came off. My servants were thrown upon one another, though no one was hurt, so true it is that my good genius always protects me. There was an element of danger in the fact that all my windows were up and that my grown-up daughter was on the bracket seat, but she instinctively clung to me and I saved her from this danger also. I came out of it without anything worse than a nervous attack." Amid all her cares, her occupations and her constant journeys, her child's happiness gave Mme. de Sabran extraordinary cheerfulness and vigour. Her gaiety and her observations made everyone laugh; she was anxious to resume the serious and important air "suitable to a mother-in-law," but in this attempt she was unsuccessful.

At length the contract was signed on July 21st. Mme. de Sabran gave her daughter 200,000 livres and undertook to provide the young couple with board and lodging. Armande de Custine, on his side, brought 34,000 livres, though burdened by several charges which reduced it to 28,000.[1] When the contract was signed Mme. de Sabran was reassured

[1] Armande de Custine had inherited from his mother a capital of 700,000 livres.

and felt an immense sense of relief. "Apart from any unexpected events, Delphine will be Mme. de Custine, notwithstanding all the powers of darkness raised against her and myself." As some relaxation after the tiring ceremony she took her children to the Parc de Meudon, where they lunched happily on the grass close to a little fountain, the joyful murmur of which invited them to rest. "For a long time I have never been so happy. We stayed, walking about, laughing and talking. Only my children can give me this sense of happiness; my mind is at rest with them. Their caresses are so real and their feelings so tender that they make me feel once more the delight of being loved. If they do not change, they will at least help me to reach the end of this sad life with a little less repugnance."

Though the contract had been signed at Paris the religious ceremony was to take place at Anisy on July 31, and then to be performed by the good Bishop of Laon. During the preceding week Mme. de Sabran was fully occupied with the final preparations. But the nearer the wedding day approached the greater became her agitation. Her highstrung nature was unable to bear all these emotions within one day. The loving woman passed from joy to sadness, from confidence to anxiety with equal rapidity. Her letters to Boufflers faithfully reflect these different frames of mind. At one time her delight is unlimited, when she remembers that she has at length attained the object of her care. She expresses her confidence in the future without reserve. "Only one who has suffered all my anxiety, my weariness, and my disgust, can have an idea of my delight. I feel younger, more vivacious, and am almost beside myself with pleasure. I am satisfied with the moment, which is rarely the case with me, and I look to the future to make both myself and my child happy." At another time she cannot avoid some apprehensions, and her anxiety is redoubled when the moment for parting with her daughter arrives. "Tomorrow is the great day which is to decide the fate of my poor little Delphine for ever. If one could count on happiness, I have every reason to believe that she will be happy. But when I think of all the elements required to compose happiness, the difficulty of uniting them and the many incidents which may disturb this fair harmony, like comets sweeping through the solar system, destroying its order and raising storms, I tremble and I think that much must be left to chance, whatever precautions we may take to chain it down."

So, on July 28, Mme. de Sabran hastily travelled to Anisy to prepare for the ceremony. She arrived at one o'clock in the morning with her daughter and at once went to bed in order, " to have a clear complexion for the ceremony by the side of my half-opened rose." She was anxious not to spoil the picture, for at her age she could not claim to lend beauty to a ceremony but could at least avoid marring it. Then the next day she writes triumphantly to Boufflers, " in three days I shall perhaps be a grandmother! At least Delphine has my leave to make me one when she thinks proper; the marriage is for Tuesday."

On Monday all was ready and they waited only for the " little husband," his father and his sister.[1] It was known that they were on the way, were to sleep the night at Soissons and to arrive at Anisy on Tuesday about eight o'clock in the morning, while the ceremony was to take place at mid-day. As Mme. de Sabran and her daughter had to rise at dawn, they resolved to go early to bed; unfortunately the prudent mother thought herself in duty bound to give Delphine a little lecture to prepare her for her new state of life. These revelations, though discreetly made, disturbed Delphine completely, and she was seized with a fit of trembling which could not be soothed. She was soon put to bed, but matters grew worse. Her fond mother took her into her own bed to warm her, with the result that neither of them closed an eye, and they spent the night in sighs, tears and mutual consolations. Though a sleepless night was not calculated to provide the " clear complexion " which she desired, Mme. de Sabran was up at five o'clock in the morning, gay, cheerful, ready to receive and to entertain her guests. They arrived at the appointed time, but in a dreadful state, worn out, while the bridegroom looked very poorly and had one

[1] Adélaide Anne Philippe, only sister of Armand de Custine; soon afterwards she married the Marquis de Dreux-Brézé, Grand Master of the Ceremonies.

cheek enormously swollen. Explanations were given and Mme. de Sabran received the following account.

On the previous afternoon, at the moment of starting, the bridegroom had been seized with violent toothache. He went to several dentists in vain. At length he found one at home and was able to have the troublesome molar extracted; but the practitioner was either clumsy or was over anxious to make a clean job of it, and pulled away a small portion of the jaw with the tooth. The result, for the patient, was further dreadful suffering and an enormous swelling. Unfortunately he looked at himself in the glass, uttered a cry of horror and fell into complete despair, declining to show himself or to be married, and proposed to fly to the other end of the world. It was hardly possible to bring him to reason and he had to be forced into the carriage. This accident had made the wedding party very late, and instead of sleeping at Soissons, they were obliged to stop at Villers-Cotterets and to get up at three in the morning to reach Anisy in time. However, all this misadventure was speedily forgotten in the business of dressing and preparing for the ceremony. Mme. de Sabran may now be allowed to describe it.

July 31, 1787.

"Everything was ready at one o'clock and in full array, and in the most gloomy silence, we went to the Bishop's chapel. I held my daughter by the hand, followed by my little son-in-law and his father. My heart never beat so loudly as at the moment when I placed her on the fald-stool, where she was to say the great 'yes' which can never be unsaid, whatever one's future wishes may be. I was not nearly so much impressed by my own wedding. I have lost my belief in happiness and I shed tears in spite of myself, throughout the service.

"Delphine did not weep, but her little face grew long, and her husband seemed by no means at ease. The Bishop gave a discourse, full of reason and sentiment, which touched everyone there. Elzéar held the canopy and as he was too small he was placed upon the largest chapel chair. He looked like one of those little angels in the pictures of the Annunciation. When the ceremony was over M. de Custine took my daughter, I took his son, and we went out in the same order and with the same gravity as we had come in, to make our way to the dining-room, where an excellent lunch awaited us. After lunch we went into the garden, and as we arrived a number of shepherds and shepherdesses, with the foreman at their head, came to pay their respects to the married couple. Each sang his own little couplet, as in the *Amoureux de Quinze Ans*; it was quite touching. After this we danced without ceremony to the village musicians. I opened the ball with M. de Custine, the father, and my children and I assure you that I have never been so light or danced so heartily. The ball and songs went on the whole day; it was extremely funny. When we were tired of dancing we played at faro and the men kept the bank, which amused us until supper-time, that is to say, until eight o'clock in the evening."

Then came the time to which Mme. de Sabran refers as her "bad quarter of an hour." She took the general aside and whispered certain pieces of advice to him, which he was to communicate to his son without delay; embarrassed by this delicate task, she blushed up to her ears and entangled herself in explanations. "I never felt so stupid in my life," she adds modestly. After these preliminaries, the bride was undressed with the usual ceremony: mother and daughter trembled alike and were equally embarrassed. Mme. de Sabran concludes her letter to Boufflers with these words:

"Farewell! Why am I not now as my daughter and why are not you as my son, after obtaining as they have done, the permission of the Church, for otherwise it is the work of the demon who places us in hell in this world and in the next, as St. Augustine says."[1]

---

[1] The letters quoted in this chapter without reference are taken from the *Correspondance de Mme. de Sabran*, published by MM. Prat & Magnieu (Plon, 1875).

CHAPTER IV

1787

Country festivities at Anisy—Philemon and Baucis—Journey to Plombières—Ascent of the Ballon d'Alsace—Arrival at Anisy—Pilgrimage to Notre Dame de Liesse—Return to Paris—Calls and introductions.

MME. DE SABRAN probably slept but little. As soon as she rose, she wrote these lines in her diary:

August 1.

"It is eight o'clock and everyone in the house is asleep except myself, who am dying with impatience for news of my poor Psyche. I hope that, like Psyche, she has been more frightened than hurt."

The excellent mother's anxiety was unnecessary. Armand had probably remembered his father's advice. At any rate, when the young couple appeared, Delphine showed no embarrassment, though all eyes were fixed on her: apart from a modest blush which increased her charm, she appeared as usual. Mme. de Sabran exclaims in delight: "My little nest is a great success; love is not as mischievous as is supposed. It is a pretty little monster which does not bite or scratch."

The next day the Bishop gave his guests an evening party in the wood near one of his farms, at Bartais. The forest was illuminated by a number of lamps which gave so soft a light, and cast such delicate shadows that the water and trees and the people seemed fairy-like. The moon was kind enough to appear; there were music and songs and a crowd of peasants, cheerful and happy. To give these rejoicings the sentimental flavour so greatly appreciated at that time, in the most solitary part of the wood had been erected a poor little hut. Thither the whole marriage party made its way, and found in it, as if by chance, Philemon and Baucis, bent beneath the weight of years; they gave excellent advice to the young couple, "and the best was their example." The couple were then escorted to the Château amid acclamations.

Unfortunately this joyous festivity was to be followed by sadness on the next day. Delphine, on waking, felt very ill, was very feverish, and had violent pains in her back, &c. "I am very anxious this morning," writes Mme. de Sabran, "the little wife is very feverish. I think that it is a nervous attack, but in spite of that, I am very anxious because she has never been so ill. Her little husband is very sad; he goes about looking as if it were his fault: he looks so guilty, that I am inclined to scold him, but I dare not: he would be justified in asking me to mind my own business." Mme. de Sabran, in her alarm, feared that it might be small-pox, the scourge of the age. Fortunately she was mistaken, and the next day she can write triumphantly, "Delphine is cured, and I think it is a case of the old proverb, 'a little sorrow for a great deal of good'; they love one another all the better for it." The happiness of her children appeared so complete that the mother was entirely delighted. "They are the most edifying and interesting couple that can be imagined," she writes, "I share their happiness, I only ask them to be as happy as they can, and I am glad to see that they take my advice." She adds the anxious qualification, as though she read the future all too clearly, "if only it will last."

"You would laugh if you could see how Delphine orders her little husband about. She rules him more despotically than her brother. They are the most amusing little couple imaginable. Love is a pretty thing in its first youth; unfortunately it soon changes and becomes ugly and ill-tempered as it grows up, like a spoilt child."

As Delphine had recovered her health the course of festivities was resumed. The Bishop gave a dinner to all his peasants. "The tables were laid in the garden opposite the Château and were well provided with legs of mutton, pies, poultry, &c.; the little Peinier and her brother represented the married couple. They arrived, followed by a great crowd to the sound of a violin marching in front and sat down at the table." During the meal a number of shepherds and shepherdesses, decked with flowers and ribbons, came and recited some verses by Elzéar, and took part in the festivity. Then, to the general delight, they saw a knight in complete armour with a lance in his hand, upon a miserable horse, followed by a very fat man vigorously lashing his ass—Don Quixote and Sancho. The delight of the company knew no bounds. The day then concluded with a rustic ball. The relations between the village and the Château were formerly often those of hate; but in very many cases, and the Bishop of Laon provides a striking example, the intimacy and confidence between peasant and overlord were no less great and this was especially marked throughout these family rejoicings.

When the marriage festivities were concluded, Mme. de Sabran went with her children to the watering-place of Plombières. She found very few people there, although it was the middle of August. The weather was very cold, people were sitting over fires as though it was January, and the visitors had fled. Notwithstanding her loneliness Mme. de Sabran did not complain of her lot. She found every pleasure in the presence of her two children and especially in the happiness which could be read in their eyes. Every morning, after the bath was over, they went for a drive; in the afternoon they read together, and in the evening, "the two little turtle-doves go to their room to coo." Then some excursions were made; among them the ascent of the Ballon d'Alsace, which delighted Mme. de Sabran. On the first day the three travellers slept at St. Maurice in the pretty little inn, where they were given excellent trout. After some hours' sleep the mountaineers rose at one o'clock in the morning and began to climb the mountain in moonlight. The beauty of the night and the splendour of the view inspired Mme. de Sabran with some philosophical reflections which she could not help communicating to the Chevalier.

September 2, 1787.

"This uncertain light illuminated the world asleep, revealing the precipices, the smiling summits of the mountains and the roofs of some distant chalets, and brought a sense of peace to our minds which I had never before experienced. . . . I sat down from time to time upon the moss, absorbed in my own reflections while my two children walked on, naturally more occupied with love than with philosophy. There is a time for everything; in the spring we cannot know what may happen in the summer, autumn or winter. At their age they only see the flowers, and do not think how long they will last or whether they have thorns."

At three o'clock in the morning they reached the summit, but the cold was intense and a furious wind made it intolerable. "My two little lovers sat so closely side by side under the shelter of their love that they soon became warm. But I, the poor widow, shivered in my little corner and felt so cold that I busied myself with collecting dry branches and cutting down brushwood to try to light a fire, which caused me incredible trouble. Meanwhile, a beautiful dawn prepared us for the sunrise. Gradually it appeared before our eyes like a ball of fire from which there speedily emanated a radiance which I could not face and before which I was tempted to prostrate myself in adoration. Those who have seen a sunrise only from the plain can have no idea of it, and I am very glad to have secured so great a pleasure at the expense of a little trouble."

When the cure at Plombières was finished Mme. de Sabran returned to Anisy with her children. There she spent a delightful life with the Bishop in addition to the enjoyment which she derived from watching her two lovers. She made delightful excursions with them and discreetly shared their happiness. She was an ideal mother-in-law.

October 29, 1787.

"This morning we began by walking more than a league through the fields and woods. My two children frisked like little goats; they jumped the ditches and streams in rivalry. But in their success they deviated from the route and caused us to lose our way and get stuck in the mud, and you know how often that may occur in the neighbourhood of Anisy. We consoled ourselves by dining with good appetites and singing afterwards in an entirely new style. Their gaiety electrifies me and I have not the courage to trouble them with my sadness. This is the only kind of deceit that I allow myself with them, and I find it easier as I wish to please them and make them happy; and truly I find it, in the long run, to my own advantage."

The young couple were so tenderly united that the mere thought of even a short separation seemed unendurable. In November Armand was obliged to go to Paris for a few days on business and Delphine was in tears. Mournfully comparing her daughter's situation with her own, Mme. de Sabran writes: " The little wife was so sad that she made me weep with her, and all because she was to be parted from her husband for four days. What a pleasant grief and what happiness to lament only an absence of four days at a distance of twenty-five leagues!"

However, Delphine began to feel anxious at the absence of any prospect of a family and conceived the idea of making a pilgrimage to the venerated shrine of Notre Dame de Liesse, which enjoyed a well-deserved reputation throughout the country, and the special virtues of which she had heard loudly praised. She talked her mother over, persuaded her husband, and everyone smilingly yielded to the whim of the attractive young wife.

Anisy
November 1, 1787.

" I feel sufficiently cheerful and sprightly, seeing that I am about to undertake a small journey, to please my children, who can get anything they please out of me; it will be a very comical journey. It is a pilgrimage to Notre Dame de Liesse. My little pietist has a special interest in it; she has read in some old chronicle that queens had gone there to discover the secret of child-bearing, and in spite of her youth and her husband's affection, she thinks this resource is necessary because after three months of marriage she is not yet with child; this whim has caused us much amusement and we propose to start on Saturday on foot, followed by a donkey to carry the luggage. We shall sleep at Laon the first day and dine on the road in some meadow near a clear stream, as our custom is. The next day, the same procedure will enable us to sleep at Liesse. We shall stay there a day and a night, the night on which I expect that the pitch of fervour will make me a grandmother, and we shall return similarly on foot like real pilgrims, singing, and laughing, etc."

Unfortunately, the weather disturbed these projects. They had hardly proceeded a league beyond Anisy, than wind and torrential rain began, to which the unhappy pilgrims were exposed for four hours; they reached Laon soaked to the skin. This mishap somewhat damped their ardour; in spite of Delphine's protests they resolved to finish the journey by carriage, and, on arriving at Liesse they did no more than hear mass, visit all the relics, the treasury, etc. Great, however, was the effect of faith; though the pilgrims had performed their vow very incompletely, and though they did not spend at Liesse the night of blessing upon which Mme. de Sabran relied, Delphine was none the less able some months later to announce the desired result in triumph.

At length it was necessary to leave Anisy and return to Paris. No one was pleased at the idea and Mme. de Sabran was even more grieved than her children. No sooner was she installed than she poured her griefs into the heart of the Chevalier and sadly describes the emptiness and vanity of her life. Her words remain true at the present day.

November, 1787.

"It is a strange life that one leads at Paris; I can never get used to it. Always on the move, always calling upon people who care no more about you than you about them; always repeating the same phrases, never daring to be what one is or venturing to say what one thinks. Such formality and restraint are deadly. I cannot be other than I am, and yet I feel that I should be otherwise."

This, however, was not the worst of it. No sooner had she arrived than Mme. de Sabran, in conformity with social custom, had to introduce the young couple to all her relations; a hateful task, but one impossible to evade. "This evening I am preparing to pay a hundred and one calls, adorned like a reliquary, with my two little turtle doves who are as tired of it as myself. It is the custom and so we must put up with it."[1] The year 1787 was perhaps the last year of happiness that Mme. de Sabran spent. She still had times of pleasure, but precarious and interspersed with so many torments and such dreadful anguish that her life, for many years, was one martyrdom. The fate of the young de Custine couple was even more gloomy, and we may say with truth that the idyll is now concluded and that the tragedy is to begin.

[1] The letters quoted in this chapter are taken from the *Correspondance de Mme. de Sabran*, by MM. Prat & Magnieu.

CHAPTER V

1788—1790

Boufflers returns from Senegal—Birth of Gaston de Custine—Delphine has smallpox—Mme. de Sabran travels to Switzerland with Elzéar—She returns to Niederviller for her daughter's confinement—Birth of Astolphe de Custine—The baptism—Journey to Plombières—Mme. de Sabran returns to Paris.

IN 1788 Mme. de Sabran experienced two great pieces of happiness. The Chevalier, after an absence of three years, came back from Senegal, cured of his ambitious dreams and determined to abandon distant and fruitless expeditions for ever. Second and chiefest, Delphine was confined of a boy in the month of September. As we have stated in the previous chapter, Notre Dame de Liesse had punctually fulfilled all the young wife's hopes. In fact, in September, 1788, just ten months after the famous pilgrimage, a boy was born named Gaston. The family was greatly delighted and Mme. de Sabran was no less happy and triumphant than the young mother. Life would have been sweet for them all if serious political troubles had not begun to agitate men's minds and to disturb the most united households. The Chevalier de Boufflers, like many of his friends, was a strong supporter of the new ideas. He adopted them with the calm hallucination of the dreamer. He was deputed to attend the States General by the nobility of Nancy, and was very proud of his important mission. He was not the only member of the family to form part of this new assembly. General de Custine, who had fought in America[1] and had

[1] He had commanded the Saintonge Infantry regiment, and had distinguished himself especially at the capture of York Town.

come back with very republican ideas, had also been nominated to attend the States General by the nobility of Metz. He had been a close friend of La Fayette from the time of their common campaign, and he soon appeared as one of the most advanced constitutional members. Armand de Custine, in the ardour of youth, was no less enthusiastic than his father and threw himself headlong into the current which swept away so many noble natures.

Mme. de Sabran, on the contrary, thoughtful, calm, and prudent, regarded the tendency of thought as full of danger and foresaw with astonishing perspicacity the ultimate consequences. Firmly convinced that the country was being led to the abyss, or, at any rate, to the destruction of the social order, with which she and her family had every reason to be content, she deplored the blindness of those about her and vainly strove to enlighten them. Boufflers, and, still more, Armand de Custine, were persuaded that the golden age had come for France, and blamed her for a reactionary attitude which declined to admit either progress or light. Discussion was often very keen in the family circle, and though the profound affection which united them prevented their quarrels from becoming violent, there were, none the less, elements of discord which disturbed and saddened their lives. Meanwhile, events moved rapidly. On May 5 the States General met and the oath of the Tennis Court took place on June 20. On July 12 Necker was sent into exile; the people rose and Bastille was captured on the 14th; on July 15 the King recalled M. Necker.

A serious illness of Mme. de Custine diverted attention from politics and the painful thoughts to which they gave rise. In a month of July, 1789, the young woman was attacked by perhaps the most serious disease and the one which, in any case, causes the most dreadful ravages, the smallpox. The case was complicated by the fact that the sufferer was again with child and serious consequences were feared. Mme. de Sabran had been repeatedly urged to have her children vaccinated. The Chevalier himself had earnestly pressed it, assuring her that in England, where vaccination was in force, smallpox was practically non-existent. He had not been able to overcome the fears of his friend. The remorse and the apprehension of Mme. de Sabran may be imagined, when she saw her beloved daughter attacked by this terrible disease. She went in terror of it herself, but she overcame her fears and nursed Delphine with admirable devotion, surrounding her with the utmost tenderness, embracing her to calm her and leaving her neither day nor night. After various changes the disease was at length overcome and the young woman gradually recovered. She was so fortunate as to bear no visible traces of this painful trial. In order to recover from the emotions through which she had passed, Mme. de Sabran went to Plombières with Elzéar, for the usual season. When her cure was concluded she did not feel anxious to return to Paris in view of the increased political agitation and resolved to make a short tour in Switzerland with her son. Delphine was heart-broken when she heard of her mother's intention. She fully expected that Mme. de Sabran would spend the summer with her during the months preceding her confinement at Niederviller [1] upon her husband's estate.

August 20, 1789.

"Good Heavens! my dear mother, it is sad indeed to abandon the hope of seeing you here. I admit that this idea was so pleasant to me that I cannot yet believe in your intention to change your first plans, but I see that you are yearning to go to Switzerland and that I must not vex you by my persuasions, so I will say nothing more except that I am very sorry to find that the persuasions of the Comtesse Auguste and the Chevalier de Boufflers are stronger than mine. At any rate promise me one thing, and promise it sacredly, that you will come and stay with me at Niederviller towards the beginning of October. You must promise that, or I shall be very unhappy. No doubt you have heard of the misfortunes of the Abbé Gibelin.[2] The suppression of the tithes has entirely ruined him and his priory no longer exists. It is really dreadful, I am very sorry for the unfortunate man. No one could expect such cruel treatment.

"Gaston is pretty well; at present he is having some trouble

[1] Niederviller is situated a short distance from Sarrebourg. Armand de Custine, upon his marriage, came into possession of the Château, the porcelain factory, and a considerable estate in the neighbourhood.
[2] The Abbé Gibelin was a great friend of the de Custine family, and we shall see that his attachment endured throughout his life.

with his teeth and you will find him thin. I feel ill as usual and my heart trouble does not decrease. Goodbye, my dear mother, your big son kisses you with all his heart and loves you as tenderly as your good Delphine."

Mme. de Sabran promised Delphine to return in October and went to Switzerland with Elzéar. They visited Basle, Zurich, crossed the St. Gothard and came back to Berne. All Delphine's letters urged her mother to return as soon as possible to Niederviller. Boufflers thought this demand unreasonable and wisely advised Mme. de Sabran to stay in Switzerland and to send for her daughter. Disturbances in the provinces became more and more frequent, country houses were plundered, their proprietors sometimes assassinated, and public security became everywhere very precarious.

"I cannot understand the imperious madness of your good Delphine," writes the Chevalier, "in insisting that you should go to her in a country where disturbances may take place at any moment, instead of coming to you to stay among these good Swiss who have surely taken a liking to you already." Mme. de Sabran certainly shared this opinion, but when her children were in question no other considerations existed for her, and she says very touchingly, "In spite of my sad forebodings and my conviction that in a very short time dreadful events will happen in France and at Paris, I am leaving Switzerland, and I leave it with as much regret as if I were going out of harbour into the middle of a storm and defying the tempest. But Delphine does nothing but cry for me. I have tried to induce her to come here, but everything frightens her, the journey, her condition, her child and perhaps the Swiss. So that I feel once more that I must pay the debt in person. I am not brave enough to torment her or myself and live separated from her, otherwise we would each remain where we are and await the accomplishment of my sad predictions. This would be very reasonable but quite beyond my strength, for I pay no attention to any calculations of human prudence when my dear ones are at stake."

She, therefore, started off with Elzéar and met her daughter once more at Niederviller. The news which she received from Paris was certainly of a nature to justify her apprehensions and to redouble her fears. After the night of August 4, when the suppression of the privileges took place, the emigration began. The Comte d'Artois and the princes of the House of Condé left France, and many followed their example. On October 1, the King refused to sanction the first articles of the Constitution; on October 5, the people marched upon Versailles, forced their way into the Château, massacred the guards and obliged the King, Queen and the Dauphin to return to the capital where they were kept under observation in the Tuileries.

Delphine's confinement took place in January, 1790; the Chevalier was informed of the fact by a charming letter from his friend. " I must tell you that this good mother has just been confined of a very pretty boy whom I have taken to my lap, as the gossips say, and have kissed very heartily after his toilet. The event has stirred the whole village and my grandmotherhood has been bruited more than two leagues abroad by salvos of cannon. More than one hundred and fifty peasants headed by Captain Pedre with his gun, came to conduct me with all due solemnity to the Church with the child. Two ranks were immediately drawn up, by the orders of the Captain. He is our local La Fayette and is certainly quite as clever as he. Then we started; a dreadful wind which seemed to have a grudge against us, carried away our hats and blew our skirts about and drove into my eyes and ears all the smoke and fire of our most impressive artillery. But these malicious blasts were soon put out of countenance; they only succeeded in displaying the readiness of all these good people and their kindness. At my side was a *Commère babillarde*, as is customary. This title is given to the woman whose duty it is to throw sweets to all the little children. She performed her task so well that at one moment I saw the father, the child, the god-father, the god-mother, the captain and the whole band thrown one upon the top of the other without succeeding in making a little Christian. At length, by dint of clever manœuvring on the part of the Captain, we reached the end of our labours; the most complete order was restored at the steps of the Church. The bells made their silvery voices heard, the parish serpent the organ and the oboes and the horn, all tried to make the loudest noise, and the priest and the schoolmaster baptised my poor grandson so conscientiously and with so much salt and water that he was violently sick and caught a cold in his eye which partly blinded him for the moment. I have named him Astolphe, that one day he may go, like his patron saint, to the moon and bring back some bottles of common-sense. Like all the sensible members of your august Assembly, everyone went home as soon as the ceremony was over. I was so deeply touched by the kindness of these poor peasants, at a time when so many others are taking up arms only to burn a Château and kill their overlords, that I had great difficulty in restraining my tears. May the man who first devised means of destroying the natural connection between poverty and wealth, weakness and strength, and that righteous and sweet conjunction of gratitude with kindness, be for ever accursed in the memory of mankind."

Delphine, as a faithful follower of the principles of Rousseau, insisted upon nursing Astolphe, and as her health was excellent no objection was offered. In spite of her great desire to return to the Chevalier, Mme. de Sabran could not resolve to enter the capital and remained at Niederviller until the month of June. There she anxiously followed the events in progress at Paris: the reform of the Constitution which overthrew the whole social organisation of France, and the profound disturbances which shook the country; she did not hide her keen anxiety from Boufflers, who had remained so long under his delusions. On May 4, she wrote to him, "So you are beginning to observe that all is not for the best in the best of all possible worlds, and to suspect that there are monsters in towns as there are in forests. We have not yet reached the end, and all that we have read in history of barbarous ages will never equal all that we are destined to undergo. The fetters which should restrain the multitude are now broken and it will use the liberty that you would give it to cut all our throats, not upon one St. Bartholomew's night, but in ten thousand of them. I tremble when I think that you are in the midst of this gulf, and that at any moment I may see you disappear from view."

In the month of June Mme. de Sabran left Niederviller with Elzéar to go to Plombières for the usual season, and on the 11th of June she writes, "I am now at Plombières which I reached without difficulty alone with Elzéar, and on my journey I only met one donkey with the national cockade, who seemed quite proud of his new decoration." At Plombières she found the old Comtèsse de Marsan. Misfortune brings people together and "they found unspeakable joy in talking with people of their own way of thinking." So these two ladies never left one another, and lamented in company the misfortunes of the age. They soon became very intimate. During this period, on July 14, took place in the Champ de Mars, the famous Festival of Federation, which seemed for the moment to restore harmony and reconcile all Frenchmen. Finally, in September, Mme. de Sabran, in spite of all her fears, gave way to the representations of the Chevalier and the prayers of her daughter, who had returned to Paris with her husband and her children. Accordingly she resolved to enter the capital. There for some months she spent her life, filled with trouble and anxiety, relieved only by the love of her daughter and the caresses of her grandchildren.[1]

[1] All the letters included in this chapter and in the following chapters not otherwise stated are unedited and form part of the collection of autographs of the Comte de Croze-Lemercier.

CHAPTER VI

1790—1791

Delphine's life at Paris—Her connections—Comtesse Alexandre de la Rochefoucauld—The Marquise de Chateaubriand—M. de Rosambo—M. de Malesherbes—The Vicomte René de Chateaubriand—The Troubadour—M. d'Esterno—Discord in the young household—Anxiety of Mme. de Sabran—She resolves to leave France—She goes to Rheinsberg

The political situation was not the only subject which caused Mme. de Sabran anxiety. Other reasons for uneasiness existed in her domestic life. The young couple whose union had given her so much satisfaction at first, and such reasonable hopes of permanent happiness, appeared, since the return to Paris, to have suffered some diverse influence; their affection seemed to have strangely cooled and there were serious signs of a misunderstanding between them. To what causes were to be attributed a change so unfortunate at the moment, so ominous for the future? Whilst they lived in the country, in the isolation of Anisy, Plombières, or Niederviller, Delphine had been a most tender and most affectionate model of wives and had devoted herself entirely to her young husband; but when they had returned to Paris she had to live like all women in her position in society, to appear at evening parties and social functions, and supper with her friends. With all the bloom and freshness of her twenty years, with her beautiful fair hair and charming figure, Delphine was as attractive as a woman can be. Boufflers called her, not without reason, the Queen of the Roses. She was a surprising success and her admirers were legion; nor was the fact out of harmony with the customs of the age and the society in which she lived.

Simple and inexperienced, Delphine was greatly flattered by the attentions which tickled her youthful fancy. She liked to hear that people thought her pretty, still more to be told so; like a true daughter of Eve she was naturally a coquette and in the intoxication of her social success this tendency increased. She certainly loved her husband, but that was no reason why others should not admire her. All the women of her society had their special admirers. Unfortunately the delicate, susceptible nature of Armand de Custine could not adapt itself to this change. He had sincerely believed that love was eternal and Delphine's flirtations vexed him. He kept his feelings to himself, suffered uncomplainingly and became estranged from his wife. She, on the other hand, knowing that she had done no harm, was worried in her turn because he did not show the affection which she thought she had deserved. She therefore sulked and flirted more than ever. In this way husband and wife were rapidly drifting apart. Mme. de Sabran had been informed of the new situation by her daughter, and her anxiety was extremely keen.

The two great friends of Delphine, who seemed to have upon her, at this time, the chief if not the best influence, were the Comtesse Alexandre de la Rochefoucauld,[1] Comtesse Alex as she was familiarly known, and the Marquise de Chateaubriand. Very pleasant, clever and distinguished, the Comtesse Alex, had "large blue eyes with black eyebrows, which suited her very well, was vivacious, daring and a good talker; a little bold, but, at the bottom, good-hearted, independent and cheerful."[2] Holding a high position, the Comtesse Alex lived in great style; several times a week she opened her drawing-rooms in the Rue de Clichy and every member of society who had not become an *émigré* hastened to her house. A constant visitor at these receptions was her cousin german, the Vicomte Alexandre de Beauharnais and his wife the attractive Joséphine, the future Empress of the French. Delphine, of course, never missed one of these evenings at which she was a striking figure surrounded by a circle of

[1] Adélaide Marie Françoise Pyvart de Chastullé, born in 1769, married June 9, 1788, Alexandre François, Comte de la Rochefoucauld, ambassador at Dresden.
[2] *Mémoires* of Mme. de Rémusat.

admirers. Delphine's other great friend was the Marquise de Chateaubriand. She belonged to a family famous in legal circles ; her father, Le Pelletier de Rosambo, was chief justice, and her grandfather, M. de Malesherbes, the first President of the Court of Aids.[1] In 1786 she had married Jean Baptiste de Chateaubriand, Councillor to the Parliament of Brittany.[2] She lived in the Rue de Bondy with her husband at the house of her father, M. de Rosambo. Introduced by her friend to the Rosambo and Malesherbes families, Delphine soon became extremely intimate with them and for her they showed much interest and affection.

It was at the house of M. de Rosambo that she met, for the first time, her friend's brother-in-law, the Vicomte René de Chateaubriand, who was afterwards to play so sad a part in the story of her life. The young officer had just arrived in Paris, knew no one and only appeared in his brother's family.[3] Delphine was naturally brought into constant contact with him and thought him a somewhat insignificant figure, so their relations were confined to common politenesses ; moreover, the young man was of a somewhat austere character, and far from approving or sharing the very lively existence of his sister-in-law and those about her, he was inclined to disapprove of it. In speaking of his brother's family, Chateaubriand says, in his *Mémoires*, " The President, Le Pelletier de Rosambo, when I arrived in Paris, was a perfect type of irresponsibility. At this time minds and morals were somewhat disturbed, a fact symptomatic of an approaching revolution. Magistrates were ashamed of their position and laughed at the gravity of their fathers. Men like Lamoignon, Molé, Séguier, and D'Aguesseau wished to fight and not to judge. Their wives ceased to be respected family ladies, and left their gloomy residences to become

[1] Malesherbes (Chrétien Guillaume de Lamoignon, 1721-1794), grandson of the celebrated attorney-general de Lamoignon, was twice minister under Louis XVI. He had two daughters : Alice Thérèse, born Feb. 6, 1756, married May 30, 1769, Louis le Pelletier de Rosambo ; Françoise Pauline, born July 15, 1758, married M. de Montboisser.

[2] Born at St. Malo, June 23, 1750. The three daughters of the President de Rosambo married : the first, the Marquis de Chateaubriand ; the second, the Comte Pelletier d'Aunay ; the third, the Comte de Tocqueville.

[3] Chateaubriand came to Paris in 1787 with his two sisters, Lucile (Mme. de Caux) and Julie (Mme. de Farcy).

society figures. The height of good taste was to be American in town, English at Court, and Prussian in the army, to be anything rather than French, while acts and words were but sequences and inconsistencies."

Though M. de Rosambo, with his carelessnesss and his objection to the new ideas, felt no great sympathy with the young Vicomte, M. de Malesherbes charmed him in spite of his surliness and roughness and he wrote concerning him:

"M. de Malesherbes was delighted to be in the middle of his children, grandchildren, and great-grandchildren. Many a time at the beginning of the revolution have I seen him come into Mme. de Rosambo's house hot with political excitement, throw off his wig, lie down on the carpet of my sister-in-law's room and let himself be mauled by a whole pack of children, amid a fearful noise. As far as his manners are concerned he seemed a somewhat vulgar man. But the first words which he spoke showed that he was a man of old family and of the higher magistracy. He was learned, honest and courageous, but so passionate and impetuous that he said to me one day, speaking of Condorcet, 'That man has been my friend; to-day I should have no scruples in killing him like a dog!'"

The Comtesse Alex, Delphine and Mme. Chateaubriand lived in the closest intimacy. These three madcaps, the eldest of whom was about twenty, thought of nothing but pleasure, parties, balls, and entertainments; they were continually together, morning, afternoon and night; anything was an excuse for meeting—the arrangement of a party, a walk in the neighbourhood with some pleasant young people, or cheerful suppers at one another's houses. Though there was nothing reprehensible in all this, it was a life hardly suitable for young women of twenty, and Delphine's husband grew more and more weary of it; but when he begin to criticise this excessive frivolity, Delphine easily proved that his causes for complaint were imaginary and had no foundation in fact. However, the examples set by Delphine's friends were of a kind to inspire anxiety.

The Comtesse Alex in particular was a woman of the age and as little of a prude as the age permitted. She had inspired two lovers simultaneously with adoration, Victor de X——[1] and M. d'Esterno: she remained faithful to her marriage vows, but she was quite ready to receive attention from other quarters. Moreover, Victor de X—— and M. d'Esterno were close friends and well aware that they were rivals. Mme. de Custine and Mme. de Chateaubriand were, of course, fully informed of their friend's intrigues and afforded her every assistance; Mme. de Custine even became the official confidant of Victor de X—— and flattered by this mark of confidence, she showed the utmost zeal in the task of performing this very dangerous part. Victor, in despair at the purity of the Comtesse Alex, was continually bringing his griefs to Delphine and asking her for the consolations of friendship. The young woman jestingly nicknamed him the Troubadour, and the name fitted so well that no other is used in the course of the correspondence.[2]

These pleasant relations had gone on for some time when the Comtesse Alex resolved to leave France for the time being, and to settle in Brussels with her father. As may be imagined, the Troubadour soon found a pretext for following his Dulcinea; M. d'Esterno, who also feared, with reason, that he would be outstripped if he remained at Paris, travelled to Brussels. These successive departures deprived Delphine of her daily society and caused her much vexation, but were a source of no less satisfaction to Armand de Custine and Mme. de Sabran. Delphine was thus left alone in Paris, separated from her friends. But she could fall back upon the post and she turned this resource to the best account. To increase the interest of their correspondence, the Troubadour and his confidant had resolved to keep it a secret from the Comtesse Álex. Delphine's conscience did not trouble her about this small piece of treachery—a confidant has a definite position and no harm could be done—as she was quite resolved to play no other part. However, a perusal of the correspondence inclines one to think that Mme. de Custine was quite prepared to assume the position

---

[1] There is every reason to believe that Victor de X—— was Prince Victor de Broglie, a son of the Marshal, but the identity is not certain.

[2] Nicknames were a mania of the age, and the three friends called the Comtesse Alex "Rose Pompon" or "Frivolity," and we shall find constant references to her under these titles in the course of the narrative.

of consoler, and really felt deeply hurt that she was not the sole object of the Troubadour's attention.

In 1791 the situation in France became daily more alarming and inspired men's minds with apprehensions increasingly serious. Mme. de Sabran who foresaw the course of events with astonishing insight, would have left the town long before if she had not been detained by the fear of abandoning her daughter. As long as she remained in Paris she might hope, by her affection, her advice and her tact, to restore harmony to the household and put an end to what was nothing more than a deplorable misunderstanding. In her absence, however, under what influence was Delphine likely to come, and what would happen to these two children who were more or less separated though they had scarcely begun family life? These considerations caused Mme. de Sabran the most painful anxiety, and her heart bled at the thought of this happiness which she had so carefully built up and which would soon, perhaps, be nothing more than a ruin. She would gladly have entrusted her daughter to a reliable friend, but unfortunately all in whom she might have had confidence had already gone into exile. She had no one to whom she could commend Delphine, no one to advise her or guide her and in time of need to save her from irreparable disaster. Armand de Custine, whose feelings were hurt, as we have seen, was quite anxious to go away, had applied for readmission to the service and expected his nomination daily, but what would become of Delphine if she remained in this grievous isolation thrown upon her own resources and almost entirely abandoned?

These very reasonable considerations caused Mme. de Sabran to hesitate for a considerable time, but she had duties to perform to others than to Delphine; she was also in charge of Elzéar, a weak, feeble creature who could not do without her. If she disappeared in the storm this unfortunate child, left without resources, would be reduced to the most miserable existence; "I become more necessary than ever," she writes, "to my poor Elzéar, who has no other than myself who can help him to extricate himself from this terrible storm in which everything will be engulfed, family, wealth, and position." These fears tortured her and profoundly troubled her mind. The death of Mirabeau,[1] and with him the disappearance of the last hopes of the monarchy, brought her to a decision. Sacrificing to her love for Elzéar her affection for Delphine and the Chevalier de Boufflers she resolved to leave France. She attempted to persuade Boufflers, her daughter, and her grandchildren to go with her, but Boufflers was detained by serious political interests and regarded the situation as by no means desperate, though he promised to join his friend as soon as possible. Delphine, also, did not take the matter seriously. She was persuaded that everything would turn out well and that her mother and Elzéar, after a quiet tour abroad, would return in peace to France and be the first to laugh at their empty fears. Hence she thought it was useless to disturb the course of her existence. In short, Mme. de Sabran's representations were useless and she was confronted with invincible opposition. She was heart-broken at leaving those whom she loved so deeply in the midst of so tragical a situation, but her love for Elzéar won the day over all other considerations. The Bishop of Laon, who was forced to go into exile in consequence of the Civil Constitution of the Clergy,[2] urged her with all his influence to follow his example. Mme. de Sabran therefore resolved to start with Elzéar. But it was not enough to wish herself away from Paris; where was she to go and in what country to find a refuge? Fortunately for her the only difficulty was the choice of alternatives. Mrs. Buller begged her to come and stay with her in London, and placed her house, her purse, and her affection at her disposal; "do please say that you are coming here, that you rely upon me, and that you understand that whatever I have is yours. Say that with the confidence of a heart which knows the meaning of friendship. You have but a narrow strait to pass and you will find health and rest." She offered to come as far as Dover to meet her and save her the anxieties of the journey. On the other hand, the Countess of Stahremberg[3] offered

[1] April 2, 1791.
[2] A law of July 12, 1790, obliged the priests to take the oath to the Civil Constitution of the Clergy, but the majority of them and almost all the bishops refused. The clergy were thus divided into two parties, the jurors and non-jurors.
[3] Louise Françoise d'Aremberg, born in 1744, daughter of the Duke Charles d'Aremberg and sister of Count Auguste de la Marck, had married,

her a charming refuge near Vienna, and wrote to her on April 6th: "My own darling, the most charming of the democracy or of the aristocracy, whom I love with all my heart, come as soon as possible and breathe the pure air of our mountains. There is no day when I do not think, in my Cistercian convent,[1] of the happiness of seeing you here. I am busy at this moment arranging a little house which I intend for you and Elzéar. It will be in the prettiest part of our dwelling, and already feels the happiness which you are preparing for it."

Finally Prince Henry of Prussia, who had seen a great deal of Mme. de Sabran during his two visits to Paris in 1784 and 1788,[2] and had been very friendly with her, insisted that she should come and join him in the Castle of Rheinsberg.[3]

After mature consideration Mme. de Sabran resolved to go to Rheinsberg, thinking that it would be a pleasanter place for Elzéar to visit, and that the assured protection of Prince Henry might prove very useful. On May 15th she started, weighed down with grief and a prey to the gloomiest presentiments. She did not think, as so many *émigrés* did, that she was only going to make a simple visit of a few weeks. Her insight left her under no illusion; she knew that her exile might last for many years, and that she would, perhaps, never see again the dear ones whom she was leaving in the middle of the storm. To facilitate her retirement she concealed the

in 1781, Louis, Count and afterwards Prince of Stahremberg, who was the Austrian ambassador to the Hague, and afterwards to London.

[1] This Chartreuse was admirably situated near Vienna on a lofty hill overlooking the whole of the town and the neighbourhood. It was formerly a Convent of Camaldules which had been confiscated by the Emperor Joseph II. and divided between the Prince de Ligne and Count Stahremberg. The new owners had done their best to make the vast rooms more or less habitable.

[2] Prince Henry, the brother of Frederick and himself a famous general, had come to France in 1784 in the attempt to neutralise the influence of Austria. He had been a great success in society, and, much hurt by the behaviour of his nephew Frederick William II., he returned to France in 1788 with the intention of remaining there. But the anxiety caused by the outbreak of the Revolution obliged him to postpone this idea and return to Rheinsberg.

[3] The Castle of Rheinsberg, some kilometres from Berlin, near Mecklenburg, had been occupied by Frederick during his youth. He presented it to his brother, who retired to it in 1789 and lived there until his death. It was a magnificent residence, in the middle of numerous lakes and immense forests.

real object of her journey, and made her way first to the Château de Raismes, near Valenciennes, the residence of the Comtesse Auguste de la Marck, taking with her Elzéar and Charles de Mellet, the son of her cousin german. From Raismes she went to Flanders and, after a short stay in Brussels, started for Germany which she crossed by short stages, reaching Rheinsberg on July 20th.

We do not propose to follow her journey or the story of her long years of exile, for the reason that Mme. de Custine is the subject of this study. She and Elzéar will, therefore, reappear only as they come into direct connection with Delphine.

CHAPTER VII

MAY TO DECEMBER, 1791

Loneliness of Mme. de Custine—Departure of her husband for the army—Correspondence with the Troubadour—Anxiety of Mme. de Sabran—Comtesse Alex—Her lovers—She returns to Paris—Departure of the Chevalier de Boufflers for Rheinsberg

It will be remembered that in the course of the year 1790, the Comtesse Alex, the Troubadour, and M. d'Esterno had taken refuge in Brussels. When Mme. de Sabran started with Elzéar for Rheinsberg, Delphine gave her brother several messages for her friends. To the Comtesse Alex, in particular, she sent her portrait and a little bonnet, the latest creation of a fashionable milliner. Elzéar had another commission more difficult to perform, to see the Troubadour, talk to him of Delphine and to write to Paris at once stating in what frame of mind he was, " whether he was happy, cheerful, or mortally sad." This was a somewhat strange commission for a brother, but the intimacy between Delphine and Elzéar was quite extraordinary, almost abnormal. It is as well at the outset that the reader should understand this situation which might not be inferred at first sight. There was between Elzéar and his sister the most rare and unusual intimacy. They had no secrets from each other, and though Elzéar was still almost a child, he possessed considerable influence and real authority over his sister. Delphine's letters are a tissue of extraordinary confidences; she informs her brother of the smallest details of her existence, tells him even the most intimate secrets of her domestic life and carries this so far as to send him copies of letters from her admirers. Her brother was to her perhaps even more than a confessor, and she reveals to him the inmost recesses of her heart. The fact is astounding but it remains a fact.

Elzéar, therefore, as he passed through Brussels, delivered the messages with which he had been commissioned and sent his sister the thanks of the Comtesse Alex, who thought her friend's portrait excellent and was charmed with the bonnet. As for the Troubadour, Elzéar could not hide the fact that his exile had tried him severely; " he is sad, pale, changed." This news caused the tender-hearted Delphine such vexation that she declares her real feelings. " He is, then, really unhappy. How deeply this idea grieves me. You may laugh at me as much as you like, but I love him more than ever; my, loneliness has increased this madness. I love all that is dear to him, even the Comtesse Alex. Perhaps you think me too kind, and you wish that I had more self-respect. Well, my ideas do not agree with yours, for it seems to me that to love truly one must put oneself absolutely aside, and live only for the object of one's affection."

Thus confronted with her brother, Delphine makes no scruple in throwing aside her position of confidant, and plainly declares herself in love with the Troubadour. She even goes so far in her irresponsible childishness as to reproach her friends for duplicity for which she was alone to blame. " I expect they are getting on very well together at my expense," she writes; " it is dreadful to have to complain of one's friends, especially when one loves them in spite of their wrong doing." She adds with bitterness, " One thing is perfectly clear, that your poor sister will never be happy or loved." Another point is clearer still, namely, that Delphine could no longer hide the vexation that she felt at the Troubadour's indifference, which wounded her self-esteem.

The life which the young woman led at Paris was not of a kind to distract her thoughts or to change the course of her ideas. She lived in almost complete isolation, hardly seeing anybody except her husband, from whom she was more than ever estranged, the Chevalier de Boufflers and a few friends from time to time. Delphine writes to her brother of the sadness of her position. " I am thus

MAY TO DECEMBER, 1791

entirely abandoned to Providence. My situation is a very suitable one for developing courage and resignation. Hitherto I have been as sad as a nightcap. I spend my day at the piano, singing sad songs, the gloomiest I can find; such are my pleasures." She was soon to find herself even more isolated and lonely. Mme. de Chateaubriand, her only remaining friend, left Paris in her turn to spend the summer at Malesherbes with her husband and her father. As for Armand, he had requested to be attached as aide-de-camp to General Lückner and was on the point of departing to join the army of the Rhine. "I have become a hermit by force," writes the young woman, "not by vocation; this life will soon make me tongue-tied."

Fortunately the Chevalier de Boufflers was a near neighbour, and she often paid him a visit with her son Gaston. One day quite an amusing incident occurred. "I must tell you an amusing trick played by Gaston. Yesterday I took him out to the house of the Chevalier de Boufflers. I was quite alone, without an attendant, and as we passed in front of the grenadier who is on guard at the house of M. de La Fayette,[1] he pulled my hand saying that he wanted to kiss the grenadier. When I tried to dissuade him from this extraordinary whim everyone looked at me. You may imagine my embarrassment when he kept crying 'I want to kiss the grenadier.' At last I let go his hand and he ran across the street by himself as fast as he could and kissed the sentinel, who was much surprised at the child's affection. Gaston was then quite content and came jumping back to me saying 'I am very fond of the grenadiers; I am a good citizen.' He is a furious democrat, but I shall be afraid to take him out again; the grenadiers will be thinking that it is I who want to kiss them." She then goes on to give some news of the only human beings about her. "Gaston is very well, as we have just seen; Astolphe is growing and becoming a very fine boy. Peïha, the dove, is cooing more than ever, but a misfortune has happened to Galaor,

---

[1] Mme. de Custine lived in the Rue de Bourbon (now the Rue de Lille), opposite the residence of the Prince de Salm (now the Palais of the Legion of Honour), which was No. 66. La Fayette lived at No. 81 and Boufflers at No. 127 of the same street—the latter with his cousin, the Duchesse de Biron.

Elzéar's dog, an animal of a wandering frame of mind; he has run away and cannot be found."

In the month of May Delphine's position became even sadder. Her husband left Paris as he had decided, to join the army of Lückner. At the moment of parting both felt certain sad presentiments and attempted to forget their past estrangement. Though their harmony was not completely restored, Delphine could not see her husband leave her without a real sense of grief.

"*Paris, May* 28, 1791.

"To-day I have been abandoned to the care of Providence; the son[1] went away this morning. He was very nice at the time of leaving me and most affectionate, while I was really heart-broken at his departure. I cannot understand it; if he had always been as he has during these last three days we should almost have been happy, but what a difference and what coldness. Still, that which astonished the mother so much has always existed; it is unexampled.

"He was very ill and much changed and I am very anxious about his health. Perhaps the warm countries in which he is going to live will do him some good. I do not know, but I am full of sad presentiments and my heart is so full that I dare not analyse them. Pity me, for I am unhappy and I fear that I may become more so. I want all your letters and those of my good mother. I send her my best love; let me hear all about her."

When the sadness of this separation had died away, as it speedily did, Delphine, to occupy her leisure and avoid boredom, resumed her correspondence with the Troubadour more vigorously than ever. A few extracts will show her character better than all the criticisms in the world. In May, 1791, the Troubadour wrote from Brussels, "I am the most unhappy of men. To love without being loved is unheard of torment and I wish for death. Why am I so unhappy as to have known this woman who has thrown her spell upon me and tortures me by her severity?" Very naturally the Troubadour thinks his young confidant charming and admits

---

[1] In her correspondence with her friends Mme. de Custine almost always refers to her husband by the name of son or brother.

that if anyone could console him it would certainly be Mme. de Custine, with her adorable character. "I may tell you without flattery, my charming friend, that you are so simple and so interesting that it is difficult to see you and not become attached to you." The Troubadour's speeches were merely conventional compliments which meant nothing more, but Delphine took them literally and showed a growing inclination to console the grieving lover. She wrote to him letters of a pressing nature, the intentions of which could not be mistaken; under the pretext of bringing him to reason she asked him to question his heart and see whether he was not mistaken concerning the object of his love. She reminded him, with some malice, of "the thousand silly things that he had written to her," of her room "which had witnessed so many sweet moments," of "the blue sofa," which he had certainly not forgotten, etc. Under these conditions could he feel for the Comtesse Alex the growing affection of which he boasted?

"Do you really think yourself, then, in love? And when you were here, when the meetings of which you told me took place, did you think you were in love with the Comtesse Alex? It is a profanation of the idea. I begin to think that you do not know what real love is; at this moment, at least. I tell you that you are not in love with anyone; you know how true my intuitions are, so you may be sure that I am not deceived. One lives and breathes only for the beloved object; all else disappears and becomes nothing and we do not know if others exist. That, I think, is what a lover should really feel.

"Write to me, my friend, for I am abandoned by all who are dear to me, mother, my brother and M. de Custine are all gone. I am terribly sad and frightened at my own loneliness. At any rate tell me that you think of me sometimes and talk of me to the Countess Alex. I think so much of absent ones that I want to know whether they are thinking of me.

"My kind regards to M. d'Esterno and my thanks for his remembrances of me. Generally people whom I like forget me at once, a result of my fortunate destiny!"

All these dissertations upon love and these variations upon the same theme had the most deplorable effect upon

Delphine's excitable temperament. Her isolation exaggerated her feelings and her sadness; she had nothing to occupy her heart and felt deeply vexed in consequence. She was angry at seeing her friend surrounded with the attentions and flattery of interested men while she, who was quite as young and pretty, was reduced to the humiliating position of confidant and adviser when she would have been glad to pay a leading part, and she revolted against the injustice of her destiny.

Though Mme. de Custine was not a faithful friend, the Troubadour, on the other hand, showed himself a faithful lover. He obstinately pretended not to understand the very obvious meaning of his young mentor's moral advice or the exhortations which she showered upon him. He continued to lament his position and regarded himself as so unhappy that he thought of leaving his beloved for ever, and talked of entering the Russian service. Delphine thought it her duty to scold him for so unreasonable an idea. "I cannot say that I approve of your projects in the least, indeed I think them very foolish. Why leave your relatives, your friends, and your country for ever, and who is driving you to such foolishness? One whom you love and whom you see, does not return your affection. Therefore you wish to flee for ever. A fine means of touching her heart! Even supposing she loved you, what do think would be the result ? I know, my friend, that she will never forget her position and you would simply make her unhappy for life. Surely that alone is enough to calm your foolishness; you have a kind and sensitive heart; think, therefore, that your happiness might involve the misfortune of the one you love. Tell me frankly, is it real love that you feel and do you not deceive yourself? The emotions of an excitable, lively temperament often pass for love. Even if it were real love, such as has never been seen, such as exists only in novels, I think I should still blame you, for the heroes of novels display a patience beyond all bounds. They are made happy by a look and are content with very little. You can see how far you are from love of this kind, for you possess supreme happiness according to them, as you see her constantly; yet you complain, are desperate and wish to flee. What has become of that gaiety which was so infectious to all about you? I thought that nothing could change it. Avoid these gloomy ideas which lead you to wish for death. It you were in love, death should make you tremble, because it would separate you from the beloved object."

Delphine always loyally informed her brother of all her love affairs and was so scrupulous as to send him copies of her correspondence with the urgent but remarkable advice to show everything to the "good mother." Mme. de Sabran was greatly shaken by these admissions which confirmed her fears only too fully and hastened to write to her daughter to try to bring her back, if possible, to sense and reason. In spite of the somewhat disturbing state of her health she found strength to give her some sound advice. " Your brother has received the bundle of all your confidences by the last post. You know that I detest the Troubadour and his letters made me frightfully angry. They seem to me nothing but empty compliments. Be careful, my child, for you are playing a dangerous game, and if I were a poet like your brother I should tell you that no fair one can ever touch the quiver or the arrows of love without pricking her fingers. Let us hope that his torch is not also concerned, for in that case the butterfly is burned and sound reason reduced to ashes like everything else. I assure you that you are too kind, and I only blame you for not being aware of the fact and not rating yourself more highly. I should like to see you a little more distant and, above all, a little more proud. Pride is the safeguard of our poor sex. If we do not respect ourselves we are not respected and in the present age respect is better than love. Here I see you smile and think that I am in my dotage, but in a few years' time you shall tell me what you think of it."

The Comtesse Alex maintained a fairly regular correspondence with Delphine and readily gave her full details concerning the course of her life. In April, 1791, she wrote her a long letter recounting the absurdities of her admirers. The document is so curious as to be worth quotation in its entirety.

BRUSSELS, 1791.

" It is quite true, my dear girl, that I have not written to you for ages and I am well aware of the fact, but I have not a moment to myself. The two inseparables never leave me all day; they arrive at eleven o'clock and stay until dinner time and then torment me because they think I spend too much time in dressing. In the evening they come at five o'clock and stay till supper. I am never free except when they make some excursion and then, I admit, it is very strange not to see them arrive. The Troubadour has been in Holland for thirteen days and M. d'Esterno has been for a week at Spa; they have come back as absurd as ever, if you understand me.

"Then they both came to me the day before yesterday looking very sad. They talked constantly in German but I saw by their faces that they had some unusual plan. I was not deceived; I took M. d'Esterno aside and worried him until he revealed the famous project, telling me that he would certainly not be outstripped in generosity by his friend. The fact is, that he has just heard of a little house, a league and a half from here, in the middle of the forest, in a very countrified district. They propose to set up house there with only an old cook to look after them and they intend to leave their servants and horses here; one of their grooms will come for orders every day. You may imagine that this proposal seemed ridiculous to me, especially in the case of M. d'Esterno, whose wife is here. I told him I hoped that they would soon be driven back to Brussels by boredom. They have taken away all the drawings that they had begun for me, to finish at the little house, saying that they will have no distractions, that society wearied them and that they would at least be able to speak at their ease of the object which formed their only occupation.

"Yesterday evening they arrived. I saw the Troubadour taking up pencils and drawings and putting them all away in his portfolio. As he usually kept them in mine, I concluded that the departure was arranged for the next day; consequently I was cross and worried and showed it. I went away to supper; when I went upstairs my chambermaid gave me a little note which he had left, in which he asked permission to write at greater length, not knowing whether that would be agreeable to me. He also told my chambermaid to come down when she heard a whistle and that he would give her a song which I had asked from him because he would not have time to write it out as he was starting early the next morning. She heard the whistle, went down and returned with the letter. He told me that he was going away and I am keeping all his letters for you to see.

"This morning, as I woke, the third letter arrived from the little house. They told me they had hoped that the country and the calm, pure air would have brought some peace to their harassed minds, but that the same uneasiness had pursued them everywhere. They thought that I was vexed and asked me to send a few words of consolation. This I did, for they are so excited that they may be capable of the worst extravagances. You see how dreadful my position is and yet you will not come and relieve the troubles of your friend. They have just told me that they will be here this evening. I will let you know what they propose to do and what they say.

"Above all, my dear Delphine, do not abuse my confidences; I have already noticed that you are not entirely frank with me, and if you wish me to speak plainly, it is this fact which has, to some extent, been the cause of my delay in writing to you. It would be dreadful to have any sense of reserve towards a friend and would entirely destroy my feelings for you. Such a thing, no doubt, is impossible, but I should be very unhappy if I found that I was mistaken.

"You reproach me for my treatment of Alex. You must admit, my dear girl, that this is a touch of prudery on your part. I have written four times to my husband, and he replied with a letter as short as usual. Goodbye, for I have no time to write at greater length to-day. I send you my warmest love, and if you can read my heart you will be very clever."

The last paragraphs of this letter betray a certain anxiety on the part of the Comtesse Alex. Her suspicions were soon confirmed. She guessed the little intrigue in progress about her and displayed some jealousy. Confronted with the demand for an explanation the Troubadour was unable to deny the evidence, but he swore by all the gods that his intimacy with Delphine had always been entirely innocent and that if the young woman had ever seemed to misinterpret his feelings it was a pure mistake on her part. The Comtesse Alex was not satisfied with this excuse from her admirer. Irritated by Delphine's double-dealing she wrote her a sharp letter reproaching her for her conduct and demanding to see all the letters from the Troubadour. But, " this was not so easy, as many of these letters were not intended for publication." To cut the discussion short, Delphine found an easy excuse; she professed that she had burned the whole of the correspondence. She affirmed, and was even ready to swear, that the Troubadour was beyond suspicion, that she had been the confidant of his feelings but nothing more, and that it was really dreadful to suspect so faithful a lover of inconstancy.

Either from credulity or from carelessness the Comtesse Alex was obliged to content herself with these somewhat lame excuses. She made peace with Delphine and the Troubadour was restored to favour and showed himself more attentive than ever. This small breach, so easily healed, none the less caused a certain coldness in their relations. Comtesse Alex began to sulk, the Troubadour stopped writing, and Delphine became the more sad and depressed in consequence. She cannot hide the terrible weariness which devours her in her letters. " I am sad to the point of death," she writes to her brother, " I mourn all day like the dove Peïha and sing your pretty song. Please write me a very sad one. Are there many Frenchmen in Prussia? there are none in Paris, and more people than ever are going away. Paris is full of strangers, and this winter there will be no society at all, a very cheerful prospect."

As a matter of fact, the emigration under the pressure of events had assumed great proportions, and the flight of the Royal Family on June 20, their arrest at Varennes, their return in the midst of a furious populace, and their confinement in the Tuileries, had raised the prevailing anxiety to the greatest height. In her loneliness Delphine had no means of distraction except to begin a fresh intrigue, an easy task for her, as her beauty attracted a thousand attentions. As usual Elzéar receives her confidences.

October 24, 1791.

"I have made the acquaintance of a delightful man, the pleasantest character possible, clever, educated, with a brilliant imagination and a great enthusiast, twenty-five years of age. Very ugly but very well made. His name is the Chevalier de Fontanges, and he is the cousin of a lady of that name whom I know. No one could be nicer or more extraordinary. He would perhaps, be dangerous to anyone but myself. Moreover, he is head over ears in love, and as my sad face inspired him with trust I have become the confidant of his sorrows. But the amusing part is that I know the lady with whom he is in love; she has taken a fancy to me and I am also her confidant. This is a little too much, and I am getting extremely tired of the part, for I am up to my ears in it. This Chevalier is a far more ardent lover than Saint Preux. The latter was an icicle compared with him and I, the poor confidant, am reduced to giving them advice and trying to bring them to reason. I am inclined to wear a black bonnet and take to crutches; you will find me in that costume when you come back."

M. de Fontanges was not the only case. Many other people gave their confidences to Delphine, even the Abbé de Vaux,[1] formerly Elzéar's tutor, "I have recently seen the Abbé de Vaux. He is surprisingly stout and fat, while he also made me his confidant, and entrusted me with the knowledge of his latest affection."

This, however, was too much and the young woman, angry at being obliged always to work for others when she would prefer her own pleasure, exclaims in mock indignation, "I rub my eyes, I wipe my looking-glass, and try to count the wrinkles which are doubtless upon my cheek. I propose to send to the parish clerk for my baptismal certificate, and shall learn, no doubt, that I am somewhere near sixty. I am as cross as old women are, and I am only appeased when I think that I am writing to my poor little brother; I feel young enough to love him, and very tenderly. I will even pardon your confidences when you have any to make, and I

---

[1] The Abbé de Vaux, who was also sometimes known as the "great Vaux," was not a priest. He had been Elzéar's tutor, and in 1793 was a professor in a college in Paris.

wish you would write me a song about my sad fate as confidant; it is a subject really worthy of a lament." She concludes with words marked by sincerity which plainly show her regretfulness. "But enough of all these loves of other people." Fortunately, Delphine is like a weather-cock, turning with every wind, and one passion has hardly been formed when it is succeeded by another. In October she admits to her brother that philosophy of the most abstract sort is absorbing the whole of her time. The miracle was brought about by chance, and a grave and serious subject inspired this madcap with the following amusing reflections. "One day when I was greatly bored, very sad and unable to find any occupation, I mechanically took the key of your brother's room and went in. I noticed the books and cast a glance of indifference upon them. I was saying to myself 'nothing interests me, I shall never find an absorbing occupation,' and was about to go out again when the critical moment arrived. A book of strange appearance caught my eye; I approached and read *The System of Nature*.[1] Some impulse drove me to open it, I ran over some pages, my interest increased, my curiosity was at its height. I carried off the book and devoured it. My passion is unlimited and I cannot tear myself away from it. It is very abstract but it interests me incredibly. You must read it; it is very dangerous, pure materialism, it makes me very sad and I assure you that it will drive me out of my senses. I am the most unhappy person in the world to find all my hopes of immortality destroyed. I already live in nonentity and have no further hold upon life, seeing that we are nothing but mechanical organisms. Men seem to me nothing more than little animals, acting only in their own interests and working each for themselves. How dreadful it is and what a fatal privilege is that of life."

Fortunately for Delphine an unexpected event was to bring some joy and cheerfulness to her life and take her away from the philosophical reading which troubled her so deeply. At

[1] *Système de la Nature*, or "Laws of the Physical and Moral World," by Mirabaud, London, 1770. This book appeared too materialist to Voltaire, who criticised it vigorously. The Baron de Holbach, who was known to be the author, had adopted a pseudonym, as he did not venture to sign his own name.

the outset of November the Comtesse Alex was anxious to see her mother, who had remained in Paris; she, therefore, left Brussels and came to reinstal herself quietly in the Rue de Clichy. No sooner had she arrived than she resumed her receptions with as much calmness as if Paris enjoyed perfect tranquillity. Delphine, delighted, in her isolation, to recover so dear a friend, ran to welcome her, completely forgetting the imprudence which she had herself committed and all the wrongs of which she had been guilty. An interesting commentary upon this is the fact that she loudly complimented herself upon the generosity of her heart, and this with a simplicity which borders upon irresponsibility.

"*November* 2, 1791.

"You really ought to be obliged to me for writing to you," she says to her brother, "for I am very busy. The Comtesse Alex is in Paris, and I do not leave her for a moment, and you may imagine that we have a great deal to tell one another. The strangest thing is the pleasure which I feel at seeing this little countess again; I love her with all my heart. I am really too kind and too frank and am not on the same level with all these people. I was made to live in a better world than this; I am unable to pretend, to hide my real feelings, and even if I am duped, I would not change my heart for that of anyone else. Pity me, for I am unhappy, though innocent, for in all this there is nothing whatever of any consequence; the only serious point is the sad reflections to which it gives rise. No doubt some ill-disposed fairy has cast a spell upon me to make me love all those who do not care about me."

The two friends made some slight reference to the past and exchanged a few remarks concerning the quarrel which had separated them, but without any bitterness. Delphine, therefore, writes upon this subject, " the Troubadour has remained in Brussels, but he has behaved very badly to me. He told stories about me to the Comtesse Alex, but fortunately did not succeed in making us quarrel. As ill luck will have it, the worse he has behaved, the more I like him. You will laugh at me, and with reason, but I cannot help it. Can one be expected to govern one's feelings?"

We do not know for what reason Victor de X. . . . had not accompanied Mme. de la Rochefoucauld ; the fact remains that he had not left Brussels. M. d'Esterno had not observed the same reserve and had shown the more haste to rejoin the Comtesse as the absence of his rival left him a clear field. He constantly met Delphine, and, as they had a certain sympathy for one another, confidences followed. " M. d'Esterno, a friend of the Troubadour and his rival, is in Paris. Our positions are so similar that we have naturally felt attracted ; he has entrusted me with all his secrets and has guessed mine or he had been told of them. At any rate, I constantly talk to him of Victor, and he constantly talks to me of the Comtesse Alex. We lament in concert the fickleness of our friends and the difference between our affection and theirs."

A short time after the return of Mme. de la Rochefoucauld the Chevalier de Boufflers resolved to leave France. He had regained his liberty, as the Constituent Assembly had broken up on September 30, and its last act had been to declare that none of its members could be re-elected. Since she had been living in Prussia Mme. de Sabran had constantly urged the Chevalier to keep his promise to come and join her. Prince Henry also insisted that he should come and try the peaceful, refined pleasures of Rheinsberg. Boufflers, who had gradually lost all his illusions concerning the Revolution, thought that he could do no better than follow his friend's advice, so he put his affairs in order, said goodbye to Delphine and started for Rheinsberg in the course of November, 1791.

CHAPTER VIII

JANUARY—JUNE, 1792

Correspondence between Elzéar and his sister—Elzéar's frame of mind—Life at Paris—The receptions of the Comtesse Alex de la Rochefoucauld—Delphine's admirers—The Comte Antoine de Lévis —the Chevalier de Fontanges—M. d'Esterno—M. de Moges.

On New Year's Day, 1792, Elzéar wrote to his sister to send her his good wishes. He took advantage of the occasion to give her a mild lecture; his admonitions are gracefully expressed and show a maturity of mind beyond his age. This admonition is so clever and so amusing that it was quite possibly inspired by Mme. de Sabran.

"*Rheinsberg, Jan. 2*, 1792.

"We are beginning a new year, my dear little sister. Heaven grant that it may be more prosperous than former years for you, as also for others, for you cannot pride yourself on being happy. If you want to have a numerous list of admirers this year, show yourself a little reserved and they will come in crowds, I promise you. You will be able to whistle them to you, as you want them.

"But this disgusting trade does not suit your frankness and transparency of character. You are too good to be admired, you are good enough to be sincerely loved. Be content with the pleasant portion which is yours. Those who are loved by everyone eventually cease to love themselves, the mind takes a false tone, the intellect becomes bewitched and the affections deteriorate. No head is strong enough to stand the heavy odour of so large a cloud of incense. It may be pleasant at first but soon it becomes customary, as perfumes may, and eventually we do not perceive its existence until age forces us to give it up. The society pleasure-lover is unwilling to abandon the habit of amusing herself and the desire for pleasure always remains; even in her old age she can only devote to religious purposes a heart as withered as her face. This is a lesson, my dear girl, which you will not find in the 'System of Nature,' but which you may discover at the bottom of your heart, if you like to look for it.

"No doubt, this annoys you, and I can hear you calling me a pedant, a preacher and a sermoniser, but be indulgent and pardon me the two pages of sound sense which I am sending you as a New Year's gift. I propose to recompense myself for it some day on the blue sofa, by talking nonsense with you to my heart's content."

But Elzéar was not content with preaching; with real powers of clairvoyance, he divined the kind of life which his sister was leading at Paris and the disturbing nature of the society which she constantly frequents. He describes it to her and analyses with unusual insight the dangers which threaten her, and to which her easy and confiding character makes her a certain victim.

"You, no doubt, are spending a brilliant winter amid the bustle of Paris. A fine carriage takes you to and fro twice a day from the Rue de Bourbon to the Hôtel de Chastullé, where all the agreeable society of Paris bows down before the little goddess, Frivolity. She, light as a pierrot, talks to one, sings with another, smiles at the third, and dances with all. Coquetry is in her eyes, seduction in her mouth, in all her gestures and in all her steps. She is admired and forgotten with equal rapidity and she forgets you also. In so frivolous a society love is merely a shuttlecock that is tossed to and fro, falls to the ground and no one picks it up.

"In this circle, which is only consistent in its constant succession of change, appears, I know not why, my transparently pure Delphine. Everyone tries to translate her words, for she speaks another language; everyone offers her false coins which she takes for real; she accepts their bills of exchange at the stipulated rate and pays for them in hard cash. They make sport of her, for they see that she always treats people seriously. They treat her badly for she has not a bad heart. Delphine does not see through them, is deceived and betrayed, and gives the most tender friendship in return for the most utter perfidy. And now, my dear, my novel is finished."

The anxiety which Elzéar felt concerning his sister was only too fully justified. At the moment when he was attempting to warn her against the danger of the society which she frequented and the desires which she felt, she was writing him a long letter in which she openly explained the numerous traps that had been laid for her. We must be just. A young woman, of unusual beauty and alone, deserves some credit for acting in self-defence. How far she resisted we do not know, but her urgent request that the "good mother" should be told everything, shows that she had, at least, the best intentions in the world.

"PARIS, *January* 4, 1792.

" Perhaps you think that I am writing to you to wish you a happy New Year, or to ask you to kiss our mother for me. Nothing of the kind! it is merely for the pleasure of talking to you, and of our good mother! This is the first year that I begin without her at my side and this should bring me ill-luck; so I foresee nothing pleasant in this coming year. I begin it very sadly, with gloomy presentiments, far from all those who are dear to me, anxious and uneasy.

"Poor little brother, when shall we be side by side upon my little sofa and able to talk freely? How often I regret you! I want to open my whole heart to you and to think aloud. I have so much to tell you that I hardly know where to begin. Let me speak first of all of Victor. He is nicer than ever and even his letters are less stiff since the little Comtesse has left Brussels. But as I hope that you will soon come back; I shall not send them to you, for it would mean copying out volumes. Enough for you to know that he has entirely cleared himself of the wrong-doing which I suspected and that I like him very much.

"Secondly, I see M. d'Esterno, who shows a confidence and respectful friendship towards me which is most touching, but he bores me to death, because he is rather stupid, poor man!

"Thirdly, the Chevalier de Fontanges, of whom I have given you and my good mother, full details. He is often brought into contact with me and is inspired with the deepest friendship for me, but it is pure friendship. I am not bored by this; it is kind but yet most extraordinary and like nothing else.

"Fourthly, an incident indeed wonderful, incredible and interesting: the Comte Antoine de Lévis has returned to Paris. He came to see me and instantly conceived the idea of appearing to be deeply in love with me. There was some magnificent acting, as he went upon his knees and uttered the tenderest protestations. In the midst of all this you must imagine your poor Delphine quite overwhelmed, surprised that anyone should think of her or take the trouble to play a comedy so well. I am really sorry that he is not sincere, for he is very nice and I am vexed that he should carry his acting so far. I see him constantly; he amuses but does not frighten me, for I do not believe a word he says. You can tell all this to our good mother, my best friend, upon whose indulgence I rely."

After exhausting the list of her chief admirers for the moment Mme. de Custine speaks to her brother of all their friends whom she constantly meets at Paris, where "life is quiet and very interesting." Everyone is calling out for Mme. de Sabran and is extremely astonished that she does not return with her son. Obviously, the anxiety which people felt had been allayed and Delphine shared the general blindness; she was persuaded that the Revolution was over and that her mother would shortly return to France. "I have seen the Comtesse Auguste.[1] I found her much changed but kind as ever. She complained considerably of you and mother. I have seen the Duchesse de Brancas, who was wonderfully kind to me and is impatiently expecting mother. The whole of society and all who are at

[1] The Comtesse August de la Marck.

Paris are delighted at her return; even Baron Gromecourt is quite lively. I have seen Mme. de Laage, Mme. de Rosambo and the Marquis de Sabran, and I should never finish if I attempted to repeat all the kind messages that they gave me for mother. Tell me about the Chevalier de Boufflers. He must have announced himself to his neighbour, for one only thinks of neighbours when one is living next to them.

"A thousand kisses to my mother; the tall son [1] is also commissioned to give her my best love and to bring her back here. All is perfectly calm and life is very pleasant, I assure you.

"M. d'Aramon is at Paris, but has not condescended to call upon me and barely acknowledges my existence when he meets me. How have I offended him? Please try to explain it. My best remembrances to Charles.[2] I have sent off all my mother's things by von Grimm.[3] My children are well.

"The Abbé Gimbelette is cheerful and lively as ever, and has also given me many fine messages, but I am not sufficiently eloquent to write them. Goodbye, write to me that you are coming back and then I shall not complain of this bad beginning to the year."

Delphine, far from taking offence at the sermon which her brother sent her for New Year, thanked him for it effusively and confessed with touching frankness, the distress of her heart, and the weakness of her nature. Though not subject to such fits of depression as Elzéar she was attacked by deep melancholy, against which she could defend herself only with the utmost difficulty. She also was the victim of a lack of moral stability for which she was hardly responsible.

"PARIS, *January* 28, 1792.

"I greatly need to write to you and to talk with you. I love you tenderly, and your last letter was charming. Nothing could be kinder or more sensible. In fact, I have almost been tempted to ask for your baptismal certificate.

[1] The Marquis de Custine, as we shall see in the following chapter, was at this time in Germany on government service.
[2] Charles de Mellet.
[3] Baron von Grimm, the famous writer, chargé d'affaires in France for the Duke of Saxe-Gotha, was returning to his own country.

"My poor little brother, you are quite right to preach to me: I want it. I have an evil mind which is always working and tormenting me. Nothing satisfies me; carelessness and discouragement have taken hold of me; I am by no means happy, I do not know why. I shall be very cross to-day; I am sorry that I chose it as the day for my letter to you, for I shall bore you to death. I am sad and I feel that it is incredibly pleasant to be able to tell you so.

"My poor little brother, why are we not together? we should be able to talk, to abuse the human race and the time would pass quickly. I am becoming fearfully misanthropic. If I were free, I would go round the world to find a true friend. I would go to every country and every state, and I expect that at the end of my search I should have had my trouble for nothing and should have found that everywhere men are the same and care for nobody but themselves. I should much like to make such a journey with you, but in Paris we should be disgusted at every step. I feel that I should always be taken in by appearances and should want your common sense to guide me."

Naturally, Mme. de Custine is careful not to abandon her laudable habits, and ends her letter with further details concerning the mental state of her admirers.

"Talking of novels, the Troubadour's novel continues as usual. He is hopelessly in love with the little goddess Frivolity and writes regularly, and his letters are not so stilted. His friend M. d'Esterno, is still here, groaning and coming to me to complain; he is a great bore, like a fish out of water, but I talk to him of the Troubadour and that makes him bearable.

"Comte Antoine continues to act the lover, but he is becoming a little too enterprising, and therefore I do not see him alone. Hence I have no doubt that he is growing rather tired of his foolish position. He is not the man to be satisfied with so little. The little Countess[1] is as frivolous as ever: she thinks she is with child: none the less, she proposes to return to Brussels, for which I am very sorry.

[1] The Comtesse Alex de la Rochefoucauld,

"You must have seen the tall son. I was hoping that mother would come back with him; she had spoken to me of her return but at present there is no further mention of it. Meanwhile, life goes on and we are separated. Yesterday I lunched with the Comtesse Auguste and we recalled past memories. I am still sad in consequence. I have never been so happy as at St. Amand; time past is gone for ever.

"Good-bye, dear brother, let me hear from you often to tell me how dear mother is. Try to bring her back soon. Paris is more peaceable than ever, in spite of all the efforts that have been made to disturb it."

As Mme. de Custine had not written for more than a month, Elzéar complains of her long silence. Delphine explains her reasons. She is unhappy through her fault and in virtue of her temperament. She cannot understand herself or the motives of her conduct. There are moments when she believes that she is going insane. Naturally her love affairs are the cause of this overwhelming melancholy. She seeks for sincere affection which she cannot find, and looks for an ideal with which she never meets.

"Paris, *March* 14, 1792.

"Well, dear brother, you have given your poor sister a nice scolding. You are quite wrong. What do you expect she has to write about? I am so sad and out of humour that I hardly feel inclined to send my sadness three hundred leagues away. I know you well enough to know that you will be saddened also and will be sorry for me, and why should I disturb your pleasure? It were better to leave me alone amid my gloom and let me forget myself.

"You will tremble when you read this tragic beginning and fear that you are to learn of some great misfortune. You may set your mind at rest; nothing has happened to me; I am quiet and peaceful as usual in my little retreat. But my heart is sick, or my head or any part of me that you please. The end of all this will be madness, for I do not see how anyone can bear the strain for long. Perhaps you imagine that I am going to explain all this; by no means, for I do not understand it myself; I do not know what I feel or what is passing within me. I only know that I am very unhappy at present. The best means of explaining my thoughts to you is to describe my actions. Perhaps you will be able to see your way through the whole.

"As for the Troubadour, our correspondence continues much as before, though I do not think it important enough to go to the trouble of copying his letters for you. However, my interest in him continues and I am always delighted to hear from him.

"The Chevalier de Fontanges, whose confidant I was, has suddenly fallen in love with me, though the fine passion which I have inspired does not touch me in the least; however, I have a warm feeling of friendship for him and rely upon him and his originality to amuse me, while his information is interesting. He is about to go away to Auvergne; so I shall have a second correspondent.

"M. d'Esterno remains here. He is under the impression that I am his friend, consequently he feels bound to come and inflict his Jeremiads upon me, which are simply wearying.

"M. de Moges, the new acquaintance introduced to me by the Comtesse Alex, also calls often, but is very quiet and tractable and an insignificant figure.

"M. de Lévis—but I must describe him to you for you do not know him. With handsome face, splendid eyes and a fine bearing, well made and very smart, he constantly thinks of his dress and his hair, and is continually preoccupied with his social success and sure that he ought to be a figure in society. He is by no means clever, but has plenty of small talk, attractive manners, cheerfulness and unconsciousness. I should think him a fickle character but good-hearted, very kind, incapable of perfidy and tactful to a degree. Such is the man whom I see most constantly, and who would like me to believe in his love. I like him and though I criticise him, I am glad to see him.

"Then I sometimes see at my house, M. de la Bourdonnais, M. d'Andlau, M. Koch, a deputy, the Marquis de Sabran, etc., and at the house of the Comtesse Alex I see the Comte de la Rochefoucauld, and Adrien de Laval pretty often. I think the latter very nice; he is an original and simple character. The only women with whom I am at all intimate are Mme. de Chateaubriand and the Comtesse Alex. If I began a list of other names I should never finish. Such is the society in which I pass my life very pleasantly. When there are no formal parties we spend the evening at one another's houses. I also see Mme. Robert Dillon and her husband, who is a pleasant fellow; mother ought to know him well. All these details are tiresome, but what am I to write about? Now try to discover why I am sad, or at any rate, terribly gloomy. I am good for nothing; I cannot read or write, which vexes me greatly, for I had drawn up an admirable plan of study. I can only say that I seem to be surrounded by the gloomiest presentiments; misfortune is prowling round me and I feel that it will catch me at last. I had better not have written to you. Goodbye, dear brother, you see that I am already half mad, for there is no sense in this letter."

"Misfortune is prowling round me," an ominous phrase which was to be terribly confirmed by the near future. There are, indeed, moments when Delphine seems to read the future with such strange lucidity as to cause deep apprehensions. Mme. de Sabran, much troubled by her daughter's letters, and by her intimacy with M. de Lévis, had urged and insisted that she should break off the acquaintance, which threatened danger, at the earliest opportunity. Delphine, who was ready to obey her mother, made firm resolutions to do so and proposed to use the next call made by the young man to put an end to his attentions. Unfortunately she had not considered her weakness of character. She describes, with some openness, her lack of firmness in the face of protestations and the incurable fickleness of her nature. But, at the same time, she asks for fresh advice, which she will listen to as carefully as before, and which she is just as likely not to follow.

"*Paris, April 23,* 1792.

"Let me, then, sit down for a talk with my good brother, my friend, the chosen one of my heart. Do you complain of my silence? No, for you have read the letter which I wrote to mother and you will pardon me. I am afraid that my foolishness must have caused her much grief. Her letter was charming; I have kissed it a thousand times and yours also. All this touches a guilty heart. You are quite right! people make a pretence only of loving me while I love them in reality. The fickleness of the hero somewhat destroys the romance. His portrait is that of the butterfly which anyone may catch who will. I have amused myself by making this thought the subject of a little drawing which I send you. How well you know me, my dear; what leads me astray is this vague sensitiveness which imagines the object of its preference and looks for it. I have a sense of void which follows me everywhere. I shall never have any but flashes of happiness, for my character is not a happy one. What am I to do? Drift with the current, as I have not the strength to swim against it. I shall never be criminal, for my goodness of heart will keep me from wrong.

"After the mother's charming letter I took the first opportunity to bring about a rupture and thought I had succeeded and complimented myself upon my performance. At any rate, I am ashamed of my weakness and I admit my wrong-doing, and you must admit that I am at least frank. Be sorry for me, love me, talk often of me to my good mother, tell her how much I need her counsel, her support and her tenderness."

With her usual unsteadiness and her extraordinary irresponsibility, Delphine immediately proceeds to describe fresh intrigues and new lovers; considerations of morality and advice though they seem at first to touch her deeply, obviously leave not the smallest impression on her mind. She feels no scruples even in jesting upon the subject.

"I spent a somewhat amusing evening to-day. I was alone and the young man of whom I have given you a rather frivolous description, the Comte de Moges, came to see me. He calls fairly often and I had not suspected his secret passion: to-day he declared himself. How different it is when one feels no interest in the person concerned! I was not moved from my coldness and did nothing but laugh and banter him. Just think! I *bantered* him! That will prove how little I care for him. Yet the poor man is fonder of me than of anyone, I am sure. How strange it is! I feel now that he would bore me to death. A lover who is not loved cuts a poor figure. At any rate, I did not deceive him. I simply told him that I did not and could not feel anything but friendship for him and I was not coquette enough to wish to torture him.

"As to the Chevalier de Fontanges, his sensitive heart has suddenly changed; he has made the most loving avowals and written the most affectionate of letters. My coldness or, at least, my simple friendship has been a great shock to him: he seems to be returning to his former affection. Love apart, I am really very fond of him. His originality pleases me and we get on so well in conversation. He is the only one who can *talk*; you know what the word implies, a task not always easy, even for the clever; we discuss philosophy together, and he is Helvetius in person. These principles delight and attract me. But he is a little too much of an aristocrat. . ."

When the subject of lovers and intrigues has been exhausted, Delphine concludes her letter as follows:—

"The Comtesse Auguste is at Raismes. She complains bitterly of your silence and of mother's.

"Tell me about your neighbour. I have a warm memory of him; unhappy people are more grateful than any others. Miss Frivolity is still here: she is with child and has grown ugly. The Troubadour is still away, but is as affectionate as ever.

"Write me a little song about my butterfly love. Find some means of tying it down. I feel as one in search of wisdom. I am tempted to go out and ask everyone, 'Do you know any means of keeping a butterfly on one flower?'

"Good-bye, dear brother: now you know all about my doings, and I hope they may give you some amusement."

Here we see Delphine's strange state of mind, her disillusionment and deep mental grief. These feelings and the uncertainty of her fate led her to order a seal at this time, which she afterwards used regularly: it bore a star with the simple legend, "Whither will it lead me?" Poor Delphine, when she put this question to herself, still believed in happiness, in spite of her presentiments, and had no idea that the star which she consulted so anxiously would lead her to the worst of fates.

CHAPTER IX

JANUARY—JUNE, 1792

Armand de Custine is sent on a mission to the Prince of Brunswick—Negotiations fail—The Comte de Ségur at Berlin—He is coldly received by the King and asks to be recalled—Armand is nominated to replace him—He is well received at Berlin, but cannot prevent the declaration of war—He returns to France and reports the results of his mission.

WE have now to ask what had become of Armand de Custine after he had joined the army of General Lückner. He did not remain there very long; in a few months he was recalled to Paris, and was asked to undertake a most extraordinary mission. There was at that moment a much discussed proposal to form a coalition against France, and to place the Duke of Brunswick at the head of the allied armies. The ministers of Louis XVI., Narbonne and Delessart, driven on by Mme. de Staël and Talleyrand, conceived the strange idea of asking the Duke, who was supposed to be the friend of France, to refuse this command and to undertake the supreme command of the French armies.

Notwithstanding his extreme youth, for he was but twenty-three years of age, and though his own experience as a cavalry captain had not marked him out for a diplomatic career, Armand de Custine was considered a fit person to undertake this delicate mission. He accepted the proposal. Custine arrived in Brunswick on June 12, but he was already too late; the Duke had received such flattering offers from the coalition that he could do nothing but decline the discreet overtures made by the young diplomatist.[1] As his mission

[1] The alliance between Prussia and Austria was signed on the 7th of February.

had been a failure it only remained for Custine to return to France, but an unexpected incident prolonged his absence and took him to Berlin. The following were the circumstances.

In January, 1792, the Comte de Ségur [1] had been appointed ambassador at Rome, but the Pope declined to receive him. The minister Delessart then asked him to go to Berlin, to see King Frederick William, and to attempt to detach him from the coalition which was being formed against France by offering him full compensation and the further advantages of an ally on the other side. Relations between Russia and France were extremely strained, and it was of urgent importance to end the situation if a catastrophe was to be avoided.[2]

Ségur accepted the mission entrusted to him and reached Berlin on January 11, 1792, the evening before the day when Custine reached Brunswick. The ambassador's only idea was to work earnestly in the interests of the peace which he thought desirable for both countries. The *émigrés*, however, were afraid that M. de Ségur might succeed in his mission; they, therefore, used every means, even the most disreputable, to work upon the king's mind and to dissuade him from an agreement. They represented that the ambassador was "a furious democrat, a political traitor, an enemy of royalty and an emissary of the Jacobins. The ministry was informed that he was coming with millions of money to corrupt those about the King, that he was bringing with him several Jacobins disguised as his servants, who would attempt to undermine the loyalty of the troops, &c.; in fact, no slander could be invented which was not used against him. Their treachery went so far as to recall certain epigrams, more or less authentic, which Ségur had formerly let fall at the Russian court, and which were bitterly satirical of the manners of Frederick William and of those about him. The King was 'personally one of the most violent opponents of the Revolution; he detested, not only its success, but its very

---

[1] Comte Louis Philippe de Ségur (1753–1832), ambassador at St. Petersburg from 1785–1789, Grand Master of Ceremonies under the Empire.
[2] The three principal points upon which the two countries differed were: Firstly, the affair of the territorial princes in Alsace. Secondly, the gatherings of the *émigrés* on German territory, and particularly in the electorate of Trèves. Thirdly, the revolutionary propaganda in Germany.

principles, and was in such fear that these might be propagated that the smallest events inspired him with panic." All the information, erroneous or otherwise, which the *émigrés* produced made a profound impression upon Frederick William.

Thus, when Ségur obtained an audience of the King, he was ill-received. The Prince received the ambassador's compliments with icy coldness, drily replied that France would be without influence in Europe for a long time to come and turned his back upon him. Ségur went back to the Embassy, heart-broken at his failure and wrote at once to Delessart to ask for his immediate recall, on January 17th. Meanwhile, he was regarded as though infected with the plague. No one ventured to approach him or to open relations with him for fear of risking the King's anger. He saw only a few official personages and his only idea was to leave Berlin as soon as possible. But as he could not abandon his post, he had to find someone to take his place. Armand de Custine was in Brunswick at that moment, where his mission had been a failure, as we have seen. Ségur proposed that he should come to Berlin and take over the business of the Embassy. The great advantage of this solution was that Custine was, so to speak, on the spot, and that both for himself and still more for his mother-in-law, he might expect a kindly reception at the Prussian Court. While waiting for the ministry to decide Ségur fell ill from anxiety at the disastrous result of his mission. The rumour immediately spread that he had attempted to commit suicide, overcome with confusion at his reception by the King of Prussia. The delighted *émigrés* disseminated reports throughout Europe of the ambassador's supposed suicide, with the most wounding observations upon Ségur, the traitor to his party, etc., etc. The Chevalier de Boufflers was then in Berlin and Ségur was an old friend of his. Though the Chevalier had every reason to avoid any estrangement from the King, he did not hesitate to show the keenest interest in the unfortunate ambassador, and called upon him daily at mid-day. Frederick William, far from bearing ill-will to Boufflers, congratulated him upon his courageous friendship.

As M. de Ségur had asked, Custine was appointed to take

his place at Berlin. He arrived on February 20, and without losing a moment, the ambassador introduced him to the ministers, to some officials, and started himself for Paris on the 27th. The next day Custine took over the responsibility for the Embassy. Frederick William was acquainted with Mme. de Sabran and was a great friend of hers and he welcomed the appointment of her son-in-law as "chargé d'affaires." He was even kind enough to announce the news to her in person. Custine had made a stay in Berlin in 1786, and had many connections there; as the King looked favourably upon him he was welcomed in society. None the less, great reserve was shown towards him, and it was impossible for him to obtain the least information. His position was, therefore, not appreciably more agreeable than that of M. de Ségur had been.

Some astonishment may be felt that Mme. de Custine did not join her husband in Berlin. It was a very natural opportunity for leaving France and meeting her family once more. But Delphine, in spite of her complaints, did not intend to leave Paris and would not, under any pretext, be separated from her admirers. Custine was under no delusion concerning the motives of his wife's refusal to join him; on April 4 he wrote to Mme. de Sabran. "I was forgetting to tell you of Delphine. She is not afraid to stay behind, but would be afraid of the journey. She gives a thousand reasons for remaining where she is, and shows so much ingenuity in devising them that I can very well see her repugnance to come here. Any-way she gives fairly reasonable excuses which I will explain."

Custine had the best intentions in the world, and, like his predecessor, was interested only in the maintenance of peace between the two countries. Unfortunately the course of events did not favour his desire. The Revolution in Sweden, and the assassination of the King raised Frederick William's indignation to its height, and the situation became considerably more serious when he received a number of anonymous letters promising him the fate of the King of Sweden. Meanwhile, important events were happening in France. Louis XVI had replaced his ministers by the Girondins, and on April 20 he had asked the Assembly to declare war upon

G

Austria who had refused to disperse the meetings of the *émigrés* and had insisted that German princes who held estates in Alsace should be reinstated in their feudal rights. Immediately after this declaration of war the King of Prussia despatched certain regiments ostensibly to the frontier. Custine called upon Herr Schulenburg to ask the reason of these military arrangements. The minister replied that "France would have it so, that for ten months French platforms had resounded with insults against crowned heads and that this must come to an end."

"It is not for the cause of the *émigrés* that the kings are taking up arms," wrote Custine, "it is wounded self-esteem which urges them on. They are all agreed that France must disappear from the map of Europe, thinking that their safety can be secured only by our ruin and that all other interests must yield to this consideration."

Notwithstanding the ill-success of his efforts Custine had sent a request to Paris that he should be given the style of minister, pretending that the dignity thus conferred upon his mission would produce a good effect in Berlin. To this his government had consented, but the Prussian ministry was of another opinion and pointed out that the moment seemed ill-chosen to improve the position of the representative of a country with whom relations were so strained. The "chargé d'affaires" received a friendly request not to assume his new title; so that, to the Prussian government, Custine was nothing more than "chargé d'affaires," while to the French government he was minister. This inconsistent situation produced the following anomaly. He was commissioned to communicate a document to the Prussian ministry which refused to receive it because Custine was styled in it as minister.

Seeing that his efforts were fruitless and that he was no more successful than Ségur in improving the relations between the two countries, Custine requested to be recalled. While waiting for the King's order, and with the object of escaping from an impossible situation, he resolved to visit Mme. de Sabran at Rheinsberg, but at the moment when he was about to carry out this intention he received a message from Count Schulenburg asking him to call upon him. The

JANUARY—JUNE, 1792

minister expressed his regret that he would be obliged to oppose his departure; he said, "The courts of Berlin and Vienna are feeling some anxiety for the safety of their ministers at Paris [1] and have decided to retain M. de Noailles at Vienna and yourself at Berlin until they are in safety." Custine was obliged to submit and to remain at Berlin as a hostage, nor was he allowed to depart until it was known that von Goltz had arrived at Brussels. As the French government had authorised Custine to return he began to prepare for his own departure. At this moment, however, his mother-in-law and his friends made every effort to dissuade him from returning to France. They told him that he was gratuitously exposing himself to the most serious dangers, that he was entirely wrong in thinking himself under any obligation to the men who directed the affairs of the country and that the only reasonable thing for him to do was to remain abroad. He simply replied, "I was sent out by this government and it is my duty to return and give an account of my mission, for which they have made me responsible. I shall do my duty." He left the archives of the French Legation at Berlin in the hands of the Spanish minister and on June 22 he arrived at Paris.

[1] The Prussian minister at Paris was Von Goltz.

CHAPTER X

JUNE—DECEMBER, 1792.

The return of Armand de Custine to Paris—Delphine has her children vaccinated—Death of Gaston—His mother's despair—Delphine goes with her husband and Astolphe to M. de Malesherbes—Armand re-enters the service and goes to join his father at Mayence.

ARMAND DE CUSTINE reached Paris on June 22, after his sad Odyssey at Brunswick and Berlin, and found the capital in a state of anarchy. Upon receiving the news of the threatened invasion of Flanders by Austria, the Assembly had disbanded the Royal Guard, banished the refractory priests and ordered the formation before Paris of a camp of 20,000 federals from the departments. The King had refused to sanction these decrees and had dismissed his Girondin ministers. The people immediately rose and invaded the Tuileries, on June 20, and massacred all who attempted to oppose them. The King and the Dauphin were forced to assume the red cap and the Royal Family only escaped death by a miracle. Two days after these horrifying events Custine returned to Paris to find his wife and children in safety, but Delphine had begun to lose the persistent optimism to which she had clung for several years.

A truly domestic tragedy was to divert Custine's attention from political preoccupations or apprehension of the future. He had found his children Gaston and Astolphe wonderfully well, and there were no premonitions of the dreadful catastrophe which was to happen. The fear, and it may be said, the terror which was inspired in the eighteenth century by the smallpox is well-known. No disease was regarded as so formidable; it was one of the scourges of humanity. Quite recently Mme. de Custine had nearly fallen a victim to it, and only her mother's devotion and care had enabled her to escape. For some years vaccination, which had at first seemed very dangerous, had made great progress, and many proclaimed the beneficial results of the new discovery. Delphine, after much hesitation, was eventually convinced. "Gaston and Astolphe are very well," she writes to her brother in the month of July, "I think I shall have them vaccinated. Imagine my uneasiness and my anxiety: I am a good mother; in that respect I shall never change, for excellent reasons." In spite of the gloomy presentiments which came over her and which were regarded by those about her as weakness, Delphine had her children vaccinated. Astolphe bore it wonderfully well and felt no ill effects. Gaston, on the contrary, though very strong, was seized about two days later, with a violent fever; symptoms of the disease then appeared which carried off the unfortunate child in a few days to the despair of his heart-broken parents.

Delphine, as we have seen, was a good mother, and was crushed by this terrible blow. Her grief was the keener as she had with her neither her mother nor her brother, the only beings in the world who could help her in her distress. One might have hoped that this unforeseen disaster would have brought the young people together and that by mutual kindness they would have attempted to diminish their grief, but nothing of the kind occurred. Armand and Delphine remained indifferent and almost hostile to one another. The grief of Mme. de Sabran when she heard of the death of her dear grandson, the child whom she had known best and whom she was never to see again, was profound. She forgot her own sorrow in order to shower the tenderest sympathy and the most heart-felt consolation upon her daughter. But not much could be done or said at a distance of three hundred leagues and at a time when many letters failed to reach their destination.

While this melancholy tragedy was taking place in the Custine family, political events were advancing. The Prussian army entered France and the country was declared to be in danger. The manifesto of the Duke of Brunswick summoning the French to submit to their lawful sovereign, and threatening Paris with utter destruction if the least injury were done to the Royal Family, roused the popular fury. During the night of August 9—10 the Commune was proclaimed, the Tuileries were invaded and the Swiss Guard massacred. The monarchy was suspended and an executive council convoked a new assembly which was to be the Convention.

Delphine long remained crushed under the weight of her misfortune and unable to write letters, but in the month of August she regained sufficient courage to write to her brother.

"PARIS, *August* 18, 1792.

"Hitherto I have not found strength or courage to reply to your charming letter, my dear and kind friend; it is graven for ever on my heart. How many tears it has made me shed! Your sorrow for me is so touching and you feel my misfortune so truly. Dear and loving brother, why are we not together that we might mingle our tears and speak of our dear child. Nothing can ever obliterate the memory of such a grief, not even the horrors by which we are surrounded. The wound in my heart is always there, the void will never be filled and I cannot explain what I feel. If you were with me I think I could make you understand. I could talk to you and discuss it with you and you would feel it all. Since that dreadful moment I have been unable to write and it is ages since you have heard from me. I am in a state of stupor with no courage for anything. I am so unhappy in every way. Pity your poor sister and love her, for that is her only consolation. Kiss my mother; I know that she thinks of me and above all that she feels what I am suffering. I had told my mother that we were expecting to go to Forges, but the gates of Paris are closed and I do not know when we shall be able to get out."

We know little of Delphine's character if we suppose that public disasters had sobered her or that her own catastrophe had made her more serious or sensible. Not without a certain sense of sadness do we see the young woman quickly forgetting her grief to talk of her love affairs and the more or less sincere affections which she inspires or thinks she inspires, and plunging once again into the eternal sentimentalism which had become her life, her only happiness and her sole occupation.

"You ask me for news of my heart and of my romances. My heart is broken and I can love no more. I have been betrayed both in love and friendship; some day you shall know all. At present I have paid too dearly for my foolishness to have any left and if I felt the least inclination to change my resolution, I would shut myself up in the Petites Maisons, for in that case my mind would surely have given way. However, I have made one conquest, tender, submissive and romantic, my husband's friend, M. de Grouchy,[1] of whom you have perhaps heard. He is a good fellow for whom I feel friendship but nothing more. He believes himself in love; it is a very long story and I cannot tell it in a letter.

"As for the Comte Antoine,[2] I can talk no more of him. He is the only person I have ever really loved and, perhaps, the only person unworthy of it. This is a fact. I have vowed eternal hatred to love. In any case, never speak of him or you will break my heart.

"At present, my dear brother, I see nothing before me but grief and anxiety. My best moments are those of despondency and sleep. I have no pleasure left in life. The sight of my son merely rends my heart, while formerly his presence almost always alleviated my grief; to-day the sight of the only one remaining to me aggravates it. I feel that my courage is at an end and that I can write no more. Have you given up writing verse? Send me some in harmony with my feelings. You have read them now and they are quite in unison with yours."

Mme. de Sabran, at this time, was taking active steps to avoid the confiscation of her property, and had commissioned her son-in-law and her daughter to take the matter up. She urged that she was not an *émigré*, that she was only staying abroad temporarily and solely for the sake of her health. She even produced a letter from Prince Henry,

---

[1] The Marquis de Grouchy, field marshal, had married at the age of nineteen Mlle. Doulcet de Pontécoulant—a love match.
[2] Antoine de Lévis.

testifying that she was only paying him a visit at his request. Delphine did not shrink from advising her mother to come to Paris and plead her cause herself. "Numbers of people in far more critical positions have taken this step;" she wrote, "I would put you up in my house and we would see what there is to be done. Distance makes everything difficult, and women never have anything to fear, especially when they ask only for justice. Moreover, if the matter is arranged your presence will be indispensable, for without it all steps will be useless. What a pity that I have not a fortune which might one day supplement yours. Ours, alas! is more involved than ever; a thousand circumstances might reduce it to nothing. Therefore we live only for the moment and scarcely dare to look into the future. All this will increase your sadness, but I think, like you, that pecuniary misfortunes are as nothing compared with those of the heart."

Armand de Custine, after his return from Berlin, had remained at Paris, where he led a sad life. Apart from the griefs that we have mentioned and the sadness of seeing his domestic life no less disturbed than in the past, he had experienced some strange political rebuffs. Though he had performed his mission at Brunswick and at Berlin with zeal and intelligence, and though he had loyally reported the smallest details, he had become an object of suspicion. While his conduct had been entirely correct, and he had been very careful to avoid interference and to lay himself open to no criticism, this fact had not saved him from proscription. He daily expected arrest, and it was a mere chance that he had not become a victim of the September massacres. As a matter of fact, dreadful scenes had stained Paris with blood. When the news arrived that the strongholds of Longwy and Verdun had surrendered without resistance and that the armies of the enemy were marching upon the capital, public exasperation reached its height against the *émigrés* and the Court, who were regarded as responsible for the invasion. On September 2 and 3, certain wretches profited by the general excitement to enter the prisons and massacre the unfortunate prisoners.

Hitherto Mme. de Custine had paid no great attention to the situation in Paris. After the September massacres she became afraid and was anxious to go away. Her friend, M. de Malesherbes, offered her a refuge with him near Orléans, where he had retreated with his children and grandchildren, the Rosambo and Chateaubriand families. Delighted to find shelter with such dear friends, Delphine accepted with pleasure and started with her husband and Astolphe on September 15. She thus hoped to escape the dangers which threatened her and her family in the capital. When she saw the turn which events were taking, she understood that she had been nursing vain delusions; that she had no more hope of seeing the dear ones whose loss she felt so cruelly; she then lost all energy and became a prey to the darkest depression. Under the influence of this deep grief she wrote the following despairing letter to her mother.

"*Malesherbes, Sept.* 26, 1792.

"I think that I shall never have the courage to write to you, my good mother. Must we, then, abandon the sweet hopes which supported us? Nothing more is left to us but the sad resource of letter writing; how can the idea be endurable? Separated for ever! Life is not worth living, if it must be without you. Hitherto I had courage, but to-day I have no more and this letter is bedewed with my tears. Condemnation to live separated from one's dear ones is a sacrifice too great for human reason to bear. Pity me, love me and write to me but send no news or any reflections upon it. Goodbye, I feel too weak to write more; if you love me your heart will easily end this letter."

The nature of this meeting in the old Château of Malesherbes may be easily imagined, together with the mournful reflections exchanged by these unhappy people, whose lives a few years earlier had seemed so fair and happy, offering an unbroken prospect of delight, and who now were crushed beneath the weight of misfortune. What had become of the gay and careless Delphine; the cheerful and amiable Comtesse de Chateaubriand; where were the joyful gatherings of the past? To-day they were ruined and exposed to danger upon every side; they had been forced to flee before the whirlwind and lived in daily anxiety of the events which the morrow might bring forth, events decisive of their fates and of their lives. News from Paris came in, sometimes favourable, sometimes disastrous. One day they learnt of the victory of Valmy,[1] which saved France from a Prussian invasion. Another day, of the meeting of the National Convention, the abolition of the Crown, the proclamation of the Republic,[2] the arraignment of the King and his trial.

However, Armand de Custine grew weary of inaction. At the end of a month he resolved to leave this refuge, entrusted his wife and son to M. de Malesherbes and returned to Paris on October 15. He immediately made his way to Pache, the Minister for War, and asked for employment with the army of the Rhine, of which his father, General de Custine, was commander. He thought he would be in greater safety with the army than in Paris, where, notwithstanding the "purity of his conduct," he was exposed to suspicion and continual affronts. It may be asked how General de Custine, whom we last saw as deputy to the States General, had come to the army of the Rhine. After the end of the Constituent Assembly, Custine found himself with no political occupation and immediately after the declaration of war, applied for a military post. He was sent to the army of the Rhine under the orders of Biron. He at once performed several brilliant achievements which secured him the rank of commander-in-chief. Profiting by the retreat of the Prussians after Valmy, he made a bold advance into Germany and captured Spiers, Worms on September 30, Mayence on October 21, and then Frankfort. It was at this time that Armand requested permission to rejoin him. He left Paris on November 10, provided with letters from Pache requesting General de Custine to employ his son in his old rank. From Mayence the young man wrote to Mme. de Sabran to inform her of his new address, and to tell her of the fruitless attempts which he had made to save the remnants of her fortune.

"*Mayence, December* 20, 1792.

"I have been through many troubles since we last met. But it is you who have been and still are chiefly affected by

[1] September 20.   [2] September 22.

the worst of these, my too loving and too unhappy mother. I do not know what place I hold in your heart, but I well know the place I deserve. I have not written to you for months, or rather, you have not received my letters, for I could not send them by post. To-day I have found a certain means of transmission; Herr von Rathkirch has undertaken to deliver my letter, so I take advantage of the opportunity. I have written to you and Elzéar twice through two brokers, but one was seized with terror on leaving Paris and the other at the frontier, and they burned my letters. I have been here three weeks; I did not want a military post and I cannot undertake to fight for those who are devouring your substance. It is no political or business reasons that have brought me here, where I expect to remain for some weeks. I will tell you the reason some day, but I wished at least to relieve my mind by telling you what is not the case.

"In the letters which have been lost I told you a great deal about the fearful times which we have had to pass through. My care to avoid interference in any matter of any kind did not save me from the list of the proscribed in the month of August. My name appeared at full length in the list that was proclaimed throughout Paris for three weeks under the name of the Civil List. It is quite miraculous that I was not included in the massacre of the Abbaye, for I daily expected to be carried off to that dreadful prison.

"But it is of yourself that I wish to speak. I need not tell you that I have done my best to gain information, foresee, and to anticipate all eventualities. For your sake and for my sister's sake, I had an interview with M. de Condorcet, with whom I had broken on my return to Berlin. He is the only member of the Convention whom I know. I will do him the justice to say that he is most indignant at the proscriptions and at the cupidity which has dictated them. He is very sympathetic in this business of ours, and at my instigation he has even approached the Committee several times to secure legal proposals of a more moderate nature, but in vain. He is now writing upon the subject; I have just read a passage from his pen, full of the bitterest sarcasms, which will be of no more use than his other attempts.

"The ministers, of whom I know two, are moderate and amenable men, but there is nothing to be hoped for in this quarter, seeing that the Convention, blackguards as they are, are obliged to be ten times more blackguardly than they would like, in order to please the mob that they have been too cowardly to overawe, when they had the opportunity, and now that the opportunity has gone they must bear the yoke. The case of the King is a striking example. Two months ago his safety seemed certain; there were not forty deputies who differed in this respect; but now you see how everything is changed. I still have hopes, but they are very weak.

"With regard to your business our only hope is in time. My chief fear is that the State debts may be paid in bills upon the effects of the *émigrés*; this would bring about a general sale. But if this is not done I can guarantee that your house will not be sold and in this way the nature of your property may save you, for the proscriptions cannot go on for ever.

"You know that Delphine is in the country with M. de Malesherbes. He has written to become the official defender of the King, but there is one phrase in his letter which makes me very sorry for him and for his task, for it will deprive him of all means of defending him successfully.

"Goodbye, mother, whom I love tenderly and shall love all my life. Farewells are painful when we do not know how long they may last. Write to me, but by a safe and sure means, without date or stamp and most circumspectly. With such a name as mine the post is not made for me. It is another reason for bringing me under suspicion. I do not know whether you saw, in the newspapers, a letter supposed to have been written by me.

"I suppose that you have not been taken in by it as Delphine was, whom I shall have some difficulty in persuading of the truth. At least you know that I am not so mad or stupid as that. I suspect some one against whom you warned me of having played me this trick. I have denied my authorship in the French and foreign papers. This may not be successful at Paris but I prefer it to being regarded as a blackguard.

"Give me full information about your health, your position and your prospects. May you find in the confidences which I think I deserve, some consolation. At least you know that if it brings me proof of your love it will overwhelm me with happiness."[1]

As will be observed, the venerable Malesherbes had written requesting the honour of defending Louis XVI. In fact, on December 13, he had written to the President of the Convention, "I have twice been summoned to the Council by him who was my master at a time when this position was the object of general ambition. I owe him the same service at a time when this position is one which many think dangerous." His request was granted and Malesherbes returned to Paris to prepare his defence of the King. He was accompanied by the whole of his family, and Delphine, who could not remain alone at Malesherbes, returned to the capital with her friends.

[1] On learning that Custine was staying near his father at Mayence, the Bishop of Laon wrote angrily, "I am delighted that you have heard from your daughter and to learn that she is at Orléans. She will be in greater safety there than at Paris, in view of her husband's opinions, which expose him to danger from the Jacobin party. What do you think of the invasion of his father into Germany? No doubt he thinks himself a conqueror, though he has merely entered doors already open. At the same time he is doing a great deal of harm in that country, and it is very extraordinary that the Prussians do not drive him out or cut his progress short. I hope he will be captured and that they will make an example of him."

CHAPTER XI

JANUARY—JULY, 1793

Delphine's life at Paris—She stays at Mello with the Comtesse Alex—She then visits Mme. de Dreux-Brézé at the Andelys—Journey to Havre—Returning to the Andelys she hears of the arrest of General de Custine—Her immediate departure for Paris.

A NEW Year then began, but the events in progress were so terrible that the usual formula, "A Happy New Year," was dropped. Hopes were persistently followed by disappointments, and the New Year attracted no more attention at Paris than at Rheinsberg. Everyone was crushed beneath the weight of misfortune. Delphine continued to write often to her mother and her brother, expressing her deep affection, and her letters, as before, are a strange mixture of love, devotion and incurable frivolity. There is the same exaggerated frankness and a series of confessions so remarkable that they seem incomprehensible.

In her correspondence Delphine gives but scanty details of her daily life; a word here and there alone reveals the anguish of the unhappy dwellers in the capital. She knows only too well that the least allusion might stop the transmission of her letters and perhaps cost her her life. She knows that all letters go through the black cabinet and constantly writes an emotional phrase or appeals to the kindness and the "sensitive heart" of the official who was to read her letter, begging him not to destroy it, as "the love of a daughter for her mother and her brother cannot be an object of suspicion." In January, to escape the terrifying events of the moment, Delphine writes to her brother at some length.

"*January* 12, 1793.

" I am tempted to lose courage and to consign everything to perdition, my good little brother. Only the hope of seeing you again supports me. My dear, what a dreadful chaos! what a sad life we lead when so little would suffice to make us happy if we were together. Let us, then, find a means of approaching one another, for I can bear this no longer. If you felt the need of it as much as I do I think we should soon be quite close to one another. My only fear is that I should die of joy.

" My darling brother, if you knew how I spend my days, I really think you would be touched. I spend them in reading your letters, admiring them and thinking over the sentiments which they express; lamenting that I get no more letters like them and growing depressed at our misfortunes and our dreadful separation. Yes, we were made to live together and to love one another; to develop for ourselves that happiness which is for so many only an ideal state, but which would be so real to us if were united. One thing has not changed, but remains invariable and that is Delphine's feelings for you, and for our good mother. These feelings cannot be affected by upheavals, misfortunes or revolutions of any kind, or even by the changeable character for which you reproach me."

How many things had happened since the last letter which would afford texts for many sermons if Elzéar were capable of writing them.

"However, that would be very unjust, for this is an excess of misfortune. You know that with a head as badly organised as mine, things could hardly be different."

This time Delphine does not speak of her love affairs; she will not make any allusion to such frivolous matters at a moment when they are all terror-stricken by the course of events; Elzéar might think that she was amusing herself. Her criticism of her head as "badly organised" is correct; after saying that in view of the gravity of events she will not even allude to her admirers, she proceeds to speak only of them and of the state of her mind. She cannot help it. Amazement is the only feeling when we observe this young woman, living amid the tragical circumstances of her age, and yet unable to talk of anything but her past, present and future love affairs. In any case, she proceeds from disappointment to disappointment and her new admirers seem no more satisfactory than the former ones. If one may believe her statement, she has had a cruel lesson from experience. "I have grown terribly old during the last six months, which seem to have added ten years to my mental life. Knowledge bought by experience is dearly gained. I must tell you that I am going through every kind of misfortune of the most painful description. I am betrayed in love, as you had predicted and betrayed also in friendship. That is the hardest blow! And so atrociously betrayed! It would take too long to give you all the details; enough for you to know that I have no real interest in life; I have quarrelled even with my husband."

Yet even in this same letter, when Delphine declares her total indifference to everything and proclaims herself the most unhappy of women, she cannot help admitting that a new friend has just appeared who is helping her to bear the hard troubles beneath which she is giving way. Of course, he is like none of the others and she is quite certain that with him she will have no deception to fear.

"One being alone consoles me a little. This is a new admirer of whom I have told you something and who is worth it. I think I told you that I had made his acquaintance at the time of the disturbances of August 10; it is my husband's friend, M. de Grouchy; you may remember what I told you. He is no mere fop, no scamp like Comte A[1] . . . he is simplicity itself, honest and upright in person and has many of your brother's qualities with much deeper feeling. He is also deeply in love with your poor sister and this in such a touching way, so different from everything I have hitherto seen, that if I had not abandoned all sentiment and all love, I think I might be touched. At any rate, he is a sure friend in whom I have the greatest confidence and who cannot be dangerous, as I have full power over him. I am sure that you would like him very much, for he is good and simple; but your poor sister is too ill-balanced a character to

[1] Antoine de Lévis.

be attracted solely by these qualities. An attractive and amiable fop has more influence over her, because he flatters her self-love more readily. This is dreadful, I know; but with you I am not afraid to speak freely, therefore you may spare yourself alarm; whether they are fops, or amiable or attractive, nothing more can interest me and I wish only to vegetate."

At this moment Astolphe was attacked by the measles. Delphine nursed him and caught the disease in her turn; she was confined to her bed for nearly a month, and thought no more of her love affairs. During her illness the trial and execution of Louis XVI took place. Immediately after the death of the King, his illustrious defender, M. de Malesherbes, left Paris and took refuge again on his estate at Orléans, accompanied by his children and grandchildren.

Armand de Custine then occupied the post of supernumerary adjutant-general to his father at Mayence, but camp life tried his health greatly. It steadily grew worse, and in the early days of January, 1793, he left the army and returned to Paris. His father had commissioned him to appear before the General Committee of Defence to secure the adoption of his plan of campaign in preference to that of Dumouriez. Armand found his wife and child at Paris, and their common life was resumed as before, except that the relations between the couple, though not entirely satisfactory, were somewhat improved. Armand's health and the danger that he had run had brought about a most happy reconciliation.

"Your brother, with whom I had had a somewhat serious quarrel, has been nicer to me than for a long time. Besides he is so unhappy in many ways that only a heart of stone could fail to be touched. So we are on affectionate terms, though more as brother and sister than as husband and wife."

The meeting of the married couple was not to be of long duration. Events became more threatening and were moving towards a tragic issue. On March 10 was formed the Revolutionary tribunal which was to judge the enemies of the Republic without appeal. Not only was the country at war with foreign powers but several provinces were devastated by civil conflicts. Armand fully realised the dangers of the situation, and was anxious at least to place his wife and son in security. He insisted that Delphine should find a secret refuge in the provinces, where she could remain and wait for better days. Her friend the Comtesse Alexandre de la Rochefoucauld had long since been obliged to close her salon in the Rue de Clichy and had taken refuge on her estate of Mello. She had established herself in the little château known as the Priory under the modest name of Mme. Alexandre, and was doing her best to be forgotten.[1] She had repeatedly urged Delphine to come and join her in this refuge, the security of which was her boast. Under her husband's persuasions Mme. de Custine at length resolved to accept the invitation, and on April 15 she started for Mello with Astolphe and an old nurse named Nanette Malriat whose family lived in Niederviller and had been deeply attached to the Custine family for generations. Meanwhile, Armand de Custine courageously remained in Paris, prepared for the worst and ready to undergo the sternest trials.

No sooner was she settled at Mello than Delphine thought herself in Paradise; in that charming residence she enjoyed the calm and repose to which she had long been a stranger, and her heart, so cruelly tried, expanded to the hope of better days. Her happiness would have been complete if she had had her mother and her brother with her. But the scanty news which she received from Rheinsberg was unfortunately far from reassuring. Her mother, torn by grief and anxiety, was continually ill, and Elzéar was in a constant state of depression, overwhelmed by the gloomiest presentiments. Delphine lived upon the hope of receiving news from these two beings who were so dear to her, and when a letter arrived her joy was unbounded.

"MELLO, *May* 1, 1793.

"O! my dear mother, what a happy moment it is when I am able to hear from you. Assuredly you will never know

---

[1] Her mother had stayed in Paris and remained there throughout the Terror. The daughter of Comtesse Alex, who married the Prince Borghèse, remembered carrying milk to her grandmother in a little tin bottle to the house where she was hiding.

the extent of my delight when I see a letter from Rheinsberg. I am seized with palpitations and am thrown into a state of excitement which would be unbearable if it lasted long, but then this is soon changed to sadness and grief when I learn that you are ill, despondent and discouraged. Farewell to courage and to happiness!

"I shall continue to look into your business, but send me that letter from the Prince that I have asked for and a copy of your passports which you had when you left here. In spite of my efforts I fear that I may not succeed, but this is a misfortune for which you must have been long prepared. Moreover, we have reached the point when the loss of fortune appears of no account.

"I will send you some of my hair, as you want it. I have not yet had Elzéar's hair made up; I wear it on my heart but I cannot at present afford to have it mounted. This will give you some idea of our present state of affluence. I have not been in Paris for the last fortnight; I am staying with Mme. Alexandre de la Rochefoucauld, fifteen leagues from Paris, in a charming house. Country air seems to me very pure and so good that for a long time I have never felt so well.

"You wish to know how I am. Pretty much the same. I retain my colour, am rather thin than fat and am perhaps better looking than I was. My hair is not so dark on my head as when it is let down. Since my attack of measles I have not been entirely well; I have fits of choking and spasms, and for the last year my nerves have been very weak. I constantly feel the violent nervous attacks which I had last year. These are sufficient details concerning my outward appearance. It is not so easy to understand my mental state. Volumes would be required and many guarantees that my words would be read, so I will not enter upon this important topic. Astolphe is with me and is quite well; my husband is at Paris."

Delphine had a very pleasant visit at Mello. She tells her brother of the calm and restful life she leads and how much she enjoys it after the hours of anguish that she spent in the capital. The Comtesse Alex is most kind to her, but there is always the slight coldness between them which was left by the incident of the Troubadour.

"*May* 17, 1793.

"I write to you from a charming place, the home of peace and tranquillity. Can you not imagine it? This place reminds me of St. Amand, the same month of the year, the same woods and the same charming streams; but there is no Elzéar to admire, to sing its praises and to walk in it. All is braided in crape and appears to me only through a dark veil. My letter will, perhaps, bring you some of the pure air which I breathe; it is so long since I have smelt the country. You cannot imagine how well I feel, I must not say happy, for in my case the two words are not synonymous. O dear! how good it is to have left Paris.

"Here I am quite close to Chantilly and can get news of your brother every day; I have my son with me. I have been here now for three weeks, regretting the days as they pass and trembling for those which are to come. Both of us; are here alone; our hearts are not in harmony, far from it; but there is no constraint and we have sufficient affection for one another to make up for other deficiencies. I am resolved to have no other sentiments; I have been too often deceived and too unhappy when my feelings were keener. A sweet indifference is the proper state of my heart; why has it not always been thus?"

Naturally, though Delphine insists that all sentimental feelings have been destroyed for ever in her, she cannot write a letter without talking of her love affairs.

"The Sigisbée[1] is as tender as ever, but he is far away. Correspondence, however, goes on in spite of my indifference, but only as a distraction. I am sure that you would like him; he is good and simple, with an excellent heart and charming sweetness. He is romantic at heart, too much so for me perhaps, as you very well say. But I rely upon him, I like writing to him, and I swear that there is nothing more in it. He thinks that my feeling goes further than this, but he is so

---

[1] M. de Grouchy, who had been appointed on the 19th of March to the army of the Cherbourg coast. He had been sent to Havre, where he was in command.

honourable that his love gives me no apprehensions. What a difference between the Sigisbée and the Agréable![1] May he be for ever buried in oblivion! I have been so deeply tried by these tests of affection that I have become completely insensible and have lost the power of love. You alone, and your dear image, can touch my heart and make me feel, to my sorrow, that I still love. I am going to have my portrait taken and will send it to you and I ask my mother most earnestly to send me yours.

"Mme. de Fontanges is at present Mme. de Pont; she remains at Paris. Mme. de Châteaubriand is at Malesherbes with all her family; her sisters are married. Mme. de Saint-Simon is with Mme. d'Orléans at Vernon; M. de Montleart is with madame, but I do not know where. Victorine is in England; Mme. d'Andlau at Paris, and the Comtesse Auguste at Bouzies. Mme. de Brancas is at Paris; my sister-in-law and her husband are at Paris; so is Mme. de Ségur. You see how everyone is scattered. The little Gibelin is sometimes at Paris, sometimes in the country. He could hardly write to you and what could he say? The great Vaux is at Paris, still at his college and still about to draw lots for the militia. Some day he will draw the wrong number.

"I send you my hair for mother. I cannot venture to tie it up with any ribbon, but I will send with it some country flowers, and I hope that they will bring with them the good country air. I place them on my heart and kiss them, and may they be a talisman for you! I like this idea and I like this present; it is pure and simple like the affection which has brought it forth. Observe that I send a thought which contains all my thoughts within itself. The white flower was picked in the middle of the field; in short, my flowers say more than I can. Farewell; dreadful word! how many griefs it alone contains."

However, the news which came from Rheinsberg was by no means reassuring. Mme. de Sabran was continually ill; she grew weaker and weaker, and those about her began to be seriously anxious. Delphine adored her mother, and the idea that her condition might be serious reduced her to despair. She begs her to struggle against illness.

[1] The Comte Antoine de Lévis.

"Preserve your life for your children and think that if you were gone life would be a burden impossible to support. I have often heard you say that will-power can do anything. Have, then, the will-power to get well and to see us again, and to teach us to love life. Think of my poor brother to whom you are still so necessary, think of your poor Delphine who has not had a moment's pleasure since your absence."

She urges her to try a marvellous drug, the excellent effects of which she has herself seen and which she used after her attack of measles; as she is unable to send it she gives her mother directions for procuring it.[1]

Delphine would have liked to rejoin her husband at Paris, but he sent her the most startling news. The capital was in a state of sheer anarchy; the Assembly had been invaded several times, and obliged to yield to the orders of a populace in arms. On June 2 it had been literally besieged and forced to vote for the arrest of the Girondins. How could Delphine have thought of re-entering the capital under such conditions? After a two months' visit to Mme. Alexandre, Mme. de Custine would no longer trespass upon her hospitality, graciously though it was offered, and went away to Normandy with Astolphe. She went to see her sister-in-law, Mme. de Dreux-Brézé, who had also thought it advisable to leave Paris, and had taken refuge at the Andelys where she lived in isolation. It was agreed that Delphine should come back afterwards for another visit to Mello. At the end of a month at the Andelys the young woman began to find time hang heavy on her hands. Then she conceived an absolutely wild idea which she, of course, thought marvellous and which she hastened to put into execution. Her admirer, whom she called the Sigisbée, was staying at Havre; this seemed a good opportunity to go and see him. No sooner said than done. Delphine put her sister-in-law off with a cock and bull story and, leaving Astolphe in her care, started for Havre in the company of a chamber-maid. She is careful to give her brother a narrative of this escapade.

[1] "This drug is to be had at Lausanne from MM. François Grasset; it may perhaps be had at Berlin, but you must take care that it is not a counterfeit. Its name is the Essence of Schevers, known as the Marvellous Essence of Altona in Denmark, prepared by Thierry Schevers of Altona, the one and only possessor of the recipe."

JANUARY—JULY, 1793

"*July* 2, 1793.

"I have been staying for the last month with my sister at the Andelys, a little Normandy town thirty leagues from Havre. The Sigisbée had been in command at Havre for some months and the idea of going to see him possessed me. I made my curiosity to see the sea a pretext, and went alone with my chamber-maid to visit the sea. I left my son with my sister. I have been here a week, most of which I have spent with the Sigisbée. This seems to me the happiest time since we have been separated. His affection is tender and respectful, and he is good and sympathetic. You would like him, I am sure, if you could see him without prejudice. He has been deeply touched by my journey and by the reason of it, for it is a wild escapade. I have walked about everywhere and seen the sea from every point of view."

The sight of the ocean, which was quite new to Delphine, inspired her with such unschooled reflections that we cannot deprive our readers of them. They show what a child she still remained.

"My stay at Havre will be memorable for a long time to come. The sight of the ships and the vast expanse of this terrible sea will be graven in my memory. By the seaside with the water somewhat rough I thought of you. How happy we should have been there together with Ossian, and how this fine sight would have inspired you! I cannot conceive how a man ever had the courage to be the first to run the risk of sailing upon this terrible element. I should like to have known that man, and feel sure that I should have loved him. Some strong passion must have induced him to venture. Gessner [1] must have spoken the truth. My interest in seeing the sea has been increased by the fact that for some time I have been reading with my sister-in-law certain novels in the style of 'Robinson Crusoe' by M. Grivel. In one of them a man is shipwrecked, and after fifty years is found on an island, happy and content and unwilling to leave it. His industry had provided him with all the wants and necessities of life. The descriptions are charming. The

---

[1] "The First Navigator" is one of the chief works of the Swiss poet, Gessner.

second novel is about a girl who is on board ship with her father who is taking her to the Indies where he wishes her to marry against her will. A young man who is deeply in love with her contrives to embark upon the same ship. A frightful tempest arises, and everybody rushes to the boats, which are engulfed. The father of the young woman is drowned with the rest; she alone remains with her lover, who, supported by his passion, contrives to construct a raft. After a thousand dangers they reach a desert island and nothing is more interesting than the means by which they contrive to exist. There are three volumes, so I will not undertake to relate the story in detail, but you must admit that the subject can be interesting. After such a course of reading, the sea has a twofold interest, and when I am out walking with the Sigisbée I imagine myself starting for a desert island."

"My poor head is thus greatly excited; it is time to leave Havre. In two days I shall be returning to the Andelys for another month and then shall go to Mello to Mme. Alexandre. Such are my proposals unless some great event changes my course or unless my great plans come to nothing."[1]

"You would laugh if you saw me in my little hotel room where I spend my time, because I know no one except the Sigisbée, who calls as often as possible, but cannot be here always. I seem just like a novelist's heroine. In the inn I am known as Mlle. Justine, and when my chamber-maid asserted that I was married, they laughed at her. However, they think me very pretty, and that should console me for posing as Mlle. Justine. Indeed, this young lady is rather an extraordinary person; she spends her time with a young man and sees no one else; certainly with the best intentions in the world."

At length it was necessary to put an end to this wild escapade, to leave the attractive Sigisbée and return to the Andelys. There Delphine was to have a terrible awakening. No sooner had she arrived than she heard that her father-in-law, General de Custine, had been arrested. She did not hesitate. As Mme. de Dreux-Brézé pretended that her state

[1] Delphine had thought of rejoining her mother at Rheinsberg.

of health did not allow her to leave Andelys, Delphine declared that she would not abandon her husband or her father-in-law in their misfortune, and that she would return to them. Thus this madcap performs a true act of heroism, for a man whom she does not love and who is, at least, indifferent to her. She knows very well that she is risking her life, but nothing can stop her, because she thinks it her duty to be with her husband. She left Astolphe to the care of her sister-in-law and of Nanette and started for the capital.

CHAPTER XII

JULY—AUGUST, 1793

General de Custine is sent to the army of the North, is then recalled to Paris and brought before the Revolutionary Tribunal—Armand de Custine is also arrested—Fouquier-Tinville's indictment of the General—Heroic conduct of Delphine—The General is condemned to death—His execution.

For a year General de Custine had played a brilliant part and had been repeatedly successful. Unfortunately in 1793 the fortune of war inflicted upon him several disastrous failures. His enemies chose that moment to ruin him. His energy, the vehemence with which he had denounced the ineptitude of the War Office, and the scorn with which he treated the incompetence of parasites had made him an object of implacable hatred. Bouchotte was at that time Minister for War; his zeal was confined to sending the armies thousands of copies of "Père Duchesne." To the absurd remarks of the minister Custine audaciously replied, "I also, citizen minister, have eyes only for the Republic; but when the success of her armies obliges me to reproach the minister for his ignorance or his incompetence in performing the difficult functions entrusted to him, I shall not be wanting to the Republic in speaking vigorously against him.

"The time has passed when generals regarded a minister as a god, even if he were a fool. I have never been one of those feeble characters; I was a Republican before the Republic, and whenever I have met one of these ministerial idols I have treated him with scorn."

He referred to the minister in the same tone in his answer

to the Committee of Public Safety, which had written reproaching him for his severity.

"The penalty of death against traitors and those who endanger our organisation ought certainly to alarm Bouchotte to a greater extent than anyone else; for of all the ill-disposed and malevolent enemies of the happiness of their fellow citizens there is none who deserves more than he, to justify the foresight of the law.[1]"

Bouchotte was now to take his revenge. It will be remembered that in 1792 Custine was in command of the Army of the Rhine, and that he had seized in succession, Worms, Spires, Frankfort, and Mayence. He had made the last-named town his headquarters. In April, 1793, after the treachery of Dumouriez, his attitude of firm loyalty secured him the confidence of the Convention, but his position was becoming very difficult, for he was menaced on all sides. The town of Frankfort was recaptured by the Prussian army and part of the French garrison was massacred. Shortly afterwards Mayence was invested. General de Dampierre, who commanded the Army of the North, had been killed on May 9, and the representatives of that army communicated the unanimous desire of the troops that Custine should take his place. He was, therefore, appointed to replace Dampierre;[2] this new command was by no means desirable, for Condé and Valenciennes were besieged. Custine, in spite of his objection, obeyed the orders of the Committee; but before taking his departure, though strictly speaking he was no longer in command, he wished to make an attempt to relieve Mayence. He made a sortie on May 17 and was overwhelmed. After this failure, for which he was bitterly reproached, he went to the Army of the North. He found the troops in a state of despondency and badly armed; his arrival was immediately followed by a succession of defeats. It was not his fault, for the situation was not of his making, but, none the less, he was regarded as responsible.[3] Condé

See Arthur Chuquet, *Les Guerres de la Révolution, l'Expédition de Custine, Mayence.* (Plon Nourrit & Co.)

[2] His place at the head of the army of the Rhine was taken by General Beauharnais.

[3] The newspapers were full of references to Custine, sometimes praising his talents, sometimes decrying them. He was not afraid to put himself forward, and wrote to the Convention upon every occasion.

had been reduced by famine, and opened its gates to the Prince of Coburg on July 12. On the receipt of this news the Committee of Public Safety summoned Custine to Paris. The General obeyed and left Cambrai on July 15.

The assurance which he displayed upon his arrival merely exasperated the hatred of his enemies. The Committee resolved that he should be accompanied by a gendarme who had orders never to leave him. The General defied the Convention and showed himself proudly at all the public places, at the Palais-Royal and in the theatre, followed always by his inseparable gendarme. He was received everywhere with noisy ovations and shouts of *Vive Custine!* The Jacobins demanded that this scandal should be stopped. The Convention obeyed and decreed that the General should be put under arrest and imprisoned in the Luxembourg. This sentence was carried out on July 22. On July 23 the news came that Mayence had capitulated, and this was followed on July 28 by the loss of Valenciennes. This was more than enough to secure the transference of Custine to the Revolutionary tribunal. He was transferred to the Conciergerie on July 28 and seals were placed the same day on the rooms in the Rue de Lille, 509, which were occupied by Armand de Custine and his wife, and where they entertained their father when he came to Paris. Seals were also placed upon a third story room occupied by citizen Gauria, the General's secretary, and upon a private room which Custine had hired in a furnished hotel.

On July 30 Custine underwent his first examination. On August 5, at ten o'clock in the morning, he was taken from the Conciergerie to be present at the removal of the seals. This was done in the presence of Louis Bonenfant, Commissary of Police for the section of la Fontaine de Grenelle. Armand de Custine and Delphine were present at the operation and signed the report. Nothing was found in Delphine's rooms which gave rise to suspicion, and her papers were returned to her. From Armand's room, on the contrary, though he had not been accused or denounced, all the papers were carried away in two cardboard boxes which were taken to the court. The seals were also removed from the room on the third floor occupied by citizen Gauria. On August 13

Custine underwent a further examination. He asked that papers should be brought from Strasburg and Cambrai which he had left there and which might help him to clear himself. This request was granted and Auvray, the usher of the court, was sent to Strasburg with Gauria. Terriard and Berceau, provided with full powers by Custine, went to Cambrai.

Delphine, when she hastened to Paris, imagined that she would only have to support her husband during the cruel troubles through which he was passing, but the reality was much worse than she anticipated. Armand de Custine had written a letter to his father at Cambrai on July 13, advising him to send in his resignation. This letter, which arrived after the General's departure, was seized and the writer was regarded as a suspect. Moreover, when he saw his father imprisoned in the Conciergerie, the young man could not contain his indignation. Regardless of the possible cost he at once printed and placarded throughout Paris the "Defence of the Political and Military Conduct of General de Custine." These two incidents provided reason enough for his arrest. He was imprisoned at La Force, and could not, therefore, help his father during his trial.

Was Delphine likely to bear the weight of this twofold misfortune? Knowing her as we do, we should hardly think it possible; yet it was so, and this young woman, twenty-two years of age, whom we have seen hitherto as merely frivolous and irresponsible, made head against the storm with an energy of which far stronger characters would, perhaps, have been incapable.

On August 14 Fouquier-Tinville, after examining the documents provided by the Committee of Public Safety and the Committee of General Security, drew up his indictment, which concluded with the words: "According to the explanation above given the public prosecutor has drawn up the present accusation against Adam Philippe Custine, sometime commander-in-chief of the Army of the North and of the Ardennes, for having wickedly and designedly abused his position as general and used it to betray the interests of the Republic by entering into communications and overtures with the enemies of France: and through these communications and overtures, having facilitated the entrance of the enemies into the possessions of the Republic and handed over to them towns, fortresses, magazines, and arsenals."

The General's trial caused considerable excitement at Paris, and the examination of the " villainous Custine" was proclaimed in the streets; the public who a few days previously had cheered the General when he appeared at the Palais-Royal, now demanded his head with no less vehemence. So great was the crowd which desired to be present at the trial that the rumour went abroad that members of the tribunal were selling tickets at twenty and even fifty francs. One individual, anticipating the condemnation and anxious to speculate upon the public curiosity had begun, on the very first day of the trial, to put up an amphitheatre in the Place de la République to sell places to those who might wish to see the "punishment of the traitor" at their own convenience. The General Council of the Commune, angry at this disgraceful speculation, ordered that the erection should be destroyed.[1]

Custine appeared before the Revolutionary tribunal for the first time on Friday, August 16, at nine o'clock in the morning. From that day until judgment was pronounced Delphine was present at every session of the tribunal, in spite of the danger to which she was exposed in consequence of the popular excitement. She could not have borne this trial but for the presence of one of her husband's friends, Guy de Chaumont-Quitry, who accompanied her every day and walked with her through the streets to preserve her, as far as possible, from insult. He was dressed as a man of the people in a *carmagnole* without a cravat and hair unpowdered and cut short. On every occasion Delphine ran great risks: "The day before yesterday," writes the *Gazette française* on August 21, 1793, "this woman, so interesting for her warm-heartedness and her filial piety, left the Palais de Justice in the middle of the crowd. There was a smile upon her face and it was thought that she was laughing. Some women, unable to feel for her position, began to shout: She laughs! but she will not laugh long. It is the daughter of Custine; her father will soon be playing at hot-cockles."

We do not propose to attempt the narrative of Mme. de

[1] Arch. Nat. Carton, W^{1b} 280.

Custine's heroic conduct during this terrible time. We prefer to leave her son to speak, who knew these events better than anyone and learned them from his mother's own words.[1]

"The first interview between the General and his daughter-in-law was touching; as soon as the old soldier saw my mother, he thought that his safety was assured. As a matter of fact, her youth, her beauty and her timidity interested the public, the people and even the judges to such an extent that the men who had resolved upon the general's destruction wished to frighten the young woman. Septembriseurs, as paid assassins were then known, were placed for several days upon the steps of the Palais de Justice and my mother was carefully warned of the danger which she ran on every occasion when she ventured to appear at the court. Nothing stopped her and she was to be seen in court every day, sitting at her father-in-law's feet. She spent her evenings and mornings in secretly canvassing members of the tribunal and of the Committees. At one of the last sessions of the tribunal my mother reduced the women in the gallery to tears with a look. These marks of sympathy so irritated Fouquier-Tinville that he sent secret orders to the assassins on the steps.

"The prisoner had just been taken back to prison; his daughter-in-law was preparing to go down the steps of the court, alone and on foot, to regain the cab which was waiting for her in a side street. Throughout her life my mother had an instinctive and unreasonable fear of a crowd; she stopped, trembling at the top of the steps and thought herself lost. 'If I stumble or fall, like Mme. de Lamballe,' she said to herself, 'it is all over with me,' and the fierce crowd thronged thicker upon her passage. Shouts came from all sides: 'It is the Custine! it is the traitor's daughter-in-law!' How was she to descend this long flight of steps, amid a mob intoxicated with rage? Some were standing with drawn swords in front of her, others without waistcoats and their sleeves turned up, were moving the women aside. She has told me that she bit her hands and her lips until the blood came, in the hope that the pain would prevent her from

[1] *La Russie en* 1839, by Astolphe de Custine.

growing pale. At length, when she thought her last hour had come, she noticed a fish-woman carrying an infant in her arms. 'What a pretty child that is,' she said with sudden inspiration; 'Take it,' replied the mother, and put it into her arms. Mme. de Custine took the child, kissed it, and went quietly down the steps through the astonished populace. She went down the courtyard, crossed it and made her way to the square without receiving any blow or even an insult. She reached the gate, returned the child to the woman who had lent it, and made her escape."

The next day the heroic young woman, regardless of danger, reappeared at the tribunal and resumed her place at the General's feet. Throughout the whole course of his trial Custine defended himself with much wit and cleverness. His answers were so keen and incisive, his arguments were so sound and reasonable and he cleared himself so readily from the absurd charges brought against him that his innocence seemed obvious. The following is a brief summary of the charges brought against him and his replies.

At the outset of the war Custine had refused to seize the gorges of Porrentruy, though ordered to do so by Marshal Lückner.

Reply.—"I did not take the gorges of Porrentruy because, in the first place, I had no soldiers, and, in the second place an order cannot be executed on Friday when it is only received on the following Monday."

Although Custine could have been under no delusion concerning the weakness of Mayence, which was bound to succumb to the armies of the Coalition sooner or later, he stripped Strasburg of its artillery for the benefit of Mayence.

Reply.—"If I sent artillery from Strasburg and Landau to Mayence, it was to fortify the town. As it was to be defended, it had to be fortified."

He had ordered officers of the Volunteer National Guard to be shot for eating grapes in the vineyards, and after the execution he exclaimed, "That is how discipline is maintained!"

Reply.—"If I had certain soldiers shot who had been plundering churches and stores or who had disobeyed the General's orders, it was to maintain discipline."

One evening, at supper in his house in Mayence, with a great number of officers around him, " towards the end of January, in speaking of the late King, he said, 'All is finished!' and then fell into a gloomy silence which was only broken by this exclamation: 'Such was not my opinion; the King should have been kept as a hostage and not executed!'"

Reply—" I might have said that if we had kept Louis as a hostage, the enemy would have attacked us with less desperation, but I have never shown any sign of pity for a man whom I have always regarded as the author of our misfortunes."

A witness reproached him for arbitrarily arresting at Mayence Dr. Hoffmann, one of the best patriots in the town. Custine replied: "I do not know whether Dr. Hoffmann was as good a patriot as he said, but the greatest enemies of liberty are often these café talkers, and club orators. It may be remembered that Dumouriex presided over Jacobin meetings in a red cap."

A witness had asserted that Custine had brought furniture to Mayence worth eighty thousand francs, to which Custine replied with a laugh: "If the witness can tell no better lies than that, he had better take a wallet and beg his bread."

The President said to the accused: "While you were with the Army of the Rhine you received communications from Mayence through a lady."

"Unfortunately, no!" replied Custine gaily.

One of the charges which made the General most angry was the comparison which the people attempted to draw between Dumouriez and himself. "There can be no connection," he cried, "between a low intriguer like Dumouriez and a man who has always served his country honourably."

One of the most violent witnesses against the General was Bouchotte's secretary, a certain Vincent. His evidence lasted for several sessions and he assumed the position of a public prosecutor. His attitude passed the bounds of decency so far that one of the jury requested the President to call the witness to order.

However, the trial dragged on and after it had lasted for thirteen days, Hébert accused the judges of being attracted by the beauty of Mme. de Custine. The President of the tribunal and the public prosecutor were even summoned to the bar of the Convention to explain the delay for which they were held responsible. At length, on August 28, at nine o'clock in the evening, after a session of twelve hours, sentence was pronounced. Custine, on the declaration of a majority of the jury, was declared convicted of high treason and condemned to death, while his property was confiscated to the Republic.

The prisoner returned with a slow step to hear the sentence read. The general silence amid the audience, and the candles which he had not seen alight since the trial, seemed to impress him greatly. He sat down and glanced over the crowd. Coffinhal informed him of the verdict, while Fouquier-Tinville read the law and asked that it should be enforced. Custine, unable to perceive Tronson-Ducoudray, his lawyer, or his other counsel, turned to the bench and said: "I have no defenders left; they are fled; my conscience can reproach me for nothing; I die calm and innocent." He looked carelessly upon the mob who shouted applause; their passion had been raised to such a height that the jurors who had not voted for death were almost torn in pieces.

Custine, after hearing the death sentence, went back to the clerk's office, fell on his knees and prayed for two hours. He asked that he might die as a Christian, and the Abbé Lothringer was sent to him, a priest who had taken the oath; Custine accepted his services as he probably saw no great difference between jurors and non-jurors. He made a long confession and requested the Abbé to write to his daughter-in-law and his daughter and handed him for the latter a lock of his hair. Then he wrote this short letter to his son.

"Farewell, my son, farewell! Do not forget a father who sees death arrive with calmness. I have but one regret, the fact that I leave you a name which my sentence might make some credulous people think capable of treason. Clear my memory when you can. If you can obtain my letters it will be easy. Live for your dear wife and for your sister, whom I kiss. Love one another and love me. I think that

I shall be able to face my last hour calmly. At any rate, I shall have to face it, so once more, good-bye.

"Your father, your friend,
"CUSTINE.

"*August 28, 1793, at 10 p.m.*"

Delphine secured permission to see the General for the last time on the evening of his condemnation. His dungeon had been changed; "they are removing me," he said to his daughter-in-law, "to make room for the Queen and because my former lodging was the worst in the prison."

The next morning, at six o'clock, he continued his confession and prayed with the Abbé who had spent the night with him. At that moment the concierge brought him a letter from Delphine, unsealed, but the General refused to read it as it might shake his resolution. At a quarter past ten he was ordered to mount the cart and started for the Place de la Révolution. The Abbé Lothringer accompanied him and often made him kiss the crucifix which he held in his hand. Custine wore the national uniform and looked, with tears in his eyes, upon the people who applauded his punishment. When he reached the place of execution he fell on his knees at the first step of the ladder, received the blessing of the priest, glanced at the sinister knife and resolutely mounted the scaffold. The people, exasperated by these marks of piety, shouted, Coward! coward![1]

---

[1] Arch. Nat. Carton, W^{1b} 280 and W A 21. See *Mme. de Custine*, by Bartoux, and the *Procès fameux jugés depuis la Révolution*, by Desessarts. An hour after the General's death, the Abbé Lothringer was denounced on the charge of sympathising with the condemned man. He was arrested and confined in the Abbaye, and was not released until the 12th of Brumaire, in the year III.

CHAPTER XIII

AUGUST—DECEMBER, 1793

Correspondence of Mme. de Custine with her mother and her brother—Armand de Custine in prison—Depression of Elzéar.

DURING the terrible period through which she had just passed, Mme. de Custine had naturally ceased all correspondence with her family. Two days after the execution of her father-in-law she wrote to her mother a letter characterised by the deepest grief, but, in order to avoid its suppression by the black cabinet, Delphine alludes only distantly to recent events. In speaking of her husband she merely says that he is always in the same place; she dared not venture to write the word, prison:

"*Paris, August* 30, 1793.

"After the long silence caused by my unhappiness, at last, dear mother, I can throw myself into your arms and weep with you. You know our misfortunes and your love for us is such that we know how you share them. Unfortunately I cannot enter into details; I can only tell you that the unfortunate Armand is still in the same place, and that I do not yet know what divine power can extricate him from it.

"Public rumour will have told you the life that I have been leading for the last five weeks. It will form a proud epoch in my life. What a dreadful position! pity your unfortunate Delphine! You can have no idea of all that she has had to go through for the last five weeks. It is torture for me to be unable to give you details, but in order that my letters may reach you, I must speak to you only of myself.

"I do not think that anyone will be hard-hearted enough to suppress this letter. I propose to give you news only of myself. My heart sinks at the thought that it may, perhaps, be intercepted, like so many others and that your anxiety may therefore be increased. I ask mercy of the man who may open this letter. I beg him to look into his heart and try to put himself in my place and to imagine that he is three hundred leagues from his mother. His heart will be softened and he will close my letter and allow it to proceed. Such, my dear mother, is my hope.

"I heard from you a month ago. To give you some idea of my dreadful position I must tell you that I had your letter in my pocket for a week without having time and still less inclination to read it. I think that this fact alone will explain into what a state of misfortune I have fallen since my return here. I am praying that we may be able to leave Paris and go and live in a very quiet corner of Normandy where we will try to be forgotten and to lessen the weight of our unhappiness, if possible.

"Be constantly near me, mother, pity your unfortunate destiny and pity your unfortunate children."

Mme. de Custine had received a letter from her brother in which he overwhelmed her with praises for her conduct. She thanks him, but asserts that she has done nothing more than her duty, and says very simply:

"*September* 7, 1793.

"You are very enthusiastic on my account, my dear, but in reality my behaviour has been perfectly simple. I have done as any honourable person would have acted and I should have been unworthy of your interest if I had done otherwise. But what would your enthusiasm be if you knew the full details! How loud would then be your praises of your poor Delphine! But, my dear, I deserve no praises. I have satisfied my conscience and that is my reward. But through what a school have I passed! How these great events form our characters and make us old! I have gained ten years in experience and your timorous Delphine has become brave and is afraid of nothing. What do you think of such a change? It is the work of real danger.

"Alas! we are by no means at the end of our misfortunes. Your poor brother is still in the same place and has less hope than ever of escaping from it; his health is terribly shaken. Our property is at the bottom of the sea and so is that of all our friends; I do not really know what we shall do; such is our position. If one could only foresee a limit to it all! if only, in the distant future, I could see a chance of our meeting! How sad is this room in which I live! I am alone all day and live on nothing but memories of the past and a little hope, a very little."

Delphine speaks with some bitterness of her sister-in-law, Adélaide de Dreux-Brézé, who could not be induced to come to her father by the most urgent representations: "Her devotion, she says, has persuaded her that she owed herself to her husband and unborn child more than to her father, and so throughout the whole of this unhappy business she has remained quietly in the country. In spite of these dreadful developments and in spite of my persuasions that she should at least come and kiss her unhappy father, nothing has been able to shake her; she did not think she ought to expose herself to fear, for there was no question of danger."

In her misfortune Mme. de Custine had learned to appreciate the affections of society at their proper value. Of all her friends very few had remained loyal to her; almost all had fled from the society of one in whom no one could show interest without compromising himself. One alone had remained immovably attached to her, had supported her in her trials and, at the risk of his life, had daily accompanied her to the law courts to defend her. This was M. de Chaumont-Quitry, and it was only too natural that he should fall a victim to his attachment to her and to his too obvious devotion. He was denounced, arrested and thrown into prison, though he was a warm partisan of the Revolution. With him Delphine lost the only support which remained to her. She writes a melancholy letter to her brother concerning this further trial:

"One consoler has come to charm my solitude, the only

one who has survived the deluge! I found him amidst my despair; his interest in us has been fatal to him. Alas! for the last two days he has been in a place like that in which Armand is, though not in the same place, and so I am deprived of him; if all these events have made us lose false friends, at any rate we have gained him; we will call him the friend in need.

"My friends, or rather those who had assumed the name, have turned their backs on us; no one ventures to come so much as to our door. The mention of our name makes them fly far and wide, for fear that the mere hearing of it will compromise them. On this side our abandonment is complete. You know that I was disposed to be misanthropic; think what it must be now! I should like to live in a savage country. As for the woman of whom you speak, Mme. de F..., she was one of the first to turn her back on me. The Frivolity [1] has behaved fairly well, and the Sigisbée perfectly. The rest have been dreadful. But let us try to forget such gloomy recollections.

"I must give you my advice now. In the first place, write nothing to the son, that is an essential point; secondly, be careful to abbreviate any names which you mention. Before all remember this.

A thousand remembrances to the neighbour of whom you do not speak. Is it true that he is at present bound to us by indissoluble ties?"[2]

How was it that Delphine was still at liberty after her audacious conduct? Why had she not been denounced, and why had she not joined her husband in prison, with the unfortunates who were there groaning? She did not know herself. In a letter of October 4 she said to Elzéar:

"*October* 4, 1793.

"No doubt you think I am in a dwelling similar to Armand; he is there still, and it is a miracle that I am not there yet. But my conduct has been open and unconcealed and far from timorous. I have no doubt that this

[1] The Comtesse Alexandre de la Rochefoucauld.
[2] There was a rumour that M. de Boufflers and Mme. de Sabran had at length legitimised their long-standing intimacy: this event, however, did not take place until 1797.

has been my safeguard. We are not yet at the end of our misfortunes; Armand cannot leave his present dwelling and his health is going totally to pieces. Mine has also been greatly shaken; I have grown thin and much altered. My life at present is so unhealthy and so unhappy. I am still separated from Astolphe, who is with Adélaide; I have been obliged to make every possible sacrifice.

"To what trials was I destined and by how many kinds of misfortune am I overwhelmed! You know the warm, indeed the too warm, interest which I take in the Sigisbée; he is in the most anxious situation.

"It is impossible to foresee how long our separation will last. I am unable to face so painful an idea, and the will to live fades away. I believe that from this fact I derive my courage.

"Remember me to mother, kiss her tenderly, and also the good neighbour. I suppose that my relations with him henceforward will allow this small liberty."

In each of his letters Elzéar shows an overwhelming admiration for his sister. Mme. de Sabran appears no less enthusiastic, and in memory of the terrible events which had just passed she designed an allegorical picture in the taste of the age. Elzéar's description of it is not without interest:

"*October* 19, 1793.

"You are my god, my goddess, my adopted angel, my saint, my patron, my dear friend, and anything else that is possible. Dear little girl, what a pleasure it was to hear from you! You have behaved like a great man and like a good woman, and I do not know whether admiration or love for you moves me most deeply. Only enthusiasm can harmonise and unite these feelings, and so I am enthusiastic without reserve.

"I should never finish if I attempted to describe all the thoughts that your letter has brought to my mind, and the feelings which it has roused in my heart. Besides, I am too full of you and your letter and your troubles and your admirable conduct to describe the impression which they make upon me. And the impression is too strong for me to analyse. My mother never talks of anything else; she is painting you and me in a magic picture, like that of 'Zémire and Azor.'[1] You are very like. She has painted you half from memory and half from a copy that she made of the miniature which is on the back of the son's box. Ruins are to be seen and volcanoes pouring lava round you while I am trying to cross the rocks to reach you. She herself, on her knees in the room, seems to be about to leap towards the picture over which the Genius of Imagination is drawing a curtain."

Elzéar's letters were not always so cheerful. The unhappy young man had always been of a very melancholy disposition, but the political events which had driven him into exile and the misfortunes which had stricken his family had vastly aggravated this tendency to hypochondria. Henceforward it steadily increased, and we see him sinking by degrees into a gloomy pessimism which was to poison his whole life and lead him into foolish extravagances. Even now he can tell his sister of his love of solitude and his passion for cemeteries.

He writes on October 3 ·

"*October 3*, 1793.

"What uneasiness, what torments, what anxiety your absence causes me! and above all your silence! When I write to you I feel like one of those poor people bowed beneath a heavy weight, who finds a milestone on which to lean his back and rest for a moment. How painful and grievous, my dear, is absence! Who could ever have told when we left one another all that we have since experienced? If we had known it, should we have been able to part? Tell the poor son how I love him and how sorry I am for him. I dare not tell him so myself, much as I should like to do so. I hope he has returned at length from his journey.

"Our mother's health is still very weak; you may imagine that all these anxieties have not made her any stronger. We do nothing but talk of you together and with our neighbour; but no one feels as I do, the torment of anxiety when added

---

[1] "Zémire and Azor," a comic opera by Grétry. The libretto is by Marmontel, who had taken the idea from the story of Mme. Le Prince de Beaumont, "Beauty and the Beast." In the last act Zémire is in the enchanted palace of Azor, and sees in a picture frame her father and sisters weeping for her absence.

to forced separation. I flee to the forests, and to the most gloomy and deserted spots. Separated from you, solitude seems to me better company than all the world, for solitude is yourself. There I constantly see you, I see and hear none but you and feel no other near me. I walk constantly and lose myself in my recollections.

"The leaves are now growing yellow, the trees are bare, and Nature is becoming sad : so much the better. I have no more love for Nature, but rather hatred ; she seems to me to be too happy. She promised me happiness, and has treacherously deceived me. I love only the night and I seek only for darkness, for bare vaults and for the sepulchres of the dead. They alone can speak my language. I shall make you sad, dear little girl ; I have given way to this outburst of melancholy which has rushed forth from my heart like a blast from the cave of Æolus. At first I had attempted to keep it back but it soon overcame me.

"Farewell ; you will at least see from this letter the state of your brother's mind, and be able to judge of his love by the extent of his sadness."

In her delight at receiving a letter from her brother Delphine does not lose a moment in replying. She scolds him for surrendering to melancholy and forgets all the dangers of her situation to plunge, with real childishness, into the wildest possible imaginings.

"*October* 18, 1793.

"A letter from you, my dear ! It has escaped the deluge and has reached me. Your letters to me are as dear as a ray of light to an unhappy wretch lost in the depths of a gloomy cavern. Let us love and thank the kindly person who allows our letters to pass ; some day perhaps we may make his acquaintance and be able to clasp him to our hearts. But, alas ! what trouble could our letters cause ? They are those of two tender lovers. Do you know, that I have sometimes regretted that I could not love you in that way ? We suited one another perfectly, at least you suited me ; your ideas of perfection would perhaps have shown you Delphine in a disadvantageous light, but our tastes and the similarity of our opinions upon a thousand matters would have brought us together. Amuse yourself with the idea that you are no longer my brother, that we are of the same age, and that we are to meet at the same country house. What will be your idea of me, and what feelings shall we have for one another? How absurd this is! I am inventing fairy tales, and for the moment, while talking to you, I forgot my dreadful position.

"Armand is still in the same place and in a deplorable state of health. I spend my days with him, but there is reason to fear that I shall be unable to give him even this consolation; our troubles increase every day and hope is rapidly disappearing.

"Your despondency has gone to my heart. Do not give way to it too much, my dear. If we were near one another we could weep together, our tears would be less bitter and would wring our hearts less. But there is nothing to support us; therefore you must will to live, that we may meet again. It is the only reason I have for clinging to life. Remember me to our dear mother and kiss her very tenderly. Is her health still weak? it causes me great anxiety.

"My Astolphe is still in the country with my sister-in-law. I have not even the consolation of seeing him. The only consolation that I have is my possession of supernatural strength; I am afraid of nothing and am calmly and courageously prepared for anything. Do you remember that a fly could once startle me? At present it takes a great deal more than that. I think that this courage is due rather to disgust of life than to any other reason.

"Farewell, brother; our hearts are at one, are they not?"

After the death of General de Custine tragic events followed uninterruptedly. It was impossible to foresee the conclusion of this gloomy period. On September 17 was proclaimed the Law of Suspects. Every citizen not in possession of a certificate of citizenship might be thrown into prison at once. The *émigrés* were banished in perpetuity and their property confiscated. The list of victims, including the most illustrious names, grew longer every day. After the Girondins, Marie-Antoinette, Mme. Elizabeth, the Duc d'Orléans and many others mounted the scaffold. The prisons were crammed with unhappy people awaiting their fate. Notwithstanding the unhappiness of the time, and the sadness of her position, notwithstanding her ruin and the dangers impending for her and her family, Delphine remained as frivolous and fickle as before. When she has lamented her separation from her brother and her consequent grief, her temperament gets the upper hand and she proceeds to speak to him of her admirers and her eternal love affairs; it is her brother, as usual, who receives her confessions.

"*December* 8, 1793.

"Your letter has arrived. It brought a little consolation to my heart which greatly needed it, for misfortune in the long run crushes the life out of us. I am glad to know that you follow me in your thoughts, that you share my griefs and that you desire to know full details of my life and feelings. I love your letters, I love your questions, and, in short, I love my Elzéar above all things. I should say that as regards the Agréable the incident is entirely closed. He behaved disgracefully and has cured me of all foolish affection.

"As regards the Sigisbée things are different. It is the most continuous, interesting and tender of romances. I like him very much, I think him worth it. But I know the weakness of my wretched head, which is entirely turned. He is at present absent, that is to say, forty leagues from Paris; a thousand circumstances prevent him from coming, much to my grief. Net even my unhappiness or the dangers around me can distract me from this fresh folly; it was fated that I should have no common sense.

"The friend in need has behaved admirably, I like him very much, and he is somewhat in love with me, but nothing is said about that. There may be some fresh conquests but these will be too long to relate, for they occur everywhere. They have never been so entirely indifferent to me, for my heart has never been so seriously occupied. You may smile and laugh at me, but you are quite wrong. Pity me, for that is all that I deserve! Everyone here speaks of my *neighbour* as I have spoken to you; it is regarded as permanent. Is it true, and why should I be the only one not to know of it? I am one of those who would be most interested and best pleased.[1]

"I have been greatly grieved to learn of the death of our cousin.[2] I must also tell you of a death, that of our poor little cousin in the Rue d'Anjou.[3] He died of small-pox in a place like that in which Armand is, though not in the same place.

"Goodbye, I have run out of paper. Write to me, my friend, it is my only comfort."

Thus it appears that the "friend in need," Guy de Chaumont-Quitry, had not been able to form an exception, and had fallen in love in his turn with the tender Delphine. It may be asked why he was no longer in prison, to which his devotion to Mme. de Custine had brought him. The reason was that he was a zealous partisan of the new ideas, that his zeal had at length been recognised and that he had been set at liberty. Thus he was able to give Delphine further proofs of his devotion, at the time when her husband's trial began.

In the month of December Mme. de Custine received from her mother a letter marked by great sadness and real despondency; she was deeply moved. Mme. de Sabran, who was very ill and overwhelmed by the misfortune which had come upon her, thought that her end was approaching and was in despair at leaving the world without seeing her beloved daughter again. The death of her cousin, Mme. de Mellet, seemed to her a warning that a similar fate awaited her in the near future. Delphine scolds her mother for her despondency and urges her to take care of herself in view of the happy hour of meeting which will surely strike some day. She tells her of her life and of the dreadful position in which she is:

"*December* 9, 1793.

"What happiness and sorrow your letter caused me simultaneously! What gloomy ideas you have, dear mother!

[1] A reference to the marriage of the Chevalier with Mme. de Sabran.
[2] The Comtesse de Mellet, who died at Aix-la-Chapelle on November 3, 1793.
[3] The Marquis de Sabran.

Let us try to put them aside for ever and think only of our next meeting. What would life be if we lost this hope? It is the only prospect to which I cling; it helps me to bear my terrible position which grows worse from day to day.

"Armand still remains where he was, without any hope of emerging. Our property is sequestrated, and the peasants are threatening us with a law-suit, claiming that the land of Guermange[1] belongs to them. No doubt they will win this; it is likely that we shall be obliged to work in order to live. For the last year we have been living only on our capital. Our position necessitates incredible expense, and if it continues only a little longer I do not know what we shall do.

"But we have experienced such great misfortunes and reverses that a fortune seems almost nothing. Were it not for Astolphe I should not mind.

"What supports me amid so many woes is the hope that we may meet again some day. Your letter cut me to the heart. What resemblance is there between you and your cousin? none at all. She was ill of a very different disease than you and for a long time; besides, it was an accidental disease which carried her off. Be courageous then, dear mother, and do not depress your unhappy daughter. Cling to life in order that your caresses may one day soothe the memory of the evils which she had suffered.

"Poor Armand was affected to tears by your kindly messages to him. He urges me to tell you of his affection and to send you his warmest love.

"It would be a real pleasure if you would send me Elzéar's portrait. To have a portrait of my Elzéar and that the work of your hands! how many advantages at the same time! Remember that my moments of happiness are very few and far between and that here you have the means of giving me a lasting pleasure.

"Astolphe is at Paris, as the place where he was living had become uninhabitable. He is very well and much grown; they say he is like me."

---

[1] The estate of Guermange, near Sarrebourg, had been given to Armand de Custine on his marriage. It included an old château and six farms.

It will be remembered that Mme. de Custine had left her son and Nanette to the care of her sister-in-law. As the position at the Andelys had become very difficult, she recalled Astolphe and his nurse to Paris. The presence of her son was a great consolation to her, but Nanette was an eccentric character and as she could not bear any ridicule of her employers she caused her mistress some trouble. When she took the child for a walk and heard pamphlet sellers crying their pamphlets against "the Custine traitors," she could not contain her indignation. She insulted the newspaper sellers and even rated them. Several times she was embroiled in serious quarrels which might have cost her dear. In spite of the remonstrances of her mistress and her own promises she was continually the cause of some fresh outbreak.

La Force, where Armand de Custine was confined, was no more disagreeable than the majority of the Paris prisons. The prisoners enjoyed a considerable amount of liberty, and a garden of considerable size was at their disposal where they were able to expatiate, but life within the prison was far from pleasant.

"There were eight or ten in a room with barred windows, pallet beds, and four very dirty walls. They had to do the household work, make the beds, sweep the rooms, be present at the different summonses, and obey the fierce jailers who were always accompanied by watch-dogs. In the evening, when the hour for retirement sounded, everyone went to his rooms, and the dogs ran about the corridors to hurry up the idlers."[1] Delphine went every day to spend long hours with her husband in his prison. She showed him much devotion and affection, and the discord which had nearly separated them in the past seemed to have diminished to a remarkable extent. But Delphine's fickleness was infinite and incurable; instead of forgetting the past and devoting herself entirely to the attractive character who was ready to receive her, she could not recover her former feelings, and was weak enough

---

[1] Dauban, *Les Prisons de Paris*. The most important prisoners in La Force were Francœur, former director of the Opera, the Duc de Villeroy, the son of Sombreuil, Achille du Châtelet, Baron de Trenck, Charost de Béthune, Lévis-Mirepoix, Vergniaud, Valazé, etc.

to let her husband pass from the world without giving him the few days of real happiness which he desired. She attempted to explain the strange state of mind which paralysed her best intentions. She wrote to her brother :

"As for Armand, though we had for a long time grown quite cold towards one another for strong reasons and though we lived apart, yet recent misfortunes have brought us together. My complete devotion to him and to those who are dear to him has touched his heart, and has made him fonder of me than he has ever been. I can feel nothing but the warmest sympathy for him, which reduces him to despair, but it is written that I should always be deprived of happiness. Now that he loves me, I am another's, of course only in heart, but this is enough to deprive us of peace and happiness. That is how we stand at present."

The unfortunate Armand had been in prison for five months. He bore his fate with stoical resignation, and in a note found among his papers he relates his mode of occupying his sad life :

"I saw very few people, but lived in retirement in my rooms amid my books. My father's death served as an excuse for this seclusion, and my companions made a point of respecting the cause most carefully. I used to walk about for two hours in the morning and two in the evening, talking a little but observing a great deal. These high walls rudely scrawled with gibbets and melancholy lines of verse, the huge bolts, the drunken door-keepers, the poor wretches dancing on the brink of a volcano, the games of prisoner's base and ball in the midst of spies and executioners provided an environment inviting to deep reflections, and inspired me with a kind of sweet reverie to which I abandoned myself without reserve."

CHAPTER XIV

DECEMBER, 1793—JANUARY, 1794

Delphine attempts to induce her husband to escape—He refuses for fear of compromising the jailer's daughter—His examination—The indictment—He appears before the Revolutionary tribunal—He is condemned to death—His last letters to his wife.

HOWEVER, the time for Armand to appear before the Revolutionary tribunal was approaching. There was little doubt as to what the verdict would be, and his wife and friends made every effort to snatch the unhappy prisoner from certain death. We must do Delphine the justice to recognise that she attempted every expedient to save her husband, even at the risk of her own life.

On her daily visits to him she was almost always accompanied by the jailer's daughter, Louise, who brought her back to the prison door and often went a short way down the road with her. Louise had been deeply moved by the sight of this handsome, gentle and distinguished young man fated to so premature a death. As soon as Delphine noticed the interest which the girl felt in her husband she resolved to appeal to this sentiment to try to save Armand from his fate. She collected all the money she could from her friends and her own resources, some thirty thousand livres, an enormous sum for the time, and promised it to the girl if she would help her husband to escape.[1] She also promised her a yearly pension of two thousand francs. Louise accepted.

"My father was of no great stature," writes Astolphe; "he was delicate and was sufficiently young and slender to

[1] M. and Mme. de Dreux-Brézé had sent twenty thousand livres.

wear a woman's dress without attracting attention. It was agreed that at the appointed time my father should put on his wife's clothes in the prison, that my mother should dress as the jailer's daughter and that the prisoner and the supposed Louise would walk out together as usual at the ordinary door. The escape was to be made late in the afternoon before the lamps were lighted."

On the very day before the appointed date the Convention decreed death as the penalty for anyone who connived at the escape of a political prisoner.

A short time before the hour arranged Mme. de Custine reached the prison and found Louise in tears at the foot of the staircase. "What is the matter, girl?" "Oh! madam, come and save him, come and persuade him. You alone can still save his life. I have been begging him in vain all the morning; he will not hear of our proposal." She then whispered to her, "he has read the newspaper." Delphine guessed the rest; knowing her husband's inflexible sense of honour, she staggered as if she had already seen him mounting the scaffold. "Come with me, Louise; you will be better able than I to convince him." They both entered the prisoner's room and a tragical dialogue began in whispers: "Then you are unwilling to escape," cried Delphine; "your son will be left an orphan, for I shall die too!"— "Sacrifice the life of this girl to save mine! Impossible!"— "You will not sacrifice her; she will hide and will escape with us!"—"There is no hiding place in France, and it is impossible to leave this unhappy country; you are asking Louise to do more than her duty!"—"Sir," said Louise, "escape! The rest is my business."—"Do you not know the law that was decreed yesterday?" and he began to read it. "I know all that, but once again I beg you to escape, I pray you on my knees; I have staked my honour, my life and my happiness upon this proposal! You have promised to make my fortune but perhaps you will not be able to keep your word. If so, I am willing to save you for nothing. We will hide, we will go abroad and I will work for you. I ask nothing of you, merely to leave everything to me."—"We shall be caught and you will die!"—"Well, and if I am willing how can you object!"—"Never!"—"What," replies

Delphine, "you think more of this noble girl than of your wife and your child!"

Nothing could shake the stoical resolution of the prisoner. "The time granted to my mother was passed in vain prayers. She had to be carried out of the room as she would not leave the prison."

In the street Mme. de Custine met Guy de Chaumont-Quitry with the thirty thousand francs in gold: "All is lost," said my mother; "he declines to escape." "I knew it; I was sure he would," was the simple reply of M. de Quitry.[1]

Armand's chance of escaping death had now disappeared. It will be remembered that on July 13, 1793, he had written a very innocent letter to his father urging him covertly to resign, a course which daily became more inevitable. This letter, on which the indictment was based, ran as follows:

"To GENERAL CUSTINE, *Commander-in-Chief of the Armies of the North and of the Ardennes, at Cambrai.*

"*Paris, 13, in the evening.*

"The courier who brought me your letter told me that he is to be sent back and will call to-morrow early to take my answer. I cannot let him go without sending you some expression of my tender and painful sympathy with the sadness of your feelings. I do not know whether my last two letters reached you; I there discussed every point to which you refer. However, nothing could be more correct or unavoidable than the steps which you are taking and which you propose to take. I should be sorry indeed for the publicity of the step to which perhaps you will soon be forced. But it will be necessary upon the assumption which you lay down. It will not, perhaps, be entirely wasted, and what I desired above all things, for yourself at least, is an explanation of your motives clearly and methodically drawn up and expressed with vigour, though also with prudence. This is an object which deserves the greatest attention.

"You have heard of the revival and present composition

[1] *La Russie in* 1839, by Astolphe de Custine.

of the Committee of Public Safety. Apparently it is able to keep silence about your despatches and the unfortunate news which you gave; at any rate the evening paper does not say that any intimation of the fact was made to the Convention.

"Farewell, dear Father, I send you my best love. Do not forget a son who suffers with you in everything, and who would enjoy more than yourself the happiness which you deserve and which, perhaps, fortune will not always refuse you."[1]

This letter reached Cambrai after the General's departure; it was seized, sent to the Ministry of War and handed to Bouchotte, who ordered his secretary to send it to Fouquier-Tinville with these few words: "You will be able to judge, republican, how suspicious Custine's letter must seem in view of the fact that it was written just before his father's act of treachery at the moment when the Committee of Public Safety arrested him in his plots."

Custine was summoned from the Conciergerie on the 12th of Nivôse and appeared before Dumas, the vice-president of the Revolutionary tribunal, with his clerk Grappard. Fouquier-Tinville was present. After a long examination and after frankly answering all questions Armand was taken back to prison. Two days afterwards, on the 14th of Nivôse (Jan. 3, 1794), after more than five months' imprisonment, the young man appeared before the Revolutionary tribunal at nine o'clock in the morning. His wife was absolutely forbidden to appear at the trial because her presence might have disturbed him. The tribunal was composed of the citizens, René François Dumas, president, Marie Emmanuel Joseph Lanne and Pierre Louis Ragmay, judges. Claude Roger performed the functions of Public Prosecutor, Jean Baptiste Tavernier acted as clerk. When the twelve jurymen[2] had taken their places before the tribunal the accused was brought in. He was perfectly calm and resolute, and his face showed not the least emotion. Citizens La Fontène

---

[1] Arch. Nat., W^{1b} 306.
[2] Citizens Gauthier, Martin, Dufour, Sillion, L'Hespir, Duglay, Devèze, Topina, Le Brun, Camet, Bene, Gannay (Arch. Nat., W^{1b} 306).

and Chauveau[1] accompanied the accused as his counsel and official defender. Then the President made the jury take the oath individually.[2] Dumas told Custine to sit down and ordered the clerk to read the indictment, of which the following are the principal passages:

" From the examination undergone by Custine *fils* on the 12th of Nivôse it appears:

" That he has, for a long time, been involved in a system of treachery organised by a perfidious tyrant and his infamous ministers at the courts of Vienna and Berlin against French freedom and national sovereignty;

" That he has been an accomplice in the conspiracy organised by his father with the traitor Dumouriez, in consequence of which Mayence, Condé and Valenciennes have been handed over to the despots banded together against France;

" In 1792 he was chosen by the infamous Delessart to act at Berlin as the agent of the Austrian Committee in the Tuileries for their negotiations with William and Brunswick to arrange for the invasion of French territory, and to be an instrument of the diplomatic villainy by which they were preparing for the ruin and dissolution of the Empire;

" That he had failed to inform the nation of the coalition between the traitor Capet and the despot William and the House of Austria; that he had failed to denounce this vast conspiracy, the secret of which he must have known, from the very nature of his employment;

" That it even *appears* that he communicated to the enemies of France copies of his correspondence;

" That on his return from Berlin he maintained the most

---

[1] Custine had chosen as his lawyer M. de la Flotterie, but he did not appear at the session, and an official defender was then nominated, Chauveau Lagarde.

[2] The following is the text of the oath: "Citizen, you swear and promise to examine with the most scrupulous attention the charges brought against Custine, the accused man present before you; you swear and promise to hold no communication with anyone until your verdict is given; to listen neither to hatred nor malevolence nor fear nor affection, to decide your verdict according to the charges and the means of defence, according to your conscience and your inward conviction, with the impartiality and firmness befitting a free man."

perfidious silence at the moment when William was bringing forward his cohorts of slaves against a free nation ;

"That in thus acting Custine has exposed the country to dangers to which it would have succumbed but for the energy with which the cowardly satellites of these despots have been repulsed."

Fouquier-Tinville then reproached the prisoner for rejoining his father at Mayence " where he became an accomplice of his treachery and of his criminal intentions and anti-revolutionary communications with the enemies of the Republic, while it even *appeared* that his father made him responsible for secret correspondence with the enemies' Generals."

It will be observed with what facility Fouquier-Tinville replaced arguments and the proofs which were wanting by suppositions which immediately became certainties to him. The treacherous formula, "it appears," opened the way to every kind of accusation, however improbable and however unjustified. Even the most innocent act of Custine, under these circumstances, could not fail to afford food for suspicion.

The Public Prosecutor continued : " Custine *fils appears* to have been sent to Paris in the month of January, 1793, *no doubt* in order to make observations and report to his father upon the execution of the plan of counter-revolution. From this moment he *appears* to have remained at Paris to act as his father's agent with the federalist faction of which he was one of the chief supporters."

Fouquier-Tinville at length reaches the letter of July 13 and exclaims : " This letter, valuable for the terms in which it is conceived, is no less valuable for its date, as at that moment Custine was most energetically occupied with the execution of the plot which he had formed against the Republic, conspiring by every means to secure the capture of the frontier towns by the slaves of the despots. The obvious conclusion is that Custine *fils* was in possession of his father's plans for the subversion of liberty."

When the indictment had been read, the only witness summoned by the Public Prosecutor was brought forward. This was Vincent, who had been brought from St. Lazare where he was imprisoned to give evidence. Vincent confined himself to declaring that the prisoner " avoided the company of patriots and was in close connection with the anti-revolutionary party; that he had been the accomplice in his father's plots for the subversion of liberty." When the President asked him what proofs he could give, Vincent replied, "that he had heard it, and that, moreover, everyone said so." He then withdrew and was taken back to prison.

Dumas then proceeded to examine Custine. Alluding to the letter of July 13 he asked him what were the griefs of his father with which he felt so deep a sympathy. Armand replied: "That he was referring to the capture of Condé, which had taken place almost at the moment when General de Custine had taken over the command of the Army of the North and that his regret was the keener as Valenciennes was threatened with the same fate, and his father's enemies would certainly impute it to him as a crime, although since his arrival at the army it had been impossible for him to open communication with these two places." The President then asked him why he informed his father of the reorganisation of the Committee of Public Safety. Armand replied that, "nothing was more interesting for a General than to know with whom he had to deal and how far he could rely upon their intelligence." He was then asked if he had had any connection with the deputies who had fallen beneath the sword of the law (Girondins). He replied "that he had never seen them except at the different Committees of which they were members and at which he was obliged to be present on his father's business; that he esteemed their talents but knew nothing of their intentions."

Armand's replies were so clear, so simple and so frank that the audience showed themselves increasingly favourable to him. Whispers were heard on every side: "Why, this young man is innocent! He will certainly be acquitted."

Pursuing his examination, Dumas asked the accused why he had been sent to the Duke of Brunswick. Armand replied that "the Council had commissioned him to induce this Prince, who was famous for his military talents, to accept command of the French armies, that he had done his best to persuade him, and if he had succeeded he would have considered that he had performed a great service to the country in preparing its triumphs over the coalition powers;

that, in any case, if Court had any ulterior purpose in the proposal he did not know of it. Nor was it likely to have been communicated to a young man of twenty-three who was usually made a mere tool in such cases." At this point Dumas read to the jury Custine's correspondence during his stay at Brunswick. By quoting passages torn from their context he gave the impression that the prisoner had been commissioned to offer the throne of France to the Duke. Armand, perceiving that he was distorting the sense of the correspondence, at once jumped up and boldly addressing the jury, cried: "Citizens, I demand that the President should read my letters as a whole. He is abbreviating them in order to ruin me; I ask your protection against this act of bad faith." His courage and firmness evoked a murmur of approbation from the audience. Dumas, seeing that he was found out, grew confused and muttered that the jury should have the whole of the correspondence and would be able to judge from the documents. But Armand insisted that his letters should be read as a whole. He wrote to the Council " that he had hoped for several days that the Duke would accept the French proposals, but that the coalition powers had made better offers than ours and that the Prince seemed disposed to prefer the throne of Poland, which was offered to him, to the command of the French armies." This very natural explanation entirely satisfied the public, and the murmurs of approval were redoubled.

At length the President asked Armand if he had known of his father's plots. He replied simply " that he had never known his father to entertain any other plans than those of serving the Republic faithfully." "It is impossible," replied the President, "and contrary to the nature of things, that such a son as yourself, habitually in correspondence with his father, should fail to be his accomplice." Chauveau Lagarde at once seized upon the last words : " In what tribunal in the world," he cried, " would anyone venture to ask for the condemnation of a prisoner upon such a presumption ! What ! it is contrary to the nature of things that a son should fail to be his father's accomplice? What jurisprudence is this? I will go further still. Even if the accused had known the designs of the guilty father, for doubtless the General must be guilty since you have condemned him, I still ask you to say whether a son is bound to denounce his father. In such a case what would become of the first virtue, filial piety? What would be the state of morality which we are trying to regenerate?"

When the discussion had concluded Roger was allowed to speak in place of the Public Prosecutor, and summed up the case. And after him the counsel for the defence spoke. Unfortunately while Custine had shown eloquence and presence of mind, Chauveau Lagarde was unequal to his task. However, he had no difficulty in demonstrating the complete innocence of his client; the Court was uneasy at the favourable manifestations shown by the public, and sent out emissaries who whispered everywhere, " if this young man is acquitted, he will avenge his father's blood." After the conclusion of the debate the jury retired to their room, and on their re-entry to the Court they gave in succession their replies to the questions which the President had submitted to them. The declaration of the majority left not the least doubt concerning the fate reserved for Custine. "It is an established fact," ran the verdict, " that manœuvres and communications have been in progress with the domestic and foreign enemies of the State, tending to favour in every way possible the entry and progress of their armies upon French territory, while there have been conspiracies against the liberty, safety and sovereignty of the people, against the unity and indivisibility of the Republic. It is also established that Armand Louis Philippe François Custine is one of the authors or accomplices in these manœuvres, communications, and conspiracies."

As soon as the jury had concluded their verdict Roger rose and naturally demanded the penalty of death. The Court immediately granted his desire, and Armand de Custine was condemned to death in accordance with Article 4, of Clause I, of Section 2, of Part 2 of the Penal Code. Moreover, all his property was confiscated to the Republic.[1]

The sentence was to be executed within twenty-four hours

[1] Article 2 of section 2 of the Law of March 10th, 1793, ran as follows: "The property of prisoners condemned to death shall revert to the Republic, provision being made for the support of widows and children if they have no other resources."

upon the Place de la Révolution. It evoked a general expression of pity from the whole audience: "Poor young man," said the spectators, as they went away, "I thought he would be acquitted."

Custine received his sentence firmly, shrugged his shoulders without saying a word and left the Court as he had entered it, with a calm and serene face.

The same evening at nine o'clock Delphine purchased permission to say a last farewell to the condemned man. The meeting took place at the Conciergerie: "My mother," says Astolphe, "approached my father calmly, kissed him silently and sat with him for three hours; they talked but little; my name alone was mentioned several times. As midnight approached my mother, fearing ill consequences from a longer stay, rose and was about to withdraw. The condemned prisoner had met her in a room which gave entrance to several cells; this common room was of some size, low and dark; both were seated near a table on which a candle was burning. One side of the room was glazed, and through the panes could be seen the forms of the warders. Suddenly a small door was heard to open which had hitherto been unnoticed, and a man came out with a lantern in his hand. This man, strangely dressed, was a prisoner about to visit another; his only clothing was a small dressing-gown or rather a kind of dressing-jacket of some length, trimmed with swansdown, white cotton drawers, stockings, and a great pointed nightcap, ornamented with a huge tassel in bright red which completed his equipment. He came slowly into the room with little steps, sliding without raising his feet, like the courtiers of Louis XV., when they crossed the gallery at Versailles. When this figure had arrived before the husband and wife, it looked at them for a moment without saying a word and continued its path; they then observed that this old man was rouged.

"This apparition, which the two young people regarded in silence, surprised them in the midst of their fierce despair. Without considering that the rouge had not been put on to embellish a withered countenance but, perhaps, to prevent a sensitive man from turning pale upon the scaffold the next day, they burst simultaneously into a terrible laugh. Nervous tension for a moment overcame their bitter grief; the long attempt that they had made to hide their thoughts from one another had severely tried their nerves; they were attacked unexpectedly by the sense of the ridiculous, doubtless the one emotion for which they were not prepared. Thus, in spite of their efforts to remain calm or perhaps because of them, they abandoned themselves to wild laughter which soon became dreadfully hysterical. The warders, whose revolutionary experiences had familiarised them with this type of laughter, were sorry for my mother, more than the populace of Paris, with less experience, had been for the daughter of M. Berthier four years previously. These men came into the room and carried my mother out in an hysterical crisis which caused continual fits of laughter, while my father remained alone, a prey to similar convulsions."[1]

After this tragical scene Armand slept peacefully. The next day, which was to be his last, he sent Delphine two touching letters which show the astonishing fortitude of the young man. At nine o'clock in the morning he wrote: "I cannot better begin my last day than by speaking to you of the tender and painful feelings with which you have inspired me. Sometimes I put them aside and sometimes they will not leave me. What will become of you? Will they leave you your house, or at least your room? These thoughts are terribly sad.

"I slept for nine hours; why could not your night's rest have been as calm? It is your love and not your grief that I desire. You know the sacrifice that I have made. I have a poor companion in misfortune who saw you when you were a little girl and who seems to be an honest man.[2] One is only too happy, in bringing one's own misfortunes to an end, to relieve those of another. You can tell that to Philoctetes.[3]

"I had forgotten to tell you that I defended myself alone and only for the sake of those who love me."

The same evening at four o'clock, Armand desired to send Delphine one last farewell. His nobility of character did

[1] *La Russie en* 1839.
[2] This prisoner was a certain Bertrand; we shall meet with him again in the next chapter.
[3] Philoctetes was the name under which they referred to M. de Chaumont-Quitry.

not belie itself at this supreme moment. As we have seen him throughout his life, so we find him at the moment of undergoing the extreme penalty; there is the same loftiness of soul, the same serenity of mind and the same scorn of death. It is impossible to read without emotion the fine words in which the young man of twenty-five says farewell to life and also to the woman whom he loved so deeply and for whom he had suffered so much, without a word of reproach or of allusion to the painful past. We feel that he is generously pardoning one who had greatly mistaken him. A nobler expression of feeling, a loftier philosophy, can nowhere be found.

"*Four o'clock in the evening.*

"I must leave you. I send you my hair in this letter; Citizen .... undertakes to hand both to you; assure her of my gratitude.

"It is all over, my poor Delphine; I kiss you for the last time; I cannot see you and even if I could I would not, the parting would be too cruel, and it is not the moment for weakness of heart. What say I! weakness of heart? How can I avoid thinking of you? The only means is to put this thought aside with a barbarity which is heart-rending but necessary.

"My reputation will be what it deserves to be and as for life, it is a fragile thing by nature. Regret is the only feeling which sometimes disturbs my perfect calm. You, who know my thoughts so well, will no doubt give them expression and turn your own mind from the most mournful of them all, for they are meant for you.

"I do not think I have ever purposely done harm to anyone, I have sometimes felt a keen desire to do good. I wish I had done more, but I do not feel the burden of remorse. Why, then, should I feel disturbed? Death is necessary and is as simple as birth.

"I grieve for your fate. May it be softened, may it even be a happy one some day! This is one of my dearest and most heartfelt prayers. Teach your son to know his father. May your enlightened care protect him from vice; as for misfortune, may a pure and energetic soul give him the strength to bear it!

"Farewell; I do not wish to set forth the hopes of my imagination and my heart in the form of axioms, but be sure that I do not leave you without a desire to see you again some day. I have pardoned those few who seemed to rejoice at my arrest. Please reward the person who gives you this letter."

Hardly had he finished his last farewell than the jailers came to lead him to his doom. His strength of mind was unshaken for an instant during this last hour. He looked quietly upon the crowd who thronged to see him go by, and showed no emotion at the sight of the scaffold itself.

" A mind capable of this fortitude," writes a contemporary, "provides a great example of courage at the moment when all human strength so often fails. Custine walked to execution like a hero. Calm and innocence showed upon his face on which nature displayed a thousand graces. He seemed not to have a thought for the death which he met, and while his blood flowed upon the scaffold the smile of his innocence still seemed to illuminate it."[1]

His proud and lofty attitude inspired even his executioners with respect. The *Glaive Vengeur* wrote:

" If the wretched young man inherited the treasonable ideas of his infamous father, at any rate he showed none of his weakness but met his punishment firmly and calmly."[2]

[1] *Procès fameux jugés depuis la Révolution*, by Desessarts.
[2] *Mémoires sur les prisons*, vol. 1, pp. 133 and 135. Bardoux, *Mme. de Custine*, Arch. Nat. W^{1b} 306. Wallon, *Le Tribunal révolutionnaise*.

CHAPTER XV

1794

Delphine is placed under arrest in her rooms—She attempts to leave France with Astolphe—She is arrested at the point of starting and confined in Sainte-Félagie—Transferred to the prison of the Carmes—Her relations with General de Beauharnais—Mme. de Beauharnais is also imprisoned in the Carmes—The General's death.

WHAT became of Delphine after the tragic death of her husband, alone, without friends or resources? Accompanied only by the poor child of three years who was now fatherless, the unhappy woman was in the most painful situation. In her distress she had not even the consolation of corresponding with her mother and her brother; her letters did not reach their destination. Any other woman would have sunk in despair, but she, with fierce energy, resolved to struggle against her destiny. She determined to live[1] in modest retirement, devoting herself to her son and to await events.

But an unexpected incident completed her misfortunes and redoubled her alarm. The trial of General de Custine and of her husband, and the bold manner in which she had compromised herself in either case, had attracted the attention and provoked the suspicion of the authorities. One day, when she was least expecting it, the commissaries for the section of Grenelle came into her rooms; acting upon the orders of the Committee of Public Safety they proceeded to make an examination and summary inventory of her

---

[1] Mme. de Custine continued to live in the Rue de Bourbon, No. 509, on the second floor. She still had a somewhat numerous household in her service: First, Nanette whose sole care was Astolphe, also a chamber-maid, a footman Charles Poupet, a cook named Goulas and his wife.

papers : seals were placed upon the chief articles of furniture, and a trunk full of papers was sent to the office of the department. Delphine was confined to her rooms as a measure of public safety; she was not permitted to leave the house in which she lived, but was allowed to welcome those whom she would. The "shoemaker at the street corner," Pierre Monnecaut, was appointed guardian of the seals and porter of the house; he was also ordered to maintain supervision over her.

This confinement, which was probably only the prelude to more severe measures, completely changed Delphine's projects; she understood that flight was the only chance left for her of escaping her husband's fate. Thenceforward she had but one idea, to flee from this accursed land and meet again the only beings who were dear to her heart, her mother and her brother. She, who for months had risked her life so often and so carelessly, who had escaped death only by a miracle, wished at all costs to avoid the dangers which threatened her, to save her life that she might bring up her orphan. Her ideas and her talents were all concentrated upon this one project, how to leave France with Astolphe.

It was no easy matter. Mme. de Custine could not start without a passport, and she was perfectly sure that to ask for one in her own name would be fruitless. During the several months in the course of which she had gone almost daily to La Force to visit her husband, she had made the acquaintance of some prisoners. One of them, a certain Bertrand, had grown greatly attached to the beautiful young woman; as he had the rare and happy good fortune to be set at liberty, he had continued with Mme. de Custine a friendship begun at La Force and saw her fairly frequently. Having neither relatives nor friends nor anyone to whom she could apply for help, Delphine's only resource was to trust in Bertrand, to explain her plans and to ask if he would help her to carry them out. He was greatly attracted by her, and though he risked his head in the venture, he did not hesitate but promised every assistance.

As we have said, the first thing was to procure a passport, an indispensable necessity. Bertrand set to work among his friends and eventually obtained a passport in the name of Mme. X——, a lace merchant who was going to Brussels on business. Naturally the description of Mme. X—— corresponded exactly with that of Delphine. When this difficulty had been overcome, the two accomplices proceeded to organise the details of the escape. One person alone was taken into their confidence, Nanette, Astolphe's nurse, and, as we shall see, she was to play a very important part in the affair.

To facilitate proceedings and avoid arousing suspicion, Delphine resolved to separate from her son. It was agreed that Nanette, who spoke German much better than French, should take the public coach to Strasburg with Astolphe and pass herself off as an Alsatian peasant travelling with her child. Delphine, the same day, was to make her way to the Maison Blanche, on the road to Villejuif, where Bertrand would await her with a chaise bought for the purpose. As soon as she arrived they would both start for Brussels; it was agreed that Mme. de Custine and Nanette would meet again at Pyrmont in Westphalia; thence they would easily reach Berlin where Mme. de Sabran, who would be informed of the affair, would await them.

The preparations for this plan were a delicate matter and had necessitated many visits on the part of Bertrand. Several times a week he came to dine with Mme. de Custine, and after the meal when the servants had retired, they talked in whispers of their great proposal and attempted to anticipate every obstacle. But this great intimacy had attracted the attention of the servants. Moreover, Delphine who could not do without some luggage for the journey, had several times sent her chamber-maid to Bertrand's house, with little parcels of clothes, linen and shoes, an act of great imprudence. The chamber-maid, whose curiosity was aroused, secretly opened one of the parcels and observed its contents. A little reflection enabled her to suspect her mistress's proposals; seized with fear lest she herself should be compromised, she denounced Mme. de Custine to the Committee of Public Safety, referring to her strange intimacy with Bertrand.

On the 30th of Pluviôse Delphine learned through her

servant Charles Poupet, who had it from the guardian of the seals, that the magistrate of the section was coming to break the seals on the 1st of Ventôse. Seized with terror and fear of the possible consequences to herself of an examination of her papers, she immediately wrote to the magistrate :

"Citizen Custine has just heard that the seals are to be broken to-morrow. She is feverish this evening with a sore throat : she therefore begs the magistrate kindly to delay for two or three days. She hopes that her indisposition will have no further consequences and will be infinitely obliged to him." [1]

At the same time she warned Bertrand that there was not a moment to be lost and that they must flee at once. The departure was definitely fixed for the 2nd of Ventôse at nine o'clock in the evening and the meeting place was to be the barrier of the Maison Blanche. Nine in the evening was the most favourable time; as it was winter, the darkness would be complete and it was also the time when the keeper took his meal. Delphine, who did not wish to compromise any member of her household, had bought a rope ladder which she was to let down from her drawing-room window, to give the idea that she had fled without the knowledge of anyone. As for Nanette, it was arranged that she should leave the house as if she was going upon some errand in the district, but that under her arm she would have Astolphe hidden beneath a great cloak. As soon as they were out of sight the two fugitives would easily reach the Strasburg coach.

Unfortunately, this carefully devised plan collapsed in consequence of the denunciation of the chamber-maid. Bertrand, who had thought it advisable to leave his own house at an early hour and to wait for the time of meeting in an inn at the Maison Blanche, was tracked by the police and arrested. The chaise was seized with the bundle of clothes belonging to Mme. de Custine. Bertrand had the presence of mind to warn his accomplice and Nanette; he sent a card to Goulas, Mme. de Custine's cook, with these words, "I have just been arrested," but the note was intercepted. While Bertrand was being arrested, Delphine sent off Nanette and Astolphe; their departure was effected most successfully and no one noticed them.

[1] Arch. Nat., F7 4658.

Mme. de Custine, full of hope and confidence, had dressed herself in the modest attire of a workwoman and was patiently awaiting the moment for departure. To occupy her last hour she was going over her correspondence: sitting on a sofa in the drawing-room, near the fire-place, she was sorting out all the papers and letters in a great cardboard box and burning all the compromising documents which might have injured her relatives or her friends. Suddenly she heard a vigorous knocking at the door of the room. She started up in fear, shut the box and kicked it under the sofa, where it was hidden by the long covering which swept the floor. The door then opened and to her horror she saw the members of the Committee of Public Safety enter with men of the section armed with sabres and guns. She was seized and searched and her false passport was found. This time she could not escape her fate. The Commissaries turned the whole room upside down and searched the cupboards and desks, but fortunately no one thought of looking under the sofa.

The President then subjected Delphine to a long examination. She was obliged at the outset to admit her acquaintance with Bertrand, but when she was asked if she was not intending to make a journey with him, and if she had not induced him to buy a chaise and sent him a bundle of linen, clothes and handkerchiefs, and shoes and other personal effects she boldly denied the fact and said that she did not understand the questions. She was then shown the articles found in the chaise, but as she had taken care to erase all marks she could not recognise any of them. She was shown the shoes and one of the commissaries, by name Curt, a hunchback and shoemaker by profession, was ordered to fit them on her feet. Notwithstanding her resistance the little hunchback succeeded and declared that the shoes fitted the citizen perfectly and were evidently made for her. "They are not mine," replied the accused with gentle persistence. Curt, however, affirmed that the shoes were of English leather, an additional crime to Delphine's charge. "That is possible," replied the young woman with amusing logic, "but as I have never ordered anything from England you see that the shoes are not mine." "Who is your shoemaker?" asked the

President. Delphine gave the name of a fashionable shoemaker. " A bad patriot," cried Curt. " But a good shoemaker," replied Delphine. " We were intending to imprison him," said the commissary, " but the aristocrat has hidden himself. Do you know where he is?" " No, and if I did I would not tell you."

Throughout this examination Delphine, to hide her agitation and to gain time for her answers, had taken a piece of paper and was drawing, with the paper upon her knees. One of the commissaries, who wished to see her work, walked behind her and burst out laughing when he saw a clever caricature representing the President and the commissaries performing their functions and Curt, ornamented with a huge hump, standing on a chair, desperately waving the shoe which was under discussion. The sketch was immediately seized and added to the other documents bearing upon the case.[1] After this burlesque incident the examination was continued. The President asked Delphine whether she had not proposed to start that evening at nine o'clock with the citizen Bertrand. She replied in the negative. The President pointed out that she was replying in the negative to every question, even when the evidence was against her. Delphine coolly replied that they could not expect her to alter the truth, and that the whole of their charge was pure fiction of which she understood nothing whatever. Confronted with this obstinacy and unable to obtain the least admission, the commissaries abandoned the examination. They questioned the servants, Goulas the cook, his wife and Charles Poupet the footman, but obtained no information of any interest.[2]

At the conclusion of the examination, seals were placed upon every room in the flat except the kitchen, the shutters and all the windows were closed and the guardianship of the seals was again entrusted to citizen Pierre Monnecaut.

As for Delphine, she was inevitably placed under arrest. It was in vain for her to protest her innocence; she could do nothing against main force. Three armed men took her

---

[1] When Fouché was Minister of Police he extracted this sketch from the police portfolios and returned it to Mme. de Custine. It remained in the family for a long time and was unfortunately lost in moving house.
[2] Arch. Nat., F7 4658.

away in a cab to the prison of Sainte-Pélagie, where she was incarcerated.[1]

We can easily imagine the anguish and terror of the young woman when she found herself imprisoned in ignorance of the fate of Astolphe, whom she thought was on the road to Alsace with his nurse. Fortunately, Bertrand, at the same time that he attempted to warn Mme. de Custine, had sent a reliable messenger to the office of the Alsace diligence to inform Nanette of what had happened; consequently she had not started but hid herself until the next day and then came back with Astolphe to live in the Rue de Bourbon in the only room in the flat which was not sealed up, the kitchen. She arranged her bed there by the side of the child's cradle and in this one room they lived while Delphine was in prison. The other servants had fled after stealing the linen and silver-plate.

A prison is never an agreeable abode, but unanimous testimony shows that Sainte-Pélagie was the most detestable prison in Paris. It was damp and unhealthy, without light or air; the cells, six feet square, were dimly lighted by narrow windows guarded by enormous iron bars; the food was abominable. As each prisoner arrived the turnkey asked, " Have you any chink (money)?" If the reply was in the affirmative a jug and basin and a few plates were brought, for which a high price was demanded; a prisoner without " chink " was obliged to do without anything.

Mme. de Custine found herself so badly off that she complained that she could not go to bed, and asked that she might be allowed to send for the things indispensable to her comfort. On the 14th of Ventôse the commissaries of

[1] "National Convention.
"Committee of Public Safety,
2nd of Ventôse, the year II. of the one and indivisible Republic.
"The Committee of Public Security, being informed that the widow Custine, living in the Rue de Lille, is under arrest at her own house, decrees that she shall be taken to the Saint-Pélagie at once, and if there should be no room there for her, to any other place of imprisonment. She will be there detained until further orders.
"Signed: DUBARRAN, DAVID, LAVICOMTERIE, ELIE, LACOSTE, VADIER, AMAT, LOUIS (of Lower Rhine)."

Arch. Nat., F7 4658.

the Commune admitted her claim; they went to the Rue de Bourbon and "after seeing that the seals were unbroken they took away two mattresses, a camp bed, a bolster and pillow, a pair of sheets and two blankets," which were sent to the prisoner.

At the end of some weeks of imprisonment Mme. de Custine, for some unknown reason, was transferred to the prison of the Carmes in the Rue de Vaugirard. There she was to meet the most distinguished members of the old and new régime. The Carmes was an extremely disagreeable prison, but little better than Sainte-Pélagie.[1] The cells were so damp that in the morning the prisoners were obliged to wring the water out of their clothes; the unventilated corridors were poisoned by a miasmatic odour; the windows, heavily barred, were further closed for three-quarters of their height by planks, and the light could only come in from above.

The relations between the prisoners were not those customary in the other Paris prisons. Politeness here was out of fashion; men neglected their dress and went about without ties, in their shirt sleeves or drawers with bare legs, unkempt and unshaven, with dirty handkerchiefs about their heads. The women dressed with the greatest simplicity; a simple cotton dress or the dress then known as a pierrot, was all they had. The food, however, was not so bad in this prison as in many others. The allowance of bread was unlimited and each prisoner had half a bottle of wine daily.[2]

The men were kept separate from the women; they only met at certain times of the day in a garden of considerable

---

[1] Before the Revolution Sainte-Pélagie was divided into two parts: One, on the side of the Rue du Puits de L'Hermite, served as a refuge for the married and single women imprisoned by the King's orders. The other part, occupied by the honourable women, was entered from the Rue de Copeau. (Sorel, *Le Couvent des Carmes*.)

[2] Sorel, *Le Couvent des Carmes*. Campardon, *Le Tribunal révolutionnaire* (Plon, 1866). Dauban, *Les Prisons de Paris*. The Convent of the Carmes had been let on March 5th, 1793, by the administrators of the national property to a certain Dufrancastel, who sub-let the greater part of it and the garden to a certain Langlois. The latter arranged open-air dances, and above the door of the convent a transparency was put up bearing the inscription "The Linden Tree Ball." In November, 1793, when the prisons were overcrowded, the Committee of Public Safety decreed that the Convent of the Carmes should be taken over from the tenant and turned into a prison. (Sorel, *Le Couvent de Carmes*.)

size. "There everybody walked about together and the men generally played prisoner's base. The Revolutionary tribunal usually chose this moment of recreation to send for its victims. If the person summoned was a man and he was playing, he simply said goodbye to his friends and the game went on without him; if it was a woman, she also made her farewells and her departure did not disturb the amusement of those who survived her. The same sword was suspended above every head and a man once spared did not expect to survive those whom he saw chosen before him for more than a day.

"Time was divided into tenths and the tenth day was known as *décadi* and corresponded to our Sunday, as no work or guillotining was done upon that day. So when the prisoners reached the evening of *nonidi*, they were assured of at least twenty-four hours of life, which seemed quite an age. The prison then gave itself up to rejoicing."[1]

Among the chief prisoners who were confined with Delphine in the prison of the Carmes we may mention the Prince of Salm-Kirburg,[2] the Prince de Rohan-Guéméné, General Alexandre de Beauharnais, the Comte de Querhoent, the Marquis de Carcadot, the Comte de Soyecourt, the Duc de Béthune-Charost, Gouy d'Arcy, Leroy de Gramont, Hercule de Caumont, the Chevalier de Champcenetz, General Hoche,[3] Guillaume Vernon, the King's valet-de-chambre,[4] &c. Among the women may be quoted the Duchesse d'Aiguillon, Mme. Charles de Lameth, Mme. Bragelogne, Mother-Superior of the Ursulines; her sister, the Marquise de Paris-Montbrun, the widow of Lescot-Fleuriot, formerly Mayor of Paris, &c.[5]

Delphine's arrival at the prison of the Carmes made a sensation; the young woman was wearing mourning for her husband, which was an act of great courage at that time. Her long black drapery showed off her dazzling complexion

[1] *La Russe en* 1839, by Astolphe de Custine.
[2] A German prince living in France. He lived in the present palace of the Legion of Honour, which he had had built and which the nation confiscated.
[3] He was transferred to the Conciergerie on the 27th of Floréal: fortunately for him, his presence there was forgotten, and he was thus able to reach the 9th of Thermidor.
[4] The warrant described him as the valet of "Louis the Shortened"!
[5] Nearly 800 persons were imprisoned in the Convent of the Carmes from Frimaire 26, year II. (December 16, 1793), to the end of Vendemiaire, year III. (October, 1794). (Sorel.)

and beautiful fair hair, and she appeared delightfully pretty. Her misfortunes and the heroism which she had displayed gave her a celebrity which made her yet more interesting. All her companions in misfortune made much of her and surrounded her with the warmest sympathy. It was fated that she could not appear without inspiring love; it was an inevitable destiny from which she could not escape. General de Beauharnais[1] had often met her some years earlier at parties given by his cousin, Mme. de la Rochefoucauld, but had taken no particular notice of her at that time. Hardly was she installed in the Carmes than the General was struck by her beauty and fell deeply and madly in love with her. As we know but too well Delphine was unduly fond of admiration, and she was not capable of defending herself for long; although she was more than ever overwhelmed by misfortune at that time and racked with anxiety, both for herself and her son, she could not resist the burning words which soothed her grief. Then Beauharnais was so young, so handsome and so tender, and so irresistible when he talked of love. This unexpected passion was for Delphine a brilliant ray of sunlight in the darkness of the prison. She succumbed to its charm without delay, and so far abandoned herself to it as to forget the horrors of her situation. Moreover, at such a tragical time was it not foolishness to think of the morrow? So the two lovers saw as much of one another as the regulations of the prison allowed. When they could not meet they wrote; their affection was inspired with an energy and a passion which they knew would be cut short in its prime. In the scanty hours of intercourse and affection which they could steal from their jailers Delphine told her lover the story of her youth and her deep affection for Elzéar. She constantly talked of this beloved brother

---

[1] General Aléxandre de Beauharnais was born at Martinique in 1760; he was thus thirty-three years of age. After going through the American war under Rochambeau, he came to France, where his brilliant talents made him very successful. He was an ardent supporter of the principles of the Revolution and was appointed a deputy by the local authorities of Blois. After fighting in the Army of the North he took Custine's place at the head of the Army of the Rhine. After the capture of Mayence he left the army, refused the offer of the ministry of war, and resigned. He retired to La Ferté, where he was arrested on the 12th of Ventôse in the year II. and taken to Paris as a suspected person.

from whom she had been separated for three years, who was her counsellor, her guide and her best friend. Under the influence of these enthusiastic accounts Beauharnais conceived a great admiration for this Elzéar whom he did not know, but of whose charm and marvellous capacities he constantly heard.

Unfortunately we do not possess the correspondence between Delphine and the General; we have only two fragments of it which Mme. de Custine sent to her brother because they concerned him particularly. These we will quote in their entirety; they show the nature of the disturbed and superheated atmosphere in which people then lived, and the height of excitement to which these unfortunate creatures might rise while they spent their lives waiting for the executioner. The following is the first letter from Beauharnais:

"Yesterday in my unjust anger, I had ceased to think you worthy to be Elzéar's sister; to day the only reason that I have for believing that this supernatural being is not a fiction, is to tell myself that he is Delphine's brother and that nature desired to counter-balance the misfortunes of our time by producing these two astonishing phenomena. I identify this admirable young man with yourself to such an extent that I would take any trouble and make any effort to merit his esteem and secure his interest.

"Ah! my dear Delphine, if, as all probability seems to say, you survive me, and if some happy day brings you back to Elzéar, tell him my name. Tell him that he and you were in my heart at my last moment, that he was the constant object of our conversation and that he helped to increase the delight of our intimacy. Interest him in my memory by telling him how loving I was; describe me to him to the best advantage, that he may maintain in your heart a permanent memory of the man who only ceased to love you when he ceased to live. Remember in future times the prayer that I now address to you. If you grant it, it will bring me belief in an eternal life where I shall enjoy the knowledge that I am still living upon earth in the hearts of Elzéar and Delphine, in the hearts of the two beings who will be dearest to me."

Another day the General wrote to Delphine as follows:—

"I wait for you to tell me how to transmit to you more easily all that inspires me. Can my blood serve you? I will shed it with pleasure if, by flowing for you, it can inflame your own and so carry my image more deeply into your memory. Then in your heart, as lover, as friend, and as brother, I should have a common place with Elzéar, with your son, and with your dearest. I should allow none of your affection to escape me and should live upon your love, even in the sighs which would deprive it of other ties. You have never replied to me upon this question, which is of great importance in view of one melancholy possibility hereafter, my request, that is, to undertake to secure Elzéar's affection for me. Remember, dear friend, the admiration which his portrait aroused in me and the impression made upon me by the good you have told me of him, and if ever you are happy enough to see him again, and be clasped in his arms, talk to him sufficiently of my remembrance to win for me his regard, so that he may undertake the task of preventing you from forgetting me for ever. Elzéar, brother of a goddess, and almost a god thyself! be my support and my protection, grant thy beneficent help to a weak mortal, the most loving, most adoring of your Delphine that ever was, and to whom, after her, you will be the dearest object in the world. Remember, my friend, that I demand the performance of this promise; in view of one possible misfortune it will give me some imaginary consolation."

Delphine and Aléxandre de Beauharnais were in the full fire of their passion when, on the 2nd of Floréal, a jealous fate conceived the unfortunate idea of securing the imprisonment of the General's own wife in the same prison. Moreover, the new prisoner was sent to share Mme. de Custine's cell. At that time, fortunately, vulgar prejudices and meannesses found no place in men's hearts, which were occupied with more serious questions. Delphine gave a warm welcome to Mme. de Beauharnais, whom she knew well, and did her best to make her lot as easy as possible. Joséphine, again, showed her fellow prisoner every consideration, and was kind enough to shut her eyes to an intimacy which she thought quite natural. The two women lived upon the best of terms, and their mutual attentions softened the rigours of their captivity. But Mme. de Beauharnais showed as much fear and despondency as Delphine showed energy and courage; she spent her life foretelling the future from cards and lamenting her fate. She was extremely attractive; her appearance, her manners and her dress had an inimitable charm and she had soon won all hearts in the prison.

The intimacy of Aléxandre and Delphine was not to last long. Another event soon put an end to their loves and plunged the unhappy Delphine into fresh despair. The Terror continued its ravages; under the dictatorship of Robespierre executions went on continually and became every day more numerous. Not only were supporters of the old régime struck down, but the leaders of every party, even the most advanced, fell one after the other. Hébert, Fabre d'Églantine, Camille Desmoulins, and Danton mounted the scaffold. A law of the 22nd of Prairial permitted the condemnation of those accused without examination or evidence, upon virtual evidence. During the last weeks of the Terror life in the prisons of Paris became far more painful. At the Carmes in particular the jailers became more brutal, and such few indulgences as they usually allowed to their prisoners were stopped. Prisoners were obliged to eat out of the dish, visitors were not admitted, and their access to the garden and court was forbidden. The jailers complacently told them that trenches were being dug there in view of a general massacre of the prisoners. The unhappy creatures were prepared for anything, and at every unusual noise they thought their last hour had come. The truth is that Fouquier-Tinville, finding that individual prosecutions were too slow and did not provide a sufficient number of victims for the guillotine, "devised a system known as batches, that is to say, cases in which one accusation involved a number of individuals." At the prison of the Luxembourg a pretended conspiracy took place which cost the lives of nearly two hundred prisoners.

The ingenious idea was then conceived of inoculating all the prisons, that is to say, of transferring to each of them a prisoner from the Luxembourg who would be thought likely to preach insurrection and to organise it. This system was carried out at La Force, Saint-Lazare, Port Libre, at the Madelonnettes, and at the Carmes. In accordance with the programme it was asserted that a conspiracy had been hatched in the last-named prison and an investigation was made. A prisoner was accused of speaking evil of Robespierre and of referring to him as "a scoundrel and a beggar"; another was accused of procuring a rope ladder to escape if he found an opportunity. That was all, but it was enough to draw up a list of forty-nine conspirators, "princes, marquises, counts, soldiers, and statesmen, nobles and priests." Their object, it was stated, had been, "to carry out a most abominable attempt upon the lives of the representatives of the people."[1]

The evening before the day of the trial Beauharnais wrote the following lofty lines to his wife:

"4th *Thermidor*, year II. of the one and indivisible Republic.

"All that can be inferred from the kind of examination to which a large number of prisoners have been subjected to-day is that I am the victim of the accursed calumnies of several aristocrats calling themselves patriots in this prison. The persecutions of these infernal machinations will follow me to the Revolutionary tribunal and leaves me no hope of seeing you again, my dear, or of embracing my dear children. I will not speak to you of my regret or of my tender affection for them, and the attachment which binds me to you cannot leave you in doubt concerning the feelings with which I shall leave life on this subject. I regret no less to leave a country which I love and for which I would give my life a thousand times, but which I am now not only unable to serve but which will see me leave it in the guise of a bad citizen. This heartrending thought urges me to give my memory into your charge; work to restore its honour by showing that a whole life devoted to the service of its country and to the victory of liberty and equality should be enough in the eyes of the people to discredit the odious calumniators who have been generally taken from the class of suspected persons. This work must be delayed for

[1] Wallon, *Le tribunal révolutionnaire*, vol. v.

the moment, for in revolutionary storms when a great people is struggling to break its chains, it feels a reasonable sense of distrust, and is more afraid of overlooking the guilty than of striking down the innocent. I shall die with a calm which may, however, be softened by one of the dearest affections and also with the courage which characterises a free man of pure conscience and honest heart whose most ardent wish is the prosperity of the Republic.

"ALÉXANDRE DE BEAUHARNAIS."

The same day the accused were summoned to appear before the tribunal. When Delphine saw the lover going by whom she was never to see again she burst into sobs and fell into a dreadful state of despair. Beauharnais consoled her and gave her an Arabic ring to keep in memory of him, bearing a talisman; she kept it all her life.[1]

The next day, the 5th of Thermidor, the accused appeared before the Revolutionary tribunal. To expedite the case, the tribunal abolished the examination, speeches for the defence, swearing of the jury, etc., and contented itself with making certain of the identity of the accused. Three were acquitted, and forty-six were condemned to death together. Among these latter was Aléxandre de Beauharnais, "formerly an accomplice in the treachery of Custine"; Salm, "the German prince who, under the mask of patriotism, was merely the secret agent of the German coalition against France;" Champcenetz,[2] the editor of the "Acts of the Apostles," etc., etc.

The same day the prisoners were led to execution.

[1] Sorel, *La Prison des Carmes*. Wallon, *Le Tribunal révolutionnaire*, vol. v.

[2] It was he who jestingly asked Coffinhal, the President of the Court, "Pardon, president, is this worked like the National Guard? Can one get a substitute?"

CHAPTER XVI

1794

Arrest of M. de Malesherbes, of M. and Mme. de Rosambo, and of M. and Mme. de Chateaubriand—Their execution—Delphine is taken to her house on several occasions to be present at the examination of her papers—One of the commissaries, Gérôme, falls in love with her and saves her from the scaffold—Kindness of Gérôme to Astolphe—Song composed by Mme. de Sabran—The 9th Thermidor—Mme. de Beauharnais set at liberty—Delphine remains in prison—Serious illness of Astolphe—Nanette asks that Delphine shall be set at liberty—Her request is granted.

THE unfortunate prisoners in the Carmes were not always without news of the outside world; sometimes by jailers, sometimes by new prisoners they were informed of such events as might interest them. Thus Delphine learned of the sad fate of her dearest friends, the only friends left to her in France.

It will be remembered that after the death of the King, Malesherbes had immediately left Paris and had retired to the country with his children and grand-children, thinking that he might be forgotten; he was strangely deluded. In the early days of December, 1793, Malesherbes' eldest daughter and his son-in-law were arrested and taken to Paris. Some days later his grand-children, M. and Mme. de Chateaubriand suffered the same fate; and finally, in spite of the protests of the inhabitants of Malesherbes, he was himself declared a suspect and went to rejoin his children in the prison of Port-Libre where they had been confined.

His son-in-law, Louis Le Pelletier de Rosambo, was the first to die. He was one of the batch of Parliamentarians who mounted the scaffold on the 1st of Floreal in the year II.

(April 20, 1794). His wife and the whole of his family were soon to follow him; all were accused of conspiracy against the state.

The intimacy will be remembered which had existed between the Comtesse de la Rochefoucauld (Comtesse Alex) and Mme. de Chateaubriand. During her visit to Brussels the Comtesse maintained a pretty regular correspondence with her friend and was not sparing of her jests upon the new régime. Among other remarks she wrote these imprudent lines: "I should like, my dear girl, to see you out of the clutches of the national power; you would find it very pleasant to live in a country of slavery where fanaticism and prejudice are still paramount, etc."

These letters, though unsigned, were dangerous to their recipient; Mme. de Chateaubriand committed the unpardonable carelessness of keeping them. They were found in the course of the search and became the young woman's ruin. In vain did she protest that the correspondence had been only between women, and had taken place before the law forbidding such correspondence was passed. She could not escape her fate, but was condemned to death and executed on the 3rd of Floréal, in the year II. With her on the same day perished her husband, the Comtesse de Chateaubriand, her mother, Antoinette Thérèse de Rosambo, a widow of twenty-four hours, and her grandfather, the venerable Malesherbes. As the old man crossed the court of the Palais with his hands tied behind his back he stumbled against a stone and said with a smile, to his neighbour, "That is a bad omen; a Roman would have gone home." He was seventy-two years of age.[1] The Duchesse de Grammont, the Duchesse du Châtelet, and the Princess Lubomirska, aged twenty-three years, were included in the same batch.

Delphine was certainly deeply moved on learning the sad fate of her dear friends, who recalled to her so many happy days and cheerful parties; but she had no time for excessive grief. The same fate seemed to await her, and she thought herself destined to rejoin at an early date the unfortunate people who had so recently disappeared. What was the

[1] Arch. Nat., W 349, dossier 703 bis. Wallon, *Le Tribunal révolutionnaire*, vol. iii.

use of pitying the dead when death was the universal fate? What did it matter whether death came a day sooner or later?

During her long imprisonment in the Carmes, Delphine was taken upon three different occasions to her house in the Rue de Bourbon to be present at the breaking of the seals and the examination of her papers. These formalities were a great joy to her; they gave her an opportunity to see Astolphe and to clasp him in her arms for a few moments. On the 26th of Floréal in the year II., the Committee of Public Security first commissioned the Revolutionary Committee of Bondy to examine Mme. de Custine's papers in her presence. In conformity with this order the supervising Committee of Bondy appointed three commissaries to fulfil this task, Chevallier, Feuilloys, and Gérôme. On the 29th the three commissaries went to the prison at three o'clock in a cab, took the prisoner and drove her to her house, where they met the other commissaries of the municipality. They examined all the documents in the desks and cupboards in the room. Delphine was confronted with a heap of papers, but persisting in her principles of defence, she confidently declared that she could recognise none of them. As the number of papers was considerable they were all placed in a great portfolio which was sealed. Fortunately for Delphine, no one thought of looking under the sofa where she had hidden her correspondence at the moment of her arrest; yet the commissaries carried their zeal so far as to take up certain blocks from the floor and to break up a desk in order to discover the secret drawers. The examination was a long one and lasted until eight o'clock in the evening, when the prisoner was taken back to the Carmes by the three commissaries.

On the 21st of Prairial at five o'clock in the evening Delphine was again taken from the prison to her house. After securing her admission that the seals were intact, the members of the Committee continued the examination of the papers. They found "certain comic and historical documents contrary to the principles of the Revolution"; several were signed, Elzéar. Delphine was asked who wrote these documents; she replied that she did not know. She was asked who this Elzear was and where he lived; she replied that she had no idea. She further affirmed that she could not recognise either the handwriting or the signature, and boldly signed the report.

On the first of Messidor, Delphine was taken from prison for the third time to be present at the opening of the portfolio containing the documents and letters seized at her house. She was shown the papers signed Elzéar Sabran; she admitted that the name was a family name, but she said that "the spelling is not of our family," and asserted that she could not recognise the handwriting. She was then shown letters signed by the Abbé Gibelin and by the Abbé Devaux. She admitted that she had known people of that name in the past, but had no idea what had become of them.[1] For the third time Delphine was taken back to prison, while the commissaries had still failed to discover the famous cardboard box under the sofa.

These visits and examinations at her house ended in a most unexpected result for Delphine. Among the three commissaries who had to take the young woman from prison and back again was a master-mason, called Gérôme. Gérôme was a young man, and his sincere republican convictions did not remove his susceptibility to the charm of beauty. He was touched by the grace of Delphine, by her distress and her tears, and swore to himself to make every effort, even at the risk of his life, to save this "pretty aristocrat" from the scaffold. From that moment Gérôme was possessed with but one idea, to save Delphine. But here Astolphe, who has related this strange adventure, may be allowed to speak.

"Gérôme had free access to the office of Fouquier-Tinville. There were heaped the papers containing the names of every prisoner in the jails of Paris. The papers were all kept in one box where they were piled up one by one by Fouquier-Tinville, who used them as they were wanted without discrimination to provide material for the daily executions. The number of papers was daily increased by different consignments from all the prisons in the town; naturally the new papers were placed underneath the old ones. Gérôme knew

[1] Arch. Nat., F7 4658.

where the fatal box was kept and for six months,[1] he never failed to enter the office when he was free from observation and to assure himself that the paper on which my mother's name was written was always at the bottom of the box. Every day he went through this infernal pile until he had discovered my mother's name and placed it at the bottom of the box. He could not venture to destroy the paper, because the number of the papers was known. On one occasion the name of Mme. de Custine appeared on the top ; Gérôme placed it beneath all the others and shuddered." [2]

Gérôme was not content with saving Mme. de Custine's life; he did yet more. During the months of her imprisonment Nanette had been able to live and to provide for Astolphe by selling her property ; but the moment inevitably came when she had nothing more. She was in the most frightful distress and death by hunger was the only prospect before the two unfortunates. Gérôme could not bear the idea of leaving in such want the child of the woman he loved; under the most ingenious pretexts and under promise of secrecy he forced Nanette to accept little sums of money which enabled her to live until her mistress was set at liberty.

Of all the passions which Delphine inspired, and Heaven knows how numerous they were, none was so sincere and disinterested as Gérôme's. A man of the people, an ardent revolutionary, he knew the vast gulf which separated him from the woman whom he dared to love but to whom he dared not confess his passion. He knew that he had nothing to hope for and that she would probably never learn his secret feelings, his obscure and whole-hearted attachment. Yet this did not prevent him from watching over her and devoting himself to her and to her child with the most complete unselfishness. The incident is too unusual and too fine to remain untold.

One of the greatest joys that Mme. de Custine experienced during her long imprisonment was caused by a tender and melancholy song which she received one day from Rheinsberg. For months she had been without news of her mother and her brother who dared not write to her for fear of compromising

---

[1] Astolphe is mistaken. He means two months.
[2] *La Russie en* 1839, by Astolphe de Custine.

her. She had no idea what had become of them. Mme. de Sabran, on her side, was living in dreadful anxiety, daily expecting to hear of her beloved daughter's death. She was reduced to reading over the list of prisoners who had perished on the scaffold in the few newspapers which reached Prussia. She had no other means of knowing whether Delphine was dead or alive. One day she conceived the ingenious idea of sending her daughter a perfectly innocent song in which she discreetly indicated how her cruel fate had touched her heart and how she hoped to see her again one day.

To the air "Jean Jacques."

"I PLANTED IT, I WATCHED IT GROW."

'Tis mine, for I first planted it,
 My Rose-tree! Ah, how brief delight!
I had to leave thee and I fear
 Thou nevermore wilt meet my sight.

Fair Rose-tree, bow beneath the storm;
 Weakness makes weak the tyrant's sway.
Then bend beneath the wintry blast
 Which else will sweep thy blooms away.

Thou mad'st me glad, thou mak'st me sad;
 On thoughts of thee I weep forlorn;
Near thee, thy blossom filled my gaze,
 But far from thee, I feel thy thorn.

Thou wast my pleasure and my joy,
 My happiness, my perfect pride,
Deep-rooted in my lonely heart
 Thy memory shall for aye abide.

O Rose-tree, guard thy tender growth,
 Be ever green and ever gay,
And cheer the winter of my life
 When winds and storms have passed away.

At length the 9th of Thermidor arrived; the fall of Robespierre and his punishment marked the end of the Terror and that dreadful nightmare came to an end. A few days afterwards the prisons were almost empty. The Revolutionary tribunal was suppressed, the Jacobin club was closed, Dumas and Fouquier-Tinville mounted the scaffold in their turn and paid the just penalty for their abominable crimes. The first person to be set at liberty from the prison of the Carmes was Mme. de Beauharnais;

she was a close friend of Tallien[1] and the famous proconsul hastened to secure her liberty. When she was told that she was free, she became quite ill with emotion and shed abundant tears, while her companions in misfortune who appreciated her charm and goodness applauded. Mme. d'Aiguillon and Mme. de Lameth were liberated at the same time. All the friends and relatives of Mme. de Custine were scattered and no one had time to think of her; Gérôme, who had been so powerful a help, could do nothing more for her; as a friend of Robespierre he was proscribed in his turn and had been forced to hide without delay. Delphine, forgotten and abandoned by all, therefore remained in prison.

But the regulations were less strict and Nanette was able to obtain permission to visit her dear mistress. Unfortunately the news which she brought was heartrending; Astolphe had been attacked by a malignant fever, had spent several weeks between life and death and had been saved only by the care and devotion of his nurse. He was still so weak that it was impossible to think of taking him out. Two months thus went by, Nanette coming almost every day to see her mistress. Delphine, however, was reduced to despair by her imprisonment and her inability to see her son; there seemed to be no reason why this painful situation should ever come to an end. Nanette, who was at her wits' end for a means of helping the prisoner, then conceived a brilliant idea. Her father had been employed for years in the porcelain factory at Niederviller. In 1793 the manufactory had been confiscated with the General's other property and the workshop had been closed. Some fifty workmen, all from the province of Lorraine, had come to Paris to look for work and among them was Nanette's father. She conceived the plan of inducing her mistress to sign a request to be set at liberty; she then found her father and asked him to sign it and to secure the signatures of his

---

[1] Tallien (1769-1820) was at first a lawyer's clerk; then he entered politics and was suspected of provoking the September massacres. A deputy of the Convention, he was sent to Bordeaux, where he carried on the most bloodthirsty of tyrannies. Converted to moderate ideas by Mme. de Fontenai he contributed to the fall of Robespierre and played an important part for several years.

comrades, which was readily done.   Nanette then handed the petition herself to Legendre, a retired butcher, who was in charge of the office for examining requests to be set at liberty.

Legendre was more occupied with the investigation of bottles than of prisoners' petitions; he threw the petition into an open box where many other requests of the same kind were reposing and thought no more about it. The petition might have remained there for months if a fortunate occurrence had not brought it to light. One evening, the 13th of Vendémiaire, three young men in the service of Legendre came into the office after a cheerful dinner. They had no light, but began to skylark in the darkness; while chasing one another they knocked over the box in which the petitions were accumulated. One of these madcaps, Rossigneux, declared that he would pick up at random one of the scattered leaves and would gain a signature the same evening to secure the liberty of the prisoner concerned. No sooner said than done. Lights were brought and it was found that Rossigneux, from amid numberless petitions, had chosen that of Mme. de Custine, supported by the workmen of Niederviller. " Bravo ! " cried the young men, " let us then set the fair Custine at liberty, the second Madame Roland."

Legendre came in at one o'clock in the morning, completely drunk, as usual, and prepared to sign anything they liked. Provided with the precious paper the three young men hastened to the Carmes, ordered the gates to be opened and themselves to be led to the prisoner's cell. But she energetically refused to open her door or to go out in the middle of the night with unknown men. The next day they came back at ten o'clock and Delphine was at length able to leave the hateful prison where she had been vegetating for eight months. It was the 17th of Vendémiaire.

The young woman's delight at recovering Astolphe was saddened by her grief at finding her unhappy child in the most wretched state of health. He was still suffering from the consequences of the terrible disease which had brought him almost to the grave and he remained " deaf and half imbecile." Mme. de Custine's position was truly appalling.

Her rooms had been devastated and pillaged; her furniture was still under seals. She had no friends and no resources and did not know how to provide for her own livelihood or for her son. The suffering and the many violent emotions through which she had passed could not undermine her courage but destroyed her health. She collapsed and was seriously ill with jaundice. For nearly five months she was in bed, nursed by the faithful Nanette, and living on supplies which came she did not know whence, and she was too ill to care.

When she recovered her health she questioned Nanette and the latter at length admitted that for the last six months she had been keeping house on money which Gérôme sent weekly from his hiding-place, expressly urging her to say nothing about it; at the same time she heard how he had saved her life. Mme. de Custine was profoundly touched by the devotion of this man whom she hardly knew and whom she thought was one of her persecutors. She made every effort to repay his great services; she helped him to hide himself and as soon as she could enabled him to leave France and seek his fortune in America.[1]

Not until the month of November, 1794, did Mme. de Sabran learn, to her delight, that Delphine was at liberty. M. de Dreux-Brézé, was at Lausanne with his wife; by means of a Swiss who had been able to travel to Paris and whom he had commissioned to look for Delphine, he at length learned that she had left the Carmes. He lost no time in informing Mme. de Sabran of this happy news.

[1] Gérôme returned to France during the consulate; he had gained a small fortune in America.
"My mother," writes Astolphe, "treated him as a friend. My grandmother Sabran, when she came back from her exile, overwhelmed him with marks of gratitude. He would never enter our social circle; he used to say to my mother: 'I will come and see you when you are alone; when there are people with you I will not come, because your friends would look on me as a curious animal. You receive me from kindness for I know your good heart, but I should be ill at ease at your house, for we have not received the same education. If I have done anything, you have done as much for me and we are quits.' My mother invariably remained a faithful friend to him and brought me up with a sense of gratitude towards him. He died at the beginning of the Empire." (*La Russie en 1839.*)

CHAPTER XVII

JANUARY—SEPTEMBER, 1795

The Chevalier Séguier gains news of Delphine and informs Mme. de Sabran—Plans for meeting between mother and daughter—They meet at Zurich—Visit to Lavater—Elzéar's appreciation of the letters of Beauharnais—Mme. de Custine refuses to remain abroad and wishes to return to France.

MME. DE SABRAN had a cousin, the Chevalier Maurice Séguier [1] who had been in the army of Condé for several years. Notwithstanding the difference in their ages they had always been deeply attached to one another and corresponded from time to time, lamenting in their letters the misfortunes of the age. In 1795, Séguier and his troops were near the Swiss frontier; it therefore seemed possible to get news from France. The Swiss received passports without any difficulty and could easily enter France and even go as far as Paris. Thus by their intervention the exiles could send letters to their relatives or their friends, and could even accomplish certain delicate commissions. The intermediary obviously ran some risk, but his fears could be overcome with money. Touched by the anxiety of Mme. de Sabran who had had no news of her daughter for eighteen months, Séguier resolved to use his privileged position in order to discover exactly what had become of Mme. de Custine since her liberation and to find out where she was living. A Swiss whom he knew was starting for Paris; he

[1] Armand Louis Maurice, Baron Séguier (1770–1831), youngest son of Antoine Louis Séguier, Attorney-General to the Paris Parliament. He became one of the pages in the King's household on March 24, 1783; in 1787 he entered the Lorraine Dragoons; in 1791 he went into exile with his family and served in Condé's army until 1797.

commissioned him to discover the young woman and bring back news of her at any cost. As a token by which he might be known, he gave him the last letter that he had received from Mme. de Sabran; when Delphine saw her mother's writing she would understand that she had to deal with friends to whom she could speak freely.

No sooner had the good Swiss reached the capital than he hastened to the Rue de Bourbon. But Mme. de Custine was no longer there and her new address was unknown. At length, after many searches and many fruitless journeys he discovered Delphine in the Rue Martel, No. 9, "at the house of one Le Fève, at the end of the Faubourg Saint-Denis, between the Rue des Petites Ecuries and the Rue Paradis." Séguier himself may be allowed to relate the interview :

"AT MÜLHEIM, NEAR FREIBURG IN BRISGAU,
"*June* 10, 1795.

"Dear mother, give me your best attention : I have to speak to you of your dear Delphine.

"Grieved that I have been unable hitherto to give you any but indirect news of your daughter, I took advantage of a journey which a reliable man was making to Paris, partly on my business and partly upon that of my friends; I commissioned him, in my own interest, to gain certain news of this poor abandoned girl, and I ordered him to ransack every corner of the town. For a long time I have had no news of him, but yesterday he arrived at last. I have just been eight leagues to meet him and have come back exhausted, and my first care is to write an account of his narrative for you.

"I give it word for word; so you may listen as if he were speaking :

"'Provided with the address which you gave me, I went to the Rue de Bourbon opposite the former Hôtel de Salm and asked for Mme. de Custine. She had left that address a long time before; different addresses were given to me where I might be able to gain information. I went from door to door and at length I discovered that she was living in the Rue Martel, No. 9; three steps and I was there. I was taken up to the first floor room and shown in. Three pretty ladies were sitting talking together.

"'Who is Mme. de Custine?'

"'I,' said one of them, the prettiest.

"'Upon my honour, sir, you have some pretty acquaintances. Very pretty, upon my word, so fresh and so white, poor woman, though she has been out of prison for some time. But you may set your mind at rest; she is living very quietly with a friend who takes the greatest care of her, and with whom she is in safety. But I will continue my story:

"'What can I do for you?' she said.

"'I should like to speak to you for a moment privately.'

"'You can speak sir, before these ladies; they are my friends.'

"'Excuse me, madam, if I confide that which brings me here to you alone.'

"'Willingly.'

"'She then led me into the next room. When I was alone with her I did not say a word, I merely twisted between my fingers the piece of her mother's letter which you had given me. She saw it, recognised it, leapt upon it and tore it from me and no sooner was she assured that her eyes did not deceive her than she pressed it to her lips and then the poor little woman burst into tears. Oh! sir, that girl surely loves her mother; I was quite sorry to see her and still am when I think of it.

"'Where is my mother?' she said.

"'At Rheinsberg with Prince Henry.'

"'And my brother?'

"'Also with her.'

"'Do you come from her?'

"'Yes, one of my friends who is nearer than she is to the frontier has asked me to go to you and take her any message from you.'

"'She is well, is she not, she and my brother?'

"'Yes, both are quite well.' And thereupon her tears began to flow faster than before.

"'Do you think it would be difficult for me to cross France and Germany to go to her?'

"'Nothing easier, madam; we will start together. You can pass as my wife and at Briesgau you will find the Chevalier Séguier, who will certainly be delighted to accompany you to Rheinsberg.'

"'She was on the point of agreeing to this arrangement when she remembered that the journey might be detrimental to her business; she is working successfully in the name of her son to recover the property of her unfortunate husband and father-in-law; during her absence difficulties might arise. I then proposed that the journey might be put off for a time and that during the interval Mme. de Sabran might be told to come to Lausanne and Mme. de Custine would then start for the same place and thus the desired meeting might be brought about. She approved of this proposal and it now remains for you, sir, to communicate with Mme. de Sabran and to settle the dates.'

"What do you think of this proposal, madam? Will you refuse to embrace your poor daughter who has no relatives or brother or husband to embrace her. Make me the intermediary of your orders; she will soon receive them. I have retained means of communicating with her."

Séguier's letter was fully calculated to soothe the mother's alarm and at the same time Mme. de Sabran received another piece of news which was an additional cause for rejoicing and gave her great hopes. The Peace of Bâle had just been signed and the cessation of hostilities between France and Prussia seemed likely to make communication between the two countries possible. Mme. de Sabran, in delight, hastened to write to her daughter, but she did not venture to give full rein to her joy and the terms of her letter show the prudence with which she avoided any possibility of compromising its recipient.

"*June*, 1795.

"After my long anxiety and suffering, my child, I take advantage of the return of wisdom and humanity to send you my love, though from a very long distance yet. May my prayers be granted by those to whom I send them. Three hundred leagues and a war between mother and daughter were a terrible obstacle to another meeting before the death of either one of us, but happily the Peace has removed part of the obstacle and I hope will soon remove the rest, when I shall have the happiness of clasping you in my arms once more. You may imagine that my love was too uneasy not to have devised some occasional means of gaining information concerning your existence, even if only by means of the newspapers where I have sometimes followed your traces.

"But perhaps you do not know that I am still staying with the good Prince Henry. He is so friendly towards France that I can delude myself sometimes with the belief that I am in my own dear country. He wishes to add a letter to mine to show you that he still remembers you and that he continues his interest in me. To him is due the Peace and to the Peace perhaps I shall owe the happiness of seeing you again. You know how kindly he asked me to come to him in less anxious times, but perhaps you do not know what attention he has shown me during the long illness which prevented me from returning to my country when the way was still open. The greater forbearance of the Government and the excellent spirit manifested by those at the head of affairs have revived in my heart the sweetest of hopes, the hope that one of us may obtain permission to come and embrace the other.

"Farewell, my child; if my letter reaches you send a reply through the French commissaries, who will certainly send your letter to the Prussian minister. Your brother and your good mother send you their best love; the moment, I hope, will come when I shall clasp you to my heart and when my tears will be tears of joy."

From that moment Delphine had but one idea, to see her mother again and as soon as possible. But how was this to be done, and how was she to meet her? Mm. de Sabran, who was quite as anxious for a meeting, proposed to make one-half of the journey to some place on the French frontier; Bâle, for instance, might be possible as a meeting-place. The thing seemed simple enough in appearance but in reality there were serious obstacles to surmount. Delphine could not leave France without a passport and her name was too well known for her to obtain one readily.

M. de Dreux-Brézé, who was living at Lausanne, was

prepared to help his sister-in-law on his side and succeeded in buying two forged Swiss passports, one for Delphine and one for Astolphe and Nanette, but Mme. de Custine rightly refused to make use of them.[1] She declined to make any journey that was not legally authorised or which might be disastrous to her position or prejudice the just claims which she had already lodged with the Government for the restoration of her property. She therefore required a passport issued by the Committee of Public Safety and made every effort to obtain one. Fortunately for her, she had rediscovered some friends and by means of their influence she was at length authorised to go and take the waters at Baden, near Zurich.

As soon as she was in possession of this precious document she made her preparations for departure; unfortunately the passport was only in her own name and she was unable to take Astolphe or Nanette with her. She therefore resolved to take them both to Niederviller which was on her road and leave them there during her absence. She then wrote to her mother and arranged a meeting at Klosterheilbronn, which was not very far from the frontier. Towards the end of July Mme. de Sabran heard that her daughter had started for Niederviller, and set off in haste with Elzéar for Bayreuth and then for Anspach, where they stayed for some time expecting a letter naming the date for their meeting. But the letter did not arrive and the travellers grew impatient and anxious. They ought to have been in the seventh heaven of delight, but for five years they had passed through so many sufferings and such cruel and terrible trials that they could not believe in happiness or the possibility of success; they were consumed with fear and anxiety, foreseeing even the most improbable catastrophes.

At length, tired of waiting and unable to contain their anxiety, they started for Klosterheilbronn, the place of meeting. They would surely find news and perhaps Delphine herself waiting for them there. But at Klosterheilbronn, unfortunately, they found no letter and no Delphine.

[1] The passports and a journey to Paris which M. de Dreux-Brézé had paid for had cost 1696 livres 11 deniers. He put in a claim for this amount to Mme. de Sabran, asking her to write to him only occasionally as his embarrassment was such that he could hardly pay the postage upon letters.

Mme. de Sabran was in despair; undoubtedly her daughter had been unable to pass the frontier. What then had become of her? Had she been arrested, and what fresh disaster was to be feared? At length, after some days of painful anxiety, a letter from Séguier arrived which filled the mother's heart with joy. Delphine, after many adventures had arrived at Bâle; he had seen her and spoken to her and found her more delightful than ever.

"*To* MME. DE SABRAN, *at Klosterheilbronn, via Anspach.*

"Franconia.

"(The postmaster of Anspach is requested most urgently to send this letter on at once.)

"If you have not yet started for Bâle, let your first exclamation upon opening this letter be an order to put the horses in at once. Your Delphine is here and I have just seen her; she is fresh and pretty and exactly like an angel escaped from hell. Envy my happiness and come and be happier than I if possible. Just think that I arrived here suspecting nothing and full of vexation caused by the uneasiness of your last letters, intending to send off an express messenger which would have been a very slow means of reassuring myself. I had scarcely arrived when I was informed that Mme. de Custine was in the same inn, not four yards away from me.

"Come, then, as soon as you can; perhaps she will not yet have reached Bâle, but a letter left at the Cygogne[1] in this town will tell you where to find her."

On receipt of this letter Mme. de Sabran did not lose a moment. She hastily left Klosterheilbronn for Bâle, her heart overflowing with joy. There she was again disappointed; her daughter was no longer at the Cygogne as she had been obliged to leave Bâle without delay. As her passport stated that she was going to Baden the authorities had insisted that she should leave the town. However, thanks to the inter-

---

[1] The Inn of the Cygogne with its sign still exists but has become the Hôtel de la Cigogne. It is situated in the lower part of the town near the banks of the Rhine.

vention of a powerful friend, the famous Lavater,[1] who lived at Zurich, and with whom Mme. de Sabran had been acquainted for many years, Delphine received permission to make her way to the latter town and to stay there until her mother's arrival.

Fortunately, before rejoining his regiment, Séguier had left a note at the Cygogne informing Mme. de Sabran of her daughter's new address. Mme. de Sabran and Elzéar took but a few hours' rest at Bâle and started off once more for Zurich. At length they arrived, overwhelmed with fatigue but supported by the idea of seeing their dear Delphine. They reached the Inn of the Epée,[2] asked for Mme. de Custine, rushed into the room upon the first floor which was pointed out to them, and fell into the arms of her whom they had never expected to see again. The three sobbed wildly, kissed and clasped one another in their arms and were incapable of uttering a word. At length, when Mme. de Sabran had partly recovered her self-possession, she could not keep this exclamation back as she looked at Delphine, "Heavens! daughter, how pretty you are!"

The delight of these first days of meeting may easily be imagined. To have lived for four years as long as a thousand centuries, to have expected every day, every hour and every moment the dreadful news of the cruel death of a beloved daughter, to see her alive and to clasp her form, to forget the fearful nightmare which had poisoned their lives, this was indeed an ecstasy of delight! The three unhappy beings who had suffered so cruelly could hardly believe the reality of their happiness; at times they thought that they were living in a dream from which there would be a dreadful awakening.

Questions followed questions and Delphine was obliged to repeat twenty times the story of the dreadful hours which

[1] Lavater, a Protestant pastor, was born at Zurich in 1741 and died there in 1801 from the effects of a wound received in 1799 when Zurich was recaptured by the French. A devotee of the marvellous, he believed in all the magicians and impostors of the age, Cagliostro, Mesmer, etc.; he also believed in himself, a belief that was shared by others, for people made long pilgrimages to see him and consult him. He was a very benevolent character and wrote a great deal. His principal work is entitled, *Essais Physiognomiques*.

[2] The Inn of the Epée, which is now the Hôtel de L'Epée, was situated in the middle of the town. It still exists with its striking sign.

she had spent, the story of the martyrdom of her father-in-law and her unfortunate husband, to relate the dangers which she had passed through during her long imprisonment and to tell of the devotion of Gérôme to whom she owed her life. Mme. de Sabran and Elzéar were never tired of listening to the story of these dreadful hours; every moment they wept with happiness; every word, every phrase, called forth a fresh flood of tears, but they were tears of joy. " It was, perhaps," says Astolphe, " the happiest moment of my mother's life."

On learning that Mme. de Sabran and Delphine had at last met Séguier wrote to his cousin:

" MÜLHEIM, *August 27*, 1795.

" At last you are to be with your Delphine: your anxieties and torments are at an end and in spite of all the monks in the world you have cried with Rousseau: ' Heavenly powers, you have given me a soul for sorrow, give me one also for happiness!' Why am I not there in a modest corner, to share your happiness, though discreet enough not to interfere with it. I should look upon you as though I were allowed a sight of Paradise, and I should enjoy your presence, as our pietists assert that we shall one day enjoy the Divine presence. I should be happy by the mere contemplation of it, while carefully avoiding, profane and earthly animal that I am, any undue encroachment."

The enthusiastic tone in which Séguier writes to his cousin may seem surprising if we do not inform the reader of the events subsequent to the meeting at Bâle between Delphine and the handsome officer of Condé's army. The young woman had produced her usual effect. Séguier was dazzled, charmed, heart-stricken and inevitably carried away; nor had he attempted to hide from the lovely traveller the effect that she had produced upon him. Hence from that moment we find him appearing as Mme. de Sabran's most attentive friend and maintaining with her a regular correspondence which treats of nothing but Delphine and her irresistible charms.

Mme. de Sabran and Delphine went to thank Lavater,

who had done so much to facilitate their meeting. Moreover, Delphine had a letter to give him from the Peruvian adventurer, Miranda,[1] whom she had known in Paris. On perceiving Mme. de Custine the great philosopher displayed astonishing insight. He could not help uttering a cry and turning to Mme. de Sabran he said: "Ah! madam, what a happy mother you are; your daughter is transparency itself. I have never seen such sincerity. One can read beneath her forehead."

The interview was charming; Lavater was delighted to welcome his visitors and made them promise to come back often. He assured Delphine that he would soon give her an answer for Miranda. Some days later he sent the promised letter, which was accompanied by this strange note:

"ZURICH, 1795.

"I cannot write more than a line to the amiable Custine-Sabran, because my health does not allow me to write much. This will be enough to tell her that her kindness and simplicity, her modesty, her purity of heart and sincerity of being have made me regard her as no less estimable than amiable a character.

"Always remain, sister and friend Custine, the strong, upright, good child which you are, self-sufficing, and the good genius who has guided you hitherto will never leave you.

"I respect all the individuals whom God has respected by His special means adopted for their guidance; my respect for them increases in proportion as they can respect God, who has guided them thus strangely.

"You brought me a letter from Miranda, by which attention I am flattered. He is a man who contains a world

---

[1] Miranda, a Peruvian adventurer, was chiefly dominated by the project of liberating his compatriots. He served successively in the armies of Russia, England, and France, and went through the campaigns of 1792-3 under Dumouriez. The raising of the blockade of Maestricht, which was laid to his charge, and the loss of the battle of Neerwinde, which was attributed to his false manœuvre, and above all the fall of the Girondins who were his friends, brought him under accusation. He was, however, acquitted. On the 18th of Fructidor he was again imprisoned and condemned to exportation, but succeeded in escaping. He died at Cadiz in 1816, after fighting for several years against the Spaniards in South America.

of men within himself. May a nation (I should like to say a *sensitive* nation, for the word *sensible* does not express my meaning) not reject this world or the world of brilliancy and energy which he carries with him ?

"I beg you to send to him by some safe means, this note which contains nothing worthy of his attention but which is, at least, an expression of my interest in him and my respect for him." [1]

Mme. de Custine was too closely intimate with her brother not to confide to him the story of her love affairs in the Carmes. She told him the whole affair and carried her confidences so far as to hand him, for reading at his leisure, the passionate letters which she had received from her lover.

Elzéar, excited by his sister's accounts and by the passages which concerned him and the exalted praises of Beauharnais, thought it his duty to copy them out; more than this, he added annotations in his own handwriting and returned them to his sister with the original letters.

Elzéar's reflections are so strange and so astounding that we feel bound to quote them in their entirety; they show better than we can do the extraordinary state of the young man's mind and his unhealthy feverishness. It is true that in this respect Beauharnais had pointed the way with remarkable clearness. The following are Elzéar's reflections upon the General's first letter:

"Sister, I was touched to the heart by the expressions which your lover uses in speaking of me to you and by

---

[1] The following is the letter which Delphine was commissioned to hand to General Miranda:

"I did not expect to have the honour and pleasure of receiving a letter from Miranda and by the hand of Custine-Sabran. You were from the outset most present to my heart, man who can never be forgotten.

"What a soul is that of the good Custine whom Providence has honoured with so many misfortunes!

"And you, energetic man, you will stand upright amid whirlwind, revolution, intrigue and plot.

"Remain always what you are now and you will always be great and unshaken.

"Finish once and for all the war by your superior genius, and make tremble all those who wish only to terrorise others. *Nil intentatum relinque*, to restore peace.

"My health does not allow me to converse at greater length with you.

"You will have a thousand stronger friends but no more sincere admirer than myself."

observing the illusions to which he was subjected by the picture which your blind love had drawn of me for his contemplation. Your love for him so increased your love for me that you were able to draw an accurate picture and he saw nothing but your brother.

"No doubt at the first moment differences of opinion and party feeling would have held me back; no doubt his reputation in every respect would have made me tremble at your imprudence in entrusting your reputation and your happiness to this man. So perhaps I should have mistaken him and avoided him for the whole of my life. But now that you have proved to me that he was a being after your own heart, I owe him a debt, because he gave you some chance of happiness, even in the shadow of the scaffold; now that you have enabled me to read his heart in his letters I will do him the justice which his love deserves; he really loved you

"Yes, Delphine, he was perhaps the only being truly worthy of you, and when this being is once found how can anyone hope to meet him a second time in this world and how can anyone be content with less? Is it possible to have either the desire or the power to look for him? Any other choice would bring down with a crash the romantic edifice which your youthful mind has constructed and would subject you immediately to the bitterness of remorse by depriving you of the only happiness left for you in life, the pleasure of regret and recollection which would be changed to poison. What lover would be presumptuous enough to rival a lover who is no more? Delphine, you will be forced to admit that after Alexandre's love, any other form of love would be degradation.

"Do not suspect me of any desire to penetrate your secrets; this would be an insult to you, because you have sworn to me a thousand times that you have none from me, and do not think that I am conceited enough to give you advice. Doubtless I do but repeat the promptings of your own heart and do you not think that he is still speaking when you hear your brother's voice? That voice will henceforward resound to remind you of Alexandre.

"The interest with which Alexandre inspires me also animates me. In life he could not bear the idea of your inconstancy, however long after his death, but now that he is delivered from this mortal yoke you may imagine that he has thrown off all earthly passions with the flesh. His love exists because it was nothing more than the acceleration of the energy of his soul, but jealousy cannot follow him into eternity. He wished to make you happy but not to tyrannise over you, and though no longer jealous for your love, he remains ever jealous for your happiness. He understands that at your age, wearied by the void in your affections and spoilt by the habit of securing love, you feel the need of some attachment. Hence his only desire is that his love may thereby be useful to you as a standard of comparison and a touchstone to judge of real feeling and avoid deception. You cannot be happy unless you recover in some other being the heart, the intellect, the charm and the graces of Alexandre. In that case you will not be unfaithful to him; what charmed you in him will also charm you in another. It will be a second Alexandre whom you will love, and perhaps, his soul will obtain, by divine favour, the power to animate another being to enable you to begin your course of happiness anew. This is the key-word to the enigmatic feeling which you experience and are unable to understand. Until that time wait and endure with patience, or rather enjoy in peace what remains to you.

"Believe the fatal experience of your brother. No consolation can ever compensate him for the fact that he failed to concentrate his happiness while his sensations were fresh, his dreams delightful and his melancholy sweet, or for the fact that his sensitiveness led him to expect other happiness than itself can give."

The second letter was accompanied by an invocation to Beauharnais himself:

"Yes, Alexandre! I swear to you before Heaven and on the altar of my heart, touched by the sentiment with which my sister inspired you on my behalf, and by the expressions which love dictated to you to describe your feelings, that I will do my best to secure that you shall not be forgotten. You are, alas! no more than a shadow, or rather, a divine spirit. Black melancholy spreads her mournful wings above me when I think that the hand which wrote this letter and the heart which dictated it are but dust and that Delphine might forget you. You might also erase your memory from the heart of Delphine; she might give a revival or conqueror to your recollection. In that case she will no longer be my sister; she would not have been worthy of loving you.

"Delphine, Alexandre is no more, and the one whom he has commissioned to plead his cause will soon cease to be. You laugh and think me far from the end of life, but in my heart I have a presentiment of my death. Though there be no outward appearance of danger, a languishing decline is carrying me to the tomb. When chance brings these words before your eyes, perhaps I shall be no more. May there never be reproaches for you! may you never have to blush between the tombs of your brother and your lover!"

On reading Elzéar's reflections, Delphine thought herself bound to take up the pen in her turn and open her heart to him and to depict the strange state of mind in which she was.

"With true feelings of gratitude I have read your annotations to the letter from my Alexandre. I have kissed your two handwritings, and my tears have bedewed them; you have made my Alexandre's letter yet more precious by adding to them your feelings for me and for him. What you say of your experience has evoked a melancholy echo in my heart; the idea that you are unhappy in matters of the heart is most painful to me. Avert or calm this torment, for I should be heart-broken by the idea, if I were again separated from you. I know misfortune so well that you would find me at one with you and we agree so entirely, that this point of coincidence would bring us nearer together.

"Your advice, your wise and tender reflections, have touched my heart, but they have told me nothing new. The reason of my unhappiness is that I feel that my powers of affection are worn out, that I can be touched only by passing feelings which defile but do not make happy. I want to love but yet I cannot; I think this fact is sufficient tribute to my Alexandre and to his memory. He is in my heart and fills it wholly; the others are hardly in my head. Be not, therefore, anxious; he will never be replaced except by his second self, and you know as well as I do that two Alexandres are not to be met with in a lifetime."

Mme. de Sabran, Delphine and Elzéar, in spite of the great joy of their meeting, were not entirely happy. A shadow often clouded their brows and spoilt their sweetest pleasures. They knew well that the happiness which they enjoyed was only ephemeral; some day they would be obliged to separate once more and to resume their life of trouble and anxiety, exposed to every distress. They would not venture to touch upon the subject which was torture to them, but the idea of a near and inevitable separation haunted them and became a constant preoccupation. Delphine at length decided to write to her brother and tell him of her great desire and make a discreet allusion to a return to France which would reunite them all in the delightful intimacy of former days.

"Your heart is no happier than mine; we are without interest, without pleasure or joy; we love one another, we should be happy together and yet we must part. At any rate, retain a constant desire to join me again; let this be our customary thought. What we really desire always comes about and as I believe that you desire it, so I shall carry in my heart a firm hope that some day we shall meet again never to part. Until that day write to me, not for the sake of writing, but to talk to me and to tell me all that fills your attention or occupies your mind. You do not feel the need of confidences because you do not know this happiness; may it be my happiness to make you acquainted with it. But soon distance and absence will perhaps make us again strangers to one another. My dear, it is for you to defy them and on your heart I rely. Rely upon mine to draw as near to you as I can. You know even my most secret thoughts; know also and never forget the love which I bear you, a love which nothing will ever be able to destroy."

Mme. de Sabran, informed by Elzéar of his sister's hints, at length opened one day the subject which she had so much at heart and spoke to Delphine of her future projects. She told her that she did not see any prospect of peace in France, that she feared new menaces and catastrophes and that she thought it the greatest wisdom to avoid a country where such risks might still be run. It would be so simple to send for Astolphe and set up house together in some pretty corner of

Germany where they would live as one family, poor and unknown but happy and contented. Why go and meet fresh disasters when they could be happily avoided?

Delphine objected, with some reason, that if she left France, she would never be able to return and that she would irremediably lose what remained of her property, as she would thus resign her right to re-enter into the possession of property which had been confiscated. Could she do this? Had she the right, merely from cowardice, to ruin Astolphe? She thought not. Moreover, was not her mother mistaken concerning the position in France? It was better than she supposed and they ought not to judge the future by the tragedies of the past, which would certainly never recur. If her mother was reasonable she would return to her own native land.

It is strange to see Delphine, notwithstanding the dangers which she had run and the collapse of her fortune, in spite of the disasters which had overwhelmed herself and her friends, showing so little ill feeling to a government which had stricken her so cruelly and so unjustly. She pardoned it and remained invincibly attached to the principles of the Revolution in spite of everything. And this state of mind, strange as it is, is by no means exceptional; it was to be observed in the case of many of her contemporaries.

Mme. de Sabran's fears of re-entering France were only too well justified by the course of events. If the end of the Terror had brought some sense of exhaustion and reaction against the revolutionary excesses, Paris was none the less very far from enjoying perfect tranquillity. Risings were of periodical occurrence and in the provinces royalists provoked numerous insurrections. In May, 1795, after the suppression of the maximum, rents considerably increased; on the 1st of Prairial a revolt broke out and the Convention was invaded by an armed crowd demanding bread, The deputy Feraud, who was mistaken for the journalist Fréron, was assassinated and his head, raised on a pike, was shown to the President, Boissy d'Anglas.[1]

These events were not calculated to inspire Mme. de Sabran

---

[1] Boissy d'Anglas (1756–1826), formerly a lawyer to the Parliament, became after Thermidor one of the leaders of the reaction. In December, 1794, he was appointed a member of the Committee of Public Safety, and on the 18th Fructidor he was proscribed and did not return to France until after the 18th Brumaire.

with any great confidence in the future. Séguier had been informed by his cousin of the long discussion which she had had with her daughter upon this important question of returning to France. He was afraid that Mme. de Sabran might yield to the desires of Delphine and urged her to beware of the seductions of this enchantress, this new " Circe " who was irresistible, as he knew only too well and who, in spite of everything, had remained an ardent republican.

"DATTINGAU, September 6, 1795.

"I adjure you, madam, to beware! You will meet your Delphine with the views and opinions which custom will make you believe invariable. But as soon as you have seen this seductive girl, she will speak to you with so sweet a voice and support her words with such glances from her lovely eyes and her persuasions will seem so true, coming from that pretty mouth, that you will be carried away.

"You laugh and say: 'I shall not be like that young fool, whose peace of mind has been overthrown by two pretty eyes.' That may be: you will none the less experience what has happened to myself, for at one time I was as firm in my purpose as you are; moreover, I supported it with all the energy of an enthusiastic young man embittered against the Revolution; yet, in spite of my obstinacy I have yielded to the charmer and I have almost forgotten the incomparable honour of five years' exile. I have been on the point of asking your pretty republican to push my cause with her friends and with her purified Senate and to get me enrolled as one of the defenders of liberty.

"If there is still time, Mme. de Sabran, in Heaven's name beware of this pink and white demon. I can see her from here, and as she has supernatural patience and has been able to tame, by her charms, some of those tigers who devour us daily, I see that she is going to persuade you to resume your life afresh in her dangerous country. Please observe that the strongest of her arguments will be a timely caress and a hand-clasp, a kiss of the kind which the late Circe gave to the too compliant companions of Ulysses, in order to keep them on her island. And if you will think over it these arguments would easily demonstrate to you the poverty of her reasons."

CHAPTER XVIII

September—December, 1795

Mme. de Custine starts for France—Her mother and Elzéar accompany her as far as Bâle—Mme. de Sabran and her son make a tour in Switzerland—Visit to the Abbey of Einsiedeln—Second visit to Lavater—Correspondence of the Chevalier de Séguier with Mme. de Sabran—Mme. de Sabran sees her daughter once again.

WHILE she was staying at Zurich Delphine received news from time to time from Niederviller; Nanette usually undertook to keep her informed of events in the old Château, but one day Astolphe undertook to give her the news himself and dictated the following delightful letter to his mother:

"Good-day, my dear little mother, come back soon. We have had some cake and if you had been here you would have had a great treat. I like you as much as you like cake, which is a great deal. M. Tournal is very well, he sends you his kind regards. Please write to me. When will you come and play hide and seek? there is plenty of room for it in the Château. Fifi is very well and loves you and so do I. I eat well, I run well, and I drink well; I like wine. My hair falls right over my face and I have a little rat's tail behind. I have grown big and I am very good. Write to me and do not be vexed any more. M. Tournal is very funny and always makes me laugh. Good-bye, mother, with many kisses."

Mme. de Sabran and Delphine could not help laughing on reading this simple letter.

After a stay of some length at Zurich, where they had

tasted of the deepest pleasures, they were obliged to think of parting once more as Delphine, in spite of her mother's supplications, persisted in returning to France. It was, therefore, settled that the young woman should start for Bâle and then make her way to Niederviller. Mme. de Sabran, who would not leave her daughter until the last moment, hired a small carriage and took the road to Bâle in sadness. The travellers again put up at the Inn of the Cygogne, where they had the pleasure of meeting Séguier, who was more than ever in love with his pretty cousin and had left his regiment to come and say good-bye to her.

The evening before her departure Delphine brought her mother a little box carefully locked. At the same time she gave her a key with a sealed letter and made her promise not to open the envelope or the box till she had gone; in vain did Mme. de Sabran ask for an explanation; Delphine remained obstinately silent.

On the next day, September 20, they were all profoundly moved; Mme. de Sabran was heart-broken at parting once more with her beloved daughter and could not restrain her tears. When the carriage arrived which was to take Delphine away to her dangerous country the bereaved mother fell into her arms; both burst into sobs and they had the utmost difficulty in parting. Elzéar and Maurice were no less deeply moved. Amid the emotions of farewell Delphine said to Séguier, " Love my poor mother, console her and care for her like a son; as the friend of her Delphine, be kind to Elzéar." Less than this would have inspired the young officer with the belief that his affection was returned.

As soon as the carriage had gone everyone retired to his room to give free vent to his grief. Towards the evening Mme. de Sabran summoned Elzéar and Maurice; she wished to open the box which her daughter had entrusted to her in their presence alone. First she opened the letter. Delphine explained in charming terms that she had been able to save from the wreck of her fortunes some few diamonds which were all that she had in the world and she begged her mother to accept them as a help for her support during her exile; for fear that her mother would refuse she had been unwilling to explain her wishes before her departure.

The box, as a matter of fact, contained all Delphine's diamonds. The reading of this letter and the sight of the jewels called tears to the eyes of all, who were deeply moved by such tender feeling. Elzéar, relating this moving scene to his sister, says:

"I had not ventured to come to mother again, for fear of rousing her grief anew by the sight of mine, but when I heard her request I came. We kissed one another like the two edges of a wound brought together in order to close it, but when we opened the box wonder gave our grief a divine character which removed all its bitterness. At first I had thought it was the box of Pandora; it was natural to suppose that on leaving us you would leave us also all your sorrows. The most that we could expect was to find a little hope at the bottom. What was my surprise when I saw in it the only diamonds that you had been able to save. These diamonds were so many mirrors of your heart and from this you may understand what our feelings were. Your tactfulness and tender feeling struck us with profound admiration and our tears began to flow once more."

In her emotion Mme. de Sabran gave Maurice in remembrance of Delphine the box which had contained the diamonds. Séguier remained at Bale for two days, sharing the grief of his friends, and then went away to rejoin his regiment. He had not concealed from Mme. de Sabran the strong feeling which he had for his cousin. Before returning to Zurich, Elzéar and his mother made a short tour to see the sights of the country, but their real object was the famous Abbey of Einsiedeln; Mme. de Sabran, who was a religious woman as far as any 18th century woman could be, had made a vow that if Delphine escaped the massacres of the Terror, she would make a pilgrimage to the venerated sanctuary of Notre Dame des Hermites. They, therefore, travelled by short stages, sometimes by carriage, sometimes on horseback and sometimes on foot and visited Thun, Lauterbrunnen, the glacier of the Jungfrau, Grindelwald, Meiringen and the famous Benedictine Abbey of Engelberg,[1] where the Abbot, who had learnt the romantic story of Mme. de Sabran from

[1] Near Lucerne. It dates from the 12th century and was founded by Pope Calixtus XI. under the name of Mons Angelorum.

her daughter, was kind enough to offer the author of it a magnificent rose-tree.

At last, on October 22, they reached the Abbey of Einsiedeln, the object of their voyage, and put up at the Inn of the Drei Könige.

The Abbey of Notre Dame des Hermites rises by the village of Einsiedeln in a sterile valley crossed by the Alpbach. Founded during the age of Charlemagne, it soon became the richest and most popular point of pilgrimage in Switzerland, averaging some 250,000 pilgrims a year. In 1274 the Abbot was raised to the rank of a prince of the Empire.[1] The Chapel of the Virgin, in black marble, rises in the middle of the Church, entirely isolated. It is surrounded by a railing through which, by the light of a lamp, may be seen the palladium of the Convent, a statue of the Virgin and the Infant Jesus in black wood, clothed in splendid garments and adorned with precious stones. Elzéar told his sister how, after long prayers to the Virgin and thanks for her divine protection, they conceived the idea of consecrating as an ex-voto the rose-tree which the Abbot of Engelberg had given them.

" In allusion to the song of the 'Rose Tree' which mother wrote for you I wrote these two lines upon a piece of paper:

" Fair rose tree! saved for us by Heaven,
Rest here beneath the eye of your preserver."

" We tied a rose to it and, after watering it with gentle tears, we religiously hung up the rose-tree to the arch. Sister, if you ever pass that way, do not forget to go and see this votive gift offered by a mother and brother in memory of you and in gratitude for the safety of your life." [2]

Mme. de Sabran was not the only suppliant to the Virgin at Einsiedeln. In the Inn where she was staying she met Mlle. de Condé, who had come to the foot of the altar to seek refuge from the troubles of life.

" We saw Mlle. de Condé,[3] ready to leave for Heaven a

---

[1] The sanctuary of Einsiedeln has lost none of its attraction for the faithful, and throughout the summer the number of pilgrims who visit it is considerable.

[2] Twelve years later Delphine made a pilgrimage to Einsiedeln in her turn. See Chapter xxviii.

[3] Louise Adélaide de Bourbon (1757-1824), daughter of Louis, Joseph de Bourbon, prince de Condé, and of Charlotte Godefride Elizabeth de Rohan-Soubise.

world stained with the murder of her parents. She had come from Fribourg to make this pilgrimage, after which she proposed to go through the Grisons and take the vows in a Convent of Turin. We found her already in a thoroughly mystical frame of mind and truly interesting by reason of her complete detachment from the world. She seemed to exhibit, in spite of her youth, an apparently blind trust in Providence. I saw her praying so earnestly in the Chapel of the Virgin that the tears came to my eyes."

On returning to Zurich, Elzéar and his mother once more put up at the Inn of the Epée, where there was so much to remind them of Delphine. On this occasion also they carried away pleasant recollections of their stay in the town. Elzéar writes to his sister:

"The time that we spent at Zurich was passed in pleasant occupations and delightful walks. In the morning in Lavater's study we attempted to discover the spell of his genius. In the evening, by Gesner's monument, we read the 'Pastor Fido.' After sunset we went home and I wrote to you or for you. We had quite settled down there with the object of gaining a full memory of your stay."

Their pleasantest moments were those which they spent with Lavater.

"He allowed us to come into his study, the sanctuary of wisdom and science. There we went over his sketches, drawings and outlines and with interest and curiosity we read the notes which he had written beneath them and his penetrating observations always struck us by their perspicacity. I composed an epistle to him reminding him of our past happiness which he had increased by contributing to it and portraying my present misfortune. He replied in some German verses full of genius. My enthusiasm for him was at its height, I was sorry to see him sinking. His health grew worse from day to day, but far from hiding his regret at leaving a life which he shared with his friends, he put no restraint on his feelings because he knew that his courage was stronger than theirs. His sole care was the consolation of his friends and his family and the provision of a proper competence for them. My mother told him one day that she had great faith in medicine but none in doctors; 'with me,' he said, 'it is the contrary; I have no great belief in medicine but a great deal of faith in doctors, for I have no others than my own children.' As a matter of fact his son and son-in-law were following this profession.

"One day we found him in a great invalid chair. He said to my mother, 'I wish I could offer it to you, but it is the throne of weakness.' It was as fine a scene as the death of Socrates.

"When I said goodbye to him, I asked for his blessing. He was in bed; I was shaken by emotion which I did not attempt to hide, and he placed upon my head the hands which I had respectfully kissed and bathed with my tears. Then he raised his swimming eyes to Heaven and his celestial look seemed to ask from the Supreme Being some portion of his treasures in order to confer them upon me. He uttered some sublime words and then embraced me. Fearing that the prolongation of this touching scene might be bad for him, I tore myself away in great depression and full of a gloomy presentiment that I should never see him again."

Maurice Séguier was more than ever in love with the attractive Delphine; he wrote constantly to Mme. de Sabran and always to speak of her daughter with growing enthusiasm. The sad and wretched life of the poor fellow had completely changed; he was in love and was clinging to the hope of a happiness which he dared hardly expect. Mme. de Sabran in anxiety at this unexpected passion, did her best to calm Maurice, and urged him, "to abandon desires which were sheer foolishness."

Séguier declared himself delighted with his foolishness and preferred it to all the wisdom in the world. He strove to prove to his cousin, by subtle processes of reasoning, that she was wrong and he was right.

" DETTINGEN, *October 20*, 1795.

"How kind it is of you to open your heart to me in this way! Your letters have made me happy for a long time. I never felt such charm in reading letters as I find in yours; they are really just what letters should be, an outpouring of your heart. Compared with them, letters dictated by the intellect seem wholly wearisome.

"You are afraid, then, that if you talk to me of Delphine I may think of her too much. An idea too constantly entertained at my age, you say, may become dangerous; with my excitable disposition I may go mad, for there is no doubt that love is a madness. Well, my good and dear friend, let me run the risk; what man in this world has not a strain of madness in him? this will be mine and as soon as I have attained it I feel in my cooler moments that I would not change it for any other form. Madness in itself is not harmful but only for its consequences and what ill consequences could madness have when it is based upon all that is good and lovable in the world? Such madness would be nothing more than enthusiasm for beauty, and such enthusiasm is really the source of good."

Séguier also complained that he received very few letters from Delphine. Mme. de Sabran was delighted to hear it, and said, "so much the better; he will forget his madness the sooner," but she was wrong: "I shall become only the more insane," the young man jestingly replied, and added, "this madness was all that was wanting to complete my position. A complete exile ought to be in rags, a vagabond and in love. Heaven be praised, I am now perfect!"

Mme. de Sabran had told Maurice that, in the course of a walk at Zurich, she had had a severe fall, had almost lost consciousness and regretted that she had not gone to sleep for ever. He jested coolly upon the subject:

"*November* 9, 1795.

"I was greatly startled by the story of your fall in the middle of Zurich and the coolness with which you tell me that you were almost sorry to emerge from your unconsciousness. Why this dislike of life? let grief have its way and think how cruel it is to wish yourself separated from a loving daughter and to be upon the point of leaving a beloved son. At the same time, I see no reason to justify your taste for the next world. Remember, Mme. de Sabran, that we can die only once; when once you are dead your regrets for your decision will be useless, for Acheron, in greed, will not abandon his prey. Then the desire to see Delphine and

Elzéar will be constant, and you will find that to satisfy your wish they will have to make the same journey. None of that, if you please; I tell you that on my own account I shall prevent them from doing so as long as I can and even if you should find time down there hang heavy on your hands I shall attempt to delay their arrival as much as possible."

The news from France, however, was by no means reassuring. The new Republican Constitution elaborated by the Convention[1] had roused the protests and the anger of the Royalists. On the 13th of Vendémiaire (October) a section of the National Guard revolted and marched upon the Assembly; Bonaparte and Barras were obliged to shoot them down near Saint-Roch.

Mme. de Sabran, who was extremely alarmed by this news, did not feel bold enough to make an immediate start for Rheinsberg. She could not make up her mind to leave the French frontier and waited in the neighbourhood of Bâle in the hope that some chance might bring Delphine back to her.

She was not mistaken; on learning that her mother was one day to be at Kehl, near Strasbourg, Mme. de Custine, at the peril of her life, left Niederviller and ran once more to embrace the mother whom she loved so tenderly. Fortunately for her this great imprudence passed unobserved and she was able to regain her hearth and home without difficulty.

---

[1] Before separating (October 26) the Convention had divided the legislative power into two Councils:—
    (a) The Council of the Five Hundred which proposed resolutions, and
    (b) The Council of the Two Hundred and Fifty or the Ancients, which passed these resolutions into law.

The executive power was entrusted to a Committee of five directors chosen from the Ancients. This Committee was selected from a list of ten names drawn up by the five hundred, and each member was to preside for three months.

CHAPTER XIX

1796

Mme. de Custine returns to Paris with Astolphe—She takes steps to resume possession of her confiscated property—Correspondence with Elzéar — Correspondence with the Chevalier Séguier—Mme. de Custine spends the summer at Niederviller.

AFTER spending some days at Niederviller, where she had rejoined her son and Nanette, Mme. de Custine started for Paris, regardless of the course of events and of possible danger to herself. She reached the capital towards the end of December, 1795. There she spent several troubled years in straitened circumstances, harassed by political agitations.

As soon as she arrived she resumed her sad and solitary life, devoting her time to her son and to painting, which had become her greatest pastime. She spent the greater part of the day in her studio; she hardly ever went out, except to interview the men in power for the time being with the object of recovering some part of her fortune and of the property of her relatives. Thanks to her prison friend, Mme. de Beauharnais, who had just married General Bonaparte, and with whom she had maintained friendly relations, she obtained some valuable introductions and made some acquaintances which were most useful to her. Thus she came into connection with Tallien, Fouché,[1]

---

[1] Fouché (Joseph, Duke of Otranto, 1759-1820), was educated at the Oratoire and was a professor in several colleges belonging to the organisation. He was appointed a deputy to the Convention in 1792 and commissioned to organise the resistance to the insurrection in La Vendée. He was then sent to Lyons with Collot d'Herbois to carry out the decree of destruction pronounced upon that town. On December 19th, 1793, he wrote: " Let us do justice after the pattern of Nature. Let us strike like

Boissy d'Anglas and Barthélemy[1] who became her "great friends." All were more or less touched by the beauty and the tears of the young and attractive petitioner. Fouché and Boissy d'Anglas especially felt greatly interested in her and became close acquaintances.[2] Thanks to their intervention her just claims, instead of meeting with unceremonious rejection, were very considerably advanced.

Unfortunately her health was bad; she now felt the reaction of the terrible trials through which she had passed. In spite of the energy which did not leave her, she often remained for hours in a complete stupor, incapable of doing anything. Her health was not her only, or her worst trial; she had to find a means of livelihood for herself and for Astolphe. Her resources were very small, she lived with a simplicity akin to poverty, and was constantly obliged to struggle with the most painful pecuniary cares.

To increase her misfortune, correspondence with her relatives became very difficult; letters only occasionally reached their destination and for the most part were confiscated or went astray. After the great delight of the meeting Delphine was deeply depressed by her new and almost complete isolation. Her brother, in spite of his promise, wrote only at long intervals; he was then staying at Venice where his mother had sent him as a distraction from the depression which haunted him. Delphine wrote to him in the early days of 1796 :

"PARIS, *January* 10, 1796.[3]

" I am now at Paris; all barriers are closed behind me and the one ray of happiness is shut out; henceforward for me there is nothing but profound darkness. But tell me, my

thunderbolts, and may the very ashes of our foes disappear from the soil of liberty." He shared in the massacres ordered by Collot d'Herbois. On his return to Paris he quarrelled with Robespierre and contributed to his overthrow on the 9th Thermidor.

[1] Barthélemy (François, Marquis de, 1750–1836), was *chargé d'affaires* in England when the Revolution broke out. He was appointed plenipotentiary minister to Switzerland and directed the negotiations which ended in the peace of Bâle.

[2] M. La Caille possessed the correspondence between Delphine and Fouché, and also with Boissy d'Anglas, but these letters did not lend themselves to publication and have been destroyed.

[3] Communicated by M. Prat.

dear, why I never get a letter from you? Have a little pity upon your poor, sad Delphine; why do you stay so long where you are? Would you not prefer to travel in that beautiful country? It would do you good in every way. Do not forget, I beg of you, when you are near Milan, to go to the islands of Borromeo and see the colossal statue of St. Charles Borromeo, and, above all, walk into his nose in honour of all the great noses of your acquaintance. Be sure not to forget that.

"Write to me often, my dear, send me sometimes verses and the song which I have asked of you. I have induced M. Girard[1] to set the others to music. Poor M. Girard, how fond he was of you! He grew quite sad in thinking of the great drawing room at Anisy. Recollections of that time are so many fairy tales to me; and if the story of this time is ever told to us it will be just as incredible.

"In consequence of what you told Eléonore[2] about the fountain of which Pliny speaks, I have begun to read Pliny and am quite delighted with him. How fortunate you are to be travelling in the country of those great men. I do not confine myself to Pliny; I read Cicero and Plutarch. Cicero is very pleasant, but he had little character and will never be my hero.

"I have heard from Eléonore. She has gone back to the lord of Merkatz,[3] which I am very glad to hear; it is a great relief to me.

"You ask about my plans. It is not this summer, but next winter that I hope to come and see mother. But how can one venture to form any plans? we are by no means sure of the morrow. Why cannot one be certain that this year will bring us together somewhere, even if it were in China?

"Good-bye; I feel sad and ill-tempered at not telling all that is in my heart. I send you my best love and I am still fond of the Griffon."[4]

---

[1] The Abbé Girard, who lived at Orléans, was very intimate with Mme. de Sabran and her children.
[2] Mme. de Sabran. Her daughter often refers to her by her Christian name after their meeting in Switzerland.
[3] The name of a little farm which Prince Henry had just given to the Chevalier de Boufflers.
[4] The name given by Delphine to the Chevalier Séguier.

o

While Delphine complained of her brother's silence, Elzéar, on his side, was accusing her of forgetfulness and ingratitude. Instead of receiving a loving letter from him as she had expected, he sent her a string of reproaches in heartbreaking depression. She replies to him:

"*February* 10, 1796.

"Your letter has touched my heart and makes me weep, but how can you tell me that I have forgotten you? How can you accuse your only friend in this world of forgetfulness or indifference? Dear Elzéar, learn to know better this poor heart which you are insulting, for it beats only for you, for my mother and for Astolphe. You are the one consoling thought; the rest is but tears, regrets and buried hopes. The thought of you alone has enabled me to live and survive so many horrors and you dare to say that I have forgotten you! It is true that I have not often written; in the first place I might say the same of you; moreover, I have been and still am ill. I have fallen into such apathy and depression that it gives me infinite trouble to write four lines. Every day my courage diminishes and profound sadness devours me. You, our mother, Astolphe and perhaps the Griffon, in a tiny, quiet corner of the world, are all that my heart requires.

"The life which I lead here is in striking contrast with my feelings. It suits me very ill. However, I live in profound retirement and see very few people, and I have no interest in life, and you know what such a life is for me. It is a kind of anticipation of death. If you wish me to recover courage you should often write to me, send me a few poems and songs and, in short, undertake to rouse my love for life.

"You talk to me of future projects; I have none, except to settle my mother's affairs. If I do not succeed I shall go next winter to Berlin. At present I am vegetating; the time is not opportune for business. I paint, am busy, dream and weep; there you have my whole history, and into the bargain I am ill. I am growing visibly thinner and becoming frightfully ugly, so prepare to love me when I am ugly as you loved me when I was pretty. I am still in bed with a feverish attack, and so shall only write you a few lines.

"Goodbye, dear and beloved one, do not lose your affection for me. I tremble to think that you may fall in love, for then you would say goodbye to your poor sister. You will tell me when that happens, won't you? I have told you everything. Do you write to the Griffon? He writes to me and I am glad to answer him; he is good and kind."

Mme. de Custine, as a matter of fact, was in correspondence not only with her mother and her brother, but she often received letters from the Chevalier Séguier; though she felt the warmest friendship for him, absence and separation had somewhat modified the feelings which she thought the handsome young officer had at first inspired. Séguier, in his letters, spoke openly of love; unfortunately the more pressing he appears, the more reserved does Delphine become; she offers him friendship but nothing more. Somewhat disconcerted by the progress of his aspirations, Maurice, however, was not discouraged and thinking that Mme. de Sabran had great influence over her daughter he begs her to plead his cause with the fickle young woman:

"*February* 3, 1796.

"I heard from Delphine on December 6, from Paris. You can imagine my delight on receiving her letter. The joy which I felt was certainly not the joy of misfortune. At that moment I was far removed from such sad delight; but when I opened the letter my great happiness was somewhat diminished. Apparently she supposed that my feelings desired freedom and obstinately informed me that I must confine myself to friendship. I may expect to lose in this respect but I shall be wrong; love is troublesome and surly, while a pleasant little friendship is the sweetest thing in the world. After this decision she talks to me of her arrival at Paris, which she calls the 'place of terror.' 'Pity me,' she says, 'may your prayers accompany me and preserve me from all the evils which thunder above my head.' Our charming Delphine must have been very pretty and interesting when she was writing these lines, with 'one elbow on the table, her head in her hand and perhaps a few tears in her eyes.'"

Delphine is not always cruel; sometimes she appears coquettish; she asks Maurice for the reasons which have inspired him with such ardent love; she cannot understand them. If it is her face, his passion is unreasonable; she must confess that she is no longer pretty; grief and misfortune have swept away the fleeting attractions of beauty.

Maurice, of course, declines to believe this painful confession, and this sentimentalism revives his hopes. He hastens to tell Mme. de Sabran of this new stage in his affections:

"*February* 11, 1796.

"She wrote me a charming letter, full of the greatest feeling. It seems that there is no peace at Paris and that the inquisition is strictly carried out; she tells me that someone had advised her to write no more letters, not even to you. 'I would rather die'; she goes on, 'what would life be to me without news of those whom I love? Never!' She thinks, moreover, that not the smallest trouble will arise, in view of the way in which her correspondence is carried on.

"Then she informs me of a discovery which she has just made, after deep reflection. The serious subject of her thoughts was the problem, What reason could have induced me to feel so sudden and so keen an interest in her? 'Could it have been my face?' she asks with an air of astonishment. 'Heaven preserve me from being loved in that way! Beauty is but a weak and fleeting advantage, &c.'

"I laughed consumedly on reading this passage. The simplicity with which she refers to the misfortune of being loved for personal beauty seems delightful. Many women would easily console themselves for that which seems an affliction to good Delphine. The unfortunate point for me is that I am far from any desire to console her in this respect; my attachment will put up with a great deal of this beauty which troubles her so much. Whatever she may say she will be placed in the first class in this respect. 'Then,' she concludes, 'if I were no longer pretty, goodbye to your interest!' The conclusion is no better than the argument; but it has this advantage, that it is more difficult to answer.

"Oh! Mme. de Sabran, my attachment for your charming daughter increases daily. I believe that, as you foretold, I am becoming insane, for, if you remember, 'love is only a form of madness.'

" At the end of her letter she tells me that her health is by no means good. Why does she not take measures to restore it? Supposing she were to feel the pleasure of illness as she has felt the pleasure of misfortune! I wish that, amid the many whom she attracts upon her path, she would throw her spell over some good doctor who would force her to get well in spite of herself. What better thing could be done in France at this moment than to care for health? In times of misfortune ought we not to think of prolonging our lives in view of a happier future? Thus to turn health to advantage is to triumph over misfortune."

Séguier's passion was fated to undergo cruel vicissitudes. The young officer thought that he was in excellent odour, when one fine morning Delphine considers that his correspondence is too ardent, and bluntly informs him that she does not wish to receive letters directly from him; in future he must send them through Mme. de Sabran. Maurice at first remained stupefied by this unexpected sentence; then, in a fit of anger, believing that his projects were ruined for ever, he resolved upon heroic and radical measures. He wrote to Delphine to say that, under the new conditions which she had laid upon him, he would prefer to cease correspondence altogether; at the same time, he tells his cousin of his sad misfortune and of the grief by which he is overwhelmed:

" My good Eléonore, it is all over with my happiness; it has not lasted long and I have had only a disappearing glimpse of it. You were right when you told me that this age was not the age for true love, that politics had killed love; what you then said on my behalf has been verified against me. Foolishly in love, making fine projects for the future and feeding upon the old sustenance of lovers, hope and dreams, one fine morning I find myself alone."

Our readers will not be surprised to learn that Séguier, after sending his final letter, fell into great despondency. Upon reflection he bitterly reproached himself for having so foolishly misinterpreted recommendations which, after all, were perhaps nothing more than the outcome of a mere whim. After this display of pride and haughtiness, he attempted to show himself humble and modest and to renew the intimacy which he had so much at heart. There was no reason for Maurice thus to be in despair or excitement; Delphine had attached no more importance to her letter than it deserved, or to the answer of her friend with its final dismissal, and she continued to write as if nothing had happened.

The unfortunate Maurice had the more need of this passion to rouse his interest in life, as he regarded his position from a most gloomy stand-point. He saw his youth expended in barren efforts and the future in the darkest colours. He wrote sadly to Mme. de Sabran:

"I have considered very closely the length of time that I have been in exile. Five years, the best years of my life from the age of twenty to twenty-five, have thus been spent in sadness and boredom; they are gone and I shall have but the memory of them to embellish my old age. Thus, during the time when one really lives, my existence will have been merely vegetation; in the time when I ought to live upon my past what shall I have to live upon, seeing that really I shall never have lived? It is very well for older people to talk of the grief of habits broken up; I think that it is to the men of my own age that the Revolution has done the greatest harm; otherwise to attempt to compare the keen enjoyment of youthful vigour with the still enjoyment of habit is illusory. When we are young we feel happiness and grasp it, but in old age what can we do but think?"

However, Delphine attempted to make some plans for the summer; she proposed to go first to Plombières for the waters and then to settle at Niederviller with her son for several months. She often thought of returning to Germany to see her mother, but it remained a matter of some difficulty to leave France and she did not know whether she could obtain a passport. Moreover, and in chief, travelling is expensive, and Delphine had barely sufficient money for her livelihood. The course of events put an end to her hesitation; the political situation remained profoundly disturbed; the Jacobins and Royalists continued to agitate the country and caused extreme uneasiness. Risings and plots continued and serious disturbances occurred in Paris and in the provinces; supervision and inquisition became much stricter than before.

It was impossible to think of leaving France. Mme. de Custine was obliged to abandon her ideas of travel and resign herself to spending the summer at Niederviller. At the same time, all correspondence was stopped for several months and Mme. de Sabran, who was dreadfully anxious, was obliged to apply to the King of Prussia to know what had become of Delphine.[1]

At length, in the month of September, Mme. de Sabran received a long letter from her daughter, relating her journey from Paris to Niederviller. She was so poor that she was obliged to travel in the public coach with Astolphe and Nanette amid all the annoyance of publicity. She tells her mother of her misfortunes and begs her, at the same time, to send a letter to Séguier, who joyfully writes to his cousin.

"ANADINGEN IN WURTEMBERG,
"*September*, 1796.

"So you have news of your dear Delphine and, more than that, have kindly sent me a letter from her. How long it is since I have enjoyed such happiness! To-day, proud of the treasure that I possessed, I felt quite above myself. We were just marching upon the enemy when it was handed to me; I never felt calmer and it seemed impossible that any harm could come to me.

"To think of our dear, sweet Delphine thus travelling in the public coach, next to some wretched red night-cap, perhaps some coarse Jacobins, pushed and jolted, finding the inns full of new recruits making their way to the frontiers, and rudely questioned by gendarmes about her journey.

"How good she is! Would you believe, Mme. de Sabran, that, in spite of her long absence and the countless events which should have effaced me from her memory, she still

[1] Letter copied by order of the King for the Comtesse de Sabran:—

"PARIS, *September* 4, 1796.

"Mme. de Custine is on her estate of Niederviller in Alsace, and a letter which I have received from her a fortnight ago shows me that she is in good health. I cannot too urgently recommend Mme. de Sabran to cease correspondence for the time being in order not to compromise her daughter's liberty. The despatch of special couriers will enable me to procure any information that she may desire and even to transmit some letters.

"DE SANDOZ ROLLIN."

thinks of me sometimes and is kind enough to spend time upon me ? If she had any money, she says her mind would soon be made up ; she would come to Germany to see you ; but she has none and is obliged to remain with her son. What a cruel world it is ! Money is the cry everywhere ; money is wanted to love and money is wanted to meet ; the poor man has no parents, or friends or lovers."[1]

Delphine's letter so electrified Maurice that he thought of defying all dangers and of making his way into France to see her, and to preserve her from the perils which threatened her. It is true that, at that moment, he was at Bâle in the same hotel of the Cygogne and in the same room where he had met Delphine a year before, and memories of this meeting crowded upon him to disturb his peace of mind. Thereupon, Mme. de Sabran, touched by her cousin's wretchedness, invited him to go and join her at Rheinsberg ; Prince Henry had given her a pretty little farm at Merkatz and Séguier would there find, not only a charming residence, but perhaps also happiness and calm. To show him that he would be no burden, she gave him " a most picturesque list of the cows, pigs, fowls, geese and turkeys which flocked round her hermitage." Boufflers added his entreaties to those of Mme. de Sabran ; Séguier was at once attracted ; he hastened to abandon the useless life which he had been leading for five years and gladly accepted the proposal so kindly offered. He announced his arrival for the month of January, 1797.

[1] Prat papers.

CHAPTER XX

JANUARY—JUNE, 1797

Mme. de Custine's sad life at Paris—She thinks of marrying again—Séguier's correspondence with Mme. de Sabran—He goes to meet Boufflers at Berlin to accompany him to Poland, but suddenly changes his mind and starts for Paris—His relations with Mme. de Custine—He fails to please her—Boufflers and Mme. de Sabran start for Poland.

MME. DE CUSTINE's life at Paris in the course of the year 1797 became increasingly difficult; she had a thousand business matters to manage, for herself, for her mother and for the Bishop of Laon. She made the most laudable efforts to try to save some remnants of their fortune, but events did not always proceed as she wished and she experienced many rebuffs. She was obliged to struggle with continual lawsuits, and was attacked by her husband's creditors, while she was unable to obtain payment of debts due to her. In short, she led a life of worry and despair and every possible anxiety overwhelmed her simultaneously.

Mme. de Sabran had been declared an *émigrée* for the second time, and finally her house in the Faubourg St.-Honoré was to be sold at a ridiculous price. If she had had any money, Mme. de Custine would not have hesitated to buy it, but thirty thousand livres were required in cash and bills for the rest; she had not a farthing. If she tried to borrow it was doubtful whether she would find a lender, and she would be charged a ruinous rate of interest with no hope of payment. "I make supplications in every quarter," she writes sadly, "but I find hearts and purses alike closed." Would it be possible for her mother to find at Berlin a banker who would advance the money, when the house could be bought in her daughter's name? Would Prince Henry or the King of Prussia consent to advance the necessary sum? The matter was very urgent, as the house would soon be sold.

It may be asked whether Delphine's health had improved, and whether she had the necessary strength to struggle with misfortune and to bear up against the thousand anxieties which overwhelmed her. Unfortunately she had not even this consolation. Worn out by harassing cares she vegetated in an almost constant state of illness and pain. In spite of herself she never lost courage; "I am really very unhappy," she writes to her mother, "but I do not despair." She then begs her mother to think of herself and Elzéar and not to give way to despondency; were it not for the hope of seeing her again she would not have strength to continue her life. It may be asked again whether Delphine felt any affection which would help her to support her distress. She assures us that it was not so and we are bound to believe her; however, we see a whole series of adorers invariably circulating round her, Médor, Lolo,[1] Bois,[2] It, &c. Boissy d'Anglas in particular was deeply smitten by the charms of the young woman, and became one of the most constant visitors at her house; but she would have given them all and many others to have, like her mother, a sure and faithful friend of twenty years' standing who would accompany her through life.

Tired of leading so miserable an existence, without interest or affection, Delphine at length thought of marrying again. After long consideration of the idea she resolved to impart her secret wishes one day to her mother.

"*January* 12, 1797.

"I remain very well pleased with Médor, but he does not satisfy the wishes of my heart, which is empty. I look for a heart which can beat in harmony with mine and I look in vain. Meanwhile my poor charms are vanishing, and the years pass by. I shall not have, when I am old and serious, as you have, one devoted friend; my present position makes me feel more than ever the necessity and has led me to entertain another idea of which I had not thought until recently.

[1] Comte Louis de Ségur. [2] Boissy d'Anglas.

I am thinking of marrying. You ask, 'Whom, in Heaven's name?' A rich man of some fifty years of age; indeed I should prefer someone older, for what I chiefly fear is that I might be thought to have taken this step for any other reason than my son's interest. But the advantages which the idea presents to me are these: in the first place, I can bring up my son as I wish; then I may be able to go and see you, I may be able to help my unfortunate friends and have a thousand small conveniences which are worth considering. What do you think of the idea?

"A good one, but where is the husband?"

"That is the point. I do not know where to find him. Will you look for one in your district?"

"Do you really mean it?"

"Yes, find me a rich old husband. What a face Médor makes when I speak of my projects, and what a face Maurice would make! but do not torment him to no purpose."

Delphine's letters continually refer to her solitude and her wish for love and affection, and some weeks afterwards she writes again:

"I am sadder and lonelier than ever, and my heart finds nothing to cling to. I should like to marry and leave this independent state, which is useless to me, but I cannot find a husband. I hardly ever go into society, and I have become quite a savage. You ought to be here to take me out and give me courage.

"My favourite occupation is to read your letters again. I see you so interested, so wholly occupied with the object of your affections and so well loved, and I compare my own position, careless of everything, loved by many but not by one alone, as I should like to be. These present loves have no intellectual charm, which is a necessity to adorn life and relieve its monotony.

"What will become of me, then, mother, when my best years are past? Am I to be always alone? I have a son whom I adore but whom destiny will remove from me. Farewell, then, to adorers and friends; books, brushes, ink and paper will be my resources. I shall be good for nothing and necessary to no one. Instead of this, if I could find a good man like the good Merkatz, I would devote my life to him, I would not worry him as you do, but would marry him for fear someone else took him. What wild ideas are these!"

Then, passing from grave to gay, Delphine, as usual, tells her mother the news of her friends:

"My friend *It* is as ever kind and good; I have seen Lolo again, he is pleasant and agreeable. I see nothing of the little B. Bois is as usual. Mme. de Roches[1] is here and I see her sometimes, but I see very few people and lead a very retired life. I feel more than ever the emptiness and unhappiness of my life.

"Farewell, mother, Astolphe is getting on admirably with his tutor;[2] he is really a treasure, most gentle and attentive.

"Farewell once more, with my best love. When shall I have your dress and your ring? I am dying with impatience to see it. Have you received the dinner service?[3] I have your box but have only found papers in one handwriting; there is not a word in your writing and neither your portrait nor that of the Chevalier are there. This discovery has made me very sad, and I have written to Thirion to know the reason"[4]

Delphine's desire to see her mother married to the Chevalier was to be realised sooner than she expected. A few days afterwards Mme. de Sabran wrote to tell her that the matter was definitely settled, and that Boufflers and she herself had decided to draw closer the intimacy which had lasted for twenty years. Delphine was delighted by this good news, and her joy was all the greater as Boufflers talked of returning to France.

"Heavens! what happiness it would be if the good

---

[1] The Comtesse Alexandre de la Rochefoucauld.

[2] Mme. de Custine had brought from Bâle a young German named Berstöcher for Astolphe's education.

[3] Delphine had sent her mother, through Séguier, a porcelain service painted by herself. Maurice described it as follows to Mme. de Sabran: "I thought I saw the whole town cemetery upon my table. There were tombs, urns and mausoleums of every kind. The famous Artémise certainly did not take her coffee from a more mournful set. I will give you no further details but leave you the pleasure of the surprise."

[4] This box contained the correspondence of Mme. de Sabran and the Chevalier de Boufflers. The latter, when he went into exile, had entrusted it to his secretary, M. Thirion, and had just written to tell him to hand it over to Mme. de Custine.

Merkatz should return to France; then you would come back as his wife. I am quite worthy to be his daughter, for I am very fond of him, so get married as soon as you can. How delighted I should be if I could witness the ceremony. Why has it not taken place before? You might then have presented me with a pretty little sister whom I would have loved as a daughter. May not this happen even yet? How delightful it would be! You will laugh at my wild ideas. Make my good father-in-law laugh with you. He must not forget that he has a grandson. What relation will he be to him? Grandfather-in-law? No, I think grand-papa is more suitable.

"Goodbye, dear mother, I am going to write to my brother and Maurice, so I must leave you, otherwise I should not have time. Kiss my new father and tell him how much I love him."

The marriage of the Chevalier with Mme. de Sabran was about to take place, but unfortunately, instead of returning to France, Mme. de Boufflers and her husband started for Poland. The King of Prussia, who was anxious to oblige Boufflers, had given him a vast concession of land in Poland, at Wimislow, where he might found an agricultural establishment and welcome a few *émigrés*. Mme. de Sabran, his faithful and devoted friend, did not hesitate to follow her future husband. She tells her daugher of the fact and, knowing the grief it would cause her, speaks only of a journey to Poland. While the Chevalier and his friend were arranging for their departure, Mme. de Sabran received a constant stream of letters from Séguier. He wrote in a state of increasing depression, and spoke of the sad vicissitudes of his affections. As a matter of fact, Delphine's letters had become rarer by degrees, were less affectionate than before and Maurice had speedily noticed that he had little to hope from the future. In despair at his rebuff he wished to find some distraction at any price. He had heard of Bouffler's projects and of his future arrangements in Poland and wrote proposing to accompany him. The offer was enthusiastically accepted.

The departure of Mme. de Sabran and the Chevalier had become a reality; Boufflers, an enthusiast and full of illusions, had persuaded himself that a fortune was to be made in agriculture, and hurried on his preparations.

As long as Delphine had thought that the Chevalier's projects were more or less vague she had not been seriously disturbed, but when she understood that he was in earnest she was terror-stricken. How could her mother, whose health was feeble, undertake so long and painful a journey? How could she accustom herself to a climate even severer than that of Berlin? Moreover, the separation would be permanent, without hope of their meeting again, as it would be necessary to cross the whole of Europe to spend a few days together. Poor Delphine "cursed Silesia, Poland, Prussia and the whole world," and could not calm her fears. She was plunged into the greatest depression.

Mme. de Sabran was hardly less disturbed, she felt sure that she would never see her daughter again, and said goodbye to her for ever. The latter replied by a very incoherent letter which shows better than any number of clever phrases the extent of her mental disquietude.

"Oh! mother, what grief your letter has caused me. Do you really think that we shall never meet again? Can your health be weak enough to let you suppose the fact? Our journey of this summer is, then, an illusion, and I shall have to mourn for many years far from you. This is the crowning point of my misfortunes, and takes away all my courage. I do not know what I am saying or doing, I have no sense of life and am in a state of depression impossible to describe. However, everyone says that there will be great changes in a short time and that the women and children will be able to come back. Will you then leave Poland? I do not love that country; it seems to me a thousand times further away than Prussia. It is in vain for me to look at the map and to no purpose do I hear that it is flourishing and inhabited; it seems to me to be a vast desert which nothing ever reaches, where letters go astray and from which no one can ever emerge. And yet my only relatives want to go there to live! Perhaps this letter will not reach you, as you are starting in a month; but you will be happy as you are to be united to Merkatz for ever, though I shall not be there to clasp you in my arms. How perfect the ceremony

would have been if your children could have been present.
But we are separated by vast distances. And is Maurice also
going to bury himself in that frightful desert? Dear
Maurice, I am very fond of him.

"You are afraid of Médor, but you are wrong; there is
nothing to fear on my account, for I am more than ever far
away from happiness. If the old husband could be found at
once, I would marry him in order to go and see you in Poland.
This would be a condition of the marriage contract. You
know quite well that I am capable of acting in this way.
Heavens! how unhappy I am. At any rate tell me this.
Supposing I find some money or borrow any and were able
to go to Switzerland, would you come?

"Oh! mother, what a weariness life is! I am completely
tired of it, so tired that I shall soon be unable to move.
Astolphe alone stirs me from my lethargy. His tutor is
admirable, full of interest in myself and tender to Astolphe;
he is already very fond of you and ought to be, for he hears
so much of you. My good friend Venain is always the
same; so is my friend It, though he is a little vexed that his
affections have not been accepted. Bois is also very kind,
and perhaps he will do as the friend. Médor is a faithful
chevalier, but you need not be afraid of him; as long as I
am away from you nothing bears any danger for me.

"Farewell, my poor heart is so full of sadness and gloom
that I do not quite know what I have been saying. I can do
no more, I am ill both in body and mind."

Some days afterwards, Delphine put aside her grief to tell
her mother the most vexatious piece of news possible. The
residence in the Rue du Faubourg Saint-Honoré had been
disposed of by the State, as the proprietor was unable to
repurchase it. It had been given to General Beurnonville in
repayment of a debt of eighty thousand francs which the
nation seemed to have owed the General. Delphine added,
philosophically, "it is hoped that in course of time this
arrangement will be no more permanent than anything else, and
that your house will return to its natural owner." This act
of spoliation was a further blow, and a severe one, to Mme.
de Sabran, who thus saw herself deprived of a considerable
sum which she had little hope of ever recovering.

The Chevalier Séguier, faithful to his promise, had left Condé's army and made his way, first to Rheinsberg and then to Berlin, to join Boufflers in arranging details for the departure for Poland. We do not know precisely what happened during Séguier's stay in Berlin, but the young man suddenly changed his plans entirely. He had just heard that his name was not on the list of *émigrés*, and thought that there was nothing to prevent him from returning to his own country. Therefore, instead of starting for Poland he resolved to go back to France. It is certain that, in spite of his protestations, he was still in love with Delphine, that he wished to see her again at any price and learn for himself what hopes he had of the future. He therefore started for France and reached the capital without excessive difficulty. His first care was naturally to hasten to Delphine, under the pretext of handing her an embroidered fichu from her mother. Unfortunately he had imagined that his presence would be enough to secure the surrender of the citadel. He showed too much boldness and enterprise, and the young woman was repelled, though strongly disposed in his favour. She relates to her mother at great length the arrival of Maurice, and the want of tact which he had shown and which would probably separate them for ever.

"Paris, *June* 31, 1797.

" You are really most kind to think of thus adorning your poor daughter; the embroidered fichu is already made up, and makes the prettiest bonnet in the world. Why cannot you see the whole, and then I should be glad indeed to wear it? Dear mother, if we have any money left you may rely upon my goodwill; all is yours and all I wish is to see you again.

" As regards Maurice, I must tell you what happened in his case. Before seeing him I used to indulge in a thousand day-dreams when thinking of him; I even went so far as to think that he alone was likely to provide me with any happiness. Oh! how my opinion has changed since I have seen him close at hand and how much he daily loses in my esteem! As soon as he arrived I received him with all possible kindness and confidence; the same evening he began to make love to me, and seemed to be vexed when I avoided the question. I thought this was a trifle abrupt. The next day he wanted some of my hair and my portrait, which was another cause for surprise. 'But Maurice, we hardly know one another; we have only seen each other for a week. What reason have you to think that you have any right to urge me to abandon my resolutions? You have been so kind to Eléonore that I love you as a brother; if in that capacity you want some of my hair and even my portrait I might perhaps let you have them.' He refused point blank, and seemed quite overwhelmed because I had not at once told him that I was head over ears in love with him.

"This incident cooled my enthusiasm and induced me to examine him more critically. His faults then struck me. I saw that he is a constant tease with false ideas upon everything, especially upon moral questions, and inclined obstinately to cling to his own opinions. This has embittered me and whenever we have met it has been to quarrel. The man who pretends to be so deeply in love only comes to spend a couple of hours with me in the evening, and then only when he is asked. The rest of the time he is always on the move; he sees a great number of society women and fine ladies. Nobody ever knows what he does or where he goes and great mystery reigns over all his movements. He is shocked that I have so arranged my life as never to be alone. 'Yes,' I replied, 'as I have had no need to be alone with anyone for a long time it has never troubled me, and since we have been separated I could not arrange it otherwise merely because it might vex you some day.'

"He is never satisfied, is always asking and is content with nothing; once again my happiness has made shipwreck.

"What a difference between his behaviour and that of Médor. The latter is compliant, good and amiable, made happy by a look, happy at being in my house and desiring to be nowhere else. He detests society and knows no other happiness than my company, though he is willing to forgo it without reproaches when his presence might be displeasing or embarrassing. He never makes the smallest objection to anything or raises the least suspicion; he is most obliging, full of little attentions for myself and for my son, offered in frankness and loyalty. Whatever he says is true and he never does anything that he cannot repeat openly. He is just going to London on family business, but will return in a month; he was quite in despair and I am also sorry for his departure. However, I have nothing but gratitude for his mode of being in love, which is exemplary, and can assure him of my permanent esteem and friendship. I feel that I daily grow more incapable of affection, and that if ever I make a choice it will be determined by reason, suitability, your approbation, and by nothing else. I am so weary of my purposeless and isolated life that I do not feel my liberty to be worth anything."

Mme. de Sabran and Elzéar were much disturbed to hear that Séguier was staying in Paris, living near Delphine and seeing her constantly, as they feared that the attachment might become mutual. Their fears were unfounded; as we have seen, the young woman had been wounded by the intrusiveness of Maurice, and their constant meetings did not modify the first impression. Mme. de Custine replies thus cheerfully to the wise advice of her mother:

"Bartholo[1] makes my head go round, more with his love than anything else. He has become absolutely *amoroso*, which is very depressing. I do not know what to do, for I like him most heartily, but nothing more than that. I have not, and never shall have, more than this for anyone and there is no more happiness for myself. I am in no way what he wants and if I had to become a contortionist to please him I would certainly give it up, but I have no ambition for that happiness. Maurice has but little feeling; his self-esteem and his selfishness are excessive, and it is just the contrary of these qualities that I require. The more I see him the less I fear him."

To Elzéar's prudent advice she replies in the same way:

"Do not be afraid of Maurice; the danger is past, I know him too well to have any other feeling for him than pure friendship. His carelessness and irresponsibility, his bitterness and obstinacy are irreparable. The last fault is particularly apparent and is most inopportune. One cannot

[1] The Chevalier Séguier.

give way to it when one has been thoroughly unhappy. What is wanted is some peace of mind and some tactfulness, the power to speak one's own thoughts, and not a language that is false both to intellect and affection; Maurice, moreover, is full of conceit and is very exacting, charming qualities with which to please a woman. He likes the world and its vanities; my tastes are quite different, for I live here as though I were a hundred leagues away from Paris; I do not even know what is going on and all that I hear comes to me as so many fairy tales."

In spite of the increasingly obvious lack of sympathy which Mme. de Custine showed, Séguier continued his visits. He either saw nothing or, at any rate he persisted in hoping for results which daily became more improbable.

Mme. de Sabran and the Chevalier de Boufflers started for Poland in the month of May, as had been arranged. Their first care, as soon as they were installed at Wimislow, was to go to Breslau, where their marriage was celebrated by the Bishop in June, 1797.

CHAPTER XXI

July—December, 1797

Elzéar leaves Venice to rejoin his mother in Poland—Astolphe's tutor, Berstöcher—Proposals for a meeting between Delphine and her mother—The Paris Revolution places difficulties in the way—Delphine's disappointment.

THE correspondence which Mme. de Custine had formerly maintained so constantly with her brother had been entirely interrupted. Elzéar had not written for months; Delphine only knew that he was still in Venice and that the most urgent entreaties could not induce him to leave the city. He made the war and the presence of the French in the neighbourhood a pretext for prolonging his stay to an unreasonable length.

Eventually, in the month of July, Delphine received a letter from her brother; he had escaped from Venice and the dangers of the war and had taken refuge in Poland, at Wimislow; the young woman was delighted to know that he was near her mother. This seemed to be the first step toward the union that she so ardently desired. She proposed to make the greatest possible efforts to visit them; if this should be impossible, they would pay her a visit at Paris, and she carefully thought over the preparations necessary to receive them:

"*July* 7, 1797

" How happy I am, my dear, to know that you are with mother. I was so uneasy and anxious to know what could have become of you, as I had no news of you. You complain of my silence, but it is rather I who should complain of yours. But do not accuse me of forgetfulness, Elzéar, for you can never be absent from my heart. You are the first thought that entered it and the first being that I have loved. If you knew how I feed upon the thought of seeing you here! Your room is prepared and everyone is expecting you and hoping to see you in our little home. Your presence would be at once authorised, for you are not on the list.[1] So you can imagine my happiness.

"If money allows I hope to come and see mother this winter; it is my favourite dream; if you should come first, we would go together, otherwise I shall bring you back with me. Life, my dear, is far too short to spend it always so far from our loved ones.

"I shall not write to mother to-day; you will talk to her of me and tell her how happy I am to know that she is satisfied with her home. Tell her how constantly I think of her and of her husband; how anxious I am to see her again and how grieved I am to be so far away. Watch over her carefully, tell me of her health and of her mode of life; in a word, write to me. My son is well, his tutor is perfection, a most pleasant and deserving young man who is already quite fond of you, and is impatiently expecting your arrival.

"Good-bye, my dear; come back and kiss your sister; come and share my home and tell me of my mother and yourself, of the past and of the present. In short, come. I have not been very well for some time; I am so unhappy that anxiety simply undermines my life; I am at the end of my courage and can do no more."

Mme. de Custine, for the past year, had engaged a tutor for Astolphe whom we have already mentioned incidentally. He was a young German named Berstöcher; she was delighted with him. He devoted much enthusiasm and care to his pupil's education and trained the unusual qualities of his mind admirably. He had grown attached to the family with unusual rapidity; although he had never shown any signs of it, we strongly suspect that he, like so many others, had been touched by the strange charm of Delphine, and felt for her a real, but discreet and respectful passion. He stayed with her until her death, never leaving her and

---

[1] The list of *émigrés*.

invariably showing her the deepest attachment. Mme. de Custine very constantly refers to Berstöcher in her letters to her mother and quotes charming details concerning him. She writes on July 13th :

"The good Berstöcher shares my troubles. Listen to what he has just done for me. I was in terrible straits for money; I had none, and could not borrow any except at exorbitant interest. He has lent me some and has invested in us a hundred louis which he had at the ordinary rate of interest. He is really perfection, an excellent man, good and sensible and very pleasant."

Sometime afterwards she writes again :

"You seem delighted with my son's tutor; I am very glad to hear it, for he is really a perfect friend. He has just made a small tour to Strasburg, where he stayed six weeks. During that time every possible attempt was made to get him away from us, and he was offered the most brilliant positions. He has refused everything in order to stay with us and if we had been banished, a measure discussed as advisable in the case of all the nobility, he would have followed us. So in this respect we are most fortunate. Moreover, my Astolphe is becoming a man of real mark, and you would be exceedingly fond of him."

Mme. de Sabran's letters to her daughter were delightful and Delphine tells her in charming terms of the good which they had done her, of the healing balm which they spread upon the raw places of her life. She owes it to these letters that she does not lose courage and can wait patiently for the time of meeting :

"*July* 20, 1797.

"I have just received a long letter from you, which has given me great pleasure, as it was the first that I have had for a considerable time. Poor dear mother, how good and kind you are! What a pity that you should be buried in the depths of Poland, when you are cleverer than a thousand others. You have such goodness and you write like an angel! I hope that in your loneliness you will work a little and write me some songs; I will undertake to get them printed. What a delight it would be to print your works. No doubt Mme. de Staël writes very well and publishes books, but you

are a thousand times cleverer than she; so write me some
books, dear mother. But you will say that I am absurd, and
laugh at my ridiculous folly.
"So you are now established in your cottage and Elzéar is
with you! You are satisfied with your books and your
farming life, though your daughter is not there to help
you.
"The state of affairs in our country is by no means settled
and very far from calm. It will influence our projects greatly,
but be very sure, dear mother, that I will come and spend the
winter with you in Berlin if I have any money; I will go
wherever you like, even to the end of the world, to see you and
embrace you; but it would be far pleasanter for me to come
and stay there with you, to look after you and to perform
the most sacred of duties. This is a fancy which I hope will
not always be imaginary."

The political situation was indeed far from secure. In
1797 the first revival of the Councils had taken place, and a
Royalist majority had been elected. Barbé-Marbois was
appointed President of the Ancients and Pichegru of the
Five Hundred. One of Mme. de Custine's new friends,
Barthélemy, whom she had nicknamed the "pale friend,"
replaced Letourneur as Director. These nominations seemed
rather disquieting to the Republic, and had by no means
produced calm and tranquillity. Delphine, thanks to her
friends in power, had not been disturbed; she was more
intimate than ever with Boissy d'Anglas and constantly saw
Barthélemy. The society of the latter seemed to give her
such increasing pleasure, that she returned to her idea of a
second marriage, and she wrote to her mother as follows:
"I should like to find a good, reasonable and sensible
husband with the same tastes as my own, ready to approve
the feelings which make up my life. A husband who would
feel that to live happily I should have to be with you and
who would take me to this happiness; a husband who
would love my son as his own, with opinions as mild as his
character, philosophical, educated and not afraid of adversity,
but rather accustomed to it. One, too, who would regard a
wife like your Delphine as some compensation for his

misfortunes. That is the being I should like to meet but whom I fear I shall never find.

"Sometimes as I go over in memory all whom I have met, I dwell upon the " pale friend." If he was no longer in his present position, if he were to resign, as they say he might perhaps do, he might leave the world's stage and live in retirement with his wife. You laugh at my absurdity and so do I; but remember my jokes on this subject; I really think it has become serious. He has been perfection to me since he has been here though, I see very little of him, because I do not like standing in the full glare of the sun. Tell me what you think of my absurdities; remember that we have to live no longer for the world but for our own feelings, for repose and for virtue. Remember that it is not pleasure but reason that is the motive. A young man arouses my pity like a child deserted on the edge of a forest. My intellect is so far advanced that I am a century older than my environment. A man of eighty would be a young man to me. I give you leave, dear mother, to laugh at me as much as you like; consider my proposals as nothing but the absurdities of a lonely heart which cannot escape from itself and often wanders astray in imaginary places. A word from you will always bring it back to the true path.

"Poor mother, when shall I be able to rest from my journeys in Poland? Do you know that I make this little excursion twenty times a day and find it killing? You know that to be with you is the first principle of happiness. Take care of yourself, dear loving mother, for the sake of your daughter and her happiness; I now know only too well the value of a good mother. The more I love my son, the more I wish to be with you; if you alone were lacking to my happiness there could be no more pleasure in life. Impress that fact upon your heart and live for your children. Do not be so melancholy or talk as you do of death and the rapid passage of time. When we are together we will think of all these sad things; at present let us think only of meeting again.

" Astolphe is well and the nurse Négle is also well; she is now cook, and Mlle. Dupont has gone. She was a fearful termagant. Venein prostrates himself before you and the friend. *It* is as good and kind as ever. Médor is as usual.

"The good Médor wishes me to tell you about him. He wishes me to say that he has given me an enormous black poodle, handsome and good-tempered. He is the king of dogs and loves me deeply; his name is Favori. The good Médor is very sad at your non-arrival; he was greatly looking forward to it. He is so good and kind and has done me so many services that I am sure you would be fond of him."

The project upon which Delphine had set her heart was to meet her mother, and she constantly tries to discover some arrangement of affairs which would allow her to realise this hope. Unfortunately the circumstances were far from favourable; it became more and more difficult to obtain passports. The political situation was greatly disturbed and Delphine's best friends were in the utmost danger. How, then, was she to get to Wimislow? Delphine then advised her mother and Elzéar to become naturalised Prussians; they would then be able to come to her without danger. The idea seemed so attractive that she was convinced her mother would hasten to adopt it and began to rearrange her little household to receive her. They would then hire a small country house near Paris where they would spend the winter as happily as possible.

Political events, however, overthrew these fair hopes. Three directors, La Reveillère-Lepeaux, Barras and Rewbell, fearing the reaction from the moderate party, had prepared a *coup d' état*. On the 18th of Fructidor (September 4) the troops of General Augereau took possession of the Tuileries, where the councils were sitting; more than half of the recent elections were declared null and void; two directors, Carnot and Barthélemy, were imprisoned, with more than sixty deputies, and deported to Guiana. Thus Delphine's matrimonial projects collapsed. She was overcome by the blow, but only ventured to hint at the disaster which had stricken both her and her friends:

"I can talk of nothing, I am so sad and my friends are all unfortunate. . . . the "pale friend". . . . this has quite crushed me. I had built so many hopes upon the latter and it is I who have brought him ill-luck."

This, however, was not all; a violent reaction took place, all the emergency laws were reinforced, and it became almost impossible to leave France or to enter it. Under these conditions how could Mme. de Custine rejoin her mother, and how could Mme. de Boufflers venture to enter France? Delphine, in the extremity of her despair, thus expressess her grief to her mother:

"*September* 13, 1797.

"My dear, I take up my pen to write to you in floods of tears. I have had your letters, and far from bringing me any consolation they bring me worse than death. Your joy, your delight at seeing us again oppresses my heart; there can be no more happiness, we must give it up. It will certainly be very difficult to obtain a passport in order to visit you, and the greatest difficulty of all is money. Thus I am constantly stricken in my dearest affections, constantly separated from happiness, agitated and tormented. Human strength, my dear, is not enough to support such grief. How nicely you had arranged the whole year! How well it suited me and how happy we should have been. You were expecting to see me at Wimislow and I would have welcomed you to Paris.

"You brought tears to my eyes when you spoke of our household arrangements and of the disturbance that it might cause me. But you do not know your Delphine; I was intoxicated with happiness and was tempted to get your bed made, so great was the pleasure of making all these preparations. I was going to give you my room and my bed, and sleep at your side in my study, where I would have a bed made up. My brother would have a charming room on the other side of the house, on the fourth floor, it is true, but next to my son's tutor. There I would have arranged his books and have been charmed to make him a pleasant little workshop. That is how the whole was settled, and now a thunderbolt seems to have crushed us. What can we do, or for what can we hope? I am sure I do not know. We must wait a month to gain some ideas or some means of conjecture.

"Dear mother, everyone was delighted at the idea of seeing you and the whole of the little household was enchanted; even the cook Négle could not sleep for joy. And now we are not to have this happiness! I have suffered so much in my life and my heart is so sore that the least wound reopens all the others and completely takes away all my remaining strength.

Be courageous, my darling, I am, perhaps, more frightened than I need be, but I was so happy that this transition has been a severe shock.

"Farewell, dear, good and excellent mother, whom I love more than myself, whom I would gladly press to my heart, in whom alone I have confidence and to whom alone I would open my heart and tell everything. And now four hundred leagues separate us! Well, we shall meet again; I have consulted a sorcerer who has assured me of the fact and my heart tells me so yet more certainly."

Not only to her mother does Delphine relate her disappointment; she resumes her long-interrupted correspondence with her brother, and opens her heart, telling him of her desires and her hopes:

"*October* 27, 1797.

"I am in despair about your health. Are you still ill and suffering? Perhaps the air of that country will do you good. Are you any taller and have you grown a beard? I am most anxious to see you again. I like your plans for study; what are you doing now? Have you any plan, any work going on or proposed? Yours is the age at which great works can be begun and great projects formed, but I do not think ambition is your failing. It would have been mine if I had been a man. I should have wished to be the first of all, to have outstripped posterity; perhaps I should have upset the world. You laugh at my tumultuous fancies, but really Nature has made a mistake and I should have been a man. I do not, however, know much of bravery. I am sure that without this quality all other virtues would be useless, and goodbye to my hero and his ambitions. But as things are it is as well that I am a woman, for 1 am not always very brave. I am afraid of the dark, of animals, of thieves and of a whole number of things. But to be a great man in my sense one must be afraid of nothing, not even of Divine Justice and still less of death. As a woman I feel that such a hero as I have depicted would turn my head; there is no foolishness which I would not commit for him. I have not been able to commit foolishness for anybody, for since we have been in a state of Revolution no great character has appeared.

"But let us leave my fancies and talk of our poverty and my sad position. What will you do now you are near mother? What will she do? What does she say? How is her health? I feel desperate to think that I cannot see her myself, care for her, console her or amuse her, and there you have the limits of my ambition."

CHAPTER XXII

1798

Mme. de Custine's desire to see her mother again—They decide to meet at Klosterheilbronn—Departure of Mme. de Custine for that town—She awaits her mother there—Her impatience and her anxiety—At length Mme. de Sabran arrives—Elzéar's illness—Mme. de Custine returns to France—Society under the Directory.

DURING the year 1798 Delphine perseveringly pursued her troublesome claims; not only did she attempt to secure the restitution of her property but she also put in claims for the property of her mother. In this latter direction she was confronted by yet greater difficulties. If Mme. de Sabran had consented to return to France much might have been done, but this was an indispensable condition; until it was fulfilled no efforts could lead to any result. In every letter this burning and vital point is discussed and often with an air of despondency.

But the loving Delphine had also another point more nearly at heart than anything, the possibility of meeting her mother and spending a few days with her. Fortunately, supervision was less strict, a sense of security had supervened and it was now possible to leave France. Mme. de Sabran, who was equally anxious to see her daughter, proposed a meeting at Klosterheilbronn, where they would spend a few delightful days of family life. The proposal was gladly accepted and it was arranged that Mme. de Custine should leave Paris when her mother started from Poland, with the object of meeting at the appointed spot, which they would reach about the same time. Delphine, therefore, started in delight on April 20 with Astolphe and Berstöcher and reached Klosterheilbronn on May 7. Her mother was not there; she waited patiently for her, but as no news arrived she became panic-stricken, fearing some accident or some misunderstanding and finally wrote on May 27 in the highest state of anxiety :

"KLOSTERHEILBRONN, *May* 24.

"I have been here since May 7. I left Paris on April 20 and stayed three days at Anspach. I have written from Kehl, from Anspach and from here and the only answer has been profound silence. I had announced my departure long ago and I learn that you have been expected here about the 10th or 12th; we have now reached the 25th without a word of explanation. I am positively ill with anxiety and vexation, spending here the little time I had to spare for you, neglecting your business and mine and all without knowing what will be the end of it. I tremble in anticipation of some gloomy event; pray reassure me by your arrival or by a letter. Time is passing and you do not appear and I am eating my heart out here in uneasiness and grief. On April 27 I heard of a fine whim of Elzéar's, that you would wait before starting for a letter telling you that I had left France. There is no sense in this proceeding, for all the letters that I had written you and my last were quite positive. This whim may cost us somewhat dearly and more incredible still is the fact that on May 1 I wrote from Kehl that I had left France and have also written from Anspach and from here. I cannot make it out, and I assure you it is quite time that this frightful mystery was explained."

Mme. de Sabran's delay was caused by serious business troubles. We know that her pecuniary situation was very precarious; great was her distress when she heard that the new King of Prussia [1] intended to stop the pension which she owed to the generosity of his predecessor and which formed the most reliable part of her income; this was a disaster for herself and for her husband. She therefore resolved to take advantage of her visit to Berlin to see her friends, such people in high positions as she knew and the King himself, if necessary, and to secure the continuance of her pension. She expected to stay forty-eight hours in

[1] Frederick William III. (1770–1840).

Berlin, but she was there for a fortnight, petitioning and making inquiries right and left. She left the town in the keenest anxiety after obtaining many promises but nothing positive.

Her stay at Heilbronn was not as delightful as she had hoped. In the first place, Elzéar fell ill of a tertian fever and caused his mother great anxiety. Delphine was then attacked by the same sickness and though not so severely as her brother, she was none the less very ill. Their meeting was thus inevitably saddened. After staying three weeks at Klosterheilbronn they started once more, Delphine and Astolphe to return to Paris, while Elzéar went to Vienna to meet his uncle, the Bishop of Laon, who had asked for him. Mme. de Boufflers went back to her husband at Wimislow. In spite of the many disappointments she had had to endure Delphine had been greatly delighted by this meeting. Elzéar and Berstöcher were no less pleased.

"The good Berstöcher is quite enthusiastic about you and mother," she writes to her brother, " we constantly speak about our stay at Kloster, it is our universal medicine. When we feel very despondent we talk of Kloster and things then seem a little brighter. Astolphe also thinks of that pleasant time. He is fond of his uncles, talks of them and even prays for them. You may tell that to his great-uncle. His grandmother is his first love; he prefers her to anyone else, but he will forget her and so shall we, as she sends us no sign of life."

No sooner had she returned to Paris than Delphine heard that during her absence the Directory had completed another *coup d'état* against the Councils (22 Floréal); she passed through new disturbances, but she was so accustomed to them that she would not have been greatly troubled if her friend Séguier had not been seriously compromised. To enable him to avoid arrest Delphine was obliged to hide him in her house. Maurice writes to Mme. de Sabran:

"*October 22,* 1798.
"(*Brumaire* 1, *year VII.*)

" Another hurricane has just blown me into the Temple ot Friendship; you may surmise that this Temple is the house of your dear Delphine. She has just been kind enough to take me in and for several days I have been breathing the same air. Whether this air will be as salutary as it should be is a point upon which I cannot certify you. At any rate, as it is what your daughter breathes it loses some of its purity when it touches my lips, and a wretched lover who is always desirous of piercing the mask of friendship naturally destroys its salubrity to some extent."[1]

This dangerous intimacy on which Séguier relied for the advancement of his cause did not secure the results that he expected. Delphine was determiued to remain upon the common ground of friendship, and he could not shake her resolution. About the same time Mme. de Boufflers received a long letter from one of her friends in Paris giving a description of society under the Directory. This friend does not sign her name but her account is so amusing and clearly describes the kind of society in which Mme. de Custine was living that we give the letter as a whole:

"*June* 2, 1798.

"I had your kind message, madam, through M. de Bonnet; I am very sorry that I missed the opportunity of seeing you at Berne, but duties that I could not possibly neglect recalled me to France. I had been banished by the Terror, but I have recovered my property without difficulty and am now taking advantage of the law authorising those who do not agree with the Republican Government to sell their property and leave the country. I am therefore busy realising my fortune and looking for a means to invest it and establish myself somewhere. I had thought of setting up house in Switzerland, but this country seems to me to be threatened by the same disturbances and I wish to get as far from revolutions as possible. I may perhaps go to Russia; I shall then pass through Berlin and have the pleasure of seeing you. How much I shall have to tell you! My stories of this country would seem to you the history of some fabulous generation, though of an age by no means heroic. M. Géréminus will be able to give you full details concerning the manners of the new society, for we have to deal with a new nation. His position is more favourable than mine

[1] The Prat papers.

and has secured his entrance to it, so that he is in a better position to judge; however, I am persuaded that a woman has a better eye for shades of colour than a man and will therefore venture some observations of my own.

"Every wealthy and educated person is now in poverty and beneath the burden of shabby clothes preserves a show of politeness and an air of dignity, I will even say of superiority, for this attitude is not readily thrown off. Politeness, courtesy, good taste and ease of manner are now to be found only in garrets, which are the refuge of French politeness and good breeding, two qualities now regarded as ancient prejudices and ridiculed by the prosperous, who cannot acquire them. The play of wit, the careful phrasing of trifles, the intellectual banter of the Court and the sound of the gentle voices of educated women are replaced by the hoarse familiarity of the middle classes.

"One of their greatest delights is eating; lunch parties are fashionable. I went to one of these orgies and will try to give you an idea of what I saw and heard. They meet at mid-day; the deputies (their wives keep house) drink a glass of brandy before starting for the Legislative Assembly; everybody, men and women, drinks to the health of the Republic. Then they begin their lunch with tea, which is supposed to be fashionable, and finish with wine, liqueurs and an uproar unbearable to ears accustomed to the old régime. This lunch lasts for about two hours. Then, while waiting for dinner they play little innocent games of kissing, slapping and tearing one another's clothes, amusements that create such an uproar as to advertise the whole district of the entertainment. At four o'clock the deputies return and dinner begins. The table is laid with dishes to the utmost extent and in the greatest profusion. Good taste decrees that the price of each dish on the table shall be explained. The most moderate calculation brought the cost of the dinner at which I was present to 260,000 francs in normal value, that is to say in assignats.

"Dinner was over at six o'clock and we then went to see the National Gardens and places such as Monceau, Tivoli, &c., which only deputies and those with them may enter. The gentlemen acted the part of the fauns and the ladies of nymphs. Republican jokes are extremely free, I can assure you; it is the only form of liberty left in France and they make the most of it.

"An extraordinary revolution has taken place among the women. As you know, Parisian women were formerly accused of the utmost fickleness and coquetry, were supposed to be incapable of any great passion, and it was even recognised, to put the matter bluntly, that they had no character or very little. Well, madam, to-day precisely the contrary is the case; the woman of to-day, as the expression goes (such terms as fashionable, or society ladies are now worn out; so we say, the women of to-day—a very suitable term, for they have no resemblance to the women of the past), these women, then are no longer coquettes, but have become bad characters. If a woman takes a fancy to a man, she indulges her desire; to say, my lover is amiable, honourable, or clever, is out of date... amiable is a term no longer used, and honourable is synonymous with stupid. Cleverness consists in making money, no matter how. The younger generation are completely corrupted, and to very few people would one entrust a louis to get change for it; even then it is advisable to pay a commission so that your messenger may regard you as a good customer and be accurate in the hope of earning something another time. This evil infection has spread everywhere; those of our own class who have retained some honourable principles and do not wish to become sharpers, will lend on usury; I could quote the names of many noblemen of your acquaintance who say quite casually: I have invested ten or twenty louis at forty per cent. per month: principles are now regarded as prejudices and nothing is so deeply ridiculed as prejudice. This is bound to happen in a country where there are no laws.

"Luxury in dress is extreme in the case of the women, and is carried to the height of extravagance, a fact resulting from circumstances. Landowners and moneyed men have been crushed; the former by the most arbitrary taxation and by their farmers, and the latter by the depreciation of the assignats; hence only personal property is of any value. To operate upon a large scale and to inspire confidence a man must have a finely furnished house, a richly-dressed wife, and must show off his possessions by giving good dinners, entertainments and balls; there has never been so much dancing as this winter.

"It is in good style to pose as an aristocrat and regret the old régime while fearing a new one. We are bound to believe in the sincerity of this style, seeing that those who call themselves aristocrats have bought the lands and wives of the *émigrés*. The marriages of divorced women increase, and this system is one of the strongest foundations of the Republic and one of the greatest difficulties to avoid. The system of equality is now in full swing; there is no idea of gradation; those whose vanity should have maintained this idea have taken such pains to hide it from themselves that they have forgotten it entirely. France is given up to fashion, and commerce is the fashion of the day. The greatest ladies walk in the mud with bundles of wares under their arms which they propose to sell for the toilets of the ladies of the day. You will admit that this is worse than equality, but the fact is that honour and prejudice are so closely joined that one takes flight with the other. Heaven grant that honour is an *émigré* and not entirely non-existent!

"This letter has grown very long but perhaps you have some leisure to spare. I am at least confident of this, that Paris cannot fail to be an interesting spectacle to you. So before closing my letter I should like to speak of two well-known women who play a great part here; Mme. Tallien, *née* Cabarrus, the divorced wife of the *émigré* Fontenay, councillor to the Parliament, and now the wife of Tallien; and of Mme. de Bonaparte, formerly Vicomtesse de Beauharnais. They are most extraordinary women, very weak characters though very courageous. The former is angelically beautiful, very clever, talented, good-hearted with keen perceptions, but great weakness of character. The latter is not nearly so clever and is rather ugly, though a creole; she has that pleasing air of indifference which attracts men. Both are kindly people and infinitely obliging. Before their marriage they were strong aristocrats. Mme. de Fontenay was in prison before the 9th of Thermidor. Tallien was attracted by her beauty and her intellect and conceived the idea of saying that she was his wife in order to save her. In this way he obtained her liberty; he acquired some glory from the death of Robespierre. Attracted by gratitude her inclination was decided by his services; her former aristocratic friends, seeing her in power, applied to her and were fully satisfied. She has always shown herself disinterested and obliging; one need only be unfortunate to rouse her interest. Her extravagance and fickleness have exposed her to every kind of criticism, but on this point she is imperturbably philosophical and nothing disturbs her serenity; she is beautiful and in power and that is enough for her.

"Mme. de Beauharnais may be regarded as a second edition of her, less pronounced in every respect but no less obliging. She has the modesty enforced by plainness of looks; more compliant, she is more touched by flattery because she is less accustomed to it. There is nothing she will not do to help those whom she thinks in love with her. On the whole it is very fortunate that these two ladies should have secured possession of members of the Government; they can soften the roughness of their manners. There are few aristocrats in Paris who are not under some obligation to them; I am perhaps the only one who has never asked anything of them; possibly that is but a matter of time, and if any one of my friends were in danger I should readily have recourse to their good hearts. Such, impartially drawn, is the picture of these two women who play a more important part in the history of manners than in political history. They are not capable of guiding an intrigue of importance; they are too deeply absorbed in their own pleasures, are wanting in perception, are vain, and have too many confidants.

"As regards the political situation of France I will speak only of domestic affairs. There is certainly a general discontent and no one likes the Government; the republican madness has died away among the element known as the people. They are discontented but not unhappy, for they have never been richer. Their chief dislike to the Government is derived from the fact that they do not believe in its stability; there is a sort of arbitrary character in the taxation which disquiets them and the Government is not thought to be sufficiently strong to guarantee their possession of what they hold. There is no sense of security and therefore a general want of confidence. A change in the Government would be welcomed, but as the people are not in distress they will show no energy to bring about a change. Hence we should be under no illusion concerning this discontent, which is due to the natural fickleness of the people and to their scorn of those in places of power. But there is a great difference between this and the energy which misfortune produces; never have the poverty-stricken been so cared for and never have working people been better off. Anyone who can work can earn what he likes; the salaries of the workmen are higher than they were ever before and all who are in poverty, that is to say, who have no means of subsistence except labour, and all with an income below a thousand francs, receive from the Government three quarters of bread daily and one and a half pounds of meat every ten days; in Paris there are two hundred thousand persons on this list; in all the great towns things are the same, and so very few beggars are to be seen.

"Notwithstanding the countless armies raised and the requisitions of every kind, the land is better cultivated than ever before. Produce is so dear that no plot of land is left vacant. The high roads are superb and the bridges and canals have never been in such good repair. Commerce is so vigorous that its mainspring breaks every three months and is replaced by some new form. The device of assignats has provided for everything, and the guillotine has been a great help. But these resources are now exhausted and finance is the real danger confronting the Government. The possibility of the conquest of Italy may restore credit for a time as was the case when Holland was conquered, but the losses are so great and the administrative expenses so vast that no taxes, however enormous, could even cover the cost of collecting them. There is a vast bureaucracy with salaries of a magnificence exceeding all dreams. Everyone can find some place in a Government office. The brother of Mme. de Polastron, who is sixteen years of age, is a clerk in the War Office and gets six louis a month, a load of wood every ten days, light, etc., and he is not the head of the department or even the chief clerk, but an ordinary clerk, and you can imagine from this how the rest are paid.

"As the Government is prepared to sacrifice everything to stop the course of discontent, it can only maintain its position by conquest. Should peace be made, what would they do with the soldiers? The lands promised to them have been sold. No extraordinary resources can be found except by war and the Government cannot exist without fresh resources, constantly renewed. Therefore they will not make peace. Negotiations should therefore be stopped; they are useless, for they can lead to nothing and merely waste time.

"Pray, madam, excuse this scribble; notwithstanding my untidiness I have no time to begin this letter again. M. de Géréminus is starting and will hardly give me time to seal my letter and to assure you how delighted I should be to see you. Pray be assured of my kindest regards; perhaps you will not guess who is writing to you but I can hardly sign my name. I will remind the Chevalier de B . . . . of the mud at St. Amand and yourself of the Terrace of the Feuillants."

CHAPTER XXIII

1799—1800

Delphine secures the erasure of the names of her mother and of the Chevalier de Boufflers from the list of the émigrés—General de Beurnonville asks her hand in marriage—Violent indignation on the part of Elzéar—The Chevalier de Boufflers and his wife return to France—Elzéar accompanies them.

IN 1799, on the 30th of Prairial (June) another *coup d'état* took place. On this occasion the Councils obliged three directors to retire and France more than ever became a prey to factions and was in a state of complete anarchy. Everyone was expecting a second Terror. When Bonaparte came forward upon his return from Egypt he was welcomed as a saviour. On the 30th of Brumaire he expelled the five hundred and seized the power the same evening, sharing it with two former directors, Sieyès and Ducos.

Delphine shows no special excitement at these upheavals. During the last ten years she has seen so many of them that she has come to consider them as a natural part of the course of events. In spite of these disturbances she continued her efforts to secure the restitution of her mother's property and of her own. Circumstances had brought her into connection with the man who had seized the residence in the Faubourg St. Honoré, General de Beurnonville.[1] He

[1] Pierre Riel de Beurnonville, born at Champignol, near Bar-sur-Aube, was the sixth son of a wheelwright. At first he was intended for the Church, but he left the seminary and entered the police force of Lunéville. At the outset of the Revolution he proclaimed the most advanced opinions, which secured for him a brilliant and rapid career. In 1792 he was commander-in-chief of the Army of the Centre; then he was twice appointed Minister for War. Captured by treachery he was confined for more than two years in the dungeons of Olmütz, and not until 1795 was he exchanged, together with the French commissaries, for the daughter of Louis XVI.

was not a bad man but he was a terrible Gascon, although born in Champagne. After the battle of Grewenmacheren, where he suffered considerable loss, he sent off a triumphal bulletin which has remained famous. He asserted that he had killed more than a thousand men and that the only loss upon his side was the little finger of a sharpshooter. This statement called forth the following epigram:

> Quand d'ennemis tués, on compte plus de mille,
> Nous ne perdons qu'un doigt, encore le plus petit !
> Holà, Monsieur de Beurnonville
> Le petit doigt n'a pas tout dit !

Delphine had been obliged to discuss business matters with Beurnonville on several occasions. Their intimacy then became greater; the rough warrior was soon subdued by the charms of the young woman, to such an extent that one day he declared his passion. Delphine laughed at him at first and would not listen, but Beurnonville persisted and proved the seriousness of his intentions by immediately requesting Delphine's hand in marriage. She asked for time to wait and consult her family.

At the bottom of her heart she did not think Beurnonville's proposal in any way absurd and even regarded it somewhat favourably. She had been thinking of marrying again for some years. The General was rich and enjoyed a high position, as he had just been appointed ambassador at Berlin;[1] then he seemed very much in love and what more could she desire. His birth and his past were certainly open to objection, but at that period these matters were not closely scrutinised. The General paid his court to the young widow assiduously; it seemed that people might soon begin to talk, and Delphine resolved to explain his proposal to her mother. Mme. de Boufflers received the news very calmly and advised her daughter to think it over very carefully, and above all, to do nothing in a hurry.

Meanwhile Beurnonville, anxious to please, was prepared to obtain Delphine's favour by any means. He knew that the young woman's most ardent desire was to see her mother's return to France, and he thought that he could do

[1] Bonaparte had appointed him to Berlin as a reward for his services on the 18th of Brumaire.

nothing that would please her better than by securing that the names of M. and Mme. de Boufflers should be erased from the list of *émigrés*. As ambassador at Berlin the task was easier for him than for anyone else; moreover, Delphine was then very intimate with Fouché, Minister of Police, and on this side also she found every facility. In the month of January, 1800, she was delighted to learn that her desire had at length been accomplished. Overwhelmed with happiness she informs her mother at once of the good news. She also hastened to communicate it to Elzéar, who was still at Vienna with the Bishop of Laon. No doubt he would also hasten back to France to enjoy the meeting so long and ardently desired. He could come the more readily as his name did not appear upon the list of *émigrés*. She advised her brother to keep the secret from the Bishop of Laon; "do not speak of what I have obtained for mother," she says, "it would compromise me greatly and them also."

Great was the delight at Wimislow when the official documents arrived reopening the doors of their country to the unhappy exiles. Their first proceeding was to realise as completely as possible all their possessions in Poland, and to return to their dear country from which they had been separated for nearly ten years. Boufflers, who was unable to contain his impatience, left to his wife the care of settling their affairs and started at once. "I would rather die of hunger in France," he cried, "than live in Prussia in wealth." Mme. de Boufflers hastened to write to Elzéar to inform him of their new proposals, urging him to return to France with them. But Elzéar was living at Vienna in a society of *émigrés* whose hatred of the French Government was pushed to the extremity of violence. The idea of returning to his country "without the King" seemed monstrous to him, as to most of his compatriots.

Just at the time that he received his mother's letter he was informed by the Comtesse Clary, who had seen the announcement in a newspaper, of the proposed marriage between Delphine and General Beurnonville. He was astounded and naturally Mgr. de Sabran showed still keener indignation. In his anger Elzéar did not hesitate to send to the Chevalier de Boufflers some vigorous observations, pointing out the danger that he and his wife were running in returning to their country and the infamy which would fall upon them all when it was known that they owed their relief to Beurnonville. Of Delphine's conduct he speaks with furious indignation :

"1799.

"It is really dangerous to return to a country abandoned to the varying policies of continuous anarchy. The experience of several years has shown us that in France the Government of to-day is not that of to-morrow. The erasure of your names from the list of *émigrés* may shelter you from danger as long as the present Government lasts, but nothing can save you if it happens, like its predecessor, to be overthrown. In that case the leaders of the victorious faction will and should proscribe all those whom their predecessors have helped. Moreover, my sister has profited by M. de Beurnonville's affection or by the desire for marriage with which his vanity has inspired him, in order to obtain this erasure. Thus the services which he renders her are, so to speak, advance payment, and as I have no doubt that my mother will persuade her to avoid so degrading and so monstrous an alliance, I see that you will all fall a prey to the vengeance of a powerful man, who will jealously reproach her for deceiving him. In a word, if you go back to France under these auspices I see but the alternatives of disgrace or persecution before my mother, my sister and yourself." He then added this supreme argument, "Do you feel bold enough, my dear Chevalier, to declare yourself the subject of a usurping Corsican brigand?"

Elzéar had been unable to contain his wrath and had written a letter of bitter reproaches to his sister. Delphine replied, explaining very simply the natural feelings of self-interest which had induced her not to reject the General's proposal at once.

"I have your letter of December 10, my dear Elzéar, and approve of all that your affection has thought advisable to write. But, my dear, you are quite wrong, both as regards myself and the facts of the case. This is not an idea proceeding from a moment's insanity ; nothing has been done towards the final step, and it is a question only of interest and reason ; my feelings have nothing to do with the matter. My intellect has examined it and my mind remains in suspense and undecided. I do not exaggerate my reputation or the happiness of my existence as you do ; I know that my reputation is at the mercy of the first scoundrel that I may meet, that I am without support, with no hope for the future, in the utmost embarrassment, and with none of the pleasures of life. I know that when the time comes for my son to choose a career, he will have no one to help him and push him forward. These are the considerations which induced me for a moment to consider proposals wholly contrary to my affection and to my point of view. There was also the further desire to be of use to my mother and yourself and my son by concluding the business that I have in hand.

"There is nothing attractive about this man, but he is generally highly esteemed. In view of the distance by which we are separated you can hardly form any correct idea of him or of the advantages which I might gain from such a union. I cannot complain, but at the same time you cannot delude yourself or doubt for a moment the nature of my real feelings. I know as well as you do what I owe to myself, but I also know my isolation, the sadness of my position and the future that awaits myself and my son. Moreover, I have never undertaken to do anything which might displease my mother, and I have always given only a conditional answer. In other words, I have referred the final decision to my mother; that is the point at which we now stand. The man in question will see my mother and she will be better able to judge of him and to break off the proposal, which I have only entertained as a necessary sacrifice to my son's happiness."

These considerations of interest, far from persuading Elzéar, increased his anger and indignation, and he applied to Maurice Séguier. He tells him of the tragedy which threatens them and the shame to which they are exposed, and begs him to impress the truth upon the unhappy woman who has been led astray by the deplorable company which she has kept. May he be able to dissuade her from an alliance which would cover them all with everlasting dishonour;

"1799.

"I trembled when I saw upon what a match Delphine's imagination was fixed; I still tremble when I think of it. How can she have dwelt upon so infamous a proposal! Why did not her heart and soul cry out against it? She actually speaks of it with coolness as a perfectly simple thing; she dares to apply the term 'reasonable' to this horror, and ventures to think that those whom she loves would accept degradation and support obtained at the price of her disgrace and theirs. She is marching towards a shame as glaring as was her heroism. This is the result of the ideas among which she has been living; it is the consequence of bad company, for such an idea could not be native to her mind; it has been implanted in her by these scandalous women, the shame of their sex, of their age and of their country,

> "Who taste in crime the sweets of peace,
> And raise a brow that never blushed.

"This mention of them will be sufficient. So, my friend, I appeal to your common-sense and high-mindedness. Impress upon her the depth of the abyss in which she will be engulfed and into which she will carry with her her unfortunate child, her parents, her friends, and all that she holds dear in this world. Show this blind and unhappy woman that even an honest servant girl would refuse so magnificent a marriage! How blind I was! I was congratulating her upon her success and rejoicing over it, without knowing to whom she owed it.

"Recall Delphine from the brink of this precipice. She will, I am sure, have pity on me; she will not say farewell for ever or raise eternal enmity between us. Iphigenia will not devote Orestes to the Furies, and the dagger which she has raised above his heart will fall from her hand."

Finally Elzéar applies to his mother and asks her how, under such conditions, she can urge him to return to France:

"Can you seriously urge me to return in this state of uncertainty, and do you wish me to sink in the mire? I have never assumed the colours of any party hitherto, and shall I begin by wallowing beneath the yoke of Bonaparte as the brother-in-law of B?,, You cannot reasonably ask me this, and you surely know what it would cost me to return to that abyss. Your pity for me and for yourself should spare us this misfortune."

Though Elzéar had spoken to his mother with unusual violence she replies gently and sensibly. She tries to show him things in their true light, and to still the anxiety which he has no reason to feel:

"Astride of the question of this stupid marriage which has never been seriously entertained, you do nothing but argue and are the very picture of an eccentric bore. You surely know me well enough to understand that I should not countenance so unsuitable an alliance for your sister. I have told you so a thousand times. Delphine is not keen upon it, and I believe what she tells me. Moreover, she has assured me that I shall decide her fate, and I certainly shall not attempt to seek my own happiness in the dishonour of my children. I will show you your sister's letters in which she talks to me of Bluebeard, which is her name for the man in question. From the portrait which she draws you will understand that she is by no means attracted to him, and would be delighted if I would rid her of him.

"You seem to fear that there may be some danger to myself if I refuse. You may lay aside your fears; I have already considered my line of action and nothing in this world can frighten me. Besides, the man in question is not a bad man; he is married and his wife is in the Indies; he is divorced, and it is upon this question of divorce that I shall base my plan of defence. Your sister has provided me with this means. This fact should be enough to show you how much she thinks of him and also that I am well able to give my refusal.

"It is not necessary that one should be an aristocrat to be in love, and I think it quite natural that anyone should be in love with your sister, whatever his political views may be. In the course of the Revolution in Brabant we saw the saddler Simon asking for Mlle. d'Aremberg in marriage for his son. These topsy-turvy ideas are the outcome of a moment's madness, and if Mme. d'Aremberg did not give her daughter she was obliged to return a polite refusal.

"One other point; it was not Bluebeard who secured the

erasure of our names. It was much rather Mme. de Bonaparte who was with your sister in prison for eight months, and who has enabled her to arrange all our business. Beurnonville is not concerned in it, except for the passport which he will have to give us, as he is *chargé d'affaires* at Berlin for the Republic. I have written all this to you not once but twenty times, and you have just told me that I have never spoken of it; it is really enough to drive one to despair."

Though reassured concerning his sister's matrimonial projects, Elzéar showed no great enthusiasm to return to France. Neither his mother's requests nor the entreaties of Delphine could decide him. He was entirely under the influence of the Bishop of Laon and of the *émigré* society in which he lived, and these people all did their best to point out the dangers and the inconvenience which his return would involve.

Delphine did not understand her brother's ideas and thought that he was anxious as herself for the long-desired meeting. She constantly wrote, urging him to press on his return. Would Elzéar be the only one to desert the "owl's nest"? Did he despise the happiness of finding himself under the same roof and breathing his native air? What did he risk by returning? He need only make a trial of it, and if the reality did not come up to his expectations he could return to Vienna. To miss the opportunity now was to miss it for ever, and he would certainly regret that he had sacrificed the whole of his life to some false idea.

Elzéar was at length convinced by these reproaches and consented to leave the Bishop of Laon and return to France.

On learning that his grandmother would soon arrive Astolphe wrote the following pretty letter to hasten her return :

"My dear grandmother, come back and give me a kiss, for I want one badly. We will come and meet you so as to see you sooner. Please ask permission from my grandfather that I may speak to him as ' tu,' so that I may not have to ask for it myself. You will come to the theatre with me, which I like very much. I am very happy, but I shall be happier when you are here. Mother will give you her room.

I still have your ring. In the summer we will go into the country and you will take morning walks with me. I shall play the piano to you to amuse you. I can draw and I am learning to dance. Good-bye, my dear grandmother, with my best love to grandfather; I love him very much.

"ASTOLPHE"

In the course of the year 1800 Mme. de Boufflers, her husband, Elzéar, Delphine and Astolphe had the pleasure of meeting together in Paris; the "owl's nest" was complete.

CHAPTER XXIV

1801—1803

Mme. de Custine's life at Paris—Her social relations—She meets Chateaubriand and falls deeply in love with him—Departure of Chateaubriand for Rome—Death of Mme. de Beaumont—Mme. de Custine buys the estate of Fervaques.

DURING the year 1801 and 1802 Mme. de Custine's life flowed by calmly and peaceably without any events of special interest. She devoted herself to the education of her son, to family joys, and to the satisfaction of her artistic tastes. The cruel trials through which she had passed had given a singularly gloomy cast to her character, and the society life which had formerly attracted her so profoundly now seemed barren and hateful. Society, indeed, both bored and frightened her. "She feared the drawing-room more than the scaffold," says her son at a later date. But if she avoided Society, she was quite ready for intimacy, and found much delight in her daily relations with her family and a few friends of proved affection. She remained upon the most affectionate terms with her mother; during the winter she saw her almost every day, even several times a day, as she had been careful to take rooms in her immediate neighbourhood. On no less affectionate terms was she with the Chevalier; hardship and the lapse of years had not deprived Boufflers of his cheerfulness and wit, and his company was always a source of great pleasure. During the summer Delphine went to her estate of Niederviller; there she spent several weeks and then went with Astolphe and Nanette to rejoin her mother at Saint Léger, a small estate near Saint Germain which Boufflers had been able to buy from his scanty income, and where he took a philosophical delight in the pleasures of country life.

The close affection which had united Delphine and Elzéar and the grief which they had felt at their separation are alike well-known to the reader. It will be asked whether their much-desired meeting had given them all the pleasure which they anticipated. The answer must be a decided negative. Elzéar had never been able to pardon Delphine for her unfortunate proposal of marriage with General Beurnonville,[1] and when he returned to France he showed a coldness to his sister by which she was deeply wounded. In spite of this, their old and warm affection would probably have surmounted this difficulty, if Elzéar, almost immediately upon his return, had not been seized by a wild affection for Mme. de Staël. It was one of those passions which absorb every faculty and stifle every other feeling in the victim of it. As he had once left his mother to join the Bishop of Laon, so he left her again to become the squire of " Corinne " and to follow her to Coppet and elsewhere. Delphine was forgotten alike and with equal rapidity.

The greatest friends of Mme. de Custine and the members of her small circle whom she constantly saw were Fouché, familiarly called by her Chéché, Boissy d'Anglas, Mme. de Rosambo, and her sister-in-law, Mme. de Dreux-Brézé, whom she nicknamed the Mouse. One of her dearest friends who will constantly reappear in the course of this narrative was the old Princesse de Vaudémont.[2] She was a proud and eccentric character. Fouché, who was quite intimate with her, called her the " queen of the owls " because she went to bed every morning and slept all day. She was passionately fond of dogs, and dogs of every species and race were to be found in her drawing-room. At Paris, in the Rue de Provence and at Suresnes, in her country house, the Princess saw a numerous company of visitors. Delphine also saw constantly the wife of the First Consul with whom she had

[1] Beurnonville's career became more brilliant even than before, and no doubt Delphine regretted more than once that she had yielded to her brother's recriminations. Under the Empire the General was appointed Count and Senator. Under Louis XVIII, he became marquis, a peer and a marshal of France. He married the daughter of the Comte de Dufort.

[2] *Née* Montmorency. Her husband was the younger brother of the unfortunate Prince de Lambesc.

maintained a pleasant intimacy from the time of their stay in the prison of the Carmes. She had also rediscovered her great friend of former days. the Comtesse Aléxandre de la Rochefoucauld. As a cousin german of Mme. Bonaparte, the Comtesse Alex was in high favour at Court and enjoyed great influence, which she readily placed at the service of her family and her friends.

But, as we have said, society played a very secondary part in the life of Mme. de Custine, and the young woman devoted most of her time to her artistic tastes. Every day she shut herself up in her studio from mid-day until five o'clock and worked at her painting, for which she had great talent. Though these different occupations were enough to fill her life and make it bearable, her heart, none the less, remained empty. With her ardent desire for affection and love she suffered cruelly and increasingly every day. Maurice Séguier,[1] for whom she had had a moment's tenderness, had been definitely rejected and the young man, in discouragement, went abroad to seek some distraction from his grief.

In 1803 Delphine was still in the prime of life as she was but thirty-three years of age. The terrible sufferings of the Revolution were forgotten and the traces which it had left upon her were almost effaced. Notwithstanding the vicissitudes of her life her dazzling beauty remained unimpaired. The Duchesse d'Abrantes said of her: " She is one of those ravishing creatures given to the world by Providence in a moment of generosity."

Delphine was well aware of her attractions and equally well aware that they were at their height and would soon decline. She had but a few pleasant years of life remaining; was she to waste them in solitude and sadness without profit to herself or to anyone? The failure of her marriage proposals had not discouraged her and she was ever seeking a twin soul to beautify her life and charm her last days. She was in this unsettled frame of mind when, in 1803, a chance meeting disturbed the whole of her existence.

There was in Paris, at that time, a man whose increasing

[1] In 1802 he had accepted a position as chief cashier at Patna, on the Ganges. During the voyage he was captured by the English and remained a prisoner for several years. He was appointed Consul at Trieste in 1806, to the Ionian Islands in 1814, and at London in 1816. He died in 1831.

reputation aroused the enthusiasm of the literary salons. This was the Vicomte René de Chateaubriand; he lent a ready ear to the excessive flattery bestowed upon him and condescended to give readings from his works before certain privileged audiences. He was not unknown to Mme. de Custine; indeed, she had made his acquaintance long before and had met him several times at the house of his sister-in-law, the Comtesse de Chateaubriand. Unfortunately for herself, she met him again at the house of one of her friends. He claimed a fresh introduction, evoked common memories with which they were in sympathy and both recalled with emotion the form of the charming young woman who had perished so miserably upon the scaffold in 1794. Delphine was charmed from the first moment and thought she had at length discovered the heart which she desired so ardently. She surrendered herself without reserve to the passion which carried her away.

Before speaking of this connection which absorbed the whole of Mme. de Custine's life and brought grief and trouble upon her, we may rapidly sketch Chateaubriand's position at this time.

In March, 1792, he had married at Saint Malo an orphan, Mlle. Céleste de Lavigne-Buisson. Three months afterwards he left Saint Malo and joined Condé's army, leaving behind him his young wife, or, as he called her, his young widow, whom he was not to see for another eight years. After a long stay in Germany he went to England and did not return to France until 1800 under a false name, waiting until his own name was erased from the list of *émigrés*. From that time he saw his wife occasionally but they did not live together again until 1804. In 1801 he had published his novel, "Atala," which enjoyed an enormous success. The fortunate author awoke one morning to find himself famous. From this date began Chateaubriand's intimacy with the clever Mme. de Beaumont, the daughter of M. de Montmorin.[1] The young woman's affection for René was unbounded; she defied all prejudices and social conventions.

[1] Pauline de Montmorin-Saint-Herem (1768–1803) had married in 1786 the Comte de Beaumont, "the greatest scamp in Paris." She divorced him in 1800. It was in the famous salon of Joubert that she made the acquaintance of Chateaubriand.

She offered him the hospitality of her country house at Savigny throughout the summer and it was there that he composed the " Genius of Christianity." The appearance of this new work aroused extreme enthusiasm, and admiration of the author became delirium. In speaking of the letters which he received at this time from his admiring female friends Chateaubriand wrote:

"If these notes were not to-day notes from our grandmothers' generation I should find it difficult to relate with proper modesty how they fought for a word from me, how they picked up an envelope written by me and with what blushing they hid it, lowering their heads under the veil of their long hair." The prettiest women were at his feet: " Among the bees which composed their hive was the Marquise de Custine who had inherited the long hair of Marguerite de Provence, the wife of Saint Louis, from whom she was descended." [1]

Apart from her royal blood, her youth and her beauty, Mme. de Custine was no despicable conquest. Her conduct during the Terror had given her a great reputation. So Chateaubriand, while naturally maintaining his intimacy with Mme. de Beaumont, began with Mme. de Custine a mysterious idyll which opened under the best of auspices. At first he showed much enthusiasm for his new conquest and appeared to be deeply in love but unfortunately an unexpected event overthrew these relations at the outset. René, for pressing reasons of which we will speak later, was obliged to accept a post as Secretary to the Embassy at Rome under Cardinal Fesch and could not delay his departure. This unfortunate incident further inflamed the affection thus threatened with an immediate separation. Though he hated the epistolary style and though his longest effusions are generally confined to a few lines, René sent Delphine at this time several emotional letters which may be quoted in view of their rarity:

---

[1] *Mémoires d'Outre-tombe.* It is interesting to notice how amenable Chateaubriand was to the most vulgar vanity and with what satisfaction he underlines everything that he thinks flattering to himself. This tendency, remarkable in a man of such powers, may be constantly observed.

*Mme. de Custine, Rue Martel, first entrance
on the left from the bottom of the street.*

"I live only in the hope of seeing you again. Of your kindness of heart, one single word to help me to pass the day! Yesterday evening I wandered through the streets of Paris without knowing whither I was going! Promise me the castle of Henry IV[1] and promise me to come to Rome."

Delphine had been so imprudent as to visit her friend in the modest room which he occupied in the Hotel d'Étampes in the Rue Saint Honoré and René writes to her in delight:

"Another day without seeing you! You will spend it very peaceably, painting, stroking Trim and forgetting that there is any one who loves you in the world. My cell is a very sad one; a miserable clouded sun, a cold wind, a room stripped of its furniture, and so already advertising my departure. Some time ago all this would have been of no consequence to me, but a saintly apparition has visited me in my dwelling and has made separation unbearable."[2]

"A saintly apparition" was indeed a somewhat risky metaphor. The other notes belonging to this period are of so little importance that they are hardly worth the trouble of quotation.

Why, then, did Chateaubriand leave Paris, where there were so many attractions, apart from the opportunity of continuing his intimacy with Mme. de Custine? He has himself given several different explanations of his departure. At this time he wrote to Fontanes, in a letter from Rome:

"Such is the point to which domestic troubles have brought me. The fear of meeting my wife has driven me out of the country a second time. The shortest kinds of foolishness are the best. I rely upon your friendship to get me out of this morass."

Thus it appears that he went away to escape the wife who was pursuing him. On the other hand, in the "Mémoires d'Outre-tombe" he writes these touching lines which may rouse some belief in the generosity of his heart:

[1] Mme. de Custine was at that moment negotiating for the purchase of the estate of Fervaques, in Normandy, where Henry IV had lived.
[2] These letters have been published by M. Bardoux, to whom they were communcicated by M. La Caille.

"The daughter of M. de Montmorin was dying and it was said that the climate of Italy might prolong her life. If I went to Rome she would be ready to cross the Alps; so I sacrificed myself in the hope of saving her." In this case, then, he left Delphine in order to prolong the life of Mme. de Beaumont. The reader may be allowed to choose which explanation he prefers as the truth.

Before leaving Paris he begged Mme. de Custine to come and see him at Rome. He wrote to her: "The idea of leaving you kills me," but this did not prevent him from starting cheerfully for the Eternal City, which he reached on June 25, 1803. Delphine was, of course, in despair at the departure of the man she loved and felt the separation the more keenly, as she well knew that Mme. de Beaumont proposed to rejoin René. As a matter of fact, Mme. de Beaumont, who remained very ill, reached Rome in the early days of October.

In July Delphine went to Plombières for the season as a consolation for René's departure. On her return, in the month of September, she went with Astolphe to Saint Léger and spent the remainder of the summer with her mother. For some months she had been negotiating for the purchase of an estate in Normandy; this business had been interrupted by her absence, but she resumed it immediately upon her return. It may be asked how Delphine, whom we have constantly seen in straitened circumstances, could think of buying an estate. Thanks to Fouché's help, she had recovered possession of much of her confiscated property, and her material prospects had become almost brilliant. There was no reason why she should not devote an important sum to the purchase of an estate. She had always been fond of the country and of the woods, and her tastes for a calm and peaceable life became stronger every day. It was therefore natural that she should seek a refuge where she could spend every summer with Astolphe and form a definite home. After many researches her friend, M. de Chaumont-Quitry, pointed out to her near Lisieux the Château of Fervaques in a delightful valley. She went to see it, was attracted by it, and immediately began negotiations with the owners. It was a somewhat historical castle, as Henry IV had lived in it when he honoured the lady of Fervaques with his favours.

After some discussion Delphine at length agreed with the vendors, and on October 27, 1803, she signed the deed for the purchase of Fervaques for the sum of 478,764 livres, plus an annual rent of 8,691 livres.[1] As soon as the deed was signed Mme. Custine went to her new possession to prepare for the necessary alterations and repairs. She wished to live in the Château the next spring, for which purpose it must be put in order. After giving the necessary instructions she returned to Paris. No sooner had she returned than she heard a piece of news which must have been doubly agreeable to her. Her rival, Mme. de Beaumont, had just succumbed at Rome to the malady from which she had suffered for many years. Chateaubriand did not wish to prolong his stay in a city which held such painful memories for him, and had asked to be recalled to France.

[1] See Bardoux, "Mme. de Custine." This estate belonged to the Duc de Montmorency-Laval and his sister, the Duchesse de Luynes.

CHAPTER XXV

January—June, 1804

Chateaubriand's return to Paris—He resumes his intimacy with Mme. de Custine—He is appointed minister at Sion—His resignation—Departure of Mme. de Custine for Fervaques—She is received with great ceremony—Her stay at Fervaques.

As we have seen at the end of the preceding chapter, Chateaubriand after the death of Mme. de Beaumont, declared himself unable to endure a longer stay in the Eternal City and wrote to the minister asking that he might be recalled to France. His request was granted.[1] He reached Paris in February, 1804, and put up at the Hôtel de France, in the Rue de Beaune, where his wife was awaiting him. Henceforward the couple resumed their common life for the first time in ten years.

At the same time he reopened his connection with Delphine which had been unfortunately interrupted by the journey to Rome. Their intimacy became even greater than before and they met every day.[2] Mme. de Custine, relieved of a hated rival, was happier than she had ever been: she could well tolerate the existing wife, knowing what she did of her lover's feelings.

---

[1] Before leaving Rome he went to offer one last prayer at the tomb of the woman who had loved him so well. Referring to the incident in his *Mémoires*, he writes:—

"Did not my grief cling, in those distant days, to the assurance that the tie which had just been broken would be the last? Yet, if I had not forgotten it, how quickly I supplied the void in my affection. Thus man proceeds from weakness to weakness."

[2] He had brought back from Rome as a souvenir a leaf picked from the tomb of Virgil. This leaf still exists in the packet of letters in the possession of M. La Caille.

At this moment, when Delphine thought she had at length found the happiness of her dreams, a new cause of grief occurred. René, who was devoured by ambition and could never remain in one place, had hardly arrived at Paris than he secured an appointment as French Minister in the Valais. He was delighted and hurried on his preparations for departure. That he might cut a better figure in the new country to which he was accredited, he resolved to take Mme. de Chateaubriand with him to Sion. While Delphine was lamenting this second separation from the object of her adoration a tragic incident occurred which cut short the young diplomatist's career for the moment.

In March, 1804, the Duc d'Enghien had been seized upon German territory, taken to Paris, condemned and executed in the trenches of Vincennes. This brutal and precipitate action aroused the utmost indignation, not only throughout France but also in the whole of Europe. It alienated from the Empire many who were anxious to serve it. Chateaubriand immediately made his wife's health a pretext for sending in his resignation. Delphine from that day broke off her intimacy with Mme. Bonaparte and was seen no more at Malmaison. While deploring the reason, Delphine was delighted at the consequences which allowed her to keep her dear René near her at Paris. They constantly met and spent such time together as they could steal from social claims and she was extraordinarily happy. He was no ordinary admirer, exacting, peevish, distrustful and greedy of flattery, but Delphine's affection excused all this and for some months she spent the only happy time with which this intimacy was to provide her.

The fact became public property and people began to talk, but far from feeling any vexation, Delphine rather prided herself upon the fact. She did not hesitate to introduce the Génie, as she familiarly called Chateaubriand, to her family. Mme. de Boufflers, who had a wide experience of the world and whose troubles had made her tolerant, yielded to this desire and when Delphine introduced her friend she received him very kindly. He, on the other hand, was not profoundly impressed by Delphine's family: he certainly thought Mme. de Boufflers charming, although " somewhat depressed by exile and privation." Elzéar he disliked at first sight; "he is too clever for me," he said bitterly and their acquaintance ended there.

As Chateaubriand had abandoned a diplomatic career, he had resolved after due reflection, actuated in some degree by the persuasions of Delphine, to remain at Paris. He set up house with his wife in the Rue de Miromesnil, No. 1119, in a little residence at the corner of the Rue Verte by the side of the vast gardens of Tivoli and Monceau, almost in the country.[1] Hitherto Mme. de Custine had lived in the Rue Martel; this was a long way from the Rue Verte and considerable inconvenience to the two friends would be the result. Delphine therefore found a simple means of overcoming the difficulty and moved to a house nearer to René's new home. The destiny favourable to lovers ordained that a flat should be vacant at the corner of the Rue Verte and the Rue de Miromesnil, just opposite to Chateaubriand's small residence. Careless of inevitable gossip, Delphine was bold enough to set up house there with Astolphe and Berstöcher. It must be admitted that she thereby scandalously advertised the fact of her intimacy, but she did not hesitate.

In the month of May, in spite of her vexation at leaving Paris, Mme. de Custine was obliged to enter into possession of the Château of Fervaques which she had bought in Normandy. The repairs and reconstructions which she had ordered were finished; it was necessary that she should examine for herself the manner in which her orders had been carried out, if she wished to see her family and her friends there in the summer as she intended to do. However, before appearing on her estate in person Delphine considered that it would be indispensable for her to have a kind of agent who would help her to manage the estate and supervise both it and the Château during her absence. In her correspondence we have often met with a certain Abbé Gibelin, whom she had known for a long time and of whom the whole family were very fond. The Abbé Gibelin had been ruined by the Revolution, but he had taken to himself a wife by way of

---

[1] At that time houses were numbered by districts and not by streets. The Great and Little Rue Verte are at the present time the Rue de Penthièvre and the Rue Matignon.

compensation and was very happy in his new estate if not particularly well off. Delphine thought of him as the future agent of Fervaques. Gibelin, when the question was put, accepted gladly and gratefully and immediately started with Mme. Gibelin to prepare the rooms. The first impression of the agent upon his arrival at his future residence was not entirely favourable, but fortunately he changed his opinion. Delphine writes to her mother: " We have had further details from the little Gibi. They are enough to make one die of laughing and we will keep the amusing parts for you to read. The following day was happier than the evening before and he began to think that the place was not so bad as it looked. Indeed, after a further examination, he thought it charming. As you know, this is the way in which great affections, or, at any rate, the most permanent affections are formed. The second impression remains indelible. So the matter is now decided; Gibi is quite happy, but what will he be when we are all there and he can count up the generations as he always does."

As soon as Gibi was installed Mme. de Custine could come when she liked. Her chief regret was the enforced separation from her dear friend, but he promised to write to her and to come and stay with her in July, and, relying upon his word, she resolved to start. She left Paris with the whole of her household, a complete change of residence. Chateaubriand, who watched the process of embarkation, saw Mme. de Custine, Astolphe, Berstöcher and Fanny the chamber-maid, crammed into the carriage, not to speak of Trim, the faithful dog, who had a cheerful habit of devouring the provisions for the journey. When everybody was packed in and stowed away the coach rumbled off to Bernay, and we may leave Mme. de Custine to tell her mother, with her charming gaiety, the story of her arrival at her new estate and the welcome which she received from the inhabitants.

"FERVAQUES, *Wednesday morning*,
"*May*, 1804.

" Well, little mother, here I am, established, fêted and fairly well satisfied and should be entirely so if you were here to see all our work and to share our glory. Really I am greatly touched by the interest that is shown in me. As you like details I will draw up my narrative with a minuteness worthy of Bertelier.

"We reached Bernay on Monday at ten o'clock and found a wretched inn and a still more wretched supper and no news from Fervaques. The next day we started again at nine o'clock. For several leagues over a dreadful road we had seen nothing, and all our hopes sank into the depths of the ruts, when, from the top of a hill, at the corner of the wood, we noticed a row of horsemen drawn up in battle array, who, at sight of us, gave us a military salute and approached our carriage. I recognised M. Jaquette, the mayor of Fervaques, who said with much grace and kindness: 'Mme. I have been unable to restrain the anxiety with which the inhabitants of Fervaques desire to express to yourself the delight which they feel at your arrival in the country.' There was I, blushing at the window, bowing graciously and saying, 'I am grateful, touched, overwhelmed, &c.' The weather was less polite and had bespattered the cavalcade, which had been hove to for two hours in spite of the rain which continued even after our arrival. Then it was a case of, 'What weather! how sorry I am to see you so wet, gentlemen!' with a countenance correspondingly regretful.

"The commander of the troop, a very well-made gentleman who rode like an angel, arranged the order of march and I was escorted thus by the whole band. I had some fear that we might be upset, which somewhat disturbed my speeches, but no one seemed to notice it, for they are so accustomed to bad roads that they think this one excellent. On the way I noticed a gentleman near the carriage riding a delightful horse, and trying to think of something to say to him I put my head out and graciously observed, 'Sir, that is a very pretty horse of yours,' 'Madam, it is yours,' was the reply. I was thus overwhelmed and entirely delighted.

"When we reached the territory of Fervaques a joyful band presented me with a bouquet; a cross on the road was adorned with flowers, and apart from the rain everything was very pleasant. I have forgotten to tell you about the country. I have seen nothing prettier or fresher or more countrified. It is a miniature Switzerland.

"Then, after much jolting, we reached Fervaques. The streets were lined with inhabitants, all happy and cheerful. Everything was there, down to fireworks and gunshots. I was accompanied to my home and there they told me that they merely wished to see me into the house and not to cause me embarrassment, and that they would come and see me at a more opportune moment. I replied that as soon as my baggage had arrived I should be delighted to receive them.

"So I am now in my Château, and I ran to the window to look at the garden; it is charming and will be prettier still when the trees have grown larger. Then I looked at the rooms and nothing was finished; thereupon lamentations began. Mine may be habitable in three weeks, but there is a great deal to be done, and a corresponding amount of annoyance to be endured. Gibi was at the window with his better half, rubbing his hands and strutting about entirely delighted. He seems to be happy and so does his wife. We chatted the whole day. After dinner I strolled round the grounds and the garden which delighted me, and I have seen nothing so pretty. M. de Quitry was not there to receive my compliments; he is away and will not be back for a day or two.

"As we drove along, the church bells rang and cannon-shots were fired. After the drive the clergy and townspeople, our mounted escort and the ladies in full dress appeared with splendid bunches of flowers and charming lines of verse which I send to you. The Mayor said to me as he came in, 'Madam, your village comes to express its happiness at seeing you here.' Their faces were beaming and they meant it very kindly. Unfortunately we had not chairs for everyone as there were at least 50 people. But it all seemed to be very informal and really kindly meant. To-morrow the farmers and workmen are coming. Finally, at ten o'clock, I was able to go to bed quite exhausted.

"Such is the faithful narrative of our day. Come as soon as you can and share our joys and give us your advice. The tower has had a respite; I think it charming and I hope you will see it and pronounce judgment upon it. And now, mother, I must stop, for I have a thousand things to do. Tell Elzéar about our reception. His head would be quite turned by this country. There is nothing prettier and it is said to be the most beautiful valley in Normandy. A thousand kind remembrances to your husband. Gibi and his wife are prostrate at your feet."

Some days after her arrival Mme. de Custine had the pleasure of receiving a letter from the Génie, short but pleasant and cheerful, in which he joked about her constant fear that her friends would forget her. He confirmed his proposals and said that he would certainly come in July; "It will be a kind of fairy tale: he travelled very far until he reached Fervaques, where there lived a fairy devoid of commonsense. She was known as Princess Hopeless because after two days of silence she always thought that her friends were dead or gone to China and that she would never see them again."[1]

Satisfied upon the question of his visit which she was expecting so impatiently, Delphine resumed her correspondence with her mother. Her letters are simple, straightforward and charmingly graceful. In every line may be felt the exquisite intimacy existing between mother and daughter, and the profound affection which united them. Unfortunately we have not the answers sent by Mme. de Boufflers, but from our knowledge of her they must have been adorable. On June 13 Delphine writes to her mother begging her to visit them and tells her of their peaceable life with which she would be charmed. At the same time she refers in touching terms to the first Communion of Astolphe:—

"*June* 13.

"I am most disappointed, little mother, that you do not think more seriously of coming here. We want you and long for you with all our hearts. Try to arrange it, then, as soon as possible. Come with all the rest, or, at any rate, with my brother; a few are better than none at all. The crowning point of our joy would certainly be to see you all here together, but it is often extremely difficult to get people

[1] *Chateaubriand et Mme. de Custine*, by Chedieu de Robethon. Plon-Nourrit & Co., 1893.

to think alike. Make an effort, preach to them and contrive it, but come and see us. Give me a definite date; as long as I am sure that you will come during my stay this year I will leave you to settle the time, and any date most convenient to you will suit me. For your own sake I should prefer that it were now, for the country is delightfully beautiful.

"What you say about your health makes me very uneasy; you say you are not satisfied with it. Try to take the 'life-giving grains of Doctor Franck'; they will do you no harm. You must then come and get fat upon our good cow's milk.

"After inconceivable fears I have at length ridden my horse. I eventually found him very nice but he is spirited and I tremble like a leaf. I hope I shall soon get used to him.

"We have had a great event since I wrote to you last, Astolphe's first Communion. He really was angelical; the priest is full of his purity, his candour, and the piety of his behaviour. There were seventy-two children and the ceremony was most pretty and touching. It was last Sunday; you would have been delighted with the simplicity of it all, and I am sure that you would have wept. We all thought of you. The little Gibi, who is our official master of ceremonies, largely contributes to the solemnity of this one.

"I have just read in the newspaper that Armand de Polignac has been pardoned. I am extremely glad to hear it, and bless the hand that brought it about. I have no doubt he will be equally delighted, for the pleasure ought to be great.

"Goodbye, mother, write to tell me what you are doing and what is to become of you. I send you and my brother kisses, also others from Gibi and Blondet; while the friend who hears this says, me too. Trim is barking, so are Gibi's little dogs, my birds are singing with deafening shrillness, and the uproar is so great that one's ears ring with it. A thousand kind remembrances to my brother and your husband."

Though Delphine wrote a great deal to her mother, she wrote still more to Chateaubriand, and took a natural pleasure in telling him of the little incidents of her life. Astolphe's first communion was the great event of the week, and she gave him a pleasant account of it. But the Génie, peevish and always ready to sermonise, did not take the matter in this way. He mounted his high horse and replied to the kindly effusion of his friend with the following dressing-down:—

"*June* 18, 1804.

" Please understand that I do not think very much of this first communion. I think you have hurried your son into it precipitately; I would wager that he does not know a word of the principles of religion. The little girls in white were dirty, and the priest is a stupid fellow; so much is clear. The ceremony is only of use when the children have been long and carefully instructed, and when they are brought to their first Communion, not as a matter of form, but from religious motives. You have made your son undergo the ceremony, though he does not even observe the simple rule of Friday, and perhaps does not even go to Mass on Sunday. Such is what you have gained by telling the whole story to a father of the Church, no doubt very unworthy but always loyal, committing great sins but knowing that he is doing wrong and repenting eternally.

"Expect me at Fervaques about the end of July."[1]

In spite of the kind urging of her daughter, Mme. de Boufflers did not announce her arrival. In fact, she did not speak of coming. This time Delphine grew angry; it was absolutely necessary that her mother should see her in her new estate:—

"LISIEUX, *June* 20.

" How is it, little mother, that we have no more news from you ? Far from coming, you do not even answer my letters. I am in despair; the month is almost at an end and you do not come. I am sad even to death ; there is no day that we do not miss you. We really must see you here this year, sooner or later. Write to me definitely; there is nothing so sad as not to know what has become of you.

[1] *Op. cit.*

"Since yesterday I have been in my own rooms. They are most pretty and I should like to see you there so much and to hear your cries of wonderment.

"My son and the friend are not yet in their own rooms; we shall have the workmen in the house for at least six weeks, but it will be very pleasant. If we had plenty of money we would finish the Château and the house would be delightful, but even so, I hope that it will not displease you. In short, like certain birds, I am beginning to grow used to my cage. We lead the most monotonous life but the time seems to have doubled its rapidity; the days go by with terrifying speed, very quietly, like the river under my windows. Do not let the finest days pass without coming. What has become of your husband and my brother? Wherever they are they will never be as well off as they would be here."

Confronted by her daughter's protests Mme. de Boufflers decided to answer. She could not come immediately as she had a thousand things to do which would keep her at home but she promised to visit her at the end of July. Delphine was in despair at this further delay and hoped that her mother would compensate for it by staying longer. In this letter she gave her some amusing details concerning the process of setting up house, about her servants and about a wonderful gardener whom her mother had chosen and who seemed to be a great scoundrel but so clever and invaluable that they could not part with him:

"*June* 22, 1804.

"I am very sorry to hear that you are not coming this month and not until the end of July. I can only hope that these constant hesitations will bring you as a birthday present, certainly the finest that could be given to me.

"Your wretched gardener is a constant source of torture; no one could be more energetic, more intelligent or a better thief. I keep an eye on him; it is only too easy at present for there is no fruit or vegetables and very few flowers. His work is the admiration of the country-side. As life goes on, scoundrels are the only people we respect, for they alone have energy and ideas of their own. Others, with their scruples and their honesty, give way to the scoundrels and go to sleep on their good consciences. So it is in this country; everybody is asleep and everything is to be done in the future; hence the completion of any piece of work is a real phenomenon in the country and raises admiration. You can imagine how that suits us. Our gardener is therefore perfect; had it not been for him the English garden would have neither finish nor beauty; he is an expert in every way. When you come you will see whether we are wrong.

"I am delighted to hear of the end of the great lawsuit. I knew quite well that he would never do anything that was not great and generous when he could act on his own initiative. Long live the Emperor, if we are not to see blood flow or people harassed and unhappy. Are you applying again to the Consuls? Tell me all about it.

"Goodbye, little mother, the frogs are making such a noise that I do not know what I am writing. They say that it is a sign of fine weather. My room is charming and I am never tired of admiring it; it is as white as Saint Léger. I send you my best love; take care of your health. Take baths, eat fruit and come and rest at Fervaques. A thousand remembrances to your husband and my brother."

At the end of June Astolphe was confirmed by the Bishop of Bayeux. Mme. de Custine writes to her mother on July 1:

"Yesterday we had an episcopal visit from the Bishop of Bayeux and Astolphe was confirmed. The divine manna, however, was not enough for him, for he eats more like an ogre than an angel. The Bishop stayed with us and we turned everything upside down to receive him. He is kind and pleasant and has confirmed nearly four thousand people at Fervaques; crowds came from the neighbourhood. The ceremony was held in a field as the church was not big enough. It was most picturesque and I assure you that the effect was charming."

Mme. de Custine was by no means isolated in her district; she had pleasant neighbours who often came to amuse her and spend a few days with her. Those most frequently seen at Fervaques were Mme. des Boulets and Mme. de Cauvigny. The first was an excellent woman but rather stupid and silly, with so little conversation that Mme. de Custine nicknamed her "my headache," a name which stuck to her. The second, on the contrary, was a charming character, lively, cheerful and clever. Her appearance was no less attractive than her mind; a pretty face and an agreeably plump figure made her equally delightful. Delphine was very fond of her and saw as much of her as possible. When Mme. de Cauvigny was at Fervaques, boredom was unknown and the hours flew by. Another well-known neighbour at the Château was Guy de Chaumont-Quitry who had pointed out Fervaques to Mme. de Custine and had induced her to buy it. But he was a character hard to please and touchy; his visits usually ended in a quarrel and "his society was an inferno." So he was not often invited. He caused Delphine an infinite amount of trouble by buying horses and carriages for her without the necessary warranty. Lawsuits were the result and the matter was not settled until the autumn. "Meanwhile," says Delphine sadly, "the law keeps my horses impounded. For two months they have not gone out of the courtyard and it is said that they will die of fat. Thus our horses and carriages disappear from view. If they had been made of sugar, we might at least have had a taste of them."

Mme. de Custine's correspondence with her mother is entirely delightful; the young woman's letters are gay and lively; she uses and abuses the inexhaustible kindness of Mme. de Boufflers, is continually asking for advice and giving her the most impossible commissions, each more urgent than the last, but all so pleasantly, with such gracefulness and affection as to seem quite natural. Berstöcher's birthday was in July and Delphine was anxious to make a present to Astolphe's devoted tutor, the friend who had given innumerable proofs of his attachment and devotion. From the outset of June she had been considering the question and was hesitating between a coffee-pot and a handsome seal. Mme. de Boufflers, when consulted, replied that the coffee-pot would cost three hundred francs. Delphine exclaimed at the figure and did not want to spend more than sixty. The friend would never pardon her for so expensive a present at a moment when she was herself short of money. She therefore inclined to the seal and sent a design to her mother. Of course it must have every perfection, must be simple, in good taste, not mean, of good gold, not too small and not too big, the handle of ivory and, above all, must not cost more than sixty francs, and had better cost forty. Mme. de Boufflers must apply to a first-class jeweller, Fourrier or Le Sage, for "the small ones are scoundrels, especially on the boulevards, where they swindle you fearfully."

Provided with these instructions Mme. de Boufflers started out docilely and a first-class jeweller undertook to manufacture the object for three louis. This time Delphine was satisfied and soon sent her final instructions:

"FERVAQUES, *July* 1, 1804.

"Well, little mother, I have decided in favour of the seal. The lettering is to be two J.'s and a B. to be arranged as artistically as possible. I should like to have thought of a clever motto to put round the letters but I cannot think; the air here is fatal to the intellect and my mind feels the influence of it. As soon as the seal is made, please pack it up and send it to Robert, Rue du Vieux Colombier, near the Rue de Gindre, No. 741 Faubourg Saint-Germain. Try to please me, little mother, and it will be very nice of you, for I do not know how to settle this birthday present otherwise."

Mme. de Boufflers performed this commission with so much cleverness that it would have been a pity not to give her some more, so Delphine finds errands for her at every opportunity. Another time she wanted some glass for the windows of the cottage, and no ordinary glass, as may be seen:

"Another errand, little mother. I am afraid it will bore you to death, but you are so kind that you will do it beautifully. I want six pieces of glass, 7 ins. by 10 ins. for the windows of the little cottage. But it must be coloured glass and each piece a separate colour so that the six are not alike; looking through one of them the effect is to be that of a storm, through another we shall see fine weather, through another moonlight, and through another, rain. Through the rest, I do not know what. As soon as you have chosen them, get a man to pack them up and send them by post to Lisieux, Rue Notre Dame des Victoires, to my address here. I do not think it will cost much, you will let me know and I will send you the money. If you can look after my glass for me I shall be delighted; nothing gets finished here except life and I must finish my cottage."

CHAPTER XXVI

July—December, 1804

Chateaubriand's visit to Fervaques—Chênedollé—Chateaubriand's second visit—Correspondence with Mme. de Boufflers.

MME. DE CUSTINE impatiently awaited the month of July as the date which the Génie had fixed for his visit. But, unfortunately, instead of the visit so often promised Delphine received a harsh, bitter letter in which her friend reproached her for betraying a secret which he had entrusted to her honour and threatened her with an immediate and irrevocable breach. The incident to which this letter referred was as follows. While Chateaubriand was at Rome, being, as usual, in straitened circumstances, he needed five thousand francs and applied to Delphine under the seal of secrecy. Mme. de Custine was naturally very jealous of Mme. de Beaumont and supposing, with some reason, that the money was intended to supply the needs of her rival, she flatly refused. However, the story was noised abroad, by what agency is unknown, and some charitable person repeated the whole of it to René. Angry at an indiscretion of which, as he thought, Delphine alone could be guilty, he wrote, as we have just said, a letter to break off their intimacy.[1]

The receipt of this letter threw Mme. de Custine into the most dreadful state of despair. Perhaps she felt herself a little guilty or perhaps her sin was one of carelessness; at any rate she wrote letter after letter to exculpate herself and to prove her innocence. At length, after repeated prayers and protestations, the Génie was mollified and peace was made. The old proposals were resumed and in the month of

[1] See *Chateaubriand et Mme. de Custine*, by M. Chedieu de Robethon.

August René started for Fervaques where he was impatiently awaited. On August 22nd he arrived and was received with all the honours. He was naturally given the finest room, that in which Henry IV had lived. He condescended to express his satisfaction and had the pleasure of being able to write to his friends that he was sleeping in the bed of the ruler of Béarn. At a later date, in his *Mémoires*, alluding to the souvenirs left by Henry IV, he wrote:

"On the chimney-piece in the Château I read these wretched rhymes, attributed to the lover of Gabrielle:

"'The Lady of Fervaques
Is worth a keen attack.'

"The soldier king has said as much to many others, transitory declarations quickly obliterated and handed down from beauty to beauty until the time of Mme. de Custine."

As René was not anxious for too intimate conversation he had written to one of his close friends, Chênedollé,[1] who lived in the district, to come and meet him. As Chênedollé did not know Delphine, the proposal was somewhat delicate. He yielded, however, to the request of his friend, came and was introduced to the mistress of the Château who, naturally only too happy to be able to please her idol, gave Chênedollé the warmest welcome and all went off excellently. Delphine on her side, always thoughtful and anxious to please, invited her neighbour and great friend, Mme. de Cauvigny, and the cheerfulness of this pleasant woman contributed to make the stay at Fervaques yet more agreeable.

Delphine was at her wits' end to devise some distraction for her guest, in the hope that he would be pleased with his visit and be anxious to return. She appeared happy, cheerful and radiant, and displayed every mark of extreme affection. Chênedollé, who observed this touching and somewhat misunderstood sentiment, felt for her and showed a real friendship for the young woman. Therefore, thanks to their united efforts, the days went rapidly by and Chateau-

[1] Chateaubriand and Chênedollé had known one another in London and had become very close friends. Chênedollé fell deeply in love with his friend's sister, Mme. de Caux, and wrote of her: "The man who has not known Lucile cannot know what beauty and delicacy there is in a woman's heart." Though Mme. de Caux, who was a widow, felt a warm affection for her adorer, she persistently refused to marry him.

briand condescended to express some satisfaction. He often said that he would come back in October for another visit and these promises overwhelmed Delphine with delight. He remained at Fervaques until August 29, but when he went away he was careful to warn Delphine that he did not like long letters.[1] However, the next day he sent these kindly words from Lisieux :

"I already feel bored so far from you and the farther I seem to leave you behind the nearer I come to you." No sooner had he reached Paris than he wrote as follows :

"*Monday, September 3.*

"I miss Fervaques, the carps, you, Chênedollé, and even Mme. Auguste. I should very much like to come and see it all again in October; indeed, it is my dearest wish. Are you as anxious to have me back again? Is our friend out of bed yet? I should be glad if he could do without my quinine.

"Try to make the billiard table level and pull up the weeds so that the pike can be seen, fatten the calves and make the fowls lay fresher eggs. When all that has been done and when M. Gibelin has put the last of the Guelfs to death, you shall tell me, and I will see if it is possible to make my way to Fervaques.

"Many thanks, may you be well and happy, and a thousand remembrances to Chênedollé. Is he still with you? Remember me also to your good son. I trust that Providence will preserve Mme. de Cauvigny's cheerfulness, plumpness and amiability."[2]

This bantering and careless letter, in which René made not the least allusion to the pleasant hours of conversation in which the poor woman had poured out her heart, wounded Delphine deeply. She replied in distress : "I cannot help feeling some surprise that, amid your long list, you had not a word to say of the grotto or of the little study and its two

---

[1] Mme. de Duras wrote one day: "M. de Chateaubriand does not spoil his friends. I am afraid he is somewhat spoilt by their devotion. His replies to letters never have any connection with their contents; I am not sure that he reads the letters he receives."

[2] *Chateaubriand et Mme. de Custine*, by Chedieu de Robethon.

splendid myrtles. I hardly think you can have forgotten it so quickly. Your friend, Chênedollé is still here, but he is going to-morrow. I am sadder than I can say, and I shall see nothing more of your favourite sights. Some parts of your letter have really hurt me."[1]

René did not even take the trouble to reply, and some days afterwards he started for Burgundy with his wife, to make a long stay with the Joubert family at Villeneuve-sur-Yonne.

In the course of September Berstöcher fell very ill. He suffered from a high fever; the doctors were unable to explain the reason, and were powerless to help him. Delphine was deeply grieved; she had a profound affection for this good, kind man, who had become a friend of the household, and the thought that he might die reduced her to despair. She spent whole nights nursing him, and at length the invalid passed the crisis and gradually recovered. But this trial had completely exhausted Madame de Custine's strength; she had suffered so much and for so many years that she could bear no more. In her turn she took to her bed with a terrible liver attack. In a few hours she was in such a deplorable condition as to cause the greatest anxiety to all about her.

M. Morin, the famous doctor of Lisieux, was hastily summoned, and though he considered her condition painful, he foresaw no serious complications. He reassured everyone, and asserted that it was unnecessary to summon Mme. de Boufflers. At length the attack passed away, and Delphine was able to get up and resume her correspondence with her mother at the end of a few days.

"*Monday.*[2]

"Well, little mother, I am still in the world, and in spite of the devil I have got through this time. I have had a fine escape. How terrified and anxious you would have been! For two days I was in such dreadful pain that I have never felt anything like it, and I am now like a poor storm-tossed bird, pale, thin, and terribly sad. They say that this

[1] *Mme. de Custine*, Bardoux.
[2] To Mme. de Boufflers, care of M. Paulin, contractor, Rue de Paris, near the Marché-Neuf, Saint Germain en Laye.

will pass, and I try to believe it. Meanwhile I take baths and drink herb tea and whey twice a day.

"So I am to see you all again! My heart sank at the thought that I should see you no more. I felt so grieved at the idea of leaving you when we were at the point of a happy meeting, and at the idea that we had come here only to remain, that I feel quite afraid when I remember it.

"Astolphe behaved admirably and was dreadfully anxious. Berstöcher was quite wild with grief and would have been overcome if it had lasted long. Just think that in the middle of all these disturbances the Prefect and Mme. de Cauvigny arrived. The latter charmed us but the Prefect was a great nuisance. I did not see him; the others undertook to entertain him; he was very sympathetic with the trouble in which he found our poor household and only stayed two days."

Delphine was the happier to find her health restored, for the reason that the arrival of the Génie was announced for the end of the month. He would hardly make excuses for anyone unable to receive him, and he had arranged to meet Chênedollé as in the month of August. Chateaubriand, therefore, arrived on October 22 as he had promised. But apparently a jealous fate strove to disturb this much-desired meeting. We will leave Delphine to tell her woes to her mother in her own person:

"You are very kind to remember the 20th. He arrived on the 19th but do not tell anyone, as he does not wish it to be known. As there is never any rose without a thorn, he found Mme. des Boulets here who suits him as well as walnut shells suit our cat. Mme. de Cauvigny had returned to Caen. His friend (Chênedollé) had had a fall from his horse and could not come at the appointed time. So he has been reduced to the society of Mme. des Boulets. I feel that he is bored and am so ill at ease that I hardly know what I am saying. To crown all this, one of our neighbours, one of Mme. des Boulets' delightful acquaintances, arrived yesterday. He is a personage who can think of nothing but horses and dress, and is rather tactless and stupid. As if that were likely to suit our poor Génie! His face is therefore long enough to break one's heart. Mme. de Cauvigny is to return to-morrow and I look forward to her visit as though she were an angel. Never have I felt the want of her pleasant cheerfulness so much. So I am here, shackled to people most truly stupid. We should have been so comfortable and happy if it had not been for these inconveniences."

The misfortunes which Delphine thus humorously describes did not rouse the pleasantest of tempers in the Génie. But still he might have had pity upon his friend who had just been seriously ill and was not entirely recovered, and to whom strong emotions were harmful. René, however, showed no consideration, and was more peevish, more exacting, and more disagreeable than ever. This went on to such an extent that one evening when they returned from a drive in the course of which Chateaubriand had not opened his mouth, Delphine in despair seized a gun with which he had been shooting in the morning and attempted to kill herself. Chateaubriand went away on the 27th without seeing Chênedollé, who had not recovered from his fall and did not arrive until his friend had gone.

In writing to her mother Mme. de Custine carefully avoided any mention of the vexation which the Génie had caused her, and tried to give the impression that she was happy. On October 28 she writes :

" He was pleasant and cheerful during his stay here, but now he is gone, and his departure makes Fervaques even sadder than the fall of the leaves."

Scarcely had he reached Paris than Chateaubriand wrote to Mme. de Custine :

" I left your owls' castle, and was sorry to do so. I should not like to see it too often, for I fear that I might contract an unfortunate attachment for it. Try to leave it soon and come back among the living. Remember that you will be my neighbour, and that I shall be able to see you as often as you like."

Delphine, however, was not deluded by these pleasant phrases, and remained impressed by the ferocious selfishness and hardheartedness which her friend had shown ; she complains and laments. René then grows vexed, in the security of a good conscience and tartly replies :

"You persecute me over much. Can I do more than I have done? I have been to see you twice against all common sense. I stayed with you as long, and even longer, than I could. I assure you that I am grieved by your unjust complaints; I really do not know what more I can do to please you. Try to understand that reason is not on your side, and be a little grateful to me for my travels, which I assure you I would not have undertaken for anyone but you. When, eternal grumbler, will you return to Paris? When will you leave your Château? I would wager that you are still frowning upon me, but I assure you that if you welcome me with a surly face you will only see me once more, for I am weary of your perpetual injustice. Let us have peace. Come and repair your wrong-doing, confess your sins, and I will receive you with mercy. But let the pardon be a sincere one. "Ever yours."

After this severe reprimand he started for Villeneuve-sur-Yonne to the Joubert family and gave no further sign of life.

When we carefully study the relations between Mme. de Custine and Chateaubriand, we can only be astounded at the inconceivable patience shown by the young woman. Gentleness, tenderness and affection on her part are met by hardness, indifference and domineering on his. The less she asks, the more he demands. Mme. de Custine's character had been matured by trials and misfortunes, and strangely softened; she had thought of possible happiness and looked to find it with René. She was accustomed to general admiration, yet she now accepts rebuffs without protest, and is mild and submissive beneath reprimands, however violent. She will not be rebuffed or rejected and bears everything in the vain hope of mollifying an unendurably vain character. It may be conscientiously said that if Mme. de Custine committed many mistakes and faults, she paid for them dearly during her association with René. Although she shows a certain dignity and does not complain, we shall see, in the course of this narrative, that deception and mental troubles eventually disgusted her with life, and the poor creature will be heard uttering cries of pain in the weariness of her torments.

As soon as Chateaubriand had left Fervaques the unbearable Mme. des Boulets considered that she could be of no more use, and returned to her hearth and home. General delight in the Château was the consequence, which was increased by the fact that the charming Mme. de Cauvigny prolonged her stay. When she went away in her turn everyone was in despair:

"*November* 6.

"We are in a pitiable state of weariness and sadness; we cannot do without her. You have no idea how good and kind and cheerful she is; our praises never stop. I was so accustomed to her sweet friendship that I can give you no idea of my present loneliness. For the first time Fervaques seems huge, the Château seems ancient, and I feel myself in isolation. She enlivened everything and was so good to me that she has absolutely spoilt me; I really cannot do without her. Astolphe and Berstöcher were charmed with her; they are both like lost children."

At the moment of separation Delphine induced Mme. de Cauvigny to promise a visit in Paris during the winter. But promises did not fully reassure her; she had experienced so many disappointments in life that she distrusted the future. She writes sadly:

"I take little account of mere hopes and even shrink from them, for they are but so many implements placed in the hands of fate to mock us. Unfortunately the present is not so happy that we can afford to give up the future. At the same time I am tempted to abandon both."

In spite of the lateness of the season, the country was still green and the walks delightful, while the valley offered an infinite variety of delightful charm.

As usual, Mme. de Custine burdened her mother with commissions of every kind. She performed these so well that it would be a pity not to give her a chance of showing her talent:

"It would be very kind of you to look out for a good servant for me. I shall have no servant at all when I come to Paris, which will be a dreadful nuisance. I want somebody very reliable and highly recommended, not too old or too young, a hard quick worker who understands her work. I cannot undertake to train any more servants. The wages are thirty-six francs a month and she will pay for her own clothes and washing. Tell Courier to look out, and give me any news you can on your side, little mother. Your hat is charming and suits me perfectly. You do my errands beautifully; on my return I will pay this enormous debt; you will tell me what I owe you, twelve livres, isn't it?"

Another time she asks for a couple of watering-cans of painted tin for the garden; then for snuffers, and little wooden spoons for the salt-cellars, &c.

In the month of November Mme. de Custine thought of leaving Fervaques for Paris. The weather was becoming damp and unpleasant and the sun was clouded; cold winds and sadness were their only distractions. Moreover, Astolphe was tired and unwell, had lost his appetite and was growing thin. In short, it was time to look for winter quarters. Mme. de Custine's delight upon her return to Paris was increased by a great surprise which her "little mother" had prepared for her. It will be remembered that Delphine had left the Rue Martel where she was living near her mother for rooms in the Rue Verte opposite Chateaubriand's house. The inconvenience of this change, though it brought her next door to her friend, was the long distance of her new abode from her family. What was her delight when she discovered that her "little mother," vexed by the separation which seemed unbearable, had pushed her kindness and goodness so far as to leave the Rue Martel and establish herself in the Rue Verte in the immediate neighbourhood of her daughter.

CHAPTER XXVII

1805-1810

Chateaubriand loses his sister, Mme. de Caux—Grief of Chênedollé—Kindness of Delphine—Stay at Fervaques — Visits — Departure of Chateaubriand for the East—Delphine's grief—Chateaubriand's return—The *Martyrs*—Death of Armand de Chateaubriand.

IN January, 1805, Chateaubriand and his wife left Villeneuve-sur-Yonne, where they had just spent several months, and returned to Paris. They no longer lived in the Rue Verte but hired a little flat in the Rue de Miromesnil, so that they were no longer such near neighbours of Mme. de Custine. René had just suffered a great loss. In the month of November his sister, Mme. de Caux, succumbed to the illness which had long undermined her health. Delphine, with her customary goodness and kindness, did her best to soften the grief of her friend. Glad to find a heart to understand and share his sadness, the Génie showed himself less surly and despotic and became almost amiable. Feeling the need of consolation he went to see Delphine every day and even dined at her house. Surprised by this change, which she had hardly expected, she renewed her interest in life and began to hope once more.

It was not only Chateaubriand who had felt the loss of his sister. For several years Chênedollé had felt a deep, though quiet, affection for Mme. de Caux. Her death was a catastrophe for him and implied the annihilation of all his hopes and purposes in life. For three months the unhappy man spent his days in digging in the hope of finding some alleviation of his overwhelming despair. Mme. de Custine was not aware of her new friend's passion, sent him letter after letter and was surprised at receiving no answer. In anxious displeasure she finally writes: "Do say what has happened. Why are you aping Colo[1] in this way ? I assure you that you must change your mode of life if you wish to resemble him in any way, for since I am here he has improved. I am not happy but I am a little less unhappy." Thus brought to book, Chênedollé resolved to confess the reason for his silence. Delphine, who was so well acquainted with sadness and grief, held out a helping hand and supported him in his distress with all the delicacy of her generous heart. Deeply touched by the sympathy which saved him from despair the unhappy man was able to write some time later :

" Mme. de Custine has given a new interest to the life which I thought irrevocably condemned to sadness and hopeless regret." [2]

René, however, who could not fail to be touched by the entire devotion of Delphine to him and to his friends, showed some condescension and talked of making a long stay at Fervaques in the spring. The mistress of the house at once invited Chênedollé, knowing that nothing could be more agreeable to her friend or more likely to keep him with her. At the same time she lets fall this phrase which betrayed the weariness of her heart :

" Our friend says that he will stay six weeks but I am not the woman to be taken in by such statements. I am more infatuated than ever and more unhappy than I can say." She concludes by these words, which are a revelation of René's character and of the suffering which he caused her : " The Génie is delighted at the idea of seeing you ; he shares your grief, and when he speaks of you one would be tempted to think that he was a kind-hearted man." [3]

In July Chateaubriand and Chênedollé met at Fervaques and stayed for nearly a fortnight with Delphine and the attractive Mme. de Cauvigny. The visit passed by very

---

[1] A name by which Mme. de Custine often refers to Chateaubriand.
[2] Sainte Beuve, *Chateaubriand et son groupe littéraire*, vol. ii. appendix, p. 332 ff.
[3] March 28, 1805. See Bardoux, *Mme. de Custine*.

agreeably, René was comparatively pleasant and all the guests did their utmost to win Chênedollé from his constant depression. At a later date in his *Mémoires* René alluded to a somewhat commonplace incident which happened during his stay but which struck him sufficiently to impress his memory. He wrote in 1833:

"Many years ago when I was at the Château of Fervaques, I occupied the room of Henry IV. My bed was enormous and I thus mounted to royalty, to which I was not born. A moat filled with water surrounded the Château and the view from my windows extended over the fields along the little river of Fervaques. In these fields I observed, one morning, a fine sow of extraordinary whiteness; she looked like the mother of Prince Marcassin. She was lying at the foot of a willow tree on the fresh grass amid the dew. A young boar took a little fine, delicate moss upon his tusks and placed it upon the sleeper. He repeated this operation so many times that the white sow was eventually hidden completely; nothing more could be seen than black trotters protruding from the covering of verdure beneath which she was buried."

After this long stay at Fervaques the Génie took his departure and was seen no more that year. Fortunately for Delphine she had some distraction. The Baron von Münchhausen, whom her mother had known very well in Rheinsberg, when staying with Prince Henry, came to see her, and both went to Fontaine-Française to Mlle. d'Andrezelle, who had been at the Court of the King of Poland. Delphine tells her mother of her journey and her visit, and the letter is worth quoting, as it gives some interesting details concerning the Court of Luneville.

"As the mother of the knight said, a ray of sunlight illuminates many things; ... the Baron is a great trouble in these matters. He wanted to stop at every public-house on the high road and now we are here, though he absorbs all the conversation, he is strangely tormented by a fear that he may not have anything to say. I am not troubled in this respect as he interrupts me every moment. I put many questions to Mlle. d'Andrezelle, of whose cleverness and memory you had spoken so highly, and asked her about the Court of the King of Poland.

T

"'How lucky you are,' I said to her, ' to have seen so many remarkable personages together.'

"'Yes,' she said, ' society was pleasant. Brilliancy had not then reached the point which it has now attained, but it was advancing.'

"'But,' I returned, ' the brilliancy of the present day is nothing in comparison with the spirit of those times, its gracefulness, its good taste, and good form.'

"'As regards form,' she replied, 'it was extremely bad, indeed it was quite indecent and licentious.'

"'But Mme. de Boufflers was so nice and pleasant, so clever and original?'

"'She was rather kind and clever, but as regards the point to which you refer I never heard her say anything striking. Mme. de Maillebois, a very capable judge, thought her rather clever and agreeable. She used to begin to compose little songs which other people finished for her.'

"'You really astonish me! I have heard charming incidents quoted concerning her. My father-in-law told me several.'

"'I then tried to recall some but they did not prove successful. Ask the Chevalier to remember the most striking and write them down for me, for I should like to overcome so strange a prejudice and restore to Mme. de Boufflers her reputation for cleverness.'

"'Is it true that she brought up a little girl with no clothes and introduced her to society in this costume?'

"' I cannot remember or quote,' replied Mlle. d'Andrezelle, ' anything concerning her except some practical jokes.' As regards the Court of the King of Poland she told me that it was as wearisome as any other, and that they constantly heard complaints and expressions of discontent. This was all that I could get out of her. You see, dear mother, that my disappointment extends even over the past. I have not yet recovered from my surprise. Goodbye; you can tell all this to the Chevalier but do not rouse any quarrel with this poor Mlle. d'Andrezelle, for I should never forgive myself if I were the cause of it. Moreover, she is very grateful for his kind recollections of her. . . . I think that the real reason for Mlle. d'Andrezelle's lack of enthusiasm for Mme. de Boufflers is that there was some jealousy between them. Mme. de

Saint-Julien told me a story about Mme. de Bauffremont, referring to that point, but Mlle. d'A. said that she thought you infinitely nicer and cleverer than the other Mme. de Boufflers, and that if she had lived she was certain from her knowledge of her character that the mother-in-law would have been jealous of the daughter-in-law." [1]

In the autumn M. and Mme. de Boufflers came to stay with their daughter. Unfortunately their means did not allow them to take a private carriage and they were obliged to put up with the diligence. This democratic system of locomotion, with its hateful lack of privacy, drew loud complaints from Mme. de Boufflers, who had never been accustomed to it and was completely shocked by the fatigue, by her neighbours, by the weariness of the journey, and by the general inconvenience. The Chevalier, on the other hand, who had been used to roughing it in the course of his adventurous existence, thought the incident charming, and laughed at the objections and outcries of his wife.

This was the first occasion on which Mme. de Boufflers had visited Fervaques. It was a great delight for Delphine to show her the whole of the "rose-coloured" Château, the park, the kitchen garden, the fish-ponds, the aged carp, and to gain her approval of the many improvements which she had made during the short period of her residence. She made many excursions into the country which was more delightful than ever at that time of year. Mme. de Boufflers was charmed and constantly poured forth exclamations of admiration and delight. Naturally the inseparable Mme. de Cauvigny was there and did her utmost to contribute to the pleasure of the meeting. "The little father" and Berstöcher suited one another admirably; they held interminable conversations and could hardly be dragged away from one another for meal times. All were happy, and when the hour of parting struck, grief was general. The autumn ended very sadly and in loneliness : " The weather, the wind, and solitude are a heavier burden than usual," wrote Delphine. In December she returned to Paris with Astolphe and Berstöcher.

For a long time Chateaubriand had projected a voyage in

[1] Communicated by M. Prat.

the East; Greece and Palestine attracted him and he was exceedingly anxious to visit Jerusalem. But hitherto he had been prevented by obstacles of every kind, especially by lack of money. In 1806 he thought that the favourable moment had come and told Mme. de Custine that he should start in the month of July, but he promised not to be away more than three months and to return to Paris in November at latest. This was a heavy blow for Delphine, and though she was prepared for disappointments of every kind, she could hardly endure it. What would she have said if she had known that René proposed to come back by way of Spain and had arranged to meet at Granada Mme. de Mouchy, with whom he was in love?

In the early days of June, 1806, Mme. de Custine started for Fervaques. She proposed to make all arrangements for the reception of René. Meanwhile she wished to have some trees and as a practical woman did not wish to pay for them. She requested her mother to open negotiations for the purpose of getting them for nothing :—

"I wish you would discover some Abbé Nollin who might give us some trees and shrubs. We should like to plant them this autumn and above all I should like a great many poplars. It may be that you will find some good creature in the world who will give us some trees. If you become intimate with M. Thouin or anyone else, you can take some trees for yourself and the rest shall be ours, the flowers too, remember that. There are people very clever at that kind of thing and I am sure there are plenty of women who fill their gardens cheaply. Good-bye, little mother, I am much afraid that my garden may remain fallow."

Anxious to give some consolation to the woman he was leaving, René kept his promise and came for a visit to Fervaques in the month of June. The prospect of his approaching departure made him easy tempered:

"The Génie has been here for a fortnight," writes Delphine to Chênedollé, "but is going away in two days. It is no ordinary departure, for he is starting on no ordinary journey. This whim of visiting Greece is at length to be realised and he is going to fulfil all his desires and destroy all mine. He assures us that he will be back in November but I cannot believe it. You know how sad I was last year and you can imagine what I shall be this year. I will say good-bye, for you will understand the state of my feelings. The dear Mouse is here. Everything has been perfect for the last fortnight, but now there is an end to it."[1]

Chateaubriand's departure threw Delphine into an access of despair and she fell seriously ill. Her letters at this period are heart-breaking in their sadness. She writes to her mother in the course of July:

"There is no rest in this world and still less happiness. I am so sad and depressed that I would not take a step to save my life. I am paying very promptly for the few happy days that I spent when I arrived here. It is very kind of you to regret the loss of the poor traveller. He spent more than a fortnight with us and he shall have your regrets, for he has not yet started on his long journey. Mme. de Cauvigny is still with me, I am glad to say, for I am not well and very sad. Here I will say goodbye, as I can write or think no more. I know nothing that gives me more pleasure than your letters."[2]

As misfortunes never come singly Astolphe suffered another attack of tertian fever and the inhabitants of the Château were no less severely tried:

"*July* 11, 1806.

"This place is something like a hospital. Our coachman has tertian fever, our cook has jaundice, and I was very ill yesterday. I had my well-known attacks of cramp, and am not rid of them to-day; it is a bad bilious attack. I have had so little pleasure for some time that I naturally feel the loss of it. But you need not be uneasy; the doctor says it will be nothing; people do not die of it; we live but to suffer. I feel so unwell this evening, and so tired and sad, that I can write no more. Please do not be vexed with me, I cannot help it. The traveller[3] must have started, and when he sees our fields again they will have lost their fresh

[1] *Mme. de Custine,* Bardoux.
[2] To Mme. de Boufflers, care of M. Le Tellier, grocer, Saint Germain en Laye.
[3] Chateaubriand and his wife started on July 15th for Venice. There they separated, and on the 30th René was at Trieste and embarked on August 1st.

green, for he is to be away until the autumn, if his journey is successful. I hope that his star is a better one than mine."

The traveller had given the fullest promises that he would not be away for more than three months and would write constantly to soften the grief of separation. Delphine was well aware, however, that the promises of the Génie were not to be relied upon.

Mme. de Boufflers was not much happier than her daughter; her husband was ill, Elzéar was also unwell, and the house had become a hospital. She was herself overwhelmed with fatigue. Delphine writes on August 3:

"Are we, then, never to have peace or happiness? Poor mother, you will never be happy, nor I either. At any rate, if we were together we might bear life with more courage. I myself have scarcely strength to get to the next day; I do not complain. My son and the friend are well. Mme. de Cauvigny will not return until the end of the month and I feel so sad, so ill and so ill-tempered that I am almost glad."

Fortunately she had a visit from the good Nanette, who was delighted with her "son's" beautiful Château, and left it with much regret when she was obliged to return to Paris. Then in September came Mme. des Boulets and Mme. de Cauvigny: "These two ladies are rivals in pleasantness; they charm this solitary abode, and it would be very gloomy without them, for I should not enliven it much. One can hardly be sadder than I am; it has become an habitual mode of existence with me which I probably shall never change, for I know of nothing which can distract me from it. Goodbye, little mother, please do not delay writing to me. All good wishes to the little father. I will answer my brother's letter which he wrote, I forget when, saying that he will perhaps come and see me if Mme. de Staël goes to Rouen, because he might go to see her from my house. Much good may it do him! But if he should come and see me I should like it to be, at any rate, for myself."

Autumn arrived, and the time fixed by the traveller for his return had long passed, and Delphine had had no news, not a word nor a letter. The unhappy woman was reduced

to despair by anxiety and grief, and actually begged news of
the object of her adoration from Mme. de Chateaubriand. By
this means she discovered that he had changed his plans and
was prolonging his travels. Chateaubriand did not return
until May, 1807. He had spent some months in Spain with
Mme. de Mouchy and merely passed through Paris and
immediately started for Villeneuve-sur-Yonne to work upon
the *Martyrs*. He did not see his friend for more than a day
or two.[1]

If Delphine had been under any illusion concerning René's
feelings for her she was now fully informed, and whatever
her grief she was obliged to resign herself to the inevitable.
It is difficult to understand why she did not definitely break
off an intimacy from which she had nothing to expect but
vexation. René, however, did not give her an opening.
Well aware of his influence over her, he did not wish to
abandon a connection which was convenient to him and was
satisfied with allowing himself a full measure of liberty,
careless of the humiliation and grief which he inflicted upon
his friend. Delphine, on her side, could not resolve to break
completely with one for whom she felt so deep an adoration.
None the less, an absolute breach would have been a hundred
times preferable in the interest of her dignity and peace of
mind. She would eventually have found forgetfulness and
calm instead of leading a life of regret, constantly tormented
by jealousy and by vain hopes of recalling the faithless one
some day.

The years 1807–1808 passed very sadly. Mme. de
Custine spent some of the winter months at Paris and
returned to Fervaques in the spring. There is no incident
of interest in her life during this period.[2]

---

[1] In 1807 Chateaubriand bought the Vallée-aux-Loups, near Sceaux,
where he spent henceforward the greater part of the year.

[2] We find in Elzéar's papers a letter from Mme. de Boufflers to her
daughter under date October, 1807. She refers to certain members of
Parisian society, for which reason we quote it :—

"PARIS, *October* 31, 1807.

"Paris is dreadfully mournful at the present time. People are dying
like flies. The poor Baron de Breteuil is at the last gasp, though there is
nothing disquieting to others in his case. At the age of ninety-six, with
gout and the stone, life is more astounding than death. Another old
man who died within twenty-four hours is M. de Menou ; he had played

Chateaubriand seems to come into no further connection with Delphine except to ask favours of her. In 1804 he had induced her to intervene on behalf of his friend Bertin,[1] who had returned to France without due authorisation. Thanks to Delphine's influence with Fouché, Bertin was not disturbed. Then Chateaubriand uses and misuses his friend's influence on his own behalf and for his protection against the strictness of the military police; and on each occasion, with untiring devotion, Mme. de Custine goes to infinite trouble that the Génie may be left in peace. In 1808, when the *Martyrs* was about to be published, the censorship raised infinite objections; René straightway applies to his usual helper and asks her to appeal once more to Fouché, which she does. The Minister makes definite promises, but Chateaubriand asserts that he has been tricking them and playing a double game, and secretly inspires attacks upon him in the Press.

In 1809 a painful tragedy took place. Armand de Chateaubriand, René's cousin, had imprudently undertaken, as agent for the Princes, to disembark on the Normandy coast. No sooner had he set foot upon the French soil than he was arrested. Charged with complicity in the Royalist conspiracy, he was taken to Paris, tried by court-martial and condemned to death. Chateaubriand attempted to save his unhappy relative and asked Delphine to accompany him to Fouché, but the latter evaded the point by asserting that sentence had not yet been pronounced. However, the next day, which was Good Friday, Armand was shot on the Plain of

his usual game on Friday evening at the house of Mme. de la Reynière. On Saturday hope was given up and he died on Sunday morning. The Duc de Rohan has also finished his painful career; death was easier for him than life, for he suffered cruelly. He died in the full assurance of religious faith. Mme. de Chimay had spent the whole summer in the task of converting him, helped by his wife and M. de Léon. He resolved to make a general confession, after many misgivings. It was a long one; his memory was failing, but what cannot grace do when the heart is really touched at the age of seventy-six. In short, he died after receiving all the sacraments and far more calmly than he would have done without its protection. His sister's example largely contributed to this result; it made a great impression upon him of which they fortunately took advantage. Mme. de la Fayette is at death's door; her last prayers were made long since."

[1] In 1800 Bertin had been accused of conspiracy against the State and had been exiled to Rome, where he made the acquaintance of Chateaubriand.

Grenelle. Chateaubriand, informed of the execution, started off in the hope of supporting his cousin in his last moments, but arrived too late. He had only time to dip his handkerchief in the victim's blood. On his return home he wrote this brief message to Delphine: " I have just returned from the Plain of Grenelle; all is over." [1]

In 1810 Delphine lost the powerful patronage which had sheltered her and her friends from all annoyance for so many years. Fouché, the Minister of Police, was suspected of intrigues with the Republicans and the Bourbons, was relieved of his post and replaced by Savary.

[1] At the end of the summer of 1809 Chateaubriand had hired a room in the Rue Saint-Honoré, at the corner of the Rue Saint Florentine. It was in this house, with M. de Las Cases, that he afterwards made the acquaintance of the Duchesse de Duras.

CHAPTER XXVIII

1810—1812

Chateaubriand is appointed a member of the Academy—He is unable to deliver his speech—Mme. de Custine goes to Switzerland with Astolphe, Berstöcher and Doctor Koreff—After a tour in Switzerland she arrives at Geneva—Monetary difficulties when she wishes to visit Italy—She visits the Islands of Borromeo—The much-desired money arrives and she starts for Turin—Adventures on the journey—Visit to Rome and Naples—She returns by Venice and Tyrol—Stay at Geneva—Intimacy of Chateaubriand with the Duchesse de Duras.

AFTER he had bought La Vallée-aux-Loups Chateaubriand spent every summer there and devoted the whole of his time to his literary work. In 1811, he published the *Itinéraire de Paris à Jérusalem*, which was surprisingly successful. Though he had always expressed great scorn of the Academy, when a vacancy was caused by the death of Chénier[1] he thought it his duty to come forward, but to his humiliation he was elected by one vote only above an obscure rival, Lacretelle. Mme. de Boufflers undertook to announce this great news to Delphine:

"No doubt you have seen in the newspapers an account of M. de Chateaubriand's nomination to the Academy. He was nominated against Lacretelle the younger, but only defeated him by one vote, Lacretelle had eleven and he had twelve. He can hardly regard this as complimentary. It is true that he constantly declared that he had no desire to be a member of the Academy and he has spoken of it with such scorn that they seized this opportunity to pay him back. At the present time he is a very discontented man

[1] Marie Joseph Chénier.

both with himself and with others, the consequence of having more intellect than reason. As a result of one of those chances which no one can explain, it happens that M. de Chateaubriand has taken the place of Chénier at the Institute and will be obliged to pronounce a eulogy upon his predecessor, which will be a very curious performance and his reception well worth seeing. Everyone is already talking of it and the room will not be large enough to hold all those who wish to be present. "The best part of it is that the 'little father' as President will be obliged to admit him. I am rather pleased for the sake of M. de Boufflers, and a little also for M. de Chateaubriand." [1]

Some time afterwards Mme. de Boufflers writes to her daughter saying that the "little father" is working hard at his speech, and has already written a thousand admirable things. The "little father" was taking unnecessary trouble. Chateaubriand's speech was submitted, according to custom, to the Imperial Censorship and modifications were demanded. The Génie, furious at so insolent a claim, refused to change a line. The result was that the new nominee was never admitted and that his speech was never delivered. The same fate befell the speech so laboriously elaborated by the "little father."

In the course of the year 1811, Delphine came to an important resolution. For several years she had been leading a wretched life, constantly disturbed by vexation and jealousy. She clearly saw that Réne did not care for her, that he abandoned her and made no secret of more splendid intimacies. None the less she adored him and cherished the hope that he would come back to her some day. Eventually, at the end of her strength, humiliated and disgusted, she abandoned the vain struggle. She resolved to leave Paris and to travel to distract her thoughts.

As an explanation of this unexpected departure she put forward Astolphe's health. The reason was very far from imaginary. The young man had always been very delicate and for some months had been causing his mother great anxiety. As he grew up he became increasingly strange and

[1] Prat papers.

nervous; he suffered from terrible headaches; the age of puberty increased his ordinary sufferings. Poor Delphine became the more anxious as she saw in the sufferings of her son many symptoms that she had noticed in the case of Elzéar, and she wondered, in her anxiety, whether the defect was hereditary. She had happened to make the acquaintance of a young German doctor named Koreff. She consulted him and he strongly recommended travel and amusement for the benefit of Astolphe. This advice was in such complete accord with her own wishes that she immediately put it into execution and announced her approaching departure for Switzerland and Italy.

Chateaubriand, at this juncture, did not change his usual selfishness. He thought it quite natural that he should abandon Delphine entirely, seeing her only at rare intervals, but, at the same time, he wished to preserve an attachment the value of which became obvious when any inconvenience crossed his path. He wished to have permanently at his disposal so reliable, so devoted and so affectionate a friend. When the journey was announced he loudly remonstrated and showed much ill-temper. He even complained, with unconscious humour, that he was being abandoned. But for the first time Delphine clung to her resolution, in spite of the reproaches and indignation of the Génie. Moreover, Mme. de Custine's journey was to be more than an ordinary tour. She proposed not only to stay in Switzerland for the latter part of the summer and autumn, but to spend the winter in Italy and make a long stay at Rome, the charms of which René had constantly pointed out to her.

We have just referred to a young German doctor whom Delphine had consulted upon several occasions concerning Astolphe's health. This Koreff was a strange personage; he was regarded as very clever and a very expert doctor, but he was ugly, by no means sympathetic, while his mocking scepticism was far from pleasant. Then he was a Jew and a dabbler in spiritualism. He rapidly gained very great influence over Mme. de Custine; indeed she came to think that his attentions were indispensable for Astolphe, and proposed that he should accompany them to Switzerland and Italy. Koreff accepted with some show of reluctance.

Chateaubriand had already looked with great displeasure upon the young doctor whom he constantly found in the house. When he heard that Koreff was to be one of the party his ill-temper knew no bounds, and he had a scene of violent jealousy with Delphine. He found a very unexpected supporter in Astolphe; the young man, as a matter of fact, had been disgusted by the influence which Koreff obtained over his mother, and showed him real hostility at all times. His animosity was redoubled when he learnt that the doctor was to have charge of his health. This lack of harmony caused Mme. de Custine much grief but she did not change her resolutions.

The four travellers left Paris at the beginning of August, and when they reached Switzerland they crossed the Saint Gothard, stayed for a time at Lugano, crossed the Grimsel, &c. Delphine rode all the way and cheerfully bore the fatigues of the journey. She wrote from Meiringen on September 2:

"I am very well; if my heart and mind were at rest I could say that I have spent some very pleasant days, but this is far from being the case. I am sadder than ever, for all the troubles of which I spoke in my last letters remain undiminished, and I am much afraid that K. may leave us before we finish our tour in Switzerland, which will be soon. I cannot tell you how much I suffer from all this, especially as I am unable to see any reason in it. It is enough to drive one wild."

She then started for Stanz and for Lucerne. From Lucerne she went to Linth. There she wrote to her mother and revealed, with charming sincerity, her sadness, her desolation and the secrets of her heart:

"*September* 17.

"I really do not know whether Ko will come to Italy. Relations between us have been so strained that I am much afraid that he will go no further. Moreover, it depends, to some extent, upon the amount of money that may be sent to him, for at Rome it is necessary sometimes to be upon an independent footing. But anything that depends upon money is always uncertain; Fate draws the purse-strings so tight. I should be deeply grieved if he did not come, as he cheers my mind. I am afraid of the air of Italy, and it is so sad to leave one's friends. This great question will soon be settled, and I will let you know at once.

"Do not say, then, that we can bend circumstances to our will as we please. That is a wholly false idea, as also is your favourite maxim : " One can always do what one likes with others, if one can do what one likes with oneself." No doubt you meant to say, " if one can do what others like with oneself." Then the epigram would be more correct. I should have been delighted with this tour had it not been for this misunderstanding, and it has deeply moved me because it shows more than anything that we cannot count upon anything, and that fate, even when it accomplishes our wishes, finds some means of thwarting them. This journey will cost me dear ; it has destroyed many illusions. Just think that the Génie is still sulking and will not pardon me. He writes letters in an unusually surly tone. Apparently someone has turned appearances to their own advantage by blackening my character, and as he has no character himself and any amount of conceit, he has taken it all in. Thus happiness collapses at every point, and thus we advance along the road of life relieved of our friends and of our pleasure.

"I can hardly believe you when you say that this tour will have cured my timidity. Since we left Bâle, with the exception of Geneva, I have hardly seen a human being except guides and inn-keepers. We have met very few travellers and, except Prince Lubomirski, whom I met once, we have lived like real savages. But I assure you that that has been the most pleasant part of it. I am afraid of Italy, simply because it will be necessary to see people. I daresay I shall escape them as I have escaped the precipices, but I shall not like them any the more for it. For in spite of my dexterity I am not in love with the exercise.

"I have an ideal of happiness in my heart without which life seems to me like a fair valley without sunlight. You see that I can speak the language of the country. This ideal happiness is of a perfectly natural kind but it is not customary either among people of our rank or in our country. My destiny will soon be fulfilled and it is only a question of living until the close of my life; this, again, will soon be a problem devolving upon my cook and my doctor, and I shall have spent life as a fish would spend it if he were placed in a splendid field bespangled with flowers and with nothing wanting but a stream."

She speaks of Astolphe and betrays the anxiety which the unhappy youth had caused her:

"How mistaken you are when you look upon me as young! That is certainly the delusion of a proud mother. And again when you say that my sadness is due to my nerves, the fact is quite the contrary. My nervous attacks are often caused only by vexation. If I were happy I should never suffer in this way. This suffering is peculiar to people who are out of their proper sphere and spend their lives doing the opposite to that which they desire. To complete my misery this unhappy temperament is transmitted from generation to generation, for Astolphe is just the same and regards himself as the most unhappy creature in the world, and the nature of his mind and character condemns my life to eternal lamentations. But this may remain between ourselves. Let us never give others the consolation of knowing that we are unhappy."

In the course of her journey Delphine passed Einsiedeln and was careful to make a pilgrimage to this famous sanctuary where her mother and Elzéar had come to pray some years before:

"I also have been to Notre-Dame-des-Hermites. I looked for your bunch of roses;[1] it had faded as all roses do and was not to be seen. I will bring you a rosary and a little image of the Virgin. I had so many vows to make that I have made none, but I was delighted with it all, with the pilgrims and the life of the place. It is really very extraordinary; I have been much laughed at because I would not come out of the shops and could not be consoled for my inability to spend a whole day at Einsiedeln. Then, in my righteous wrath I said that I would write to you and that you surely would no more understand than I can how anyone could tear themselves away from so simple a spot and one so attractive by reason of its associations.

The change of scene and the open-air life produced an

[1] See page 186.

excellent effect up Delphine's health. She was wonderfully well and faced every danger calmly. She had become brave and boasts of it:

"Where the horses can pass I will go, even on the slope of some dreadful glacier; I have not the slightest fear. All the same I much prefer my own fireside and the pleasant talk of my friends."

The journey was continued, but under some difficulties. Astolphe continued to show the most violent antipathy to Koreff, when an unexpected accident fortunately improved the situation. As the young man was going upstairs he struck his head violently; "he was so tall that all the houses were too low for him." Koreff nursed him with so much care and skill that the invalid eventually laid aside his repugnance. Thus things were going well, when Mme. de Custine found the most disquieting letters awaiting her at Geneva from her agents. The farmers were not paying their rents and no money had been sent her to continue her journey. This news overwhelmed her: "I spent my day weeping," she writes, "a poor resource." At length she resolved to take up her pen. She scolded her agents, spurred on their zeal and insisted on their sending her a little money. While waiting for the money to arrive our travellers remained at Geneva and were obliged to meet certain people and in particular Mme. de Staël who was overwhelmingly gracious, to the great displeasure of Delphine:

"When we arrived," she writes, "we had seen Mme. de Staël. We hoped to see her as little as possible, for as I am not her friend I should think it very hard to be compromised on her account. But as she has no sense of proportion she could not see my point and overwhelmed us with invitations and kindnesses. I did not wish to act in a cowardly way and could not altogether remain in obscurity, so this will make our stay here somewhat disagreeable."

This forced intimacy was so painful to Delphine that, as a means of escaping, she conceived the idea of making a tour round the lake to see the famous vintage of Vevey. It was a five days' excursion and on the way a new idea came into her head. How would it be if they went to see the Islands of Borromeo, the famous islands that none of them had seen?

1810—1812

The proposal was naturally carried unanimously, but no one had any money. Fortunately Delphine was not to be baulked by this small inconvenience. She admitted her embarrassment to the inn-keeper at Bex and he advanced her twenty-five louis on the strength of her face. So the band started off for the Simplon in the most beautiful weather possible. The Islands of Borromeo seemed to them a, terrestrial Paradise.

At length they returned to Geneva and Delphine was delighted to find the money that she expected. She left her carriage there lest it should be spoilt upon the journey, and also for fear that such a fine vehicle might cause her to be overcharged in the hotels. She took a simple travelling carriage and the party left Switzerland to cross the Mont Cenis, but not without incident:

"TURIN, *November 2*.

"We started from Geneva in a travelling carriage. This is a kind of large coach with seats for five, and on the box there is a kind of hood for the coachman and the servants. Thus we travelled through fair Savoy towards fair Italy. The first day passed by without incident but on the second day, about mid-day, we met the diligence in a very narrow road; the diligence is the scourge of carriage travellers. In spite of the amount of room which we took up it attempted to pass us. Its wheels were locked in ours with a dreadful crash; we all cried in alarm and were thrown out of the carriage, although we asked them to wait until we had lowered the hood which the weight of the diligence was crushing remorselessly. At our shouts the postilion whipped up his horses, and as our weight was not equal to that of the enormous diligence, it broke the front of our carriage as it drove away. Our driver, in a fury, rushed after the diligence, which was forced to slacken its speed at a short distance on account of a little hill. We heard a lot of shouts and oaths and expected that the matter would not finish without the interchange of blows, when we saw our poor driver coming back with his face covered with blood. Ko went to him at once and saw that he had lost the end of his nose. The man said that he had grappled with the postilion and that the latter flew at him and bit off the end of his nose. You may

U

imagine how horrified we were; the poor man will be disfigured in spite of the care of Ko. He is admirable upon these occasions, as you know.

"We laid a formal complaint, but the course of law is so dilatory and so hampered by a thousand forms of procedure that we would willingly have given the ends of all our noses to be out of it. At length, after an infinite number of examinations and reports and cross-examinations of the physicians we started off again, at the expense of paying for the breakages and costs and having a coachman with a false nose and a mask of bandages which gave him the air of a spectre. We had a comical entry into Turin, as everyone looked at our strange driver and pitied him and us.

"Apart from this we are all well. We had a real summer's day for crossing the Mont Cenis, though the evening before was frightful, with torrents of rain and deafening thunder. I have seen nothing of this town except a very long street, so long that it looks quite narrow, although it is wide. The houses are dull and grey, which gives them a sad appearance, and to crown all, we are in a house where it is impossible to see, even at mid-day; yet it is the best hotel. I am going to the theatre and will therefore say goodbye as I have to dress, and I really do not know how to set about it. Write to me at Rome, *poste restante*."

Unfortunately we do not possess Delphine's correspondence with her mother during the journey in Italy. We only know that she spent the whole of the year 1812 there, at Rome and at Naples. In these places she met charming people who made her visit very delightful, and she spoke of it years afterwards. Although she was forty years of age and had gone through more sufferings than most people, she had preserved a wonderful pureness of feature and great elegance of figure. At Rome she made the acquaintance of Canova, who admired her greatly. She liked talking with this great artist, and was charmed by his simplicity and his Venetian stories. One day her son, who became uneasy at this increasing intimacy, attempted to cross-examine her and said suddenly: "With your romantic imagination you are capable of marrying Canova." "Do not be too sure of that," she replied, "if he had not become Marquis of Ischia, I might be tempted."

At length, in November, 1812, it was necessary to think of leaving this happy land and of making their way to Switzerland, in order to return to France. Unfortunately the weather was frightful and travelling was correspondingly difficult. On November 30, the travellers were at Venice. From there Delphine writes to her mother:

"The season is dreadful, and we shall therefore return to Geneva through Tyrol in order to avoid the Mont Cenis, which we should have to pass, as the Simplon road is blocked. It is very little out of our way and will bring us back through our dear Switzerland. I am delighted with Venice; it resembles nothing that we ever saw before. I like the gondolas, the Palace of the Doges, the Square of Saint Mark, in fact, the latter seems to me the most astonishing sight of all. If it were not so cold it would be delightful, but the damp is unbearable, wood is very scarce and expensive, and so we freeze all day; otherwise we should be entirely happy. What a nuisance not to have found your letters! I was hoping that you would let me hear something about the Génie. I have not a word from him and am quite anxious. Where is he now? People should not leave one another in this world if they wish to meet again. However, I hope that I may see you again soon. I expect to be at Paris for the Kings and meanwhile I send you my love. Remember me to the 'little father' and to Elzéar."[1]

From Venice Mme. de Custine reached Zurich; she was there on December 30. She sends her mother an account of the journey which she was obliged to make in order to avoid the Mont Cenis:—

"ZURICH, *December* 30.

"We are now at Zurich, little mother, and shall soon have finished a journey which is very difficult at this time of year. We have crossed Tyrol, part of Bavaria, part of Suabia and are now in Switzerland. We are making our way to Geneva, where I hope at last to hear from you. I am very anxious, both about you and all my friends. It is so

[1] To Mme. de Boufflers, Rue de Faubourg Saint-Honoré, No. 114, after the Little Rue Verte, house of M. Amelot, Paris.

long since I had a letter. Where is the Génie, where can I write to him or find him? I hope ▪I shall learn all this at Geneva. I expect to be at Paris about January 20, but at this time of year travelling is not rapid owing to the ice and snow and the shortness of the days. It is tiring to be in the carriage before daybreak and often at four o'clock in the morning every day for three months. But these are small troubles compared with those of the heart, which are very different.

"We have been somewhat startled by this climate after the gentle breezes of Italy. Fortunately my health has not suffered from it so far and we are all well. Whenever sickness attempts to seize one of us Koreff gives it a fright and it goes away. A good doctor is an invaluable talisman. You will be astonished when you hear in detail all the privations that I have been able to bear.

"So I am about to begin another year far from you. This fact makes me sad and the year begins on Friday, a bad omen. May it obliterate this painful impression by bringing us some happiness. I send my love to the little father and Elzéar and we all send you our kisses, little mother, which is allowed on New Year's Day. But it is a sad fashion of wishing one another a Happy New Year. Send word to Nanette that we are all well and shall see her again soon."

There were serious reasons why Delphine had not heard from the Génie. A new affection filled his life and absorbed him almost entirely.[1] It was at the end of 1811 that Chateaubriand had been attracted by the Duchesse de Duras and had begun with her an intimacy which lasted for several years.[2] She was the daughter of the Comte de Kersaint, who had been one of our most distinguished sailors. As a deputy to the Convention he had voted against the death of the King and had emphatically resigned his position. He therefore mounted the scaffold on December 5, 1793. During the Revolution and the first years of the Empire Mme. de Duras lived in retirement in her Château d'Ussé and devoted herself

---

[1] At the end of 1809 Chateaubriand hired a flat in the Rue Saint-Honoré, at the corner of the Rue Florentin, in the house occupied by M. de Las Cases.

[2] Claire de Coetnemoren Le Chat de Kersaint (1777-1829).

solely to the education of her two daughters. In 1812, thinking she could not complete their education in a remote country house, she resolved to return to Paris. A short time after her return she met Chateaubriand at the house of M. des Las Cases, and both were immediately attracted. For his benefit she opened her salon, where he reigned without a rival, and she used on his behalf all the political influence which she possessed. Henceforward René did not abandon Mme. de Duras until the day when he left her in turn to replace her with Mme. Récamier.

CHAPTER XXIX

1813

Mme. de Custine establishes herself at Geneva—The sadness of her life — Elzéar is arrested and imprisoned at Vincennes — Delphine hastens to her mother—She returns to Geneva and finds Astolphe ill—She sets up house at Berne.

THE year 1813 began under somewhat disquieting auspices. The news from the armies was alarming, and the Russian campaign ended in disaster. Europe was in coalition against France and no one could foresee the result. Instead of starting for Paris and reaching it in time to see the Kings, as she had hoped, Mme. de Custine, greatly anxious at the course of events, changed all her plans and established herself at Geneva, where she thought she would be in greater safety. But the winter was severe and she felt the cold terribly. Her sensitiveness in this respect had become a really serious weakness. After the mild climate of Italy she could not bear Switzerland, and had it not been for the watchfulness of Koreff she did not know what would have become of her. On March 19 she writes to her mother:

"We have had a second winter and I have suffered horribly. Meanwhile time is passing and the days go by. I always live in hopes that the future days will be better than those which are past, and thus we journey through this sad vale of tears. When I do not leave my refuge and am sitting by the fire with my friends I forget our grief, and the evening passes like a dream, but if I have to put my head out-of-doors things are very different. Then I think of our friends at Rome and of the pleasant life which I led there; or of our friends at Paris whom I should so like to meet again; or of you, my dear little mother, to whom I have so much to tell."

As the days went by the news became more alarming. On April 18 Delphine writes again:

"We are sadder and more dispirited than ever; mind and heart are alike in the depths of despair; for twenty years I have spent no sadder days than these. We live like hermits and do not emerge from our hole, and this the more readily as no one notices it. We are quite sure here that we shall leave no regrets behind us. Oh! Rome, what regrets we left in you and how many we carried away with us. Our health is only tolerable; the friend has been ill and is still suffering with rheumatic pains. This climate is detestable for rheumatism, for the teeth, and I think for everything. Goodbye, I am so sad, so unwell and so depressed and gloomy that I can write no more to-day."

From time to time, to keep her hand in, Delphine commissions her mother to do small errands for her. One of these was very dear to her heart, as it concerned the purity of her complexion. The cold winds had roughened her skin, and at Paris a certain ointment of "Mme. de Bonaparte" was sold which was a sovereign remedy for the skin. Her mother must send her a small pot at once by a Swiss, M. de Chateauvieux, who was returning to Geneva. This remedy cost ten or twelve francs a pot, and she must see that it was quite fresh and pack it up so that the bearer should not know what it was, otherwise, "the news would be all over Geneva."

The good M. de Chateauvieux performed his commission and called to see Delphine, bringing the precious pot and, at the same time, to give her news of M. and Mme. de Boufflers. He could not find praises enough for the little father and constantly spoke of him. He was charming and said with delightful simplicity, "but M. de Boufflers is still quite young. And this in spite of his eighty-five years of age. Admit that he is amusing, his kindness and politeness are extreme. It is only people of that age whom I can care for; there are no others who are really good-hearted."

The cold, anxiety concerning her health, and the sadness of her life were trifles compared with another grief which overwhelmed the unhappy family. Elzéar, as we have seen, had grown intimate with Mme. de Staël, and when he was not at Coppet he carried on a regular correspondence with her. In April, 1813, this correspondence was seized, and as Fouché was no longer there to protect Delphine's brother, the unhappy young man was arrested and confined in the fortress of Vincennes by the orders of Savary. Mme. de Boufflers was astounded at this unexpected severity and feared every kind of catastrophe. Already she had visions of her unhappy son paying with his life for his imprudent correspondence. She induced her friends to intervene and used all the influence she possessed, but to no purpose, for Savary remained inflexible. When Delphine heard of her brother's misfortune she did not hesitate for a moment; she decided, whatever might be the cost, to entrust Astolphe to the care of Berstöcher and Koreff, and started for Paris to support the courage of her mother in this hard trial. There she spent six weeks in a round of audiences and petitions. At length, from Marshal Oudinot, whom she knew very well, she secured a promise that Elzéar should soon be restored to his family. She therefore started off somewhat reassured and rejoined Astolphe at the end of June. She found him ill in the house of her friends, the Odier family, who had kindly taken him in and nursed him as well as they could during her absence. A window sash had been the cause of his illness. It had not been sufficiently raised and the young man had put his head out of the window and struck the sash violently when he was withdrawing. A few days afterwards he was seized with a violent feverish attack. To complete the disaster Koreff was at Berne and was also ill. Astolphe was greatly changed, had grown pale and thin, and became feverish every evening. Mme. de Custine announced this disastrous news to her mother and concluded her letter with these disturbing lines: " I am sad and wearied to death; unhappy because I have left you and have learnt nothing of you. In short, you can have no idea of my depression; I can only write you one word to-day. When will fate weary of persecuting me? Let me hear from you often, very often, I beg. Do not tell Nanette that

Astolphe is ill; tell her that I arrived safely and that I will write to her by the first post."

The next day she wrote as she had promised to her dear Nanette. But, with touching solicitude, she says nothing about Astolphe's condition, being anxious to spare her grief and apprehension. The constant devotion which she shows for this old servant who had become the friend of the family is certainly touching:

"GENEVA, *July* 6.[1]

"We have arrived safely, Nichette. I have given your letter to your son and he will soon reply; he was very glad to see us again. We shall stay for a few days here and then we shall go to Berne, where you must write to me under the name of the friend *poste restante*. Let me hear all about you and all about my mother. Take care of yourself and hope that we may meet again sooner than we expect to do. I can only write a line, for I have a thousand things to do, and am rather tired after my journey. Tell my mother that I am not writing to-day because I feel a little unwell, and that I will write by the first post and am a little more satisfied than yesterday about the matter of which I spoke to her. Give her these lines to read and tell her that I send her my best love and have constantly thought of her and the poor prisoner. I hope she will write often.

"Farewell, Niche, we all send you our love."

At length Astolphe's health improved and all apprehensions were relieved by another piece of news at this time. Elzéar had been set at liberty; it is true that he was exiled to a distance of fifty leagues from Paris, but that was a trifle. Delphine was in exultation and wrote to her mother expressing her delight at this happy termination of a dangerous adventure.

The inhabitants of Geneva themselves, when they discovered that Delphine's society was no longer likely to compromise them, showed themselves more sociable: "The good news has produced a strange effect upon them; you have no idea how kind they have been since Elzéar was set

[1] To Mlle. Nanette Malriat, Rue de Miromesnil, No. 19, Faubourg St.-Honoré, Paris.

at liberty. There has been a general rush to congratulate me."

However, Mme. de Custine grew steadily more weary of the stay at Geneva: "The place is bewitched," she writes, "and I hate it as much as I hate its tiresome people." As Koreff was still at Berne and his absence was a source of anxiety, she resolved to go and see him, and naturally took Astolphe and Berstöcher with her. She was delighted at once by the warm welcome extended to her by the people of Berne.

"*July* 30.

"We are delighted to have left Geneva. The sight of other people and other countries makes us feel how fully justified we were in detesting the people of Geneva. I must make an exception in favour of the Odier family, who have been charming, but for the rest I can say nothing. I hate the town, and the cold politeness of the people is even more insulting than their kicks. Here there is a general kindliness which puts you at ease at once, although we have not yet seen many people, in the first place, because Astolphe is not yet well, and then because I have been ill in my turn. We have been kindly received, with all Swiss goodness, at the house of M. de Freudenreich. The whole family is as pleasant to us as people can only be in this country. What a difference between them and those wretched Geneva people!"

Astolphe's health improved by degrees, but the poor youth had been terribly tried. He writes a moving description of his sufferings to his grandmother on October 4:

"*Berne, October* 4.

"I have really been in a sad condition. Can you imagine anything worse than to have intelligence enough to understand that one is stupid, to be just capable of realising one's nonentity? This is what I have felt for many months. I was totally incapable of clear thought or keen feeling. Suffering had placed a mute upon the strings of my soul, and I was cut off from the world by a veil of sadness. I had even come to fear any piece of good news or a happy event, thinking that I was unworthy of happiness, as I was incapable of enjoying it or even realising it. These bad days are past, like many others. Our Aesculapius has eventually cured me, after exhausting all the means which his art provides. In consequence he has put two blisters on my neck, two on my arms, and two on my back, and has given me back the use of my head and my heart. For the last few days I have felt quite well, my sight is no longer blurred, and there is no band of iron round my head. But it is now four months since the accident took place."

Reassured henceforward concerning the fate of her brother, Delphine thought that she might be able to enjoy in peace the delights of her new residence. She was disappointed. She had hardly recovered from the cruel emotions through which she had passed than a new and pressing care came to disturb her peace of mind. Astolphe was summoned to France by the Conscription. The young man had been already obliged to appear before the military authorities on one occasion, but his state of health had then secured his immediate dismissal. But the Imperial Army had suffered so many losses that it was more than ever in need of young soldiers. Astolphe's exemption was annulled, and he was again summoned to Geneva for a second examination. No doubt he would have been declared fit for service on this occasion, and a departure for the army was equivalent to his death sentence. Mme. de Custine was in despair that there was no means of withdrawing; he must either appear or buy a substitute. Delphine seized at this latter alternative: "We are trying to find one," she writes, "but at what a price!" Once again the poor woman gave way beneath the weight of the miseries and misfortunes which came upon her without mercy or relaxation:

"I am overwhelmed with grief, anxiety and despair. Our woes are infinite; I have no longer strength or will to bear them. I am thoroughly disappointed and weary."

A few days afterwards Astolphe's case was settled and the substitute was found. Though Delphine was reassured for the moment she had many other griefs, and could not regard the future without a sense of terror:

"BERNE, *October* 20.

"Our health is improved; Astolphe is well and I am tolerably so. That is no longer the worst point. It is the future that disturbs the present; it is so dark and obscure that we cannot see our way and to think of it is to feel a cold hand upon one's heart. What are we to do or where are we to go? My heart is torn by a thousand anxieties and I have no rest. Do not leave my letters lying about, burn them. What has become of Nanette? Please see her as often as you can, for I am afraid something has happened to her.

"I have just received a letter from the Génie of a pleasanter nature than usual.

"It is raining in torrents and one can hardly see. I feel as sad as the weather and have not a gleam of hope in my heart, either for the present or for the future. Take care of yourself and avoid your dreadful colds; wrap up well when you are going out, but not too much indoors."

It was fated that Delphine should never have a moment's rest upon her painful path, and that every day should bring its own sorrow. After the imprisonment of Elzéar, the illness of Astolphe, and his summons to join the flag she thought that she might be able to enjoy a little rest. She was mistaken. In the course of her journey to Italy she had grown deeply attached to Koreff and thought that he shared the feeling; the idea that this new tie might be broken had never entered her mind. What was her grief and despair when the young doctor came one day and informed her that he would be obliged to return to Germany where matters of business and his future prospects required his presence. It was not a final departure, he would soon return and resume their pleasant intimacy, but for the sake of their common interests it was surely his business to make certain of the future. Delphine was crushed; it was the last stroke of fate and, perhaps, the most cruel. She made every attempt to dissuade Koreff but could only secure his promise that he would return.

Koreff therefore abandoned the little colony in November, 1813, and started for Germany. Delphine was overwhelmed with grief at his departure and remained inconsolable for months. She did not hide from her mother the mental anguish with which she was struggling. She writes to her on November 29, from Berne:

"Here we are still and here we propose to stay. I wish you were with us. I am sad and more than sad at the departure of our friend. He leaves a gap which no one can fill and a void in our affections which is even more felt than the lack of his society. You can have no idea of what he has been to us, especially since we have been so unfortunate. He will return, that at least is his desire and our hope, as soon as he has settled his monetary affairs. But who can say what the future will bring forth? And who can settle anything now? However, we must hope for the best and we must deceive ourselves in order to live. He writes to me by every post, but what a difference between writing and speaking at the present time! However, the thing is done and the only remedy is his return; all my thoughts cling to it.

"I do not feel any too well; the climate and vexation are undermining my health. You may be quite sure that I wrap up well. This country is a small Siberia for cold; but these things are very trifling and if we had no other sorrows we should be happy.

"Just think that I met Mme. Simons here (Mlle. Lange), she is still charming and talked to me of you and of Elzéar. I think that you hardly know her more than I. What people one meets on a wandering life; it is quite amusing. As you may imagine, she will not do to fall back upon, but she has amused me for the moment.

"We live in complete retirement, especially since our friend has gone. We read and write and wait for post days; that is the whole of our existence. I cannot eat or sleep; I go out for an airing to get used to the climate, and I bless the end of each day hoping that the next will be better."

The days went by and Mme. de Custine's grief remained unchanged. Nothing brings any consolation to her broken heart and her letters are but one long lamentation. On December 10 she writes to her mother:

"Pardon me if I write at such long intervals, but I am so

sad and unhappy; I might say so much and I can write so little that in my depression I had rather be silent. Since our friend went away life is but one long dark night. He often writes, but vast is the difference, and in a time of storms it is a grief not to hear the same thunder roaring. He thought he was acting for the best; he looked to the future, a mistake of his age; he thought he was securing his future happiness and mine. Do not speak of his journey to anyone, I beg, and above all not to Nanette.

"We spend the saddest of lives since our friend went away; there is no amusement or distraction. We hardly ever go out and we pass the time in order to reach post days, for they can bring some relief from all our misfortunes. It is something when they bring letters from the absent ones, but what we want is news of their return. The pitiless march of time will, perhaps, bring this day and will dry many tears. But when this will be I cannot say.

"Farewell; my health is poor and my cheerfulness has gone. Astolphe, whose youth should be the delight of us all, is older than Methuselah. With me it is the contrary; the older I grow, the stronger I feel in mental courage and youth. You will laugh at this, and with reason, for it is ridiculous, but, at the same time, it is true."

CHAPTER XXX

FEBRUARY—OCTOBER, 1814

Astolphe meets Monsieur at Vesoul—The Prince's Court—The *aristocrouches*—Arrival at Paris—Astolphe's embarrassment—He begs his mother to come and meet him—Mme. de Custine returns to Paris—Stay at Fervaques.

IN February, 1814, Mme. de Custine was still at Berne with her son. She then heard that the Comte d'Artois had just arrived at Bâle and was preparing to return to France in the train of the foreign armies. Although the future was still very dark she feared that the days of the Empire were numbered. Possibly the Bourbons would return to the throne and then it would be advisable to be one of the first to meet the new régime. If she desired nothing for herself, Astolphe must at least have his share of these advantages. Forgetting her past ardent republicanism she resolved to go to Bâle and ask for an audience of the Comte d'Artois, and to present her son who, she said, was burning to serve the good cause and die for his legitimate princes. The Comte d'Artois liked Mme. de Sabran greatly, and was neither spoilt nor impressed by the abundance of his partisans. He received Delphine very kindly and willingly granted her the permission which she asked. Astolphe was authorised to follow him and to form part of his modest Court.

Mme. de Custine returned to Berne in high delight and Astolphe prepared for his departure without losing a moment. He was delighted, thought himself a personage of some importance and already saw himself playing a part which was to be extremely brilliant. His first care was to order from the tailor of Morges a fine aide-de-camp's costume, bedizened with gold lace. Then he said farewell to his mother and Berstöcher, who remained in sadness at Berne, and started, full of enthusiasm, to join Monsieur, who meanwhile had established himself at Vesoul. To part from her son at such a moment was a cruel sacrifice for Delphine, but her anxiety for the future had outweighed all other considerations. None the less her uneasiness was great and she shed abundant tears at the departure of her son, whose precarious health she had watched for so many years with anxious love, and who was leaving his mother's protection for the first time.

Astolphe, like a good son, attempted to soothe his mother's anxiety. He wrote to her from Neuchâtel on March 1 :

"Try to calm your anxiety, for you must take care of yourself, and worry of this kind always wears people away. Providence has disposed of me in taking me from you, and will watch over what it has taken ; believe this and have the courage to believe it. I am going to ask you for something which would seem futile to a freethinker, but I think a great deal of it ; it is to pray for me twice a day, a quarter of an hour in the morning and a quarter of an hour in the evening. You can say whatever you like ; the nature of the words does not matter, provided they are offered in the hope of obtaining only eternal benefits. Ask what may be necessary for the elevation and purity of my soul, and never miss this daily half hour, whatever may happen."

Astolphe had barely passed the frontier than his illusions and his enthusiasm collapsed. His early letters show how completely he was disenchanted ; he even wonders whether his mother, in her blind affection, had not been unduly and regrettably precipitate.[1] In the first place, he is horrified at the dreadful situation of France ; the countries which he crossed seemed to produce nothing but Cossacks ; flocks and herds and the tillers of the soil had given place to hordes of brigands. He is then astounded to perceive that the party to which he had just attached himself was completely for-

[1] Astolphe's correspondence with his mother in 1814, from which we borrow the following details, was published by M. Bonnefon in the *Revue Bleue* (October, 1907). It had been communicated to him by M. La Caille.

gotten in the country and had no standing there. Even the foreigners seemed to know nothing about it. The allies were at the gates of Paris, and had not spoken a word about the Bourbons. Many talked of peace with Bonaparte, others of peace with the Senate and a Regency. If peace were made without mention of the Bourbons, he would have compromised himself to no purpose, and have sacrificed his whole future in order to pay his court to the Comte d'Artois, a very poor compensation. These prudent reflections had considerably cooled the young man's ardour, and he proceeded to rejoin the Prince very deliberately. It must be admitted that he was rather tempted to return to Switzerland than to travel away from it. However, as he could not remain indefinitely in this situation, he made up his mind and presented himself before the Prince at Vesoul. He was very kindly received, but the court was indeed a strange assembly :

"Here we have a court in full form and full magnificence, and my awkwardness therein is a sight to behold. My sword between my legs, my hat under my arm, with a uniform cut by a tailor of Morges, I am an extremely ridiculous figure. I have not yet dropped my hat, but I keep catching myself in my spurs, and I never have a hand free to do anything. Fortunately, there are plenty of people no less badly rigged up, and no one pays the least attention to it."

Astolphe would probably have been unable to bear his new life if he had not found in attendance upon Monsieur a charming young man, almost of his own age, Alexis de Noailles. The two young men became close friends and spent a great part of their time together.

No sooner had Astolphe found time to make acquaintance with the Prince's adherents than he perceived with grief that his apprehensions had been fully justified ; his disillusionment was great and complete. Brought up by his mother in liberal ideas, he was astounded by what he saw and heard. The general tone of those surrounding the Prince was deplorable and the old soldiers of Condé's army were so ridiculous in their boastful manners that they were known as the *aristocruches*.

The Court was already divided into two hostile parties, the Pietists and the Unbelievers, who were at daggers drawn. At the Prince's table the talk "ran only upon horses, dogs and good cheer":

"Our party is supported by such feeble creatures that I blush for them. When I hear the entry announced of a Knight of Saint Louis and a woman of rank I am always tempted to run away at full speed. They see none but low-class people, men and women of no account. They talk of cutting off somebody's fears, whipping somebody else and branding others, but the song that is heard on every side is, 'We want the old régime, unadulterated,' the old régime with its abuses, as M. de Narbonne says."

The Prince was not so narrow-minded as his partisans: "Monsieur was saying the other day that clear-sightedness or comprehension were of no use to the people, and that the Russians were the happiest nation in the world."

All this talk disgusted the young aide-de-camp, and the more capable he became of judging the character of Monsieur's party the more he regretted the decision which he had so lightly made at his mother's instigation.

"We are about," he writes, "to attach our name to a party which probably will not be that of France and which we can no longer abandon without dishonour and disgrace. We are proceeding to tie our hands and deprive ourselves of all means of effectively helping the country. If I had thought that a French Prince needed the support of five hundred thousand foreigners to reconquer France, I should never have espoused his cause."

All that he saw inspired him with such discouragement that he very seriously thought of leaving the Comte d'Artois and going back to his mother: "The greatest mistake one can make is to persist in a mistake; to sacrifice opinions, fortune, mother, and country to pay one's court at Vesoul seems to me the height of madness."

At the moment when Astolphe was seriously considering the idea of returning to Switzerland events rapidly changed; the situation and prospects seemed to become more favourable for the Bourbons. The Prince, after many representations, was at length authorised by the Russian commander to establish himself at Nancy, and he therefore went thither immediately, followed by his partisans. This fortunate change in events modified Astolphe's intentions and he also went to Nancy. During the days which he spent in this town the young man quotes a strange incident which throws a lurid light upon the behaviour of the various nationalities who overran his country. He relates that a foreign officer was stopped five leagues from the town by a party of well-armed peasants. They asked his nationality. "Prussian," he replied. "Then," answered the leader of the peasants, "you are our brother. Had you been a Russian or Austrian we should have shot you." The Russians devastated the countryside, plundering and burning without mercy, and the exasperation of the inhabitants reached the point of despair. As events became more favourable the Comte d'Artois and his suite made their way towards Paris under the protection of the foreign armies.

"*April* 1.

"The march of events has been miraculous. We advance, driven on by a fair wind; all is favourable and all succeeds. We have made mistakes but no matter, we shall be great men."

The nearer he approached to the capital, the more was the young man horrified by the sight of France and the dreadful poverty to which the people were reduced. The following touching description to his mother is worth quoting:

"The memories of our journey have left me profoundly sad. The state of Champagne and the neighbourhood of Paris on the east and north is enough to make one weep. The Cossacks have committed horrible outrages; our poor people are crushed and brutalised by misfortune and have not even the strength to complain. Every moment I am obliged to tell myself, 'This is France, I am in France,' to believe the fact. Since we left Vitry and made our way into the country we seem to have lost the sense of hearing; there is not a cry, not a song or a word to be heard in the streets or in the high roads. Men are to be seen sitting before their houses, which are deprived of doors, windows, and furniture, and Russians go galloping through the streets. And for fifty leagues the sight is the same everywhere. Everything smaller than a town or city has been utterly devastated; numbers of villages have been burnt and the whole country is a desolation. Fear and stupor are painted upon every countenance. I had no idea that such devastation was possible. I was greatly struck by the resignation of all whom I questioned concerning their losses."

At length Astolphe entered Paris with the Prince on April 12. The next day he wrote to his mother and informed her of the state of public feeling, of future possibilities and of the rumours which he had heard:

"I have never seen anything so extraordinary as the boulevards and they never seemed so beautiful to me as yesterday. But the indifference and carelessness of these people who dress to amuse themselves and run to see any new sight, not so much from curiosity as in order to show themselves off, filled me with profound pity. I cannot say how astounded I was, as we passed before the Théâtre Français, to see the crowd pressing in at the door as usual. "What," I thought, "our Princes are returning to Paris to-day, Bonaparte is leaving Fontainebleau for the Isle of Elba, and half Paris, not knowing how to spend the evening, is hastening to crowd the seats to hear Mlle. Duchesnoy screech or to see Mlle. Mezeray make faces. These people would more readily lose their kings than their actors.

"Furthermore, everyone says that Civil War is a chimera, that Bonaparte is more completely crushed than if he were dead, and that his own cowardice has contributed to dethrone him even more than the weapons of his enemies. For the sake of the peace of France I hope he may be assassinated during his voyage. At present it is generally admitted that admiration of the great man is dishonourable. This is the popular notion among the people and is to be heard everywhere. I should fear him still more if he were dead; the memory of him might be fatal to us.

"You will be interested to hear that people are resuming their titles and that etiquette has been in full swing since yesterday in all its wearisome severity, a thing to avoid. To my tailor I have resolved to appear as a count; they say that princes have to wait a week for a pair of trousers, dukes a fortnight, and counts and marquises three weeks. Such is my fate. I asked my tailor this morning what was the fashion in coats and he replied indignantly, 'Sir, what fashion could there have been for the last three months? We have had other things to think about.'

"No one knows what the position of the Bourbons was in France, and 'Monsieur' is an unintelligible title. People ask what Louis XVI was, get up the genealogies of our princes, and speak of them like pictures rediscovered in some old church."

The next day Astolphe writes again. On this occasion he has completely changed his views concerning the Parisians, and is quite ready to recognise his mistake:

"*April* 14.

"I am now going to make amends. I slandered the Parisians in my last letter; their enthusiasm is beyond belief, it is fabulous. Nothing like it has ever been seen; everybody has gone mad. The finger of God is to be seen everywhere. Providence is about the streets; atheism has always been frightful but now it is ridiculous; heroism is the order of the day. On the day of the Battle of Paris women walked about the Boulevards dressed as if for Longchamps, waited for the allies and cheered the Russian Emperor. And yet cannon-balls and shells were raining upon Paris and struck the house of Mme. de Vaudémont among others, but no one felt any fear. Everyone is ruined, for the farmers can pay nothing, but no one considers the fact and there is enthusiasm general and immense."

No sooner was he in Paris than Astolphe went to pay his respects to his grandmother, but he did not seem wholly satisfied with his reception:

"I have seen my grandmother," he writes, "good fortune makes no more impression upon her than misfortune. In her eyes I hold a very brilliant position, but she was not more affectionate on that account. I opened my mouth to tell her that I had left you six weeks ago; without allowing me time to finish she said, 'What, you have been six weeks in Paris!' Her mind wanders. M. de Boufflers is greatly changed, but she not in the least. Nanette is wonderfully well."

Some days afterwards he was invited to dine with Mme. de Boufflers and on this occasion his reception was somewhat warmer:

"I have been dining to-day with your mother and was much better pleased; I suppose one needs to get accustomed to them. The Troubadour was there and I was delighted with him; he is a converted character."

Astolphe did not confine his visits to his family, he also paid his respects to Chateaubriand whose patronage was not to be neglected. He had just published his pamphlet, "Bonaparte and the Bourbons," which had caused a vast sensation and the author seemed likely to play an important part. The Génie received Astolphe kindly and promised his support. The young man's ideas were now completely changed. He no longer regretted his journey to Vesoul or the fact that he had been among the first to join Monsieur's fortunes. He hoped that he would speedily reap the fruits of his conduct but he will not put in any claim, being persuaded that everything will be offered to him.

"*April* 16.

"Can you imagine," he writes, "that a month ago we were only partisans and that we are reigning in France to-day? I can congratulate myself upon my conduct hitherto. At the same time to ask for anything would be to run the risk of losing all my advantages. The dress I wear will carry me wherever I ought to be; it is the envy of all Paris and only those who were first at Monsieur's Court have the right to wear it. We are called the First Royalists. We say that six weeks ago we were only fit to be hung, and we are now making a reputation which is bound to increase."

The young man, however, speedily perceived his mistake; no one thought of him or troubled about him, and he wrote in bitterness:

"In this country one is so easily set aside that we must labour constantly at the oars, not merely to advance but to maintain our position."

Astolphe felt somewhat lost in this society, which was wholly strange to him, and amid the universal upheaval he does not know in what direction to turn ; in his letters he begs his mother to come and join him as soon as possible:

"It is dreadful for a Frenchwoman to be so far from Paris to-day," he says ; " I need you greatly. I am lost in the vast and dangerous world without your advice and support."

Naturally, the scramble for places made him uneasy. Astolphe was anxious to secure an appointment, but the question was, which ? His whole life was at stake and he could not decide without consulting his mother. Then he wants tact and cannot ask. He had attempted to secure an appointment on the staff of the Duc de Berry but failed. It will be the same in every attempt he makes. A woman and a mother is far cleverer :

"You can be very useful to me here ; women alone know how to make requests. People have so great an idea of you that you will have great influence in this business. Madame has spoken of you to several people. You can ask a private audience of Monsieur and my business would be settled in that one visit."

The Génie, whom he consulted, advised him to take service in the King's Household. Astolphe's particular desire was to be attached to the staff of Monsieur, but he would never venture to ask for a place. Mental isolation, want of guidance, the disappointments which he experienced, and above all the rise of his natural temperament, brought a new fit of melancholy and misanthropy upon the young man. Like his uncle Elzéar, he often feels a vague depression which he cannot forget and an invincible dislike for society. He confesses this disquieting defect to his mother:

" I cannot find anything anywhere to satisfy me, and the future which appears before me seems a hundred times more dreadful than misfortune. The Court will be the death of me if I have to attend it as I have been doing since my stay here. It is the Palace of Stupidity and I should die of it. Oh! for Switzerland and Italy. We did not know how happy we really were at Rome. How deeply I regret my liberty. I am most depressed and feel overwhelmed with all the wretchedness of happiness."

Somewhat anxious concerning her son's health and fearing that isolation might have an ill-effect upon him, apart from his strong desire to see her, Mme. de Custine resolved not to prolong her stay in Switzerland and left Berne with Berstöcher, reaching Paris at the end of May. She hastened to comply with Astolphe's desires and began an interminable series of interviews and requests, discouraged by no rebuffs. But place-hunters were numberless and bewildering; she received kindly words and promises for the future but nothing more. After several months of this painful anxiety, in which hope was constantly followed by disillusionment, Astolphe's depression made him ill, and his mother seized the opportunity to carry him away with her to Fervaques, which she had abandoned for two years. The good air and the delight of seeing the old Château again would restore their health. In September they are once more installed at home, expecting M. and Mme. de Boufflers, who had promised them a visit:

"FERVAQUES, *September* 7.

"Astolphe is now fairly well and so is the friend. But so much cannot be said of the weather. For the last two days we have had a hurricane and cannot put our noses out of doors for fear of being blown away. If I were near you I might let myself go before the wind and try this new mode of locomotion, but meanwhile, the gale is breaking and shattering everything. My poor trees and flowers are a miserable sight, and you will see nothing of them. Tell your husband that he must respect my cabbages, the only things which the blasts have spared. We are also keeping for him the beetroots and turnips, which are admirable; but come soon, for time is also a great devourer of vegetables. I am so sorry to hear of your headaches; you should adopt some treatment for them and persevere with it. Try taking camomile in the morning when you wake up. You ought not to let this trouble become permanent."

CHAPTER XXXI

OCTOBER, 1814—JULY, 1815

Astolphe starts for Vienna as attaché to M. de Talleyrand—The Congress—Mme. de Custine's friends—Her life at Paris—Return of Fouché to France—Death of the Chevalier de Boufflers—Astolphe's health causes his mother anxiety—Return from the Isle of Elba—The Hundred Days—Fouché in office—Return of Louis XVIII—Dismissal of Fouché.

IN October, 1814, Astolphe was again in Paris with his mother, after a stay at Fervaques, where he had recovered his health. Notwithstanding many reasons for discouragement, he redoubled his solicitations to secure some position which he thought he had deserved for his zeal in the Bourbon cause. However, no one thought of him and he received nothing but vague promises and fair words. Very fortunately for him, his friend, Alexis de Noailles, had just been appointed attaché to M. de Talleyrand, who was commissioned to represent France at the Congress of Vienna. Noailles proposed that Astolphe should come with him and undertook to secure him a position in the Prince's suite, which would provide him with occupation and bring him forward. Mme. de Custine advised her son to accept, and the two young men started cheerfully for Vienna at the end of October. Astolphe wrote to his mother immediately upon his arrival:[1]

[1] Astolphe's correspondence during the Congress of Vienna has been published by M. Bonnefon in the *Revue Bleue* (August, 1910). It had been communicated to him by M. La Caille. From this correspondence we borrow the following letters.

"*November* 2, 1814.

"The journey which we have just finished entirely resembles a dream. To see the towns, rivers, and mountains fly past one, to be amid an unknown people, to hear an unknown language, and to experience changed customs and all without leaving one's seat is astounding. I seemed to have turned a somersault in my sleep and to have fallen out of my bed into Vienna. The period of this journey seems not to have been part of my life; the last week had neither hours nor nights, nor days. We seem to have come from Paris to Vienna with one jolt; we have seen nothing but our own carriage and here we are, arrived, without eating or sleeping or stopping for a moment except to repair the carriages.

"We arrived this morning at six o'clock. Alexis has seen M. de Talleyrand, and has spoken to him of me. He replied graciously but without any definite promises. 'I do not know how we can use him,' he said, 'but bring him to me. After all he will always be useful to go into society and tell us his observations.'"

Astolphe's somewhat modest responsibilities were, in fact, confined to this occupation. But he dined every day at the Prince's table and heard the most interesting and brilliant conversation in the world. At Vienna Astolphe met once more the famous Koreff. After leaving Mme. de Custine at Berne he had made his way into the good graces of the Prince von Hardenberg,[1] Chancellor of Prussia, and had become his secretary. It was a great relief for Mme. de Custine to know that her son was in the neighbourhood of the doctor in whom she had such confidence.

Astolphe was most warmly welcomed by the society of Vienna. The Prince de Ligne, who had been very fond of his grandmother, treated him like a son and gave him the run of his house. He also made the acquaintance of Princess Clary, Princess Lubomirska, the Duc Dalberg, M. de la Tour du Pin, Von Humboldt, the Duchesse de Sagan, etc. At Vienna he also made the acquaintance of

---

[1] Hardenberg (Charles Augustus, Count, and then Prince of), 1750–1822. A Prussian statesman and the favourite of Queen Louise.

Frau von Varnhagen von Ense, wife of the second secretary to the Prussian Legation. Her cleverness and her charm had made her really famous and her salon was very select. We shall meet with her again in Frankfort in a subsequent chapter.

Astolphe's letters during the Congress are interesting. He pokes fun at "all these big-wigs gathered round a green table, professing to rule the world and unaware that the nations are no longer inclined to be governed by the selfishness of pen-holders."[1]

"Germany has reached the year '89 and this is a fact which all our old big-wigs of the Congress decline to understand. We ourselves preach legitimacy, moderation, and justice upon the housetops. But we are somewhat in the position of the fox who had lost his tail and I am afraid we produce no great impression. We are going to have balls, entertainments and masquerades and it is said that the Emperor of Russia will appear as Mars with all the gods of Olympus and all the nymphs of fable; in short, nothing will be wanting except hope. There is a gloomy background to all this outward show."

As a matter of fact, enjoyment took the first place and serious business was left in the background. "The days at Vienna," wrote von Varnhagen, "seem to be of a particular character, changing into enjoyment everything that comes in contact with them; the most ordinary and daily actions, eating, drinking, walking, and lounging, become so many pretexts for entertainments and rejoicings." His wife expressed the same idea when she wrote:

"I now begin to understand what a Congress is. It is a meeting of people who are so happy that they are unable to separate."[2]

The Prince de Ligne summed up the question in this humorous formula: "The Congress dances but it takes no steps."

While Astolphe was staying at Vienna Mme. de Custine, relieved of anxiety concerning him, set up house again at

[1] "What can be expected of the Congress?" said Talleyrand to Astolphe. "They are too frightened of one another to quarrel and too stupid to come to an understanding."
[2] *Rahel*, by Jean Edouard Spenlé. Paris, Hachette, 1910.

Paris and began to see something of her family and friends, from whom she had been separated for the last two years. Naturally she saw the Génie, and intercourse was resumed as in the past. From time to time he came to lunch with her, but his appearances were few and far between. He was more than ever absorbed by his intimacy with Mme. de Duras and by politics, for which he found an increasing attraction; his ambition was to be a minister. Astolphe, who had been informed by his mother of René's ambitious projects, wrote very sensibly:

"I am sorry to hear what you say about the Génie, both on his account and on yours. Is it for the pleasure of overcoming difficulties that he wishes to become minister? Minerva has made him a poet, and I do not think that she will make him a minister. Even granted that it led to happiness, it would not be a wise step."

The friends whom Delphine saw most frequently were her dear Princesse de Vaudémont, eccentric as ever, but a faithful friend; and also the Duc d'Otrante, who had just spent several years out of France. He was in Italy with Murat when he heard of the Emperor's resignation. As he had not abandoned his intention of playing some part he hastened to return, and established himself with his children in his Château of Ferrières. Thus he was able to keep an eye upon events, and to turn them to advantage if a favourable opportunity should occur. From that moment he maintained a very intimate and affectionate correspondence with Mme. de Custine, but dealing almost entirely with political questions. To this correspondence we shall make but the briefest allusion.[1]

Mme. de Custine would have spent the winter comparatively peaceably if she had not had the misfortune, in the month of January, to lose her stepfather, the Chevalier de Boufflers. For several years his health had been growing feeble—misfortune, trial, poverty, and, above all, old age, had undermined his energetic temperament; no one would have been able to recognise the broken wrinkled old man, scarcely

---

[1] This correspondence has been published by M. Bardoux in his volume upon Mme. de Custine. It was communicated to him by M. La Caille.

able to walk, who had lost his memory, as the smart and fiery Chevalier de Boufflers, the author of " Aline, Queen of Golconda," the life and soul of the Court of Lunéville," to whom all women were kind. Unfortunately he was nothing more than a shadow and a memory, and when he passed away, in the arms of his wife, in the month of January, 1815, it was a happy release. Mme. de Boufflers' grief was profound ; she lost the faithful companion of her life, the man whom she had loved for thirty-eight years with unfailing tenderness. She was left alone without means, ill and almost blind, to bear the burden of infirmity and the difficulties of a precarious life. Elzéar and Delphine certainly loved her tenderly, but their lives were absorbed by so many cares that the poor woman had but too much reason to fear the sadness and isolation of abandoned old age. Delphine watched over her mother with the best of care, but she herself was so preoccupied in many directions, and overcome by so many keen disappointments, that she could not give the poor, desolate woman the daily support that she would have liked.

For a long time she had noticed with anguish an element in Astolphe's temperament which recalled Elzéar's defects. Though gifted with the greatest talent the young man had a dark, uneasy, and restless mind, which was a bad omen for the future. With touching care his mother had made every effort to train him and to provide him with occupation; she had hoped to turn him in the direction of ambition, but all her efforts had failed. Not without profound terror did she observe a want of equilibrium in Astolphe's faculties, and her letters show the anxiety which she felt. Her son was no less unhappy for the grief which he caused the mother whom he adored:

"In your letter there is something so dreadful that I cannot read it without trembling," he writes to her one day, "and it is I who am the cause of this trouble. This is the idea which is killing me. Teach me to make you happy so that I can be happy; we are doing one another harm for we agitate and distress one another. We must be calm."

On another occasion he writes:

"I have your letter ; I knelt down and prayed after reading it to ask God to make me worthy of such a mother. I cannot tell you how I grieve when I think of the mischief I am doing to all of you. My strange state of mind makes me a burden to everyone. I feel that I weigh upon them and cannot relieve them of myself."

After spending some months in a fairly satisfactory state of health Astolphe was again troubled by his headaches. Delphine certainly felt reassured by the presence of Koreff, but she could not fail to be disturbed by this repetition of a brain trouble which certainly announced some morbid condition. Astolphe's letters were very disquieting :

"Vienna, *January* 27, 1815.

"My indisposition is a serious illness rather for its cause than for its effects. People are often in much greater pain without being so ill as I am. This astounding sensitiveness of the brain requires infinite precautions. It is not enough to cure it; a repetition must be prevented, for such illness eventually has a terrible influence upon the character. The fact is that for the last two years I have not been entirely well. For it is not only health that a brain disease can cause us to lose and I may for a time to come remain under this irritability. I should like to have a case made for my head, a cap lined with iron wire with a covering of varnished cloth or something of the sort. If I were King I would call the whole of my Council together to devise some form of head-protection."

"*February* 1, 1815.

"For the last three weeks I have only been out of my room twice. Koreff forbids me to take the air absolutely, saying that in such weather it might be the worst possible thing for me. This imprisonment has already done me more good than anything that I might have seen or done out-of-doors. None the less I am very sad in a room which is as gloomy as all those of Vienna, with no one to see except occasional visitors. But I feel that my mind is growing clearer, that my courage is rising and I lean in full confidence upon the hand that guides me, feeling that I am not dependent upon myself and that by my own mere will I cannot succeed in driving away any of the thoughts that trouble me."

However, Astolphe had found a family who were very kind

to him and whom he continually praises in his correspondence, the Schlosser, with whom he spent a great part of his time.

"*May* 10.

"I have your No. 48, which is quite heart-breaking because it depicts the sadness of your life so thoroughly that I cannot tear my thoughts from it. Meanwhile I am watched very tenderly and loved like yourself at Berne by my good friends, the Schlosser, who are such people as are not found every day. They have that unspoken kindness which goes so entirely to the heart and is so little known in France. I like them more every day; we do not spend a day without meeting, for we dine together. This reminder of family life amid the somewhat incoherent existence of Vienna has done me inexpressible good; it is saving both mind and emotion, which were alike wandering. The bachelor's life is a dreadful thing; bachelors are the cancers of civilisation."

While Astolphe was ill at Vienna most serious events had taken place in France and at Paris. In March, 1815, a brief note from Fouché told Mme. de Custine that Napoleon had disembarked in the Gulf of Juan and was marching upon Paris in triumph. At this news Delphine was overwhelmed, took fright and was at first anxious to flee to the provinces or abroad, but her friend dissuaded her from departing and his influence was strong enough to persuade her.

"*March* 12, 1815.

"Do not think of leaving Paris, I urge you," he writes, "you have friends here and we will support you mutually. Be assured that the military government which has invaded us will be of no long duration."

Three days afterwards, in a secret interview at the house of the Princess de Vaudémont, the Comte d'Artois in the name of Louis XVIII offered Fouché the Ministry of Police. He refused, saying that it was too late. The next day, as it was feared that he might misuse the revelations which he had heard, an attempt was made to arrest him, but he was on his guard. He possessed the key of the garden of Queen Hortense, the wall of which adjoined his own grounds. He crossed the wall by a ladder, leapt into the garden and took refuge with a friend.[1]

Four days later, although he detested the Emperor, and though his letters show the keenest hostility to him, Fouché accepted the Ministry of Police which Napoleon had offered him, almost as soon as he was installed in the Tuileries. On this side, then, Mme. de Custine could be at her ease, as long as Fouché was there she knew that she was safe. She therefore waited at Paris and watched the course of events.

The situation was by no means so reassuring to her friend Chateaubriand. The famous pamphlet, *Bonaparte and the Bourbons*, naturally marked him out for the vengeance of the Bonapartist party. As soon as the march of the Emperor upon Paris was known René was panic-stricken and his friends perhaps even more so. Mme. de Duras, who was more than ever attached to him, begged the King to find him a place on a foreign mission, and he was appointed to the Legation at Stockholm. Instead of going to his new post he thought the simpler plan was to follow Louis XVIII to Ghent, where he performed the functions of Minister of the Interior.

Fouché was under no illusion concerning the probable duration of the new reign. This remark concerning the Emperor is attributed to him:—

"He has returned from the Isle of Elba even madder than he went and he will not last three months." The Duc d'Otrante also did his utmost to provide for the future. He showed himself most kind to the nobility, mollifying the rigorous measures. At Ghent his name was always mentioned with emotion and people were never tired of praising his kindness.[2] After Waterloo and the abdication he and Talleyrand appeared before Louis XVIII at Arnouville. Talleyrand returned as President of the Council, and Fouché, at the instance of the Royalist Party and in spite of the repugnance of Louis, became Minister of Police.[3]

[1] M. Gaillard, a former member of the Oratory like himself, whose appointment he had secured as Councillor to the Court of Appeal of Paris. Bardoux, *Mme. de Custine*. [2] Bardoux, *op. cit.*
[3] "What a figure the most Christian King cut between those two unfrocked monks," wrote Duc Victor de Broglie. Pozzo di Borgho, when he saw them get into a carriage, said, "I should much like to hear what those lambs are saying."

No sooner was he installed in the ministry than Fouché was obliged to take measures against his former friends. Carnot, among others, was obliged to withdraw to the interior of France. " Where do you wish me to go, traitor ? " he wrote to his former colleague in the executive power, " Wherever you like, idiot," replied Fouché. Throughout this period the Minister regularly informed Mme. de Custine of the course of events and his letters are remarkable for his great depth of view and his rare insight into the future. Although he had been summoned to power at the instance of the Royalist Party he had numerous enemies and his position speedily became very difficult. He sought support upon every side; he knew that Chateaubriand was very hostile to him and imagined that he could bring him to a better frame of mind if he could have a close and intimate conversation with him at the house of a common friend, and asked Mme. de Custine to be this benevolent intermediary. Delphine, ever kind and ever ready to serve, lent herself to this purpose and brought René and the Duc d'Otrante together at dinner. The latter came anxious to please and ready to make every concession, but the former, who had been unwilling to accept the invitation, showed a lofty and disdainful air which was not calculated to favour effusiveneses or confidence. Neither the efforts of Delphine nor the exertions of Fouché could overcome the stiffness of René; the dinner was a very dull affair and the party separated soon afterwards knowing that the meeting had brought them no nearer together. Chateaubriand, referring to this dinner in his *Mémoires*, says: " He did not utter a single word which showed any originality of ideas or any unusual insight. I came out shrugging my shoulders at crime. M. Fouché has never pardoned my dryness or his failure to make an impression upon me."

The Duc d'Otrante did his utmost to maintain himself in power; he had speedily forgotten his conduct during the Terror and he imagined that his admirers were no less forgetful of it. However, he had become another man ; he was kind and generous, especially to his friends. Knowing that Mme. de Custine was anxious to go to her invalid son in Germany, he brought her a passport with his own hands and put his purse at her disposal. The marriage of Fouché with Mlle. de Castellane seemed to strengthen his position for the moment. Louis XVIII signed the contract.

But the Minister of Police had an implacable enemy in the Duchesse d'Angoulême; moreover, the Royalist Party which had regarded him as indispensable as long as there was any danger and had looked upon him as their saviour could now find no epithet too insulting for him and loudly called for the dismissal of the infamous Jacobin and the regicide. Eventually the King yielded, and after holding office for three months Fouché was dismissed. As some compensation, he was appointed Minister in Saxony. Need we add that two friends remained immutably faithful to him in his misfortune, Mme. de Custine and the Princesse de Vaudémont. The Minister left Paris on October 4, 1815. In his farewell letter to Mme. de Custine he said : " I have not gained the success which I desired ; I have used argument to men who would only listen to passion ; possibly also my ideas were too large for the heads into which I attempted to get them."[1]

[1] Bardoux, *Mme. de Custine.* Fouché settled at Dresden, but after a few months there he came under the operation of the law which exiled the regicides who had performed public functions during the Hundred Days. He resigned himself to this further misfortune and retired to Prague in 1816. After vainly attempting to secure permission to reside in England, he was allowed by the Emperor of Austria to settle at Trieste. There he died on December 25, 1820, after a short illness through disease of the chest.

CHAPTER XXXII

July—December, 1815

Astolphe leaves Vienna and settles at Frankfort—He goes to Schlangenbad to take the waters—Marriage proposals—Albertine de Staël—Astolphe begs his mother to come to him—Mme. de Custine settles at Frankfort.

DURING the course of these events in France, when Fouché disappeared from the scene in which he had played so sad a part, Mme. de Custine was troubled by the most cruel anxieties. She was more than ever uneasy concerning Astolphe, and the news which she received was far from reassuring. The young man was still at Vienna and still unwell; in spite of Koreff's care his condition did not seem to improve. The letters which his mother frequently received from him were evidence of extreme mental trouble, and we may say even of cerebral disturbance. On May 31 he wrote:

" I have a great deal more that I might say but I give up the attempt in despair. Such correspondence is worse than absolute silence. My heart is full and I cannot relieve it; if I could speak I would not tell you a single thing, for I live far from the world and pass by men on the great high road of life, or rather, on a little path by the side of the high road.

" I am wholly occupied with a book upon St. Martin which has just been lent to me and by which I am delighted. It is a series of isolated thoughts but they reveal a whole soul, a new world where one can rest as in a newly discovered land. In reading St. Martin curiosity is aroused, not by his words but by his actions. If he were alive I should go to him and beg him on my knees to instruct me, not by words which would teach me nothing, but by allowing me to live with him. I have a great and most urgent need to become a disciple and until I have found my Messiah I shall have no rest. Perhaps my misfortunes are due to the fact that I am looking for him on earth. I should have lived eighteen centuries earlier to be entirely happy but faith replaces this happiness and so I am trying to make progress in prayer."

Astolphe's religious enthusiasm was nothing new. A year previously a rumour had gone about that he proposed to take Orders and was so positively stated as to make his grandmother anxious. To a pressing inquiry Mme. de Custine had replied: "What you ask me concerning Astolphe is mere gossip at present, but I may tell you between ourselves, he is quite capable of such an action. I do not know how the rumour arose for, at the moment, the only evidence for it is an exaggerated pietism. We certainly shall not be accused of influencing him in this direction. I do not know what will be the outcome."

Astolphe's physical sufferings and his fits of mysticism were not the only symptoms which caused Mme. de Custine profound anxiety. There were, unfortunately, other more serious considerations. During his stay at Vienna Astolphe had become intimate with a young German named Wilhelm von . . . who had immediately gained unbounded influence over him. In his letters Astolphe continually speaks of this new friend and calls him his "brother." With maternal insight and prudence Mme. de Custine had been much disquieted by the progress of this intimacy and this passionate friendship which she could not understand. She feared, with reason, the consequences which might result for the weak character and the ill-balanced brain of her unhappy son. She had given him the best of advice, but he had found a thousand reasons for refusing it. At this moment Wilhelm was recalled to his family and went away to Darmstadt. His departure produced a fit of complete despair in Astolphe. The young man had but one idea, to leave Vienna and settle nearer to the friend who had become inseparable. The project, however, was out of the question for the moment; communication was very difficult and very expensive and Astolphe's pecuniary resources were so limited that he had been obliged to take rooms in a poor little lodging on the fourth floor. These disappointments aggravated his malady, his headaches increased and he became extremely feverish. Fortunately his landlord's family were good people who looked after him most carefully; Koreff did not abandon him and came to see him every day. However, medical science could do nothing for a purely nervous disease.

Since the departure of Wilhelm, Astolphe had taken a complete dislike to Vienna and the mere idea that he could not go away increased his sufferings to a remarkable degree. He thought that all was lost when Alexis de Noailles, who came to see him constantly, told him that he was starting for Frankfort with M. de Talleyrand and was commissioned to offer him a place in the Prince's carriage. At this news the invalid leapt out of bed, his fever disappeared, and he recovered his strength and was ready to start at once. The idea of "escaping from his prison" and drawing nearer to the friend whom he deeply regretted had been enough to cure him, at any rate to outward seeming. On the appointed day he entered the carriage with his companions but Koreff insisted that a Brother of Mercy should accompany him. He wrote to his mother on July 23:

"I have almost literally left my bed to enter the carriage, with a blister which I have had on my neck for five months and a cautery on my skull for three weeks. We travelled in an open landau, unprotected from the mid-day sun or the cold at night. Three years ago it would have been a pleasure but to-day it was torture. However, in four days and four nights I reached Frankfort where I took leave of dear Alexis and his patron and my Brother of Mercy.

"I cannot yet understand how I contrived to bear the journey. The first day I thought I should be obliged to stop twenty-five leagues from Vienna. My poor head ached unbearably and my legs were so weak when I got down. But I said nothing of it, as I wished to go as far as possible, and by dint of strong coffee I bore up so well that my travelling companions continually complimented me upon my appearance. However, I counted the post-houses with inexpressible anxiety. The last two nights I was feverish, but no sooner had I taken my morning coffee than I recovered. Alexis was most kind throughout the journey and we had much agreeable conversation. I was forgetting a parasol which I held for these two hundred leagues as the sun became unbearable."

At Frankfort our travellers separated; while Talleyrand and Alexis de Noailles continued their journey to Paris, Astolphe remained alone amid the Prussians and Austrians until he could go to Darmstadt to meet his friend Wilhelm. Noailles, before starting, was so kind as to leave him the sum of 100 louis for his expenses.

Astolphe's letters to his mother precisely reflect the religious excitement by which he was overcome. They cannot be summarised, and some extracts will give the best possible idea of the invalid's state of mind:

"FRANKFORT, *June* 17.

"I am starting this evening for Darmstadt where I shall spend a week, for my soul's health. I want it, for I feel like a spring run down. I have never felt the weight of life so much as to-day; indeed, my heart is not strong enough to beat with joy at the moment of meeting with my brother. I am totally changed and become a new man. Pain has remodelled me, and excitement gives me a temporary strength, but my usual condition is one of lethargy.

"I am astounded at the sweetness there is in suffering. My heart melts into tears which my eyes cannot shed, and yet my soul is at rest. Peace is with me. I see no limit to our griefs, and I fear that you will never reach that point of courage. The great art of living is to allow God to work in us and to give Jesus Christ always the first place in our hearts. I do not recognise this gift in you, and for this reason am particularly frightened. My life is nothing but one long prayer for you and for the friend who needs so much to leave the hurry and disturbance of our present age. But I feel that we can leave it when we wish, and the largest square in Frankfort for me is a cloister. I abandon myself to the torment of absence and disappointment, and the discipline is far more efficacious in me than that of monasticism. My soul is becoming as supple as a reed, and I bow, in spite of myself, before the Almighty Being that I adore more profoundly as my weakness is more complete. The less I exist the more I need the One who ever exists."

For several months Astolphe had had no news of his mother and was very anxious. However, he thought that she was in safety in one of the provinces. When a letter at length arrived and told him that Delphine had not left Paris during the Hundred Days, he was startled by fears of what might have happened. He writes to her from Schlangenbad where the doctors had sent him to take the waters:

"SCHLANGENBAD, *July 22*, 1815.

"I would have kissed your letter if I had not been ashamed of myself. Heavens! to remain at Paris! I should have died if I had dreamed of it. How fortunate that I was living here where we get no news. I am well aware of the danger in the provinces under Bonaparte, but we have been told that Paris was on fire at least ten times. None the less I thought that you were far away, and it is both useless and impossible to describe what I have suffered.

"My health, though better, is not completely restored. It needs you. My brother has done me much good, and I remembered, after spending several days with him, that there were still some joys in the world for me. Oh! mother, what have I suffered! It was too much! God has had pity on me. Besides, you hurt me. I see you there before me and after a long absence you appear as a spectre. For several months I have been endeavouring to drive away your apparition which was killing me, and it has returned with your letter.

"I live here in the most complete solitude but it does not seem to me in any way sad. The waters are not strong but extremely gentle in their operation, and do me the greatest good. I am ordered entire rest of mind and soul. I am also ordered entire happiness."

These letters, in which Astolphe depicts his mental troubles in such startling colours, were torture to Mme. de Custine. Persuaded that marriage would be the best and most rapid remedy for the sufferings of the unfortunate young man, she did her best to distract him from this solitude which was so fatal to him. Through his uncle Elzéar, Astolphe had made the acquaintance of Mme. de Staël some years before and had constantly seen her daughter Albertine and had not hidden the deep impression which she had made upon him at first sight. Mme. de Staël, on her side, seemed to regard Astolphe favourably and had hinted upon several occasions that a marriage proposal would not raise objections from her. Mme. de Custine, in her anxiety, clung to this idea and wrote to Astolphe begging him to give up these wild dreams and gain some common sense and to come in touch with the reality of life by making a flattering marriage which seemed to offer every chance of happiness.

Astolphe replies in the same sense as his mother and recognises that a happy marriage would be the most complete happiness for him, and that Albertine is the only woman who has really made any impression upon his mind. He admits that in this union he finds all that he could desire. A family which is not French, a circle of friends intellectual with the only kind of intellect which pleases him, no narrow-mindedness or vulgar commonplaces, etc. But on reflection he raises some objections. How can he decide upon so serious a step without seeing the girl again, and how could he see her again forthwith? He could, indeed, have gone to Coppet but his action would be too obvious and the step too compromising. Then Astolphe has other scruples; he does not like society and does not wish to go into it. How would this very pronounced taste in himself agree with the education and the tastes of Mlle. de Staël? The more he considers the matter the more his uncertainty increases. He certainly desires marriage but, at the same time, he is afraid of it; he wishes it but he does not want it. He writes: "I am more afraid that I may regret missing this marriage than I am anxious to bring it about. I fear that I may let slip a unique opportunity of becoming happy and thus making you happy, and that I may reproach myself with it all my life." So he cannot decide to act but he will not give up the idea: "Keep Albertine's future always in view. Do not raise any objections but also do not attempt to accelerate the affair. These things are generally settled automatically or, at any rate, without interference.

For three months the correspondence between the mother and son turned only upon this eternal subject. To every one of his mother's entreaties Astolphe replies by new fears and hesitations. At length Mme. de Custine, in despair, tells her son that there was a talk of a marriage between Mlle. de Staël and Duc Victor de Broglie. Astolphe heard the news with no great emotion and replied philosophically: "I do not know whether Albertine would have made me happy but I have never felt any desire for marriage except with her. I neither can nor could think of another for long. Therefore I am entirely resigned and shall be even somewhat relieved when the matter is settled." He goes on to declare, however, that if the marriage takes place he will never see either Victor or Albertine again.

Astolphe, however, was not entirely absorbed by his matrimonial projects, and his life at Frankfort was not entirely void of interest. A proposal had been mooted that the new Federal Diet might meet in this town, and in expectation of this event many diplomatists had already come into residence, among others the Prince von Hardenberg, Herr von Varnhagen,[1] etc. Naturally Koreff had accompanied his Prince, and Astolphe had the pleasure of meeting his friend and his doctor again. The young man went to receptions, and his intelligence and the variety of his knowledge secured him a warm welcome everywhere. Mme. de Custine was delighted to see her son living in a select literary and elegant society.

Astolphe, during his stay, had the pleasure of meeting Goethe several times. When his mother heard that he had been introduced to the great poet she was delighted; the thought that he was to meet this illustrious man in society inspired her with enthusiasm, and she fondly writes to Astolphe that in such society he would improve prodigiously. He writes:

"I laughed when I read the expectations that you have formed of Goethe. Surely you know that nothing is more

[1] While Varnhagen went to Paris to take his part in the negotiations for the second treaty of 1815, his wife settled for a time at Frankfort.

difficult than to approach and interest this extraordinary man. He has been kind to me and I shall be able to claim acquaintance wherever I meet him but nothing more, though that is a great deal. Besides, what do you suppose that he could discover in me? I am like the storm-tossed lake in which no reflection can be seen. Schloffer, who tries every question, does not advise me to become more intimate with Goethe. You would have been more successful with him than I for he is very fond of beauty and naturalness. Unfortunately he is not staying in Frankfort.

At the outset of September Astolphe suffered a further attack and the unhappy young man, over-burdened with anxiety, writes thus sadly to his mother:

"I am ill again; my head is heavy and stupid with a sense of cold and sickness, a most annoying condition. Farewell to my future and my proposals, for nothing can be done in this intermittent state of illness and health. I live like a pendulum and move, sometimes to the good, and sometimes to the bad, unable to advance directly."

After some days the malady increased and became terribly severe. Then a cessation occurred. Astolphe was able to recover himself and to write under the impression of the dreadful days through which he had passed:

"FRANKFORT, *Wednesday,*
"*September* 20.

"I will begin by saying that I am better, surprisingly better, as usually happens after my attacks, but this has been one of the worst. I have been quite insane. They say that the equinox is my bad time; this much is certain, that I was out of my senses for three days, for I do not remember a single word of my thoughts then. I saw nothing but darkness behind me, and if I had not a long letter which I wrote to you in a fit of grief and despair I should think that I had been asleep. I do not send you this sad picture of my mental suffering; I am assured that it is physical, but the fear of going insane is a new torture which is more severe than all the others. I feel as if my mind was suffocating; such is my mental condition."

Astolphe was extremely anxious to see his mother again.

In every letter he begs her to come and meet him at Frankfort. They might spend the winter so pleasantly with a few good friends, far from the storms of politics: "You must need a change from Paris," he wrote, "you can live here more cheaply and rest your eyes from a sight which must be dreadful. How you must be suffering! There are days when the grief of separation from you makes me absolutely homesick, for you are my only native land."

Mme. de Custine would have been delighted to yield to her son's wishes, and would have been far less uneasy if she had been near him, but there were many reasons to keep her in Paris. In the first place her hardly-tried mother had been plunged in grief by the death of her life's companion; then France was passing through a terrible crisis and everyone felt his resources diminishing daily.

Delphine, in particular, was in a very precarious position; she could draw no money from the farmers and had great difficulty in meeting her son's expenses and living herself.[1] The journey from Paris to Frankfort was very expensive, and then was it reasonable to have three households, one at Paris, one at Fervaques, and one at Frankfort? Moreover, the roads in Germany were blocked by the Russian armies and travel was unusually dangerous. Not a day passed on which isolated travellers were not plundered and held to ransom by Russian soldiers. After much hesitation affection outweighed prudence, and Delphine decided to start. She was obliged to borrow a considerable sum of money to be able to make the journey. By way of economy she gave up her rooms in Paris and stored her furniture.[2] But as she did not wish to disappoint Nanette, who adored Paris and could not be resigned at leaving her, she hired for her a pretty little room until she should return.

---

[1] Astolphe's letters are full of requests for money; in one year he spent 4,200 francs. His illness was a very expensive matter, for Koreff's prescriptions were "ruinous." At Frankfort the hotels were very dear, "and then one eats so much in Germany." Then he adds, "I had a servant who could only save for himself and became wildly extravagant whenever I was concerned. He cost me sixteen louis from Vienna to Darmstadt and three from there to Switzerland. What made me especially angry was the way in which he saved for himself."

[2] The Prussian soldiers billeted upon Mme. de Custine were excellent people and helped her to move house.

Astolphe was delighted by the news of his mother's forthcoming arrival. He hastened to find her a suitable room, and was greatly helped in his search by the Princess von Stolberg : " She is full of kindness," he writes, " she says that it is mere selfishness, and I daresay it is. She is dying of curiosity to see you. She is a pleasant person, by nature a bore, but not devoid of common sense or intellect; she is what is known as very high class, for she was formerly a lady canon, which explains everything."

After much searching Astolphe at length found a flat facing the sun which seemed suitable at a pinch. There was a fine ante-chamber which might serve as a dining-room, a drawing-room, a bedroom, and then on the same landing, though separately, there was a room for Berstöcher, a kitchen, another room for Jenny, the chamber-maid. The household linen and crockery were provided, but not the knives and forks. The whole flat, with the stable and Astolphe's room, was to cost nine louis and fifteen francs a month : " It is not dear for Frankfort or for this year when the meeting of the Diet which is, however, quite uncertain, has inspired all landlords to ask enormous prices. Finally forty francs a month would be expended upon wood. This is enormous, but it is a German calculation, for all Germans like to roast themselves."

The Princess von Stolberg urged Delphine to bring some bed covering, saying that the " counterpanes here are very poor and that she should have some silken covering for her feet. I said that I thought you had nothing of the kind, whereupon she cried loudly, a Parisian lady ! She advises you to bring your eiderdown, which perhaps will not be out of place in the carriage."

Astolphe also urgently asks his mother to bring him his little cloak of oiled silk, which he has been wanting continually as it is so convenient. Mme. de Custine started in December and reached Frankfort without difficulty.[1]

---

[1] These letters are addressed to the Rue de Miromesnil, No. 19, Faubourg Saint-Honoré. All the letters addressed by Astolphe to his mother for the years 1814, 1815, and 1816, of which we have just quoted numerous extracts, have been communicated to us by M. La Caille, who has placed at our disposal, with the utmost kindness and courtesy, his magnificent collection of autographs.

CHAPTER XXXIII

JANUARY—DECEMBER, 1816

Mme. de Custine's stay at Frankfort—She there spends the whole winter of 1816—Intimacy with Frau von Varnhagen von Ense—She returns to Fervaques — Correspondence with Frau von Varnhagen.

As we have seen in the preceding chapter, Mme. de Custine reached Frankfort at the end of December, 1815, and took up her residence with Astolphe. Apart from the great delight of seeing her son again she had the pleasure of renewing acquaintance with her dear Koreff, and resumed the kindly relations so suddenly interrupted two years before at Berne.[1] Through Astolphe and Koreff Delphine rapidly made several acquaintances and soon had good friends around her to soften the sadness of her exile.

"The life which I lead here," she writes to her mother, "is by no means agreeable from the social point of view, but I have formed a pleasant little circle of acquaintance; the Minister Humboldt is the most important figure. No one could be more clever or more graciously clever. This pleasant society distracts my thoughts though it does not console me for the absence of my friends." The absence of friends was not complete, as one of them pushed her friendship so far as to come and meet her at Frankfort. Before

[1] Some years later Chateaubriand met at Berlin Herr von Hardenberg and also Koreff, whom he had detested since the journey to Italy. He writes of him in his *Mémoires:* "Herr von Hardenberg, a fine old man, as white as a swan, as deaf as a post, going off to Rome without permission, finding amusement in too wide a direction, believing all sorts of chimeras and, finally, devoted to magnetism in the hands of Dr. Koreff, whom I met on horseback riding in remote places between the devil, medicine, and the muses . . ."

leaving Paris Delphine had said goodbye to the Princesse de Vaudémont and, half in jest and half in earnest, had urged her to come and meet her at Frankfort, confidently boasting of the pleasures of a winter in that town. The old Princess had given a non-committal answer, and great was Delphine's surprise and pleasure when she saw her arrive one fine morning escorted by her menagerie. The Princess spent the whole winter in Germany and was a great resource to her friend. But Mme. de Custine was to make a new friend at Frankfort bringing a fresh charm to her life and adding a real pleasure to her time of exile. We have mentioned upon several occasions the name of Frau von Varnhagen whose acquaintance Astolphe had made at Vienna and whom he had recently met again at Frankfort. This extraordinary woman, whose salon was famous in Germany during the earliest years of the nineteenth century, deserves more than a passing mention.

Rahel Antonie Frederica Levin was born at Berlin on March 19, 1771. She was the daughter of a Jew who had a jeweller's shop in the Jägerstrasse; she was severely brought up, and to mental suffering cruel physical pain was often added. But the girl was endowed with unusual intelligence and an energetic soul and struggled desperately against her fate: "Such gifts as I have received," she wrote one day, "are not cheaply gained, they must be paid for with suffering." It was Goethe who discovered in the girl unexpected views of nature, of the world and of life, and who rescued her from the moral Ghetto where she was fading. Of the garret where she passed all her youth she says: "It was my mausoleum, where I loved, lived, suffered and revolted. There I learned to read Goethe. In his presence I grew up and to him I vowed eternal reverence. There I spent nights, sometimes awakened by pain; there I looked at the sky, the stars and the world with some dim hope and, at any rate, with a heart full of desire. I was innocent, no more so than to-day, but I believed that the world was kind and good, or at least, might be so. I was young.[1]

[1] Jean Edouard Spenlé, *Rahel*, Paris, Hachette, 1910. M. Spenlé has drawn with incomparable charm a delightful figure of Rahel. From his interesting and curious book we borrow the details here given concerning her.

At first she gathered in her attic in the Jägerstrasse a few intimate friends with whom the whole range of human learning was discussed. As Rahel's reputation increased she received in her salon the most illustrious representatives of Berlin society, and people fought for introductions. The young woman, with her irresistible charm, her delicate and, at the same time, powerful intellect, turned all heads.

"Few women," says M. Spenlé, "have faced life with a more lucid, more courageous, and more untrammelled courage." Frederich Gentz wrote to her: " You are romanticism in person and this you were before the term was invented. Your character throws more light upon the matter than piles of dissertations could do."

" Until 1806 Rahel's star shone most brilliantly. It may be asked by what means this woman who had passed the age of thirty succeeded in gathering around her so diversified a society and what was the real charm in her personality and her conversation." [1]

When Herr von Varnhagen, who was afterwards to marry her, met her in 1803 for the first time he drew this portrait of her which is strikingly true to life:

"I saw a light and graceful little person come forward, a delicate rounded form with hands and feet extraordinarily small. Her face was framed in thick black ringlets and struck me by its high intellectual distinction. It would have been difficult to say whether her dark eyes, alert and penetrating, gathered more from their environment than they gave out. The expression of suffering gave especial sweetness to her open countenance. Dressed in a dark costume there was something shadowy and furtive about her, though, at the same time, she was at her ease and decided. I was particularly struck by the grave sweet tone of her voice, which rose like a bell from the depths of her heart, and also by her very original manner of expressing herself in a way perfectly natural, with happy and unexpected turns of phrase. She showed simplicity, brilliancy, and candour by turns. At the same time a certain accent of sincerity seemed to warn the most decided objector that he would waste his time in attempting to blunt or turn the keen point

[1] M. Spenlé, *op. cit.*

of this mind which was as if moulded in bronze. Yet her presence radiated kindliness and put the simple and modest at their ease forthwith."

She had made a journey to Paris in 1801, and preserved the following impressions of Paris and the French:

"I also am in love with France, with Paris and everything that there moves," she writes to a Parisian friend. "I am charmed by everything that you do, by your movements, by the people you see and by the hats which you wear. How I love Paris! I only realise the fact when I leave it. What an exquisite place to stay in, and how well everything is arranged for the conveniences of life. And then my dear Frenchmen are so kind, so polite, and so easy of intercourse. . ."

When she returned to Germany by way of Brussels she wrote again these charming lines:

"You cannot imagine how grief-stricken I feel at Brussels. Though French is spoken there I find myself suddenly outside France, and seem to be suddenly transported into a land of barbarism. That which a German leaves when he comes to France he carries with him in the depths of his heart; he need but meet two or three compatriots to find himself at once at home; but that which we leave in France we can nowhere recover. I would compare it to a pure atmosphere; we only appreciate it when we have lost it and we begin to fade for want of it, for it is the essential element of life."

Herr von Varnhagen had been in love with Rahel since 1803, but from 1806–1814 he was on campaign with the Austrian army, and not until September, 1814, was he able to marry the woman he adored.[1] He was thirty years of age and she was more than forty-two, but his worship of her continued to the last day.

"Certain chance words of yours," he said to his wife, "have taken root in me so deeply and have thrown out such vigorous shoots that I was completely changed. You are to

[1] On the very day of her marriage Rahel was converted to the Lutheran religion. Herr von Varnhagen, in 1814, had left the Prussian army to enter the diplomatic service, and by the influence of the Chancellor, von Hardenberg, he had been appointed second Secretary to the Legation.

me what the Bible is to the believer. He carries it ever with him in his thoughts and in the thousand events of his life, discovering constantly secret coincidences with himself and lessons for him alone. It penetrates his knowledge and the whole circle of his joys and griefs, and becomes a torch illuminating his whole life."[1]

No sooner had Astolphe been introduced to Rahel than he came under the charm of her personality and mind. "I am bound to her for ever," he writes, "though I am not in love with her." Something of the same effect was produced upon all the friends of the household: "The fact is that men instinctively felt in the case of Rahel an excessive superiority, a moral and intellectual energy unduly great, a perspicacity and firmness of thought almost masculine, and a critical power and insight which seemed to place her above the passionate homage of love."[2]

Custine soon became one of the most constant visitors at Rahel's salon, and as soon as his mother was at Frankfort he dragged her off to Frau von Varnhagen. At this time Rahel was forty-five years of age and Delphine forty-six. At their first meeting the two ladies felt irresistibly attracted; they gave their feelings full vent and became intimate friends in a few days. Rahel had a passion for friendship: "I am ready," she said, "to serve my friends with my blood." She introduced her new friend to all her acquaintances, among others to Frau Schlegel, Count Flemming, Prince Gustav von Mecklenburg, Herr and Frau von Humboldt, etc. They saw one another constantly and were inseparable. During the day they would take long walks in the neighbourhood of the town or talk for hours at a time, or Rahel would introduce Delphine to the principles of the German language. In the evening they were always together in her drawing-room.

Thus the winter of 1816 was one of the happiest periods in Delphine's life. Her intimacy with Rahel made her stay

[1] "Varnhagen was not an attractive character. Up to the time of his marriage his life had been a series of mistakes, checks, and failures. He had entered life under an evil star and had been early embittered. A mass of suppressed animosities had grown up within him, animosity to those about him and to the destiny which had not given him the rank he desired." (*Rahel*, by Spenlé.)

[2] Spenlé, *op. cit.*

at Frankfort delightful. Then she had the satisfaction of seeing that Astolphe, under the influence of this irresistible charmer, was less gloomy and disappointed. With indescribable joy she saw that he was beginning to cling to life; he would even follow his mother and her new friend in their walks and share their conversation, while the intimacy of these kindly women soothed his nerves and calmed his imagination. Full of pity for this gifted and unhappy being Rahel surrounded him with kind intentions. She soon conceived a very warm friendship for him and they corresponded for a long time.[1]

"Frau von Varnhagen's conversation," says Astolphe, "was not a more-or-less brilliant speech, it was an action peculiar to herself, always unexpected in its nature because it was actuated by the needs of the moment and the temperament of the person talking with her. Talking, indeed, is not the word; whatever was said to Frau von Varnhagen was a confession, voluntary or not. Never did so beneficent an illumination reach a suffering heart. She could interest a circle as much as a single friend. Her mind was never at a loss because it was more than a mind; it was genius at the service of an intimate friend or of society. No small event of the day was too small for her nor was anything above her in the great events of life. Her thoughts became all things to all men; she did not reserve herself for books or political intrigues, she never played a part or thought of what impression she might produce. "If one has not sufficient cleverness to waste," she said, "one is not clever enough to perform one's desires."

The charming stay at Frankfort which was to leave so kind and pleasant a remembrance in the hearts of Mme. de Custine and Astolphe was drawing to a close. Spring was approaching and the pleasant society which the chance of events had brought together was upon the point of separating. Mme. de Custine was most disappointed at leaving the friend under whose influence she had so rapidly fallen, and who had been able to strengthen her courage, tried by so many suffer-

[1] The correspondence between Frau von Varnhagen and the Custines, mother and son, has been published at Florence. There is a Belgian edition of 1870 (Henri Merzbach, Court bookseller), and from this we have made numerous quotations.

ings. However, she was preparing to return to France with her son when Koreff advised her to take the waters at Karlsbad. He insisted so urgently that she yielded. She left Frankfort in the month of June, 1816. The farewells were heart-breaking and she shed tears abundantly, embracing her dear Rahel and apparently some premonition told her that she would never see her again. Rahel was no less deeply moved; at the moment of parting she gave Delphine some earrings and a silver chain, and these she always wore in remembrance of the friend whom she loved so affectionately.[1]

While Mme. de Custine and Koreff started for Bohemia Astolphe, whose health was still feeble, went to Ems to take the baths, upon the advice of Koreff. After a very tiring journey over dreadful roads Mme. de Custine reached Karlsbad and began the season. Life in a watering-place is very monotonous, but Delphine was fortunate enough to meet some of her Frankfort friends and soon formed a little circle of her own. Fortunately the waters suited her marvellously and she revived like a well-watered plant. Mme. de Custine and Rahel had felt the grief of parting too deeply not to write to one another constantly. Delphine continually tells her friend of the grief which she feels at their separation:

"KARLSBAD, *July* 25, 1816.

"Your kind letters have been a real pleasure to me and have done me infinite good. They make me feel that I am talking with you. They are like yourself, with your gracefulness and charm. How sorry I am that you have not come here! not upon your account, for I know nothing more insipid or wearisome. Had we been together we would have defied all that and, rules notwithstanding, would have spent some happy moments. I have been so ill, so sad, so bored and harassed that I have not opened a book or written a line. I recall with deep regret the lessons that you gave me and the beautiful moments that will never fade from memory. What progress I should have made!

"M. Berstöcher is greatly obliged for your kind remem-

---

[1] Frau von Varnhagen was herself upon the point of leaving Frankfort. Her husband had been appointed Chargé d'Affaires at Karlsruhe.

brance; he is taking the waters and is fairly well. It is a kind of frenzy from which people cannot escape and when it attacks you you cannot calculate when it will stop. There is a man who drinks eighty glasses daily from the hottest spring. We have not reached that point yet; we have not passed the dozen and that from the ordinary spring.

"Good-bye, my dearest; think of me sometimes and keep a little corner for me in your warm and friendly heart."

After the season of six weeks at Karlsbad, Mme. de Custine thought that she had done with doctors, but that was not Koreff's opinion. He insisted that she should take sixteen baths at Teplitz to complete her cure. At first she refused, but as Koreff said that he would accompany her she gave way to his arguments and started with him. The waters of Teplitz, in Bohemia, were situated in the most delightful country in the world and the whole of German, Prussian, and Austrian society were accustomed to meet there. The Clarys, the local magnates, had a magnificent residence there in the middle of a beautiful park. Mme. de Boufflers was closely acquainted with them and they did their best to entertain Delphine. She was continually invited to their entertainments. In the morning, after the bath and walk, they played at bowls in the park or rowed in the gondola on the magnificent lake, or drove about the country. In the evening the local artists gave a performance in the theatre of the Château; after the theatre there was a concert and a ball.[1] Thus the cure at Teplitz was a very pleasant time for Mme. de Custine.

At the conclusion of the season she bade an affectionate farewell to Koreff, and they promised to write as usual, twice a week, long letters which would soften the grief of separation. Delphine then met her son at Frankfort, and both started for France. As her financial situation did not allow her to remain in Paris, Mme. de Custine merely visited her mother and went on to Fervaques to spend the winter there with Astolphe. Paris had no attractions for her as the Génie thought of her no more and only saw her at rare intervals. She writes to Rahel:

"Paris is so different when one has been away for two

[1] Spenlé, *op. cit.*

years that one can leave it without regret after a few days. One feels so strange there as to think oneself still travelling.'

No sooner had they reached Fervaques than Astolphe hastened to write to Frau von Varnhagen, and as others always like to know the country in which one lives, he gave her a rapid and graceful description of the country and the Château of which he was so proud:

"Imagine a valley which can be crossed in five minutes' walk, but is deep enough to resemble a mountainous country, though sufficiently different from the plain to have a character of its own. There are a few trees in the depth of the valley, pastures all round to the foot of the hill, then cultivated land, some clumps of trees, and orchards thick as forests, hiding the houses which they enclose with magnificent hedges running along the roads. Amid this little green haven imagine a great Château, too low for its length, for it is 200 feet long; the second story is an attic, but relieved by a slate roof, very pointed, and of the style of architecture known in France as Henry IV, which is not without a certain dignity and nobleness. The walls are of brick, a red restful to the eye, and the more so as it is interrupted by panels of white-cut stone in relief, forming, as it were, pilasters in the style of the Medici. In all this there is no trace of luxury; it is solid and severe, though not gloomy. Round the Château are many young trees.

"Apart from the river which flows at the bottom of our garden, we have, on the garden side, moats, five feet wide, along the whole of this side of the Château. The outbuildings, stables, and coach-house, sheds and gardeners' house, are connected with the Château, and spoil the view of the courtyard which they narrow. Were it not for these encumbrances it would be a truly English garden."

Astolphe also gives us news of the life at Fervaques. His letters to his grandmother are charming, simple and natural, and show the true nature of the young man when his mind was not darkened and troubled by disease:

"FERVAQUES, *November* 19, 1816.

"Here we have all the elements for a letter by Mme. de Sevigné. There is winter, a great Château, bad roads, an old

Abbé, the visitors and bores from time to time and now and again the pains of rheumatism. As you will see the only thing wanting is the gracefulness of the *Dame des Rochers* to write you the most amusing letters in the world. However, modesty aside, I do not think that Mme. de Sevigné would write to-day as she did in her own age. Temperaments in those days were kindly and a delicate and easy mind could find nutriment and occupation in the world about it. If we would recover that spirit to-day, we must throw off the fetters which we have bound upon gracefulness and true freedom of thought.

"I have fallen into all the habits of the household as if I had never left it. After wandering about the world for six years it is strange to come home again and be so little astonished or impressed. It is the resumption of life after a parenthesis, the length of which memory cannot measure.

"Apart from some small disorders we have found everything here as we left, except that the trees have grown as tall as the Château. Everything was still green and was almost spring-like upon our arrival, but the next day we had a dreadful storm and a thing which I think is unprecedented, the thunder and lightning were followed by so heavy a fall of snow that in a few hours the whole country was covered a foot deep. A second storm melted it.

"I love our green valley at all times of the year, and if I did not regret anyone here I should be perfectly happy. It is the first time for a considerable period that I find myself in a position which I am not anxious to leave at the first moment; if I were only able to find a few more inhabitants for our great Château you would not see me leave it in a hurry.

"We are reading Mme. de Beaussets and also Dante, a canto of whom I translate every evening, more or less badly, to my mother, Gibi, and Berstöcher, who form a little circle in our great drawing-room."

It thus appears that Gibi was still at Fervaques, which he had resolved never to leave. Astolphe draws a rapid and amusing sketch of this old family friend:

"He is a remnant of the eighteenth century and its

philosophy. Mentally and physically he is ossified, an image seen through a microscope. When I think, as I listen to him, of all the illustrious people of his age and the friends of his youth, Diderot, d'Alembert, Marmontel, etc., I seem to see a table cleared after an entertainment and a well-gnawed bone thrown to the dog as the room is made tidy."

At a later date Astolphe tells his grandmother more of their calm and gentle existence :

"FERVAQUES, *December*, 1816.[1]

"I would write to you oftener, but in a life where we do not rely upon chance to provide our pastimes our occupations are definite and numerous, so that the days go by and I seem to have time for nothing else.

"We are making small plantations, which are as much trouble as large ones. We walk a great deal in all kinds of weather, for that is the only means of keeping well. And I study and work as seriously as I can. In the evening we all read together. This life has made me realise that time is too short only for those who have nothing to do. I have seen people busy with so-called serious affairs apparently unable to find occupation for their days, whereas we, leisurely as we seem to be, find them only too short. How many mistakes do men make in their mode of arranging their lives! Society rests upon a basis of give and take. Need we be surprised that all lives are based only on miscalculations.

"The winter is by no means disagreeable. The valley is always green, countrified and isolated, though not lonely. We live in peace and never feel ourselves cut off from the world. The rest which we enjoy is really a triumph over circumstances, for men show so little resource in this respect. We try to conduct the little world round us in as orderly a manner as possible, though things are by no means no sooner said than done. My mother pays much more attention to housekeeping than she seems to do; she takes an interest in everything, and supports the solitude and monotony of our life with a courage habitual to her on great occasions.

"The little Gibi flits about the corridors and even the

[1] To Mme. de Boufflers, Place Beauvau, corner of the Rue des Saussayes, Paris.

garden on sunny days, and I go riding when the roads are not too slippery. I have found many pleasant things to do here and even more material for thought. The misfortune of the present age consists in the fact that everybody is in a hurry and crowding to the same point. It seems to me that by retiring each of us for a short time to our homes, we confer a double benefit. In the first place we relieve pressure in the centre of the crowd and we fill a place in the area which is deserted by the crowd and which would otherwise be lifeless. General unrest is merely the sum total of individual unrest, and if everyone did his best to secure peace, regularity and morality at the little point which forms his own circle, we should not be in our present condition. But people think only of rising above their positions instead of accommodating themselves to their environment. The man who may be able to do some good does nothing but harm by his efforts to produce a general improvement. Let us begin with ourselves and our own little surroundings before attempting philanthropic measures of State revolution.

"Fortunately we hear nothing of the revolutionaries here. Our revolutions are confined to the almanac; we hear of the others only when they are over, and even then they change the habits of the country to a degree that is hardly perceptible. I really believe that the mistakes which politicians make in their calculations are due to the fact that, clever as they are, they have not left Paris for twenty years and they think that to-day feeling in that town will provide a measure of information upon every subject. Here is another mistaken point of view. I might discourse at length upon the subject, but I await your arrival, when we can talk at our ease. In letter-writing, however much we may desire, it is impossible to say what we mean as we would like to say it. That at least is true of us men, for in re-reading your last letter I see that grandmothers alone should be allowed to write letters."

Since her return to Fervaques Mme. de Custine was absorbed by the anxiety which pursued her constantly and hardly left her the faculty for thought. Her attachment for Dr. Koreff has been mentioned; they had separated at Teplitz at the beginning of September after promising to write as usual, namely, twice a week. Delphine had religiously kept her word. She received no answer. At first she thought there was some temporary delay or some mistake in the post; she restrained [her uneasiness and continued to write, but September, October and November went by and she received not the smallest news. In great despair, imagining that the worst had happened, Delphine spent hours of the utmost anxiety. At the end of December, unable to bear the apprehension which tortured her heart and supposing that her letters had been intercepted, she resolved at any cost to confide in her friend Frau von Varnhagen and ask her to send to Koreff, by some certain means, a letter which she would enclose. She declared her grief to her friend in the most touching terms as follows:

"FERVAQUES, *December* 25, 1816.

"My dear friend, I cannot describe my delight at hearing from you; it was like a ray of sunlight in a dungeon. My soul is overwhelmed with gloom and sadness which is increased by loneliness. Your gentle words have strengthened my heart against the dreadful woes of separation. You may well conceive the state of my depression but this is to be absolutely between ourselves. Allow me to observe secrecy to anyone rather than yourself.

"Can you imagine that I have not had a single sign of life from Koreff since I left him at Teplitz. That for many years when we have been parted I wrote to him twice a week and he as often to me without fail; that he is a friend of ten years' standing at least, tried by time and by the thousand griefs which he has felt and shared—in short, by feelings which one might reasonably believe to be indelible. We parted with grief and regret, promising to soften the irksomeness of separation by resuming our former correspondence; not a word from him has reached me. I have written to him ten times without showing ill-temper or discouragement and have even sent him letters by different routes but without success.

"My life is absorbed by this grief; I cannot lose a friend so lightly upon whom I thought I could rely, because he has given me proofs of his loyalty which I shall never forget.

Life is not worth living if those to whom we look for support disappear at the moment when their help is chiefly needed.

"I continue my studies but with no great zeal and read St. Martin, but my mind cannot rise above the griefs by which it is crushed. You ask me what I am doing and how I am getting on here. Now you know, but to outward seeming things are going well. I still love my trees and Providence has kindly left me this taste; I put the best face possible upon everything but my mental suffering prevents me from doing much."

Rahel, pitying such real grief, readily undertook to perform her friend's desire. She forwarded her letter to Koreff who decided to answer. He made excuses to explain the motives for his silence and found more or less plausible reasons, but the essential point was that he persuaded Delphine. She was consoled and reassured for the future and hastened to thank Frau von Varnhagen.

"At last, thanks to you, this little tie has been reunited.[1] Outwardly it may mean little but it means a great deal to my happiness. You know and understand that there are minds which comprehend everything and shed a light which embellishes life and gives it brilliancy and colouring and real value, and so I felt myself in the depths of gloom until I had received some word from him."

Delphine could not remain unoccupied and she found a thousand means of filling her days which left her not a moment's freedom. She devoted herself more than ever to painting and every day she spent long hours in her studio. Then she read a great deal and delighted to discuss her reading with Astolphe and Berstöcher. She also supervised with much zeal the interior decoration of the Château, nor did she neglect the beauty of the park and flower gardens. She was very fond of flowers and wished to have them always about her. Not only did she garden herself, but she planted trees; she even had the kindly thought of naming them after the friends whom she preferred. She writes to Rahel on January 2, 1817:

"We are planting all our friends and you first of all. We

---

[1] The reunion, however, was not so complete as might be thought. From this time Koreff's letters became less frequent.

have given names to a number of trees, and you are near a little waterfall in a green field between Koreff and Count Flemming. I call this plantation the 'sentimental metempsychosis.'"

Finally, correspondence completed the occupations of the day, and Delphine usually found in the evening that she had not finished her self-imposed tasks.

Frau von Varnhagen had promised to pay a visit to Fervaques and Delphine reminded her of it, while telling her also of the life which she led in the old Château and the hopes which supported her:

"We constantly speak of you, and the idea of seeing you some day is like a distant light guiding the traveller astray. When despair is about to seize our hearts a little light appears and we take courage for the morrow and successive days in order to reach the day which will bring you here. You know that you are already established in our garden as a tree; it is a tulip tree which beautifies even the springtime. You have no idea what a comfort this piece of childishness has been to me. You will laugh at all this foolishness but you will understand it, for you understand everything. You say in your charming way that people should not be alone when they are no longer young; at any rate, ought one to be old? but one is for so long a time no longer young and not entirely old that the interval is a painful one. My chief consolation is the fact that time passes with frightful rapidity, and though the days are sad we see them slip away like the waters of a torrent. My loneliness does not trouble me so much as news of my friends reaches us. The situation of this dwelling is very agreeable and the climate is moderate and healthy.

"Astolphe is better in mind and perfectly well in health; so is our dear Berstöcher, apart from his insomnia; he spends whole nights without sleeping. My own health follows the character of my feelings, and is good or bad according as I am encouraged or in despair. I study German, I paint, I look after the inside of the Château and I garden a little, for I am passionately fond of trees and flowers and plants. With all this and with kindly letters from Germany life is still possible."

CHAPTER XXXIV

1817—1820

Visitors at Fervaques—Proposed marriage for Astolphe—Mme. de Custine spends the winter of 1818 at Paris—Return to Fervaques—Intimacy of Astolphe with Mme. de Genlis.

IN the spring of 1818 Delphine had the great delight of receiving a visit from two of her friends from Frankfort, Prince Gustav von Mecklenburg and Count Flemming. For the latter in particular she had always felt a great liking. She also had frequent visits from her mother, the Princesse de Vaudémont, Mme. des Boulets (the headache) and Mme. de Cauvigny was always pleasant and charming. Then Guy de Chaumont-Quitry came fairly often, and, always good-tempered, but more eccentric than ever, had begun to regard Fervaques as his own house, and sometimes appeared in the Château before his arrival was known and left it again unperceived. "He is amusing," writes Astolphe, "because he has preserved a veneer of good humour amid the general shipwreck of all that was truly good and real in his heart. His history is a picture of our Revolution in miniature, and has suffered from the splashes of our misfortunes. He belongs to one of the most noble families in France, entered the Revolution as a Jacobin and then abandoned his liberal principles. He is a lofty character, proud of his nobility but even more greedy for power. In short, he is an indefinable mixture of false energy and enthusiasm, pride, activity, and real kindness, for in spite of this detestable portrait he is not only endurable but agreeable."

Life would have been very pleasant at Fervaques if the

mistress of the household had not been greatly troubled by pecuniary cares. The year 1818 was a year of famine and everyone suffered correspondingly. The harvest was bad, the farmers could not pay, and ruin and poverty were widespread. Mme. de Custine's position became more difficult as she had borrowed money in order to be able to go to Frankfort and look after her son and the loan was to be repaid this year. When rents did not come in and life became more and more expensive her anxieties increased. Despite the fact that she lived with the strictest economy, she could scarcely make both ends meet. Her mother could not help her for she, also, was troubled with all kinds of cares, especially pecuniary anxieties. Astolphe writes to his grandmother on June 6 :

"FERVAQUES, *June* 6, 1818.

" My mother has read your last letters to me and we are all most sorry for your difficulties, your disappointments, your lawsuits, and your anxieties and sufferings and so on. We are the more sorry to hear all this as we had long been rejoicing in the idea that we should see you here in the spring and be able to show you Fervaques in all its beauty. It becomes charming when the fresh green appears and, though men may lose their heads, the earth does its best to repair our madness. You do not hold out any hope of seeing us and this uncertainty depresses me. Our district, though it suffers much, is none the less one of the best in which to live, at any rate, to judge from what one hears and reads of all others.

" We have lighted upon a very unhappy year, but it is better, I think, to spend it at home than elsewhere. There, too, one spends one's money well but in another way. The harvest looks promising; warm weather is required which we have had for the last few days, but we have many long months to pass in which we shall hear of nothing else and the monotony will dull the senses of those who are not dead of famine. Half the country people have not eaten bread for several months; this winter they have been eating pea flour from which they make soup. As this is growing scarce or is even failing in certain districts, distress has increased, and the poor are eating bran mashed up with skimmed milk. The sight of such poverty is very painful. Our Normans, true Normans as they are, have a very valuable quality to-day, namely, patience. Elsewhere people would complain more though suffering less, and you may well imagine that hunger does not induce contentment but provides a prey for bad advisers and ill-counsels.

"I personally have everything to be thankful for, as my health is well maintained and I am growing slowly stronger. Besides, it seems to me that, at the present time, anyone who can avoid hunger and boredom has no reason to grumble—these are the two maladies which have overcome the human race. Boredom devours those who have something, hunger those who have nothing. As I am neither bored nor hungry I am as well as anyone can be here on earth. My mother's health is better than last year. You will find her complexion clearer, and she is more lively and vigorous. All we require here are a few more people to love.

"Our return here for a short time was quite necessary. In six years of absence many abuses grow up, and it is necessary to play the master in order to root out these evils. I use the term play, for I never feel that anything really belongs to me, and I think that I am but playing a part when I act as owner. My life has been chiefly spent at the window, and I cannot believe in the reality of things."

As we know, for several years Mme. de Custine's great desire was to see Astolphe married, and it certainly was not her fault if several proposals made for this purpose had come to nothing. In July Mme. de Custine wrote to her mother to ask her aid in her matrimonial projects, and she gives an amusing description of the fine matches in her district. It was essential that Astolphe should marry wealth, they were "too beggarly for him to marry for inclination:"

"FERVAQUES, *July* 10, 1818.[1]

"You do not write very often, little mother; I feel very anxious about your lawsuits, your health, and your journey. I can only console myself when I think that there is no lawsuit concerning Fervaques. The weather is magnificent

[1] To Mme. de Boufflers, care of Mme. Bourgne, Plombières.

and the country charming; what a pity that you are not with
us! How much gossip we might have about the past and
the future.

"As regards the future, Astolphe is more inclined to marry
and will certainly think of it seriously this winter. We have
recently heard of an admirable match. It is Mlle. de Saint
Aulaire, the daughter of the man whose wife you know. She
is enormously rich. It is said that Mme. de Caumont wants
her for her son but that there is nothing in it. Please find
out the truth if you can do so on the quiet and make some
inquiries about the young woman's face and character. Mlle.
de Goyon would also be a good match but what are her
prospects? you do not say a word of these. Mlle. de Hautefort is a fine match and I know that nothing has been settled
for her, but then she is hunch-backed, and she might have
no children. Think seriously of Mlle. de Saint Aulaire; the
more I think it over the more excellent does the idea seem.
She is said to be very rich, try to find out the truth of this;
she ought to be in possession of her wealth as it is derived
from her mother, who has been dead for some years. Mlle. de
Duras is tempting in many respects but her present fortune
is very small and her future prospects are remote. And then,
her mother wishes to keep her, which would not suit
Astolphe; he would be heart-broken at leaving me as this
would change our whole course of life; it is the greatest
objection to Mlle. de Duras. Or Mlle. de Goyon would do
very well also.

"So open a campaign in this direction; we absolutely must
find someone this winter and someone with wealth, for otherwise we had better stay as we are. This is the fruit of our
reflections and our solitary meditations. So try to help us
in this great work. I tell you again that Astolphe wishes
above all things to be independent and real liberty can only
be secured by wealth. Meanwhile let me hear from you, for
our real and only delight is in your letters."

In January, 1818, Mme. de Custine, who was in despair at
her inability to find a wife for Astolphe, considered that she
was wrong in burying him in the country and thought she
had better let him show himself in society where his talents

would make him a general favourite and enable him to procure the heiress that he desired. Although her pecuniary resources were still most modest she resigned herself to the sacrifice and took a little flat for six months in the Rue d'Anjou Saint-Honoré, No. 38. She furnished it with the furniture which had been stored since her departure for Germany. A few days after her arrival she wrote a melancholy letter to Rahel:

"*January* 11.

"What a cry of joy went up when your dear letter arrived, and after reading it what old remembrances of friendship rushed in upon me! She is always the same, says one, she is charming, says another, she will come and see us. But I think what a charming person she is and what a pity that she lives so far away. In short, this kind of conversation went on the whole day and through all the troubles of Paris life which are known as pleasures people continually repeated the same words in order to speak of Rahel.

"So you also feel the burden of life. Every day makes it so heavy and makes us so weak that we feel that the end cannot be far off. I go out very little; I spend my evenings with my dear Princess,[1] whom you saw at Frankfort and who has not forgotten you. Think what it would be if she had had time to love you as we have had."

The hopes which Delphine had conceived of the result of a stay in Paris were by no means realised, and in the month of May she went back to Fervaques, where Astolphe's position remained unchanged. As soon as she was in the Château she wrote to her mother:

"Fervaques, *May* 9, 1818.

"I have reached harbour, little mother, in spite of the roads, which are frightful from Bernay. I have come back here to find winter, and am sitting over the fire and lamenting the springtime of Paris. If the roads do not soon dry you had perhaps better go as far as Lisieux when

[1] The Princesse de Vaudémont.

you come; in fine weather all the roads are good, but we have had no fine weather yet.

"The ram has arrived safely and well. He recognises me and seems in excellent health. He follows me about like a dog. I have named him Orléans. His arrival in the district, his origin and the donor of him are generally known, and people came from all sides to see him. All he wants is a wife; an animal which was promised to me will certainly arrive, but will be too old for him as it is eighteen months of age. Tell Mme. de Vaudémont my regrets in this respect, and if this dear and good princess could give me a sheep of the age of the ram I should be most delighted. Tell her that, thanks to her, I am becoming a shepherdess; I do nothing but keep my sheep, and I think it is just as good an occupation as many others.

"I think that Astolphe is at Saint Léger; I long to see him, for conversation with Gibi is not very inspiring. My health is none too good, but the friend is very well. He is so glad to be here that everything is for the best. I hope I may soon hear from you.

"I feel here as if I were isolated at the end of the world. Nothing is to be heard but the croaking of the frogs and the song of the cuckoo, and the distant barking of dogs in the farms. I have done nothing yet but unpack and put things straight and rest while looking after my sheep. This occupation would seem more important if I could use the plural. You will be surprised to hear that my ram was not at all tired by the journey and ate out of my hand at every change of horses. He is wonderfully well.

"Good-bye, little mother, let me hear from you soon about your goat's milk and your baths. I am anxious to know that you feel better. The friend sends you his kind regards."

Astolphe soon returned to his mother at Fervaques and was no less delighted to return than she. To Mme. de Boufflers he wrote:—

"FERVAQUES, *Monday, May* 18.

"We have had a very good journey and a triumphant entry to Fervaques three days ago. I always feel better here than anywhere else; an inward feeling tells me that I am in my proper place, but elsewhere my experience is exactly the contrary. The reason is that here I desire only what is attainable, and surely this is one of the thousand definitions of happiness, and perhaps not the most incorrect. Fervaques is made deeply attractive by the thought that you will be coming to see us this year. I am sure that a visit will do you good. The peacefulness of this district is as catching as the bustle of Paris, with its unsullied verdure which restores the soul to its natural condition of peace and contentment.

"When I write to you I write exactly as I think, for you have a unique talent for putting minds and hearts at their ease. I have given my mother your little crown of Sainte Geneviève and have told her of our pilgrimage. All of it has charmed her. She does not seem to be wearied here and brings order and neatness into every department. Her energy is displayed for the smallest things. Besides she sees that I am happy here and so hides any possible feelings of regret that she might have. In a mother's heart anything may be found and all may be hidden, and we are sure to obtain from it whatever we require when we require it. Hers is the only generosity that does not crush us, for sacrifices made by other people always leave us dissatisfied with ourselves."

On June 3, Delphine writes again to her mother. Astolphe's marriage is again under consideration:

"FERVAQUES, *June 3*, 1818.

"*By Lisieux in the department of Calvados and not in that of Orne, as you always address letters.*

"I am very glad, little mother, to hear that you have at last received our letters and I hasten to reply to your long epistle though I do not think it long, for it was charming. Astolphe has returned from his little journey which was not made in pursuit of some fair one but merely to drink his fill of the fresh air, the solitude, and the sweet odour of springtime. Of this he has had his fill and his health is all the better for it, and he has come back very well and happy. I am much grieved about our marriage proposals. The old neighbour who might have helped us in all this is dying and we see no means which might lead us to this fine match. The general information is admirable ; she will have an income of forty thousand livres on her marriage and she will not marry before the age of eighteen, which will be next October, but she has refused all proposals hitherto, saying that she wishes to make the acquaintance of her admirers and choose the one she prefers. With this we quite agree, but how can we get a glimpse of such a marvel or meet her ? To this question I see no answer unless Mme. de Vaudémont, when she goes away from here, goes to visit the aunt of Mlle. de Mou . . . as she did last year and takes Astolphe with her. But her visit will not be for some time and I am afraid that others may be cleverer than ourselves. It would be an advantage if the young lady could be impressed with us, not with any definite proposal, but by the words of someone who would praise Astolphe so as to make her anxious to meet him. What a pity that Mme. Dubourre is so talkative; as she has lived for so long at Rouen she ought to know all about this. Might it not be possible to get some information out of her in the course of a conversation ? You can act upon this idea as you please, but with cleverness, skill, and discretion. Can we not make the acquaintance of some other people in Rouen ? This marriage is just what we want. The young lady is said to be very nice and well educated. She has an estate three leagues from here but never visits it. It is confined to farms and pastures.

" All my animals are well ; I had another calf yesterday and my ram is splendid. Does not the Princess grow weary of her solitude ? I do not recognise her in this respect, and I rely on you to turn her inclination.

" Goodbye, little mother. M. de Quitry, who is here, prostrates himself before you. He is as good and foolish as ever. Goodbye, I have no news of anyone else, the absent are always wrong in our dear country. For this reason try to be here as soon as you can in person. For in imagination you have been settled here for a long time."

The spring, summer, and autumn of 1819 passed by as usual. Delphine remained at Fervaques attempting to find a wife for Astolphe, but unsuccessfully. She lived the same calm, peaceful life, seeing a few intimate friends such as Mme. de Cauvigny and the Princess de Vaudémont, who had fallen into the pleasant habit of an annual visit, looking after her trees and plants and doing her best to live economically. During the last days of October Chateaubriand paid a short visit to Fervaques; he only stayed two days and on his return he stopped at Versailles and somewhat mysteriously spent twenty-four hours with Mme. Récamier.[1] His journeys to Fervaques were often to serve as a cloak to mysterious love intrigues.

In December, 1819, Delphine resolved to spend a few months in Paris, certainly not on her own account, as she would have preferred to remain at Fervaques, a course urged by prudence, for she had very little money. But Astolphe's marriage was at stake and some sacrifice was necessary. Astolphe went in front of her by some days. She writes to her mother:

"I am very glad that you think Astolphe is growing stouter, at present he is very well. You have nothing more to say to me about our great marriage proposals; is it a case of another delusion? However, it will not be our fault this time, for we have not hesitated to come to Paris, though it would have been more reasonable to stay here as we are not overburdened with money. Apparently I shall stay at the Hotel Grange-Batelière. When furnished rooms are required that is certainly the best. The arrangements about food are inconvenient, as I shall have to leave my cook here, and in this way we can hardly have people to dinner or lunch as usual, for an extra person means six francs. However, as it is for so short a time we may be able to endure it. But it is dreadful to be thus reduced to extremities. If something is not settled this winter for Astolphe we shall have to shut ourselves up here for a long time, even for the following winter. This will be better than constantly running into debt. It is not a pleasant thing to have to say to anyone, but there is no help for it."

In the course of the summer Delphine had written several

---

[1] See *Trois Amies de Chateaubriand*, by M. André Beaunier, p. 165. Charpentier, 1910. M. Beaunier has most cleverly analysed and related Chateaubriand's love affairs, and we have found his book of great service.

times to Chateaubriand but had received no answer. The
Génie was far too busy with politics and his love affairs.
However, Delphine wrote to him as soon as she returned to
Paris, and could not hide how much she had been wounded
by his silence :

" I do not know whether I ought to tell you that I have
arrived from Fervaques and should like to see you. Perhaps
you are as ill-tempered to those who are present as to those
who are away. It is a strange atmosphere which makes it
impossible to write a line to a friend or allows one to receive
three or four letters without returning a sign of life. It
seems to me inconceivable, and I would never have believed
that you could have been so influenced.

" Astolphe will come and see you on Sunday, but when
shall I see you ? " [1]

As soon as he had begun to spend the winter in Paris
Astolphe went into society and became a considerable
favourite. He had met Mme. de Genlis again. This famous
literary woman was well aware that Mme. de Custine
positively hated her, but this fact did not prevent her from
beginning an intimacy with Astolphe, flattering him and
professing her readiness to act as his guide and counsellor.
About this time they exchanged small poems and letters
which appear most ridiculous, especially in view of the
morality of Mme. de Genlis. The following is a specimen of
this correspondence :

"*January 3*, 1820.

" So I have brought tears to your eyes, dear Astolphe,
how deeply the thought touches me ! How I sympathise
with the state of your mind and feelings, and how deeply
I am attached to you. The union of two hearts formed by
sympathy and virtue—this is the only true union ; it is a
heavenly union, and could not be disturbed by any talk
about difference of age. A moment's separation can give no
pain at the end of a dangerous exile, and I have now passed
all dangers. Nearer than you are to eternity, I see this
ravishing prospect more clearly, and as I contemplate it the
duration of human life seems so small that it has neither

[1] *Chateaubriand et Mme. de Custine*, by Chedieu de Robethon.

measure nor proportion, even as a point has no parts or magnitude. My soul is naturally more animated and lofty than yours, and the thought of its immortality makes it ever tremble. These are emotions and delights which youth cannot know; what earthly impressions can equal them ? Such is the consequence of old age in conjunction with belief." [1]

In her anxiety for Astolphe Mme. de Genlis also attempted to find him a wife. She knew the daughter of General Moreau, a charming young person of considerable wealth. Introductions took place, and negotiations seemed to be proceeding admirably when Mme. Moreau raised a claim that the young couple should live with her. Mme. de Custine regarded separation from her son as an impossible condition, and on this point the parties could not agree and the proposals were broken off.

[1] The La Caille collection.

CHAPTER XXXV

1821-1825

Astolphe's marriage—Visit of the Génie to Fervaques—The birth of Enguerrand de Custine—Chateaubriand in London—Astolphe goes to see him—Chateaubriand at the Congress of Vienna—He is appointed Minister for Foreign Affairs — Mme. de Custine desires a peerage for her son—Death of Léontine de Custine—Pretended visit of Chateaubriand to Fervaques—He is dismissed from office—Astolphe's unfortunate adventure.

IT was not until the following year that Mme. de Custine at length had the delight of seeing Astolphe married. On May 12, 1821, he married Mlle. Léontine de Saint Simon de Courtomer, a charming young person but of delicate health.[1] Mme. de Custine had now reached the summit of her ambition and she cherished the hope that the future would at length recompense her for the many tribulations she had experienced in the past. The young couple settled at Fervaques and passed a happy summer.

Chateaubriand[2] had even promised that he would come and share his friend's happiness in October and Delphine was delighted at the idea of having him for a few days, but, in place of the Génie a letter reached Fervaques bringing sadness and disillusionment:

"PARIS, *October* 20, 1821.

"Another hope overthrown! I had told you that I would come to see you after October 15, but all these plans have

[1] Aimée Léontine de Saint Simon de Courtomer, daughter of the Marquis de Courtomer and of Jeanne Frottier de la Coste.
[2] He had been appointed Prussian Ambassador and had started for his new post on January 1, 1821. But he only made a very short stay at Berlin and returned to Paris for the baptism of the Duc de Bordeaux. On July 30, when M. de Villèle left office, Chateaubriand resigned.

been upset by the near opening of the Chambers. However, as I cling to everything in life in order to avoid total shipwreck, it is possible that I may be free at Christmas and I suppose that you will then have left the country. You are very happy to be able to live there. A thousand remembrances to my friends and even to the old Château. I like its walls, its streams and the old Henry IV room. To yourself my assurance of that friendship which follows you everywhere and with which I have wearied you for I cannot say how many years."

However, the Génie kept his promise. At the end of November he spent four days at Fervaques, to Delphine's great delight. Immediately upon his return he wrote:

"*November* 27, 1821.

"I left peace and happiness behind me at Fervaques. Here I have found a collection of all the harassing troubles in the world. Sickness, politics, storms, etc. I am much to be pitied, and the four days of your quiet home have made these usual troubles even more unbearable. If you regret me I shall ever regret you."

These troubles, however, were to have a happy issue, as Chateaubriand was appointed Ambassador to London on January 22, in place of the Duc Decazes. He started for his new post on April 2, and pleasantly relates that when he reached Dover he was welcomed with the usual salute of sixteen guns as he entered and as he left the town, and by four officials at the door of his hotel. It is extraordinary how sensitive Chateaubriand was to all these questions of outward show and with what satisfaction he relates them.

On June 19, 1822, Mme. de Custine had the delight of welcoming a grandson. Great rejoicings took place at Fervaques for the birth and baptism of Enguerrand de Custine. In the following month Astolphe, who perhaps found that his own place in the house was somewhat occupied, had another fit of his wandering impulse and started for England and Scotland. As soon as Delphine heard of his intentions she informed Chateaubriand. He replied kindly that he would see what he could of Astolphe, would find him rooms, and hoped that he would take his meals at the Embassy. He adds:

"*July* 2, 1822.

" How happy you are to be together in your great Château in the month of October, and why cannot I be with you? I am overwhelmed with attention in this country and I prefer Fervaques.

" Yours ever."

All went off as had been arranged. Astolphe reached London and became René's guest, who introduced him to society. On August 23, he wrote to Delphine and told her of her son, and concluded his letter as follows:

" I shall see you at Fervaques this autumn; as you know, I always come back again and cannot forget my eternal affections."

Whether it was that Astolphe was inclined to see the worst side of things or whether his experiences were unfortunate, he showed himself little pleased with England and Scotland. He said that England was the temple of boredom and that in England were to be found only narrow-minded men, prejudiced and ridiculous, and ill-tempered women. In short, he returned much disappointed after a tour of several months.

When the Congress of Vienna became a serious question Chateaubriand was particularly anxious to act as the representative of France and used all his influence to secure the post that he so ardently desired. From London he wrote to M. de Villèle: " It is the object of my strongest desires. Serve me that I may serve you. When I have negotiated with Kings I shall have no rival."

At the same time he urged Mme. de Duras to use her utmost influence with the King and his ministers. To Mme. Récamier he was no less pressing; she had succeeded the duchess in his affections and he wrote to her:

" This congress has the immense advantage that it will bring me back to Paris and these intrigues merely signify that I am dying of my desire to see you. I bring good luck to the Royalist Party and I cannot help observing that their affairs are prosperous wherever I go and are unfortunate wherever I do not appear." [1]

Mme. de Duras, who was still fond of him and was too great a lady to bear malice, used her influence with the King and with M. de Villèle, and at length secured that he should represent France at the Congress. When he left Paris on October 5, full of confidence in his superior genius, he said to Mme. de Custine in his farewell letter :

"I shall pass from the second rank to the first." At the Congress he did nothing at all. On his return M. de Villèle offered him the portfolio of Foreign Affairs which had fallen vacant by the resignation of Mathieu de Montmorency. He accepted and became a member of the Ministry in 1822.

Mme. de Custine had been long troubled by Astolphe's lack of occupation. She attempted to find him a position suitable for his name and his birth with some employment which would distract him from his disastrous day-dreams. She had thought of a peerage for the moment but the lack of success which had attended her efforts in 1814 and 1815 had shown her that she was not in such high favour at Court as she had supposed, and she was awaiting a favourable moment to bring forward her son as a candidate. He was then thirty years of age, well born and capable ; what more could be desired ? When she saw that Chateaubriand was in the Ministry she thought that the day was won. She hastened to her friend and begged him to think of Astolphe. René promised everything that she desired ; not only did he assure her of his complete support but he seemed vexed that she should doubt his word, and she went away full of hope. In the month of January a batch of peers were to be made and Delphine anxiously renewed her solicitations. René replied to her on January 27, 1823 :

"The person I have most at heart is Astolphe. If peers are made he will certainly be one, but the question is whether there will be any. I rather doubt it. In any case, sooner or later, a peerage cannot escape him."

From that moment Delphine had no rest. She understood Chateaubriand's indifference in spite of his promises and his fair speeches. Astolphe's peerage was the smallest of

[1] Bardoux, *Mme. de Custine.*

his cares. She thought that her chance of success would be better if she insisted and redoubled her requests. At heart she was angry at the lack of energy shown by her friend and did not spare him her reproaches. She even attempted to rouse his pride by reminding him of the conduct of the man whom he detested. She reminded him that at her request Fouché had given a peerage to M. de Brézé. "You must admit," she said to him, "that it would be remarkable if you cannot do as much for Astolphe." To these reproaches René replied with the calm of a good conscience: "You do not believe in my indifference, and as for my kindnesses you laugh at them. I have no favours to give and I will do for Astolphe what I would not do for myself."

While Mme. de Custine thus lived in the hope of a peerage which never came she was troubled by grief and anxieties within her family circle. Her daughter-in-law, who had always been delicate, fell ill and could hardly pass the winter. The climate of Normandy is somewhat damp and did not suit her. But as she was unable to bear a long journey they resolved to take her to Saint Léger to Mme. de Boufflers in the spring. Soon it became obvious that her illness could have but one conclusion. In June the unfortunate young woman took to her bed and died on July 7 at the age of scarce twenty years. The body was taken to Fervaques and buried in the little cemetery of Saint Aubin.[1]

This death was a sad blow for Delphine; not only did she lose a daughter-in-law whom she loved tenderly but she feared the influence of solitude upon Astolphe. She could not, however, abandon herself to her grief; she had to think of the orphan and of the anxieties of the moment. Upon this frail being she poured all her love and tenderness. She took refuge with Enguerrand and Astolphe at her dear Fervaques.

Chateaubriand does not seem to have shown any very lively sympathy with the misfortunes of his friends. No other proof of this fact is needed than the mournful and bitter letter which Delphine, usually so sweet, wrote to M. Bertin aîné,

[1] The village of Saint Aubin is larger than Fervaques and contained the Church and cemetery. At a later date, under Louis-Philippe, Fervaques increased at the expense of Saint Aubin, a new church was built in Fervaques and the church of Saint Aubin was closed.

requesting him to send to René a few words which she was writing to him asking his support for the peerage:

"FERVAQUES, *September* 18, 1823.

"May I ask you to send this letter to our friend (Chateaubriand)? I cannot write to him without sending my letter through his offices where he leaves it lying about and this I cannot endure, so kindly do me this small service. I have been hoping that since we were so unhappy M. de Chateaubriand would think a little more of us and would find some means of occupying Astolphe in order to win him from his natural grief, but no power can oblige him to think of his friends."

René had held out hopes of a visit to Fervaques in the month of November and Mme. de Custine awaited his arrival daily. At length a letter announced that the minister was able to tear himself from his overwhelming labours and was about to arrive. At that moment he was deeply in love with Mme. de C . . . , for, in spite of his fifty-five years, he was as foolish as a schoolboy in these matters. Delphine was to provide him with the opportunity for a meeting with her. As a Minister of Foreign Affairs requires an *alibi* and as he could not leave his post without stating his destination when the war with Spain had taken a critical turn, he publicly announced that he was overworked and was going to Fervaques for a few days' rest with his old friend. This was perfectly natural and in no way reprehensible. To make the pretext more realistic he even warned Delphine of his arrival and then started. But instead of proceeding to Lisieux he went to Dieppe in company with his adored mistress. Delphine received a despairing letter from the Génie stating that he was hastening to her in pleasurable anticipation of his visit when a fatal accident shattered his plans. His carriage broke down and while it was being repaired a messenger arrived from the ministry to recall him to Paris, and he was obliged to abandon the prospect of the pleasurable meeting to which he had so looked forward. " Be sure that I am not discouraged," he added hypocritically; "in spite of this mishap, if you prolong your stay at Lisieux I do not give up hopes of coming to see you." He probably projected another escapade with Mme. de C . . . which Delphine was unconsciously to help.

She does not, however, seem to have been so entirely taken in by this trickery as her friend hoped. Rumours of it reached Fervaques and Delphine complained, for the Génie wrote to her on December 2 :

" You are repeating a story in your last letter which is current here. There is no sense in it. I was going to Fervaques intending to see you and I was recalled. Although I merely left Paris for twenty-four hours I find a thousand stories in circulation and political rumours going about. Would you believe that, notwithstanding your injustice, and public gossip, I am thinking of journeying to Fervaques at this moment? I shall probably be unable to arrange it but I cannot give up so pleasant an idea." [1]

Chateaubriand did not appear at Fervaques either in November or December. In December he wrote again to Mme. de Custine :

"Do not think that I have forgotten you, for your memory is one of the pleasantest and most imperishable in my life." Such protestations of eternal affection meant nothing to Chateaubriand; they were simply formulas of politeness which he showered unscrupulously upon the friends he deserted. Mme. de Custine well knew their worth. She did not lose sight of Astolphe's peerage, and as René did not come to Fervaques she wrote to him and renewed her request. On December 2 he replied :

" I have told you a hundred times and I repeat once more, that in my opinion a peerage is the right career for Astolphe and he cannot have long to wait for it. From a peerage one can advance anywhere ; a little patience only is required. He is by no means so old as I was when I began my political life. No doubt I should have been more happy at Fervaques, if I could be happy anywhere. Loneliness pleases me and life often wearies me. It is a misfortune which was born with me and I must bear it as there is no remedy." [2]

---

[1] See *Trois Amies de Chateaubriand*, by M. André Beaunier, pp. 175–177.

[2] All the quotations from Chateaubriand's letters given in this chapter are taken from "*Chateaubriand and Mme. de Custine*," by Chedieu de Robethon.

The course of events during 1824 were to overthrow Mme. de Custine's hopes for ever. On June 6, the Day of Pentecost, Chateaubriand was unceremoniously dismissed. As soon as she heard of her friend's misfortune Delphine, who bore no malice for his ingratitude, sent him the following touching letter:

"You know that whatever my own troubles may be they take a second place to yours, so come and rest yourself at Fervaques."

A short time afterwards an event took place which was to shatter the career of Astolphe and to poison the last years of his mother. The narrative may be found in a letter from Herr von Varnhagen von Ense. He says:

"A dreadful accident has just caused a sensation throughout Paris. One fine morning, in the neighbourhood of this town, a young man was found lying senseless in a field, stripped of his clothes and bruised in different parts of his body. The young man was no other than Custine; he seemed to have been the victim of a crime. He was not publicly referred to, but his name was whispered in secret and his calumniators were glad to undermine the reputation of a man who had enemies among the liberals as well as in the aristocracy. In disgust at such evil-mindedness he withdrew from society for a time and devoted himself seriously to literature and to travel."

"This much is certain," says M. Chedieu Robethon, from whom we borrow these details, "that the affair was the outcome of one of those deplorable incidents which leave a permanent stigma on a man's career. Custine was taken in by some disgraceful assignation which he had made at his own instance, and which was accepted merely to inflict an exemplary punishment upon him. Arriving at the meeting-place punctually Custine found five or six adversaries before him. He was ill-treated, beaten, stripped of his clothes and left in the middle of the field, and returned to Paris in a cabman's coat, whereupon his chief anxiety was to give information to the police. This imprudent step made the scandal public, and an investigation was begun. The truth of the fact was the more quickly established as the aggressors belonged to a crack army corps and were ready to come forward. They were not prosecuted."[1]

Mme. de Custine, in despair, withdrew to Fervaques while her son travelled. She took with her the little Enguerrand, who was all that remained for her to love in this world.

[1] Koreff repeatedly affirmed that Astolphe was wholly irresponsible. See *Chateaubriand, Interprétation medico psychologique*, by Dr. Évariste Michel.

CHAPTER XXXVI

1826

The death of Enguerrand de Çustine—Mme. de Custine starts for Switzerland—She sees Chateaubriand for the last time—Her death on July 14—Her burial at Fervaques.

IT was written that Mme. de Custine should be spared no human grief. She had seen her daughter-in-law die in the flower of her youth and had seen the brilliant future which she had dreamed of for her son collapse most lamentably. The poor woman had then concentrated her affection upon the orphan entrusted to her care, a delightful child, whose precocious intelligence and caresses had entirely won her heart. She watched over him with devoted tenderness, and surrounded with anxious solicitude the only being which made life of any value. Unfortunately her instincts were only too correct; the fate which had pursued her for so many years could not even leave her this last wreck of her fortunes. Enguerrand, whose health was very delicate, was soon attacked by the disease which had carried off his mother. At the end of October, 1825, brain fever set in, and for more than two months Delphine saw the poor little being whom she adored writhing in dreadful anguish and holding out his helpless arms to her; powerless and heart-broken, she was obliged to watch over this dreadful and interminable agony. When the sufferings of the poor martyr had ceased Delphine was crushed and broken, physically and mentally.[1]

On this occasion the measure was complete; crushed by this further misfortune and unable to struggle, without hope or object in life, she waited anxiously for death to free her from an existence which had become burdensome and had lasted too long. Her wishes were soon to be granted; the liver disease from which she had been suffering for years became more acute, and she foresaw that her end was approaching. Feeling very ill at the beginning of the summer Delphine declared that before dying she wished to visit Switzerland again, where she had spent such happy moments. But the truth is that she could not contemplate leaving this earth without saying a last farewell to the man whom she had deeply loved and who had caused her so much suffering. Chateaubriand was at that moment at Lausanne with his wife, who was ill. Those about the dying woman yielded to her desires and, after saying farewell to her mother, she started for Geneva with her son and Berstöcher. On the evening before their departure Astolphe wrote to Rahel these words, which are impressed with heartfelt grief:

"I had a wife, I had a son, and I have lost them. My child was as beautiful as an angel and seemed likely to be no less clever than good. Sixty-four days of brain fever wasted him before my eyes, and this dreadful spectacle has ruined my poor mother's health, on whose account I feel the greatest anxiety.[2] These misfortunes have not blunted the remembrance of our friendship. I saw you at a time when

[1] Enguerrand was buried by his mother in the Cemetery of Saint Aubin; on a marble stone may be read:—

Here lie
Léontine de Saint Simon de Courtomer
Born February 12, 1803
Married May 15, 1821, Astolphe Louis Léonore
Marquis de Custine
Died July 7, 1823
and
Louis Philippe Enguerrand de Custine
their only son
Born June 19, 1822
Died January 2, 1826.

[2] Mme. de Boufflers survived her daughter by six months. She died on February 27, 1827.

all I knew of life was hope, and you represent to me all that I have lost in the course of experience. When shall we meet again, and when will your keen mind help mine to grow young once more and to plunge again into that stream which ever brings refreshment to you? We are starting to-morrow for Geneva, where I hope the change will restore my poor mother's health."

Chateaubriand, who had been informed of Delphine's arrival, spent a few hours with her at the Hotel d'Angleterre at Sécherons.[1] Speaking of this interview in his "Mémoires" he wrote:

"I have seen her who confronted the scaffold with such courage. Whiter than fate, dressed in black, her figure wasted by death, her head dressed in its own unique silken adornment, I have seen her smile at me with her pale lips and her fair teeth, when she left Sécherons, near Geneva, to breathe her last at Bex, at the entrance of the Valais."

Satisfied with her interview with René and anxious only for death Mme. de Custine settled at Bex and there awaited her end. "She retained her beauty," says her son, "so far as to strike even strangers who had not known her in her youth and who were consequently uninfluenced by the charm of recollection." Delphine seemed to enjoy her stay at Bex and revived under the influence of its pleasant climate, when she suddenly expired on July 15 in the arms of Astolphe and Berstöcher. The latter immediately wrote to Chateaubriand:

"All is over, sir; your friend no longer lives. She yielded up the ghost this morning without suffering at a quarter to eleven. She had been out for a drive yesterday evening and there was no premonition of so sudden an end; indeed, we had no idea that her illness would end in this way. M. de Custine, who is too overwhelmed to write himself, had been yesterday morning to one of the mountains near Bex to order a daily supply of mountain milk for our dear invalid. I feel too crushed to enter into fuller details, but we are preparing to return to France with the dear remains of the best of

---

[1] A little village, then in the neighbourhood of Geneva but now one of the suburbs of the town.

mothers and friends. Enguerrand will rest between his two mothers."

The mortal remains of Delphine were transported, according to her wish, to the smiling valley which was her favourite residence and where the dear ones who had preceded her were already lying at rest.

"I heard," wrote Chateaubriand, "her coffin pass through the long street of Lausanne during the night to its eternal resting-place at Fervaques."

It might be thought that this sudden and premature death would have roused some remorse in the heart of Chateaubriand, but such a supposition would imply a mistaken view of his character. Two years later, when he crossed Lausanne once more on his way to Rome, he simply remembered that on this road passed away the Marquise de Custine who had wished him well. On his return to Italy in 1833 he stayed at Bex to change horses. Remembrance of the dead came back to his mind, but the memories of the past inspired him only to write these lines, disgusting in their crudity:

"At Bex, while the horses were being put into my carriage which had perhaps drawn the bier of Mme. de Custine, I leant against the wall of the house where my hostess of Fervaques had died. She had become famous before the Revolutionary Tribunal for her long hair. At Rome I also saw some beautiful, long, fair hair which had been found in a tomb." Such was the funeral oration which the Génie thought worthy of the woman who had given him the best of her life. Poor Delphine!

Delphine was buried near Fervaques, on the hill which overlooks the "rose-coloured" Château in the humble cemetery of the Church of Saint Aubin.

Here lies
Dame Louise Eléonore Mélanie de Sabran
Widow of Monsieur Armand Louis Philippe François
Marquis de Custine
Born at Paris March 18, 1770
Died at Bex in Switzerland July 25, 1826.

Beneath this white marble stone Delphine sleeps her last sleep near her daughter-in-law and her dear grandson. She had vainly sought happiness in life, and only in death had found peace and rest. The epitaph which Mme. de Boufflers had composed for herself should have been inscribed upon her tombstone:

>   At length I reach the haven
>   Where I would be ;
>   Death gives me yearned for peace
>   Eternally.

INDEX

INDEX

ABBAYE, the, 91, 115 note¹
Abrantes, Duchesse d', 242
Aguesseau, 46
Aiguillon, Duchesse d', 150, 163
Alembert, d', 6
Alex, Comtesse. *See* Rochefoucauld, Comtesse Alexandre de la.
Alexandre, Mme. *See* Rochefoucauld, Comtesse Alexandre de la.
Amat, 148 note¹
Ancients, the, 215
Andelys, 102–4
Andlau, M. d', 74
Andlau, Mlle. d', 12 note¹
Andlau, Mme. d', 101
Andrezelle, Mlle. d', on the court of Lunéville, 273–75
Anglas, Boissy d', 181, 192, 202, 204, 207, 215, 241
Angleterre, Hôtel d', Sécherons, 370
Angoulême, Duchesse d', 311, 322
Anisy, 6 and note², 7, 20, 26–28, 30–33
Anjou, Charles Comte D', 2 note
Anspach, 171
Antoinette, Marie, 11–12, 16, 123
Aramon, M. d', 71
Arcy, Gouy d', 150
Arenberg, Comtesse Auguste D', 20–21
Arenberg, Duke Charles D', 50 note³
Arenberg, Mlle. D', 237
Arenberg, Mme. D', 237
Arnouville, 320
Arragon, Hildefonso of, 2 note
Artois, Comte d', and Mme. de Custine, 16–17, 303; emigration, 41; the court at Vesoul, 305–7; entry into Paris, 308–9; the court, 310, 311; and Fouché, 319
Assembly, the, 42, 81–82, 84, 102, 190
Augereau, General, 217
Aunay, Comte Pellitier d', 46 note²
Auvray, usher, 109

BAGATELLE, 17
Bâle, Madame de Custine at, 172, 286, 303; Peace of, 169, 170
"Ballon d'Alsace," ascent of the, 32
Barbé-Marbois, 215
Barras, 190, 217
Bartais, 30
Barthélemy, Francis Marquis de, 192 and note¹, 215–17
Bastille, capture of, 38
Bauffremont, Madame de, 275
Bayeux, Bishop of, 258
Bayreuth, 171
Beauharnais, Josephine. *See* Bonaparte, Madame.
Beauharnais, Vicomte Alexandre de, 45, 107 note²; imprisonment, 150; letters to Madame de Custine, 151 and note¹-53: letters to his wife, 155–6; execution, 156; Elzéar's reflections upon his letters, 176–9; notes by Madame de Custine, 179–80
Beaumont, Comte de, 243 note¹
Beaumont, Comtesse de, 243–8
Beaumont, Madame le Prince de, 121 note¹
Beauvau, Marshal de, 14
Bel Oeil, Château de, 10–11
Bene, citizen, 132 note²
Berceau, 109
Bernard, Abbé, 6, 12–13, 18–19
Bernay, 251, 252
Berne, Madame de Custine's stay at, 298
Berry, Duc de, 311
Berstöcher, M., tutor to Astolphe, 204 and note²; 207, 213, 214, 250, 251, 295, 296, 332, 339, 369: journey to Klosterheilbronn, 221–23; illness, 265, 266; at Fervaques, 269, 275, 342, 346, 347; in Berne, 298, 304; return to Paris, 312; letters to

INDEX

Chateaubriand on death of Madame de Custine, 370-1
Bertelier, 252
Berthier, M., 139
Bertin, exile of, 280 *and note*¹
Bertin, aîné, M., letter from Delphine, 363-4
Bertrand, Madame de Custine and, 139 *note*², 143-8
Béthune-Charóst, Duc de, 127 *note*¹, 150
Beurnonville, General de, 207; account of, 231 *and note*¹, 241 *and note*¹; proposal to Delphine, 232-9
Bex, 289; death of Madame de Custine at, 370-1
Biron, Duchesse de, 55 *note*¹
Biron, M., 90
Blanche, Maison, 144, 145
Blondet, 255
Bonaparte, Madame de, and Madame de Custine, 45, 191, 238, 241-2, 249; imprisonment in the Carmes, 153, 162-3; kindness of, 227, 228
Bonaparte, Napoleon, 190, 191, 305; return from Egypt, 231; departure for Elba, 308; march upon Paris, 319; and Fouché, 320
Bonenfant, Louis, 108
Bonne Espérance, Abbey de, 22
Bonnet, M. de, 224
Bordeaux, Duc de, 359 *note*¹
Borghèse, Prince, 98 *note*¹
Borgho, Pozzo di, 320 *note*³
Borromeo, Islands of, 193, 288-9
Bouchotte, General de Custine and, 106-7, 132
Boufflers, Chevalier de, friendship for Madame de Sabran, 4, 12, 17, 38-40, 50, 193; letter from Madame de Custine, 7; letters from Madame de Sabran, 10, 13, 16, 18, 20; 22-29; 33-5; governor of Senegal, 15, 37; and Madame de Custine, 44, 54, 55, 240; and M. de Ségur, 80; marriage with Madame de Sabran, 119 *and note*²; 124-5, 204-5; at Merkatz, 200; departure for Poland, 205-6, 208, 211; name erased from list of *Émigrés*, 233; return to Paris, 239; mentioned in the letters, 257, 258, 274, 283, 291, 292, 309, 312; visit to Fervaques, 275; illness, 278; death of, 316-17
Boufflers, Madame de, 274-5
Boufflers, Madame de. *See* Sabran, Madame de

Boulets, Madame des, 258, 266, 269, 278, 348
Bourdonnais, Madame de la, 74
Bouret, M., 4
Bourgne, Madame, 350
Brabant, revolution in, 237
Bragelogne, Madame, 150
Brancas, Duchesse de, 70, 101
Breteuil, Baron de, 279 *note*²
Brézé, M. de, 363
Broglie, Duc Victor de, 320 *note*³, 329
Broglie, Prince Victor de, 48 *note*¹. *See also* Troubadour
Brun, Le, 132 *note*²
Brunswick, Duke of, 78, 85, 133, 135
Buller, Mrs., 6 *and note*¹, 8, 9, 50

CAILLE, M. La, 192 *note*²
Cambrai, 109
Camet, 132 *note*³
Canova, 290-1
Carcadot, Marquis de, 150
Carmes, the, Madame de Custine's imprisonment in, 149-50, 155, 159-60; description, 149 *note*²; chief prisoners, 150; effect of the Terror, 154; release of the prisoners, 162-3
Carnot, 217, 321
Cases, M. de Las, 281 *note*¹, 293
Castellane, Mlle. de, 322
Caumont, Hercule de, 150
Caumont, Madame de, 351
Cauvigny, Madame de, at Fervaques, 258, 263-4, 266-7, 269, 272, 277, 278, 348, 356
Cauvigny, Prefect, 266
Caux, Madame de, 263 *note*¹, 271
Cenis, Mont, 289-90, 291
Centaure, warship, 1
Champagne, poverty of, 307
Champcenetz, M. de, death, 156, *and note*²
Champcenetz, Chevalier de, 150
Champcenetz, Madame de, 11
Chartreuse Convent, 51 *and note*¹
Chastullé, Hôtel de, 68
Chateaubriand, Armand de, death, 280-1
Chateaubriand, Madame de, wife of René, 243, 248, 249, 265, 271, 277 *note*³, 270
Chateaubriand, Marquis de, 46 *and note*³, 157, 158
Chateaubriand, Marquis de, 45, 46, 47, 48, 55, 75, 101, 157-8, 243

INDEX

Chateaubriand, Vicomte René de, *Mémoires* quoted, 46-7, 245-6, 248 note¹, 273, 333 note¹, 370-1; *Atala* 243; intimacy with Madame de Custine, 243, 244, 248, 262, 279, 284-86, 291, 292, 316, 340, 369-70; Secretaryship at Rome, 244; *Genius of Christianity*, 244; letter to Fontanes, 245; letters to Madame de Custine, 245, 254, 256, 264-5, 267-8, 360, 364-5; return to France, 247-8; and Madame de Boufflers, 249-50; letters from Madame de Custine, 255, 264-5, 357; and the Duchesse de Duras, 264 note¹, 281 note¹, 292-3, 316, 320, 361, 362; visits to Fervaques, 263, 266-7, 272, 276, 356, 360; at Villeneuve-sur-Yonne, 268, 271; death of his sister, 271; tour in the East in 1806, 275-9; the *Martyrs*, 280; *Itinéraire de Paris à Jerusalem*, 282; nomination to the Academy, 282-3; and Madame Récamier, 293, 356, 361; *Bonaparte and the Bourbons*, 310, 320; relations with Astolphe, 310-11; follows Louis XVIII to Ghent, 320; and Fouché, 321; appointed Prussian Ambassador, 359-60; appointment to London, 360-61; at the Congress of Vienna, 361-2; Foreign Minister, 362-3; dismissal, 366
Chateauvieux, M. de, 295
Châtelet, Achille de, 127 note¹
Châtelet, Duchesse du, 158
Chammont-Quitry, Guy de, 110, 118, 125, 131, 139 note³, 246, 253, 259, 348, 355
Chauveau, *See* Legarde
Chênedollé, M., at Fervaques, 263-6, 272; and Madame de Caux, 271; letter from Madame de Custine, 276-7
Chénier, Marie Joseph, 282, 283
Chevallier, 159
Chimay, Madame de, 279 note²
Civil Constitution of the Clergy, 50 and note²
Civil List, the, 91
Clary, Comtesse, 233
Clary, Princesse, 314
Clarys of Teplitz, the, 340
Clermont-Gallerande, Madame de, 11
Coburg, Prince of, 108
Coffinhal, 114, 156 note²
Commission of General Security, 109
Commission of Public Safety, 132,
135, 142, 144, 146, 148, 171; General de Custine and, 107, 108
Commission of Public Security, 159
Commune, proclamation of the, 86
Conception, Convent of the, Paris, 2
Conciergerie, the, 108; meeting between Armand and Delphine, 138-9
Condé, army of, 133, 135, 166 and note¹
Condé, Mlle. de, 186 and note³-87
Condé, Prince de, 41
Condé, siege of, 107-8
Condorcet, M. de, and the proscriptions, 91-2
Confiscation, Law of, 137 note¹
Conscription, Law of, 299
Constituent Assembly, the, 66, 90
Constitution, reform of the, 42
Content, warship, 1 note¹
Convention, the, 91, 92, 132; Laws against conniving at escape, 130; invasion by the crowd, 181; and the Republican Constitution, 190 and note¹
Coppet, 296, 328
Cordons-bleus, procession of the, 15
Councils, revival of the, 215; *coups d'état*, 217, 223, 231
Courier, 270
Courtomer, Marquis de, 359 note¹
Courtomer, Mlle. Léontine de Saint Simon de, 359, 363
Cromecourt, Baron, 71
Croze-Lemercier, Comte de, 43
Curt, shoemaker, 146-7
Custine, Armand de, marriage, 20, 24-9, 30-4; politics, 38; children, 40-2; jealousy, 45, 47-9, 54; rejoins the Army, 55-6; in Germany, 71 note¹, 73; mission to the Duke of Brunswick, 78, 80; appointment in Berlin, 80-3; refusal of his wife to join him, 81; return to Paris, 84; and the revolution, 88, 90, 98; letter to Madame de Sabran, 90-3; reconciliation with his wife, 97; remains in Paris, 98, 99, 102; his rooms in Paris sealed, 108; arrest, 109; in prison, 116, 118, 119-20, 123, 125, 126, 127, 128; plans for escape, 129-31; the letter on which the indictment was based, 131; examination, 132-3; the indictment, 133-7; last meeting with Delphine, 138-9; letter to Delphine, 139-40; death, 141
Custine, Astolphe de, early years, 42, 55, 84, 89, 97, 98; *La Russie en*

INDEX

1839, quoted, 111–3, 129–31, 138–9, 150, 160–1, 165 *note*[1]; mentioned in the letters, 120, 123, 126, 207, 213–14; in Paris, 126–7, 191, 250, 275; plans for flight from, 142 *and note*[1], 145; brought back by Nanette, 148; the house in the Rue de Bourbon, 159; health, 163, 277, 278, 288, 296–7, 302, 323–5; Niederviller, 171, 199; question of his property, 180–1; letters to his mother, 183, 304–9, 311, 317–18; Klosterheilbronn, 221–3; letter to Madame de Sabran, 238–9, 349–50, 353–4; at Saint Léger, 240, 246; at Fervaques, 251, 269, 341–44, 353–4; his First Communion, 255–6; Confirmation, 258; his mother's illness, 266; tour through Italy and Switzerland, 283–90; and Dr. Koreff, 285, 288; in Berne, 298; summoned by the Conscription, 299; attached to the Comte d'Artois, 303–4, 305; in Paris society, 310–12; Attaché to M. de Talleyrand, 313–5; correspondence during the Congress of Vienna, 313–14, 316; departure for Frankfort, letters, 325–6; marriage projects, 327, 350–2, 354–6; letter from Schlangenbad, 327; impressions of Goethe, 329–30; joined by his mother, 331–3; and Frau von Varnhagen, 334, 337–9; improvement in health, 347; on Chaumont-Quitry, 348; Madame de Genlis and, 357; marriage, 359; visits England and Scotland, 360–2; and M. Chediéu Robethon, 366–7; narrative of Varnhagen, 366; last journey with his mother, 369; letter to Madame de Varnhagen, 369–70; Custine, Enguerraud de, birth, 360, 363, 367; death, 368, 371

Custine, Gaston de, 37, 39–40, 55, 84–5

Custine, General de, 20, 22; Madame de Custine's marriage settlement, 23–5, 28–9; with the army of the Rhine, 37, 90, 97; arrest, 104; and Bouchotte, 106–7; with the army of the North, 107–8; arrest, 108; the indictment, 109–10; interview with Madame de Custine, 111–12; charges and replies, 112–14; letter to his son, 114–15, 131

Cygogne, Inn of the, 172 *and note*[1], 173, 184, 200

DALBERG, Duc, 314
Dampierre, General de, 107
Danton, 154
David, 148 *note*[1]
Decazes, Duc, 360
Delessart, M., 78, 79, 80, 133
Desmoulins, Camille, 154
Devèze, 132 *note*[2]
"Didon," 16
Dieppe, 364
Dillon, Madame Robert, 75
Directory, *coup d'état* of 22 Floréal, 223; society under the, 224
Doges, Palace of the, 291
Drei Könige, Inn of the, 186
Dreux-Brézé, Marquis de, 27 *note*[1] 101, 129, 170–1, 171 *note*[1], 363
Dreux-Brézé, Marquise de, 101, 102, 104–5, 118, 120, 123, 129, 241, 277
Dubarran, 148 *note*[1]
Dubourre, Madame, 355
Duchesnoy, Mlle., 308
Ducos, 231
Dufrancastel, 149 *note*[2]
Dufour, citizen, 132 *note*[2]
Dufort, Comte de 241 *note*[1]
Dugazon, 17
Duglay, citizen, 132 *note*[2]
Dumas, trial of M. de Custine, 132–6; death, 162
Dumouriez, 97, 107, 113, 133, 174 *note*[1]
Dupont, Mlle., 216
Duras, Duchesse de, Chateaubriand and, 264 *note*[1], 281 *note*[1], 292–3, 316, 320, 361, 362
Duras, Mlle. de, 351

ÉGLANTINE, Fabre d', 154
Einsiedeln, Abbey of, visits of Madame de Sabran, 185–87, 287
Elizabeth, Madame, 123
Émigrés, 41, 62, 79; laws against, 123
Engelberg, Benedictine Abbey, 185–6
Enghien, Duc d', execution, 249
Epée, Inn of the, 173, *and note*[2], 186
Esterno, M. de, and the Comtesse Alexandre, 48, 60, 66, 72; goes to Brussels, 48, 53; and Madame Custine, 57, 70, 74

FAMINE of 1818, 349–50
Fayette, M. de la, 38, 55, *and note*
Fayette, Madame de la, 279 *note*[2]
Federal Diet at Frankfort, 329
Federation, Festival of, 43
Ferand, deputy, 181
Ferrières, Château de, 316

INDEX 379

Fervaques, Château de, 246-7, 250-61, 263-70, 272, 275-76; purchased by Madame de Custine, 312, 340, 341, 352-6. 371-2
Fesch, Cardinal, 244
Feuillants, Terrace of the, 230
Feuilloys, 159
Fève, Le, Madame de Custine lodged in the house of, 167
Fifi, 183
Five Hundred, the, 215; action of Napoleon, 231
First Royalists, 310
Flemming, Count, 337, 348
Fontaine-Française, 273
Fontanes, letter from Chateaubriand, 245
Fontanges, Chevalier de, 63, 70, 74, 77
Fontanges, Madame de, 101
Fontenay, Madame de, 163 note [1], 227-28
Fontène, La, 132
Force, La, 109, 127 and note [1], 143, 155
Fouché. See Otranto, Duc d'
Fouquier-Tinville, trial of General de Custine, 109, 111, 114; trial of Armand de Custine, 132, 134; methods, 154, 160; death, 162
Fourrier, 260
Francœur, 127 note [1]
Frankfort, 90, 107; Astolphe at, 327-31; Madame de Custine, 331-32
Frederick William II., 51 note [2], 79-81, 199, 205, 222
Fréron, journalist, 181
Freudenreich, M. de, 298
Friday, 17

GAILLARD, M., 320 note [1]
Galissonière, Marquis de La, 1 note [1]
Gansay, citizen, 132 note [2]
Gauria, secretary, 108, 109
Gauthier, citizen, 132 note [2]
Gazette Française, article, quoted, 110
General Committee of Defence, 97
General Council of the Commune, 110
Geneva, 288, 291; Madame de Custine established at, 294, 297-8; last meeting between Madame de Custine and Chateaubriand, 369-70
Genlis, Madame de, letter to Astolphe, 357
Gentz, Frederich, 335
Géreminus, M., 224, 230

Gérôme, attempt to save Madame de Custine, 159, 160-1; proscription, 163; Madame de Custine's gratitude, 165, and note [1], 174
Gesner, monument, 187
Gessner, 103
Gibelin, Abbé, 39 note [2], 101, 160, 250-1, 253-5, 264, 342-4
Gimbelette, Abbé, 71
Girard, Abbé, 193
Girondins, the, 84, 123, 135
Glaive Vengeur quoted, 141
Goethe, 329-30, 334
Goltz, M. von, 83
Goulas, 142 note [1], 145, 147
Goyon, Mlle. de, 351
Grammont, Duchesse de, death, 158
Gramont, Leroy de, 150
Grange-Batelière, Hotel, 356
Grappard, clerk, 132
Grasset, François, 102 note [1]
Gretry, 121 note [1]
Grewenmacheren, battle of, 232
Grimm, Baron von, 71, and note [3]
Grimsel, the, 285
Grindelwald, 185
Grivel, M., 103
Grouchy, Marquis de, friendship with Madame de Custine, 87, 96, 100-104, 119, 120, 124
Guermange, estate of, 126 and note [1]

HARDENBERG, Prince von, 314, 329, 333 note [1]
Hautefort, Mlle. de, 351
Havre, visit of Madame de Custine, 103-4
Hébert, 113, 154
Henry, Prince, and Madame de Sabran, 51 and note [2], 66, 87-8, 168, 170, 200
Henry III. of England, 2, note [2]
Henry IV., castle of. *See* Fervaques
Herbois, Collot d', 191 note [1]
Hespir, L., 132 note [2]
Hoche, General, 150
Hoffmann, Dr., 113
Hortense, Queen, 319
Humboldt, Frau von, 337
Humboldt, Herr von, 314, 333, 337
Hundred Days, 322 note [1], 327

"IPHIGÉNIE EN AULIDE," 12

JACOBIN CLUB, the, 162
Jacobins, the, 108, 198, 199
Jaquette, M., 252, 253
Joséphine. *See* Bonaparte, Madame

INDEX

Joubert, family, Chateaubriand and, 265, 268
Joubert, salon of, 243 note [1]
Juan, Gulf of, 319
Jungfrau glacier, 185
Justine, Mlle., name taken by Madame de Custine, 104

KARLSBAD, 339–41
Kersaint, Comte de, 292
Klosterheilbronn, 171, 172; meeting between Madame de Sabran and Madame de Custine at, 221–23
Koch, M., 74
Koreff, Dr., 284–6, 288–90, 292, 294, 296, 298–302, 314, 318, 323, 325, 329, 331 note [1], 333 note [1], 339, 340, 344, 345–6, 367

LAAGE, Madame de, 71
Lacoste, Elie, 148 note [1]
Lacretelle, 282
Lambesc, Prince de, 421 note [2]
Lameth, Madame Charles de, 150, 163
Lamoignon, 46
Landau, 112
Langlois, 149 note [2]
Lanne, Judge, 132
Laon, Bishop of. See Sabran, Monsignor de
Lausanne, 369, 371
Lauterbrunnen, 185
Laval, Adrien de, 74–5
Lavater of Zurich, 173 and note [2]; visits of Madame de Sabran, 174–5, 187
Lavicomterie, 148 note [1]
Legarde, M. Chauveau, defence of M. de Custine, 133 and note [1], 136–7
Legendre, 164
Léon, M. de, 279 note [2]
Lescot-Fleuriot, 150
Letourneur, 215
Lévis, Comte Antoine de, return to Paris, 70; Madame de Custine and, 72, 74, 75, 87, 96, 101, 124
Lévis-Mirepoix, 127 note [1]
Liesse, 34–5
Ligne, Hélène de, 11
Ligne, Prince de, 11, 314; description of Bath, 8–9
Ligne, Princesse Charles de, 10–11
Linth, 285
Longwy, 88
Lothringer, Abbé, 114–5, 115 note [1]
Louis XV, 1–2, 138
Louis XVI and the de Sabrans, 12; recall of M. Necker, 38; refusal to sanction the first Articles of the Constitution, 41; flight to Varennes, 62; and the Girondins, 81–2; trial and execution, 97
Louis XVIII, 319, 320
Louis of the Lower Rhine, 148 note [1]
Louise, the jailer's daughter, plans for Armand's escape, 129–31
Louise, Queen, 314 note [1]
Lubomirska, Princess, 158, 314
Lubomirski, Prince, 286
Lucerne, 285
Lückner, General, 55, 56, 78, 112
Lugano, 285
Lunéville, Court of, 273, 317
Luxembourg, Marshal of, 4
Luxembourg, the, General de Custine imprisoned in, 108: a pretended conspiracy, 154–5
Luynes, Duchesse de, 247 note [1]
Lyons, destruction of, 191 note [1]

MADELONNETTES, the, 155
Maestricht, 175 note [1]
Maillebois, Madame de, 274
Malesherbes, M. de, President of the Court of Aids, 46–7; and Madame de Custine, 89–90; "defence of the King," 92, 93; return to Orleans on death of Louis, 97: arrest, 157
Malesherbes, Mlle. de, 46, note [1]
Malriat, Nanette, nurse to Astolphe, 98, 127, 148, 161, 331; plans for flight from Paris, 142 note [1], 144, 145; obtains release of Madame de Custine, 163–5; at Niederviller, 171, 199, 240; correspondence with Madame de Custine, 183, 296–7; visit to Fervaques, 278; mentioned in the letters, 292, 302, 309
Marck, Comte Auguste de la, 50 note [3]
Marck, Comtesse de la, 39, 52, 70, 73, 77, 101
Marguerite of Provence, 244
"Mariage de Figaro," 11
Marmontel, 121 note [1]
Marsin, Comtesse de, 43
Martin, citizen, 132 note [2]
Mayence, 90, 107, 108, 112, 133
Mecklenberg, Prince Gustav von, 337, 348
Médor, 202, 203, 207, 209, 216, 217
Meiringen, 185
Mellet, Charles de, 52, 71 and note [2]
Mellet, Comtesse de, 125 and note [2]
Mello, retirement of Madame de Custine to, 98–102, 104

INDEX

Menou, M. de, 279 *note*[2]
Merkatz, 193, 200
Meudon, Parc de, 26
Mezeray, Mlle., 308
Mirabeau, 25, 50 *and note*[1]
Miranda, General, 175 *and note*[1], 176
Molé, 46
Monceau, 225, 250
Monnecaut, Pierre, 143, 147
Montagne, Collège de, 19
Montault - Navailles, Mlle. de, 12 *note*[1]
Montleart, M. de, 101
Montmorency, Mathieu de, 362
Montmorency-Laval, Duc de, 247 *note*[1]
Montmorin, M. de, 243
Montreuil, 15
Moreau, General, 358
Moreau, Madame, 358
Moges, Comte de, and Madame de Custine, 74, 76–7
Morges, 303
Morin, M., physician, 265
Mouchy, Madame de, 276
Münchhausen, Baron von, 273
Murat, 316

NANCY, 307
Narbonne, M. de, 78, 306
National Convention, 90
National Gardens, 225
National Guard, attack on the Assembly, 190
Necker, M., exile and recall, 38
Neervinde, 175 *note*[1]
Négle, cook, 216, 219
Niederviller, porcelain factory at, 20 *note*[1]; Madame de Custine's visits to, 39 *and note*[1], 40, 98, 163, 171, 183, 198–200, 240
Noailles, Alexis de, 83, 305, 313–14, 325–6
Nollin, Abbé, 276
Notre Dame de Liesse, 34–5, 37
Notre Dame-des-Hermits, 185, 186, 287

ODIER family, 296, 298
Olmutz, 231 *note*[1]
Orange, Princesse d', 10
Orléans, Duc d', 123–4
Orléans, Madame d', 101
Otranto, Joseph, Duke of, friendship with Madame de Custine, 147 *note*[1], 233, 241, 246, 280, 316, 319–22, 363; account of, 191 *and note*[1], 192; fall of, 281, 296, 322, *and* *note*[1]; and Louis, 319–20; and Napoleon, 320; a dinner with Chateaubriand, 321
Oudinot, Marshal, 296

PACHE, M., 90
Palais de Justice, 110
Paris, reform of the Constitution, 42; the federal camp, 84; gates closed after August 9–10, 86; the Proscriptions, 91–2; reaction after the Terror, 181; emergency laws reinforced, 218; advance of the Allies, 305–7; entry of Comte d'Artois, 308–9: battle of, 309; return of Madame de Custine, 312; arrival of Napoleon in March, 1815, 319; the Hundred Days, 327; Frau von Varnhagen's appreciation of, 336–7
Paris-Montbrun, Marquis de, 150
Passports, forged, refused by Madame de Custine, 171
Paulin, M., 265, *note*[2]
Pedre, Captain, 41
Petites Maisons, 87
"Philemon and Baucis," 31
Pichegru, 215
Pietists, the 306
Pin, M. de la Tour du, 314
Plombières, 32–3, 39, 43, 246
Polastron, Madame de, 229
Polignac, Armand de, 255
Polignac, Comtesse de Diane, 15, 16
Polignac, Duchesse de, 11, 24
Porrentruy, 112
Port-Libre, 155, 157
Poupet, Charles, 142 *note*[1], 145, 147
Présentation, Convent of the, 13
Provence, Beatrice of, 2 *note*
Provence, Blanche of, 2 *note*
Provence, Eléonore of, Wife of Henry III, 2 *note*
Provence, Marguerite of, 2 *note*
Prussia, alliance with Austria, 78; entrance of the army into France, 85–6; retreat, 90

QUÉRHOENT, Comte de, 150

RAGMAY, Pierre Louis, 132
Raismes, Château de, 20, 52, 77
Rambouillet, 16–17
Rathkirch, Herr von, 91
Récamier, Madame, 293, 356, 361
Republican Constitution, the, 190
Reveillère-Lepeaux, La, 2

382 INDEX

Revolutionary Committee of Bondy, 159
Revolutionary Tribunal, 97, 108, 110 132, 150–6, 162
Rewbell, 217
Reynière, Madame de la, 279 note [2]
Rheinsberg, Castle of, 51 and note [3], 66, 168
Richard, King of the Romans, 2 note [2]
Robert, 260
Robespierre, 154, 155, 162, 191 note [1], 228
Robethon, M. Chedieu, 366
Rochambeau, 151 note [1]
Rocheforte, Madame de (afterwards Duchesse de Nivernais), 5 note [3]
Rocheforte, Princesse de, 10
Rochefoucauld, Comte de la, 48 note [1], 61, 74
Rochefoucauld, Comtesse de la, 2 only; friendship with Madame de Custine, 45, 61–2, 68, 72, 74, 77, 119, 204, 242: salon, 47–8, 74–5, 151; goes to Brussels, 48, 53; and the Troubadour, 56–7, 58, 59; correspondence with Madame de Custine, 59–61; return to Paris, 65; retirement to Mello under the name of Madame Alexandre, 98, 99, 104
Roger, Claude, 132, 137
Rohan, Duc de, 279 note [2]
Rohan-Guéméné, Prince de, 150
Rosambo, M. de, 46–7, 157–8
Rosambo, Madame de, 46 note [1], 47, 71, 157, 158, 241
Rossigneux, 164
Rosseau, principles, 42
Royal Guard disbanded, 84
Royalists, the, 198, 280
Russians, the, in France, 306–9, 315, 331

SABRAN, Comte de, 1, 3
Sabran, Elzéar de, childhood, 3, 5, 10–12; influence of the Abbé Bernard, 13, 18–19; and the Queen, 16; at Delphine's wedding, 28: travels with his mother, 39, 40, 49–52; carries his sister's messages to Brussels, 53–4; letters from Madame de Custine, 56, 59, 62, 63–5, 69–77, 86–7, 95, 100–1, 103, 117–19, 122–4, 128, 192–5, 210–13, 219–20; letters to his sister, 67–9, 120–2; ill-health, 121, 222–3, 278, 311; Beauharnais' admiration for, 151–3; papers signed by, 159–60; Delphine's enquiries after, 168; journey to Klosterheilbronn, 171; meeting with Delphine at Zurich, 173–4; reflections on the letters of Beauharnais, 176–9; Delphine's notes, 179; Delphine's wish to return to France, 180–2; parting with Delphine at Bâle, 184–5; visit to Einsiedeln, 185–7; second visit to Lavater, 187; leaves Venice for Wimislow, 212; attitude towards the proposal of Beurnonville, 233–9; return to Paris, 239; affection for Madame de Staël, 241, 328; Chateaubriand's impression of, 250; mentioned in the letters, 254, 255, 257, 258, 291, 292, 302; arrest, 296–7; exiled from Paris, 297; affection for his mother, 317

Sabran, Garsende de, 2 note
Sabran, Madame de, 2–4; friendship with the Chevalier de Boufflers, 4; illness and visit to Spa, 7–8; letters to Boufflers, 10, 13, 15–18, 20, 22–9, 33–5, 41–2: and the Abbé Bernard, 12–13, 18–19; and the Abbé de Vaux, 19–20; at St. Amand, 20–22; and General de Custine, 23–5, 28–9; the marriage, 30–2; at Plombières, 32–3; return from Switzerland, 40: in Paris 1790, 43; anxiety caused by Delphine's behaviour, 44–5, 48, 49–50, 59, 67, 75; exile, 50–2; and Frederick-William, 81; and Madame de Custine's return to Paris, 82–3; death of Gaston, 85; confiscation of her Paris property, 87–8; and Madame de Custine, 90; illness at Rheinsberg, 98, 101; letters from Madame de Custine, 98–9, 102, 116–7, 125–6, 201–11, 214–19, 251–61, 265, 269, 273–5, 285–90, 291, 294–302, 354–6; marriage to the Chevalier de Boufflers, 119 note [2], 124–5, 204–5; appreciation of Delphine's courage, 120; song composed by, 161–2; and the Chevalier Séguier, 166–9; letters to Madame de Custine, 169–70; 279 note [2], 282–3; journey to Klosterheilbronn, 171; then to Zurich 172–3; meeting with Madame de Custine, 173–4; visits to Lavater, 174–5, 187; fears of re-entering France, 180–2; parting with Madame de Custine at Bâle, 184–5; visit to the Abbey of Einsiedeln,

INDEX 383

185-7; meeting with Madame de Custine at Kehl, 190; letters from the Chevalier de Séguier, 195-200; letter from Frederick William, 199; declared an *Émigrée*, 201; departure for Poland, 205-6, 211; loss of her Paris house, 207; leaves Poland for Klosterheilbronn, 221-3; attitude towards Beurnonville, 232, 237-8; name erased from list of *Émigrés*, 233: return to Paris, 239-40, 270; Chateaubriand introduced to, 249-50; visits to Fervaques, 275, 348; visit of Astolphe to, 309; death of M. de Boufflers, 317; letters from Astolphe, 343-4, 349-54; at St. Léger, 363; death, 369 note [2]
Sabran, Marquis de, 71, 74, 125
Sabran, Monsignor de, Bishop of Laon, 3, 6, 12, 19, 20, 26, 28, 30-2, 33, 35, 50, 93 note [1], 201, 223, 233, 238
Sagan, Duchesse de, 314
Sage, Le, 260
Saint Amand, mud baths of, 20-2, 73, 230
Saint Gothard, 285
Saint Léger, 246, 353, 363
Saint Louis, 2 note
Saint Mark, Square of, 291
Saint Maurice, 32
Saint-Aubin, cemetery of, 363, 369
Saint-Aulaire, Mlle. de, 351
Saint-Julien, Madame de, 274-5
Saint-Lazare, 134, 155
Saint-Pélagie, Madame de Custine imprisoned, 148 and note [1], 149; description, 149 note [1]
Saint-Preux, M., 63
Saint-Simon, Madame de, 101
Salm-Kirburg, Prince of, 55 note [1], 150 and note [2], 156
Santa Maria, battle of, 1
Savary, Minister of Police, 281, 296
Schevers, Thierry, 102 note [1]
Schlangenbad, 327
Schlegel, 337
Schloffer, 330
Schlosser family of Vienna, 319
Schulenberg, Herr, 82-3
Sécherons, 370
Septembre massacres, 163 note [1]
Séguier, Antoine Louis, 166 note [1]
Seguier, Chevalier Maurice de, gains news of Delphine for Madame de Sabran, 166-9; letters to Madame de Sabran, 172, 174, 188-90, 195-

200, 204 note [3], 223-4; and Madame de Custine, 182, 184, 193-200, 207, 223-4; the parting at Bâle, 184-5; goes to Merkatz, 200; proposed departure for Poland, 205-7; return to Paris, 207-11; letter from Elzéar, 235-6; after career, 242 and note [1]
Ségur, M. de, 79-80, 202, 204
Ségur, Madame de, 101
Sevigné, Madame de, 341-2
Sieyès, 231
Sillion, citizen, 132 note [2]
Simon the Saddler, 237
Simons, Madame (Mlle. Lange), 301
Simplon, the, 289, 291
Society under the Directory described, 224
Soissons, 27, 28
Sombreuil, 127 note [1]
Soyecourt, Comte de, 150
Spa, 7-8
Spenlé, M., 335
Spires, 90, 107
Stäel, Mlle. de, 328-9
Stäel, Madame de, 78, 241, 278, 288, 296, 328
Stahrenberg, Comte de, 50 note [3]
Stahrenberg, Comtesse de, offer to Madame de Sabran, 50-1
Stanz, 285
States General, 37, 38
Stolberg, Princess von, 232
Strasburg, 109, 112
Suspects, Law of, 123
Sweden, assassination of the King, 81
Swiss Guard massacre, 86
Système de la Nature, 64 and note [1]

TALLEYRAND, M., Congress of Vienna, 313-15; and Louis XVIII., 320; departure from Vienna, 325-6
Tallien, M., 163 and note [1], 191, 227-8
Tallien, Madame. *See* Fontenay, Madame de
Tavernier, J. Baptiste, 132
Tennis Court, oath of the, 38
Teplitz, waters of, 340
Terriard, 109
Terror, the, effect in the prisons, 154; end of the, 162
Théâtre Français, 308
Thirion, M., 204 and note [4]
Thouin, M., 276
Thun, 185
Tivoli Gardens, 225, 250
Tocqueville, Comte de, 46 note [2]

Tournal, M., 183
Trenck, Baron de, 127 note [1]
Trèves, 79 note [2]
Tronson-Ducoudray, 114
"Troubadour," the, 47-8, 53-5, 60-2, 65, 66, 72, 100, 310; correspondence with Madame de Custine, 48, 56-9, 74
Tuileries, imprisonment of Louis XVI., 62; invasion of 20th June, 1792, 84; invasion of August, 9-10, 86; *coup d'état* of 18th Fructidor, 217; return of Napoleon, 320
Turin, 290

UNBELIEVERS, the, 306
Ussé, Château d', 292

VADIER, 148 note [1]
Valazé, 127 note [1]
Valenciennes, 107, 108, 133, 135
Vallée-aux-Loups, 279 note [1]
Valmy, 90
Varennes, 62
Varnhagen von Ense, Frau von, salon, 315, 337; account of, 334-6; friendship with Madame de Custine, 334, 337-9, 366; letters from Madame de Custine, 340-1, 345-7, 352; letter from Astolphe, 369-70
Varnhagen, Herr von, 315, 329, 335-7, 337 note [1], 339 note [1]

Vaudémont, Princesse, friendship for Madame de Custine, 241, 309, 316, 319, 322, 353, 355, 356; in Frankfort, 333-334
Vaux, Abbé de, 63 *and note* [1], 101, 160
Venain, 207, 216
Venice, 291
Verdun, 88
Vergniaud, 127 note [1]
Vernon, Guillaume, 150
Versailles, 138; the attack on, 41
Vesoul, the Court of, 304-7
Vevey, 288
Vienna, Congress of, 313-5, 361-2
Villèle, M. de, 359 note [1], 361, 362
Villeneuve-sur-Yonne, 265, 268
Villeroy, Duc de, 127 note [1]
Villers-Cotterets, 28
Vincent, 113, 134-5
Volunteer National Guard, 112

WATERLOO, 320
"Wilhelm," 324-5, 327
Wimislow, 211
Worms, 90, 107

YORK TOWN, 37 note [1]

"ZEMIRE AND AZOR," 121 note [1]
Zurich, 291; meeting between Madame de Sabran and Madame de Custine at, 173-4

www.ingramcontent.com/pod-product-compliance
Lightning Source LLC
Chambersburg PA
CBHW022047160426
43198CB00008B/145